AN OUTLINE

OF

THE EQUITY PLEADING AND PRACTICE

WITH FORMS

AND

The Federal Equity Rules

Prepared for the use of the students of the Law School
of the University of Virginia

BY

WILLIAM MINOR LILE, LL. D.

Professor of Law

SECOND EDITION

UNIVERSITY OF VIRGINIA
GEORGE W. OLIVIER
ANDERSON BROS.
1922

Copyright, 1922
By
William Minor Lile

MAY 9   1922

Preface To First Edition

This small volume is the result of many years of effort to collect the fundamental principles of the Equity Pleading and Practice for the use of the author's students in class-room instruction. The topic is one that can successfully be taught to students only by confining the instruction chiefly to the procedure of some particular jurisdiction. Numerous attempts to use the larger well-known texts in the class-room have proved hopeless failures. The author has therefore drawn very freely upon the system of procedure as it exists in Virginia, where the procedure at law and in equity is still almost as distinct as when Lord Bacon occupied the woolsack — and where the equity procedure probably conforms more nearly to that of Bacon's day than that of any American state.

In the treatment of the subject of Receivers, free use has been made of Mr. High's scholarly treatise, for which due acknowledgment is made. If, in so elementary a work, the subject of Receiverships seems overstressed in comparison with the briefer treatment of other topics of equal or greater importance, the explanation is that it was found impracticable to handle the subject in less compass, even in most elementary fashion.

Detailed reference is made throughout to the new Federal Equity Rules—and these rules have been reproduced in full in the Appendix.

It is hoped that the complete record of a chancery suit, as exhibited in the Appendix, may assist the student in visualizing the actual procedure in court, and in cultivating a closer acquaintance with those forms which he is expected as a practitioner to have at his fingers' ends.

In order to fulfill its primary end as a guide to the student, through what seems to the average undergraduate a dull and uninviting territory, the value of the work to the experienced practitioner has been sacrificed, by the omission of many minute points of practice.

W. M. L.

University of Virginia,

    May 1, 1916.

Preface To The Second Edition

In this second edition, effort has been made to incorporate the later important decisions of the Supreme Court of Appeals of Virginia, and the material amendments to the equity practice introduced by the recent Code revisal. The Virginia Code citations have been transposed to conform to the reversal of 1919. In collecting the later decisions, and in the transposition of the statutory citations, the author's labors were materially aided by the industrious and intelligent co-operation of his young friend and former pupil, Mr. Thomas D. W. Duke, to whom grateful acknowledgment is made.

In this edition there has been a substantial revision of the original text. The chapter on Jurisdiction is practically new, and one hundred or more new sections have been added. A few additional forms have also been inserted—including the more important pleadings in suits for the sale of infants' lands. A table of cases has also been added.

As indicated in the preface to the first volume, the work is meant primarily as a hornbook for undergraduate students and inexperienced practitioners—to which circumstance is to be attributed the omission of many matters of statutory detail. When the student becomes a practitioner he will presumably make a more detailed study of the statutes, in their original form, as found in the Code, along with the very full and helpful annotations of the revisors.

W. M. L.

University of Virginia,

February 1, 1922.

Table of Contents

Table of Contents

Chapter XXXII

RECEIVERS.

Chapter XXXIII.

RECEIVERS—CONTINUED.

Chapter XXXIV.

APPEALS.

———

Appendix I.

———

Appendix II.

THE FEDERAL EQUITY RULES.

Lectures on Equity Pleading and Practice

CHAPTER I.

Equity Courts.

Preliminary—function of procedural rules.—The student cannot better begin his studies of the equity procedure than with a knowledge of the purpose, and a conviction of the necessity, of fixed rules and methods for all judicial proceedings. Judge Story has thus admirably expressed the function and operation of these rules in his classic treatise on Equity Pleading: [1]

"It is obvious that in every system of jurisprudence professing to provide for the due administration of public justice, some forms of proceeding must be established to bring the matters in controversy between the parties who are interested therein before the tribunal by which they are to be adjudicated. And for the sake of the dispatch of business, as well as for its due arrangement with reference to the rights and conveniences of all the suitors, many regulations must be adopted to induce certainty, order, accuracy and uniformity in these proceedings. . .

"Indeed, . . . there are many rules altogether founded in artificial reasoning, but which nevertheless may be affirmed, with few exceptions, to be greatly promotive of public justice and subservient to private convenience. If, here and there, any of them work an apparent hardship or mischief, it will, on close examination, be found that they also accomplish much general permanent good; and in this respect they partake only of the infirmity of all general rules, which must, in particular cases, give rise to some inequalities and shut out some individual equities and rights."

---

[1] Story's Eq. Pleading, §§ 1-2.

§ 1. Jurisdiction statutory.—The judicial system of each State of the Union is fixed by local legislation.

The Federal system depends on the constitution and laws of the United States.

§ 2. Equity courts in Virginia.—The equity or chancery jurisdiction in Virginia is vested in the circuit [1] and corporation [2] courts of the different counties and cities, with special provisions made for the cities of Richmond, Norfolk and Roanoke.

§ 3. Federal courts of equity.—In the Federal system, the original equity jurisdiction was from the beginning vested in the United States Circuit courts, until by a quite recent statute the Circuit courts were abolished, and all original jurisdiction, both at law and in equity, was vested in the District courts—courts which had formerly possessed no general equity jurisdiction.

§ 4. The Virginia and Federal judicial systems—continued.—In neither the Virginia nor the Federal system are there separate courts for the administration of the equity jurisdiction, as distinguished from the jurisdiction at law. But the courts named in the preceding sections possess general jurisdiction at law and in equity. Although the two jurisdictions are thus administered by the same courts, equity suits are instituted and conducted according to the equity practice, and actions at law according to the practice at law. The records are kept distinct, and there is no further mingling of the two systems than in the administration of both by the same judicial machinery.

For a knowledge of the judicial systems of other states, reference must be had to their local legislation.[3]

---

[1] Va. Code 1919, § 5890.　See id. chs. 245, 246, 247.

[2] Id. §§ 5907, 5910.

[3] Of the States still maintaining the distinction between actions at law and suits in equity, in the following the two jurisdictions are exercised by the same court, as in Virginia and in the Federal

The Pleading and Practice in Equity Courts.

§ 5. Equity pleading and practice in Virginia.—In Virginia, the procedure in courts of chancery is based on that prevailing in the High Court of Chancery in England at the time the colonies declared their independence, as modified by statute, or by departures here and there, established by long custom and judicial sanction.

§ 6. The same — in the Federal courts—old equity rules.—Up to February 1, 1913, when radical alterations were made in equity practice, the procedure in the Federal courts of equity probably conformed more nearly to that formerly prevailing in the English High Court of Chancery than even does the procedure in the Virginia courts. This procedure was to a large extent, as it still is, regulated by what are known as the *Federal Equity Rules,* promulgated from time to time by the United States Supreme Court for the regulation of procedure generally in all Federal courts of equity. In most respects, these rules were largely declaratory of the former English practice.

§ 7. The same—new Equity Rules.—But in response to a very general demand for reform in the equity procedure of the Federal courts, the Supreme Court of the United States on November 4, 1912 (effective February 1, 1913), promulgated a new code of equity procedure for the Federal courts, making extensive and radical alterations of the old procedure—all looking to economy and dispatch in the maturing, decision and final disposition of equity causes. These later rules completely super-

---

system: Florida, Georgia, Illinois, Maine, Maryland, Massachusetts, Michigan, New Hampshire, Pennsylvania, Rhode Island, Vermont, and West Virginia—including also the District of Columbia. In the States following, the two jurisdictions are exercised by separate tribunals: Alabama, Delaware, Mississippi, New Jersey and Tennessee. In the rest of the States, under the so-called "code system," the distinction between the law and the equity jurisdiction (but not between law and equity) has been abolished, so far as such abolition is possible, so that both legal and equitable rights may be administered in one and the same action.

sede the former Equity Rules.[4] They are reproduced in the Appendix.[5]

The Machinery of a Court of Equity.

§ 8. Court officers.—The officers normally in attendance upon all sessions of a court of equity are:

1. The *judge*—usually termed the *chancellor;*

2. The *clerk*—sometimes called the *register,* or *prothonotary;* and

3. The *sheriff*—(in Virginia, of the county, or-the *sergeant* of the corporation).

In addition to these, every equity court has attached to it, (1) One or more *masters* (or *commissioners* as they are termed in Virginia); and (2) One or more *receivers*—sometimes permanent, but more usually appointed specially in particular cases. The court has the discretion, which is frequently exercised, of appointing special masters and special receivers to serve in special cases. In absence of statutory provision, there are no jury trials in the equity courts.

§ 9. The same—duties.—The *clerk* is the secretary of the court, and custodian of its records.

The *sheriff* is the ministerial officer of the court, whose chief duty is the service or execution of process, (original, mesne or final), on parties and witnesses—and to attend the sessions of the court as tipstaff.

The chief function of the *master*[6] is as accountant of the court, and the investigator of special matters of fact involved in litigation before the court, and particularly in the settlement of complicated accounts, and, in creditors' suits, the ascertainment of liens and their priorities. He is also, in a sense, the

---

[4] For a luminous discussion of the question whether the regulation of court procedure is a legislative or a judicial function, and as to the constitutionality of statutes delegating to the courts the promulgation of rules of practice and procedure, see 2 Am. Bar. Ass. Rep. 46. See 2 Minn. Law Review, 81.

[5] In Florida the Federal Equity Rules are adopted as rules of the State courts, "in absence of provisions of the law or rules of practice of this State." Gen. Stat. Fla., § 1877; Farrell *v.* Forest Invest. Co. (Fla.), 74 So. 216, 1 A. L. R. 25, full note.

[6] See Va. Code 1919, §§ 6266-6279; post, ch. xix.

business agent of the court, as its representative in the sale of property under the court's decrees.

The *receiver*[7] is more commonly the financial agent of the court, particularly charged with the collection and disbursement of funds, and in the care and management of property in *custodia legis*.

---

[7] Id. §§ 6280-6294. See *Receivers, post,* chs. xxxii-xxxiii.

CHAPTER II.

Jurisdiction.

I. POTENTIAL—ACTIVE.

§ 10. Jurisdiction—several senses.—As the term jurisdiction is used in several different senses, it becomes important to distinguish these at the outset. Indeed, so marked is the distinction, that for our purpose we may classify jurisdiction as of two kinds—the one *potential,* and the other *active.*

Later we shall consider another classification, from a different point of view, namely, jurisdiction *in personam* and *in rem;* and, again, the distinction between jurisdiction and *venue,* or place of suit.

THE SEVERAL KINDS OF JURISDICTION:

A. Potential—B. Active.

§ 11. (1) Potential jurisdiction.—By potential jurisdiction is meant the power granted by the sovereignty creating the court to hear and determine controversies of a given character.

For example, the Virginia statute declares that the circuit courts of this state "shall have original and general jurisdiction of *all cases in chancery* and *civil cases at law.*" [1] Hence we may say that by virtue of this statute our circuit courts have *potential* jurisdiction, generally speaking, over every conceivable chancery cause affecting persons or property, regardless of the residence of the parties or of the location of the subject-matter of the controversy.

It is to be observed that such jurisdiction looks to the *subject-matter* of the suit only, with no reference to the *person* of the defendant, nor to the *place of suit*—nor again, to the meth-

---

[1] Va. Code 1919, § 5890. (Similar jurisdiction is conferred on the corporation courts: Id. § 5907.

ods by which the jurisdiction may be acquired or exercised in a particular case.[2]

§ 12. (2) Active jurisdiction.—In order, however, that the court thus invested with potential jurisdiction may rightfully exercise that jurisdiction *in a particular case,* certain conditions of fact must appear—these conditions varying with the character or purpose of the proceeding. These conditions of fact may be demanded either by the settled principles of the unwritten law, or by the mandate of the statute law.

It is, for instance, a principle of all civilized jurisprudence that howsoever general the potential jurisdiction of any court, before this jurisdiction may actually be exercised by proceeding to judgment, either the *parties* to the controversy or the *subject-matter* thereof must be brought, by proper proceedings (presently to be mentioned), within the judicial cognizance and control of the court. We may, therefore, define active jurisdiction as the *right to exercise the potential jurisdiction in a given case.* In other words, active jurisdiction connotes potential jurisdiction, plus such conditions of fact in the particular case, as are necessary to enable the court, under existing rules, to hear and determine that cause.

A. Potential Jurisdiction.

§ 13. Potential jurisdiction lacking.—This jurisdiction has been defined. Where such jurisdiction is lacking in a particular case, it is a settled rule that any judgment or decree rendered therein is *coram non judice,* and void for all purposes.[8]

Thus, if the Hustings court of the city of Richmond (a court without general equity jurisdiction) should entertain a suit for specific performance of a contract, or should assume to enter a

---

[2] This statement is not strictly true as applied to the jurisdiction of the Federal courts, whose jurisdiction is a limited statutory one— nor to other courts when exercising a special limited and statutory jurisdiction. See *infra.* § 18.

[8] Elliott *v.* Piersol, 1 Pet. 328, 340 (sheriff levying execution issued thereon liable for damages); Pennoyer *v.* Neff, 96 U. S. 714; Shelton *v.* Sydnor, 126 Va. 625; cases *infra.*

decree of divorce—or if the District court of the United States should assume jurisdiction of a controversy between two States (a jurisdiction vested exclusively in the United States Supreme Court)—any judgment or decree resulting from such usurped jurisdiction would be not only voidable but void, and therefore subject to collateral attack.

§ 14. The same—not cured by waiver or consent.—It is an equally well settled rule that where, in order to hear and determine a given cause, the court must usurp a power not vested in it under the instrument of its creation, no act or neglect, and no waiver or consent, of the parties, howsoever solemnly given, can diminish or enlarge the powers of the court. The maxim here is "consent cannot confer jurisdiction." [4]

§ 15. The same—no plea necessary.—Since there can be no waiver of the objection in such case, it necessarily follows that if the defect of jurisdiction appears on the record—or, perhaps better, if the record does not disclose a case within the jurisdiction of the court—exception to the jurisdiction may be made by any party, at any stage of the proceeding, and in any form, oral or written, and even for the first time in the appellate court. It is equally true that even though no such objection be made, the court will of its own motion dismiss the suit whenever and at whatever stage of the proceedings the absence of jurisdiction comes to its attention.[5] And, further, any decree in such proceeding is subject to be collaterally assailed, whenever and wherever it may be brought in question.

§ 16. Test of potential jurisdiction.—The test of potential jurisdiction of the case made by the plaintiff's bill may always be made by demurrer. If the pleading is not demurrable, the potential jurisdiction exists. Not that a demurrer is essential, since we have already seen that where the jurisdiction is,

---

[4] Heigler *v.* Faulkner, 127 U. S. 482; Litz *v.* Rowe, 117 Va. 752; Thacker *v.* Hubbard, 122 Va. 379; Moore *v.* N. & W. R. Co., 124 Va. 628, 636; Shelton *v.* Sydnor, 126 Va. 625.

[5] Green *v.* Massie, 21 Gratt. 356; Catron *v.* Bostick, 123 Va. 355; cases *supra*.

in fact, lacking, objection may be made informally, or the court will itself raise the objection. What is meant is that if the bill will withstand attack by demurrer, the case is *coram judice,* and the jurisdiction proper.[6]

§ 17. Jurisdictional allegations—general jurisdiction.— Where the court is called upon to exercise its general equity jurisdiction, no special jurisdictional facts need be alleged, beyond those allegations necessary in the statement of an equitable cause of action. In such cases, the jurisdiction is said to be 'presumed', but perhaps it would be more correct to say that in such cases jurisdiction *exists.* The 'presumption' of jurisdiction is appealed to rather in questions of active jurisdiction,[7] discussed in a later section.[8]

§ 18. The same—limited jurisdiction.— But the rule is just the reverse where the bill is addressed to the supplementary jurisdiction of equity—a jurisdiction not inherent in the equity courts, but conferred by special statute, and to be exercised *only under prescribed statutory conditions* of fact. Such jurisdiction is generally termed a *limited statutory jurisdiction.*

Here the bill must affirmatively allege, and the plaintiff must

---

[6] This is not always true, however, where the bill is not addressed to the general jurisdiction of the court, but to a *limited statutory jurisdiction,* for the exercise of which special conditions of fact must appear—as, for example, in suits for divorce, or for the sale of infants' lands. In this class of cases, the bill may on its face set out a proper case for the exercise of the limited jurisdiction, and, therefore, withstand a demurrer; and yet the defendant may deny the existence of one or more of the essential jurisdictional facts, and thus raise the question of proper jurisdiction. Thus the bill for divorce, in addition to other proper allegations, may (as it must) allege that one of the parties has been domiciled in this state for one year, as required by statute. The defendant may traverse this allegation, and thus raise the jurisdictional question by plea or answer. It is clear that such a plea need not be in abatement, since even in the absence of any plea, the court will raise the objection, *ex mero motu,* if observed, and the objection is one that may not be waived. The burden here is on the plaintiff to prove, and not on the defendant to disprove, the jurisdictional allegation. See § 18, *infra;* Yates *v.* Yates, 115 Va. 678; Blankenship *v.* Blankenship, 125 Va. 595. See *Bills for Divorce, post,* ch. xxix.

[7] Blankenship *v.* Blankenship, 125 Va. 595; Shelton *v.* Sydnor, 126 Va. 625.

[8] See *infra,* §§ 35-38.

prove, the required jurisdictional facts; and the jurisdiction may legally be exercised only in substantial compliance with the statute—otherwise the case is *coram non judice;* and, in spite of the consent or waiver of the defendant, any decree therein entered, beyond dismissal of the bill, is void whenever and wherever questioned.[9]

This is but an application of the familiar principle, that where statute gives a new right, unknown to the common law, and along with the right prescribes the method of enjoying or enforcing the right, the statutory method is *exclusive,* and must be followed substantially as given.

B. Active Jurisdiction.

§ 19. Active jurisdiction—how acquired — waiver.— Where potential jurisdiction exists, active jurisdiction, which, as we have just seen, is the right actually to exercise the judicial function of hearing and determining a particular cause, may be acquired in two ways: (1) By valid and compulsory process of the court; and (2) By the voluntary submission of the parties.

Since the process of the court is not effective beyond the territorial limits of the sovereignty by which the court is created, it follows that if neither the defendant nor the subject-matter be within such limits, so as to become subject to the court's process, the court, though possessing full power to deal with controversies of that kind—in short, potential jurisdiction —is unable to exercise its grant of power in the particular case, and consequently is without active jurisdiction; and the cause must be dismissed, unless the defendant voluntarily submits himself to the jurisdiction. So, in any case where there is an absence of proper process, legally served.

---

[9] Coleman *v.* Va. Stave Co., 112 Va. 61; Brenham *v.* Smith, 120 Va. 3011; Roberts *v.* Hagan, 121 Va. 573; Parker *v.* Stephenson, 127 Va. 433; Yates *v.* Yates, *supra;* Blankenship *v.* Blankenship, *supra;* Williamson *v.* Berry, 8 How. (U. S.), 495; Hoback *v.* Miller (W. Va.), 29 S. E. 1014; Roche *v.* Nesters, 72 Md. 264, 7 L. R. A. 533; Cooper *v.* Sunderland, 3 Iowa 114, 66 Am. Dec. 52; authorities *supra.* The Federal courts exercise a special and limited jurisdiction as here described.

Hence the methods of acquiring and exercising active jurisdiction, as prescribed by law, may, to a large extent, be modified or waived by the consent or voluntary appearance of the defendant, without in anywise affecting the powers of the court in the exercise of its potential jurisdiction. *Consent may therefore, as a general rule, confer active but not potential jurisdiction.*[10]

§ 20. Active jurisdiction lacking—how objection made.

—Where the court, though possessing complete potential jurisdiction, fails to acquire active jurisdiction of the defendant, or of the particular *res* against which the proceeding is directed, in the manner required by law—as by lawful service of process, by proper attachment proceedings, or by a lawful summons by publication, or in such other form as may be required by law—any judgment or decree rendered in such proceeding is without due process of law, and therefore as completely invalid, and the proceeding as truly *coram non judice,* as if the potential jurisdiction itself were wanting.

In such case, as in that of the absence of potential jurisdiction, the objection may be made informally by motion, or in case of non-appearance of the defendant, the court will itself raise the objection, if observed, and no formal plea is required. The authorities are too abundant and uniform to require citation.[11]

II. ERRORS NOT AFFECTING JURISDICTION.

§ 21. Distinction between 'mere error' and lack of jurisdiction.

—The student should carefully observe the distinction between a merely *erroneous order* or decree, due to a judicial misconception of the legal or equitable principles upon which the rights of the parties depend—whether in the substantive law of the case or in the rules of procedure, the court hav-

---

[10] Moore *v.* N. & W. R. Co., 124 Va. 628.

[11] See Wade *v.* Hancock, 76 Va. 620; Lavell *v.* McCurdy, 77 Va. 763; Hilton *v.* Consumers' Can Co., 103 Va. 255; Mallory *v.* Virginia Colony Feeble Minded, 123 Va. 205; Applegate *v.* Lexington, 117 U. S. 255, 270; Wilson *v.* Seligman, 144 U. S. 41; Scott *v.* Streepy, 73 Tex. 547, 11 S. W. 534.

ing plenary jurisdiction of the parties and the subject-matter—and, on the other hand, affirmative action by the court in a cause of which it has *no jurisdiction*, either because the jurisdiction is inherently wanting, or has been improperly acquired. The distinction, in result, is the distinction between a *void* and a *voidable* judgment or decree.

Errors of the sort first named may render the action of the court *voidable;* but *until avoided*, either by proceedings in the same court or on appeal (of which more hereafter), the erroneous decree is valid and binding, and may not be questioned collaterally.[12]

Errors of the second class, going as they do to the foundation of the court's powers, render the whole proceedings in the case, not voidable only, but void.

III. ULTRA VIRES ORDERS AND DECREES—'JURISDICTIONAL ERRORS.'

§ 22. Decree in excess of powers.—For its power to adjudge a cause, not only is the court dependent upon investiture with both potential and active jurisdiction, but its powers are further limited in *extent and scope.* That is to say, though possessing complete jurisdiction (potential and active) of the parties and the subject matter, the court may yet go so far beyond its prescribed or accustomed powers or methods as to render its action, in that particular, as completely invalid as if potential jurisdiction itself were lacking. Such errors as these the courts are fond of designating "jurisdictional errors."[13]

The border line between what are judicially termed "mere errors," noticed in the preceding section, and "jurisdictional errors" just noted, is not very well defined, and there is much overlapping of the two classes of error.[14]

----

[12] Neale *v.* Utz, 75 Va. 453.

[13] See Windsor *v.* McVeigh, 93 U. S. 274, 282; Nulton *v.* Isaacs, 30 Gratt. 726, 740-742; Lavell *v.* McCurdy, 77 Va. 763; Lancaster *v.* Stokes, 119 Va. 149.

[14] "Jurisdictional error", as applied to this class of errors, is not a happily chosen phrase. *Ex hypothese*, the court has *complete jurisdiction* of the cause, and therefore power to declare the law of the case (*jus—dicere*). The error into which the court has fallen, in so far

IV. Jurisdiction and Venue.

§ 23. (1) Potential jurisdiction and venue.—A discussion of the venue, or the locality of suits, is deferred to the succeeding chapter. But for the purpose of exhibiting the sharp contrast between questions of jurisdiction and of venue, it may be observed here, by way of anticipation, that the term *venue* denotes the *particular county or corporation* in which a given controversy is, in the first instance, properly triable. In short, *venue* has to do with *geographical* or *territorial* considerations, whereas jurisdiction is concerned with questions of *inherent judicial power.*

Thus, as already shown, every circuit and corporation court in Virginia (subject to a few statutory exceptions, to be noted later), is invested with complete equity jurisdiction; and consequently, so far as concerns questions of jurisdiction, every such court has the power to hear and determine *any equity cause brought before it*—and this, without regard to the county or corporation in which the parties reside, or the controversy arose, or in which the subject matter is.

§ 24. The same.—But in order to relieve a defendant from the intolerable nuisance of being haled to a distant county and compelled to submit the trial of his case to a court remote from his residence, the statutes, as we shall see in detail later, have assigned, with some minuteness the particular county or corporation in which suits are to be brought—the county or the corporation of the residence of the defendant, or of the locality of the subject matter, or in which the cause of action arose, being the preferred venue.

When, therefore, exception is sustained to the potential jurisdiction, the cause is in the wrong *court;* if sustained to the

----

transgressing its legitimate powers as to render its action wholly invalid—as if the court, on a bill for an injunction, should decree that the defendant (or both plaintiff and defendant) be hanged— seems more properly to touch the *extent* and *scope* of the court's power, than its jurisdiction. The term jurisdiction is a much abused term at best—see, in corroboration, *infra*, §§ 29, 35. For sake of clearer delimination, the phrase *ultra vires* is here used to indicate the so-called jurisdictional error. See *supra*, § 21.

venue, the cause is brought in the   wrong *county or corporation.*

§ 25. The same—more especially of venue.—The statute, then, investing all courts named, with plenary equity powers, is strictly a jurisdictional statute; but the statutes prescribing rules by which equity causes are to be, as it were, distributed territorially for hearing among the more than one hundred equity courts of the State, are not in any sense statutes of *jurisdiction,* but of *administration* only. These statutes of administration, or venue, affect, not the powers of any court, but are primarily addressed to the *parties* to particular controversies. They do not confer jurisdiction on any court whatsoever. And, as they are meant largely for the benefit of the defendant (preferring as they do the defendant's home county or corporation), the courts have construed them as merely conferring a privilege on the defendant to insist upon the statutory venue—a privilege of which he is required to avail himself at a very early stage of the proceeding by a plea in abatement.[15]

§ 26. (2) Active jurisdiction and venue.—The distinction between the potential jurisdiction of the court and the venue of the suit, considered in the sections preceding, exists as well in connection with the active jurisdiction and venue. As already observed, the active jurisdiction is concerned with the question whether the court has properly acquired the right and power to compel the particular defendant to respond to its *subpœna,* and to obey proper orders and decrees rendered in that particular controversy. On the other hand, the question of *venue* concerns only the exercise of the privilege of the defendant to insist, for example, upon the controversy being tried in his own county or corporation—provided, and provided only, that he asserts his privilege by a plea in abatement at a very early stage of the litigation. If not so asserted, the privilege is lost, and the court will proceed to judgment.[16]

§ 27. Mistake in venue—not jurisdictional. — Enough

---

[15] Va. Code 1919, § 6105. See *infra,* §§ 26, 27.

[16] *In re* Moore, 209 U. S. 490. The distinction here is admirably discussed by Sims, J., in Moore *v.* N. & W. R. Co., 124 Va. 628.

has been said to indicate that a mistake or error in the venue is in no sense jurisdictional. Even if the objection be timely made, an error of the court in overruling the objection would be a mere error, and the judgment or decree valid until reversed by proper proceeding on appeal, or otherwise.

So, on the other hand, it has sufficiently appeared that a mistake in the jurisdiction, potential or active, is fatal and no right or protection whatsoever may be predicated thereon.[17]

§ 28. The same—exception to rule that mistake in venue is not jurisdictional.—It has already been pointed out [18] that where the court is proceeding under a *special statutory and limited jurisdiction,* unknown to the common law, then any substantial departure from the course of procedure specifically prescribed by the enabling statute, will invalidate the judgment. The statutory right must be enforced substantially by the statutory remedy. It follows that if the statute giving the right prescribes a particular venue, the venue and the jurisdiction become coterminous; and therefore a mistake in the one becomes a mistake in the other, with all the consequences heretofore noted.[19]

V. Plea to the Jurisdiction.

§ 29. Plea to the jurisdiction—(1) potential. — The Virginia statute [20] declares that where the . . . bill shows on its face proper matter for the jurisdiction of the court" [i. e., potential jurisdiction] "no exception for want of jurisdiction shall be allowed unless it be taken by plea in abatement." [21]

---

[17] McDonald *v.* Mabee, 243 U. S. 90; authorities *supra.*
[18] *Supra,* § 18.
[19] Examples would be suits for sale of lands of infants and lunatics: Brenham *v.* Smith, 120 Va. 30; Roberts *v.* Hagan, 121 Va. 573; divorce suits: Blankenship *v.* Blankenship, 125 Va. 595; enforced sale of real property in partition proceedings: Roberts *v.* Hogan, *supra—* all of which are statutory rights with prescribed statutory remedies. See post, *Suit for Partition; Sales of Infants' Lands; Divorce; post,* § 29.
[20] Code 1919, § 6105.
[21] With the further provision that "no * * * plea in abatement shall be received after the defendant has demurred, pleaded in bar, or anwsered to the * * * bill, nor after the second rules subsequent to the service of process on such defendant." Id.

It seems clear that the term *jurisdiction* here is inaptly used as denoting *venue only*, since, as we have seen in the foregoing discussion of jurisdiction, if the court is in fact without potential jurisdiction, the defect cannot be supplied by waiver or consent. Mere failure to plead in abatement therefore—thus waiving the objection—cannot confer a jurisdiction which the court cannot under its own constitution, under any circumstance, exercise.[22]

§ 30. The same—(2) active jurisdiction.—The same principle is applicable where the objection goes to the *active* jurisdiction. If the court, howsoever general its jurisdiction, has not properly acquired jurisdiction of the particular defendant or subject matter—because, for example, of the failure to serve process, or service of an invalid process—there is a complete absence of jurisdiction of *that particular cause,* and the cause is as completely *coram non judice* as if potential jurisdiction were itself wanting.[23]

But as the defect of jurisdiction here may be waived, a general appearance and pleading to the merits would operate as such waiver.[24] If the defendant appears, therefore, he should do so *specially*. But having appeared *specially*, he may make the objection by mere motion, without pleading in abatement. If he does not appear at all, a judgment by default would be invalid because of the fatal defect of jurisdiction.

It seems clearly to follow that the statute quoted, declaring

---

[22] Deatrick *v.* State Life Ins. Co., 107 Va. 602. Where the jurisdiction is a limited and statutory one, a plea may become necessary to traverse the jurisdictional allegations, but, as already pointed out (*supra* § 28), such a plea is in *bar* and not in abatement. Jurisdiction of suits for divorce, for example, exists only where one of the parties has been domiciled in this state for one year. If the bill alleges (as it must) the required period of domicile, the jurisdiction may be assailed by a plea or answer denying that jurisdictional allegation. Such a plea however, would not be in abatement, but in bar. It could not give the plaintiff a better writ. Even in absence of any plea, in abatement or in bar, the court must decline the jurisdiction and dismiss the bill, on failure of plaintiff to establish, affirmatively, the necessary jurisdictional facts. Yates *v.* Yates, 115 Va. 678; Blankenship *v.* Blankenship, 125 Va. 595.

[23] An exception is made by Va. Code 1919, § 6103—where a mere *defect in the return* must be pleaded in abatement.

[24] See *infra,* § 31.

that no exception to the *"jurisdiction"* shall be allowed unless taken by plea in abatement, has reference solely to the *venue*, and that the term *jurisdiction* here denotes *venue* and nothing more.[25]

§ 31. Exceptions to jurisdiction—special appearance.

Where the exception goes to the *potential* jurisdiction of the court, it is immaterial whether the defendant appears generally or specially. As the objection cannot be waived expressly, *a fortiori* is an implied waiver by a general appearance ineffectual for any jurisdictional purpose.

Where, however, exception is to be made to the *active* jurisdiction, the right to such exception will be waived by a general appearance and pleading to the merits. Even appearance for purposes of exception to the (active) jurisdiction only, without more, if the purpose be not made clear, may be taken as a general appearance, operating as a waiver. Hence it is always safer, in such cases, for counsel to advise the court that the appearance entered is special and not general.[26]

§ 32. Contrast between jurisdiction and venue—resume.

—To sum up the several distinctions between *jurisdiction* and *venue*:

1. Jurisdiction connotes the powers of the court—venue the place of suit.

---

[25] This statute has existed, practically in this form, in Virginia, since the Code of 1849, and probably from an earlier period. It has been very generally misunderstood by the profession, and has been the source of much litigation—due largely to the unhappy use of the term *jurisdiction* where *venue* is meant. It is believed, after an examination of a large number of cases, that it has uniformly been applied as embracing *venue* only—though rather by interpretation implied than express. So far as known, in no case has the court held, in the plain language of this note, that *the term jurisdiction here denotes venue only,* and that it is only objection to the venue that is required by this section to be pleaded in abatement. But there seems no escape from the conclusion.

[26] See Rhode Island *v.* Massachusetts, 12 Pet. 657; Central Transp. Co. *v.* McGeorge, 151 U. S. 129; Goldey *v.* Morning News, 156 U. S. 518—special appearance to object to the service of the process, and for motion for removal to Federal court; Wabash, etc., R. Co. *v.* Brow, 164 U. S. 281; Hitchman, etc., Co. *v.* Mitchell, 245 U. S. 229; Hilton *v.* Consumers' Can Co., 103 Va. 255.

2. Jurisdiction is a question of law—venue is a question of fact to be established by testimony.

3. Jurisdiction must appear from the allegation of the bill —venue need not so appear.

4. Jurisdiction (potential) may not be conferred by consent —venue may.

5. Error in jurisdiction is fatal—error in venue, not pleaded in abatement, is harmless.

6. Exception to the jurisdiction may be made by demurrer or plea or answer, or orally, or by the court *ex mero motu*— exception to the venue may be made by plea in abatement only.

7. Jurisdiction (potential) contemplates *subject-matter* only —venue contemplates *locality* only; error in the one is in the selection of the *court*—in the other in the selection of the *place*.

8. Jurisdiction is essential to confer venue; but venue is not essential to jurisdiction.

The foregoing comparison between jurisdiction and venue, enables us to reconcile the apparently conflicting principles constantly recurring in the books, namely, the rule that "consent cannot confer jurisdiction," and the rule that "objection to the jurisdiction must be pleaded in abatement, at any early stage of the proceeding."

VI. Jurisdiction as between Law and Equity.

§ 33. Equity exercising common law jurisdiction. — Notwithstanding the principle announced, that the decree of a court without potential jurisdiction is null and void, this result does not follow from the mere circumstance that in the exercise of its concurrent jurisdiction, a court of equity has erroneously taken jurisdiction of a cause regularly brought before it, but properly cognizable only in a common law court. The proceedings would be erroneous, and liable to be set aside on appeal, but would not be void nor subject to be questioned collaterally [27]

---

[27] 1 Pom. Eq. Jurisp. 131; Lemmon *v.* Herbert, 92 Va. 653; Goodman *v.* Winter, 64 Ala. 410; Mellen *v.* Moline, 131 U. S. 352, 367.

no more than would the judgment of a law court be void because the court had inadvertently recognized an equitable claim or defense. *A fortiori* is this result true where, as in Virginia and in the Federal System, the two jurisdictions of law and equity are vested in the same court, though exercised separately. The court, however, will itself take note of the error in the choice of the forum, if observed, and waiver or consent of parties will not cure the error so long as the case is *sub judice,* even in the appellate court.[28]

§ 34. Action at law erroneously brought in a court of equity—transfer.—By the original equity practice, a suit brought in equity but properly cognizable at law only, or *vice versa,* could not be transferred to the proper court—or to the proper side of the court, even where both jurisdictions were ex-exercised by the same court—but must have been dismissed, and the suit brought *de novo* in the proper court.

Recent statutes have wisely altered this rule, both in the Federal and the Virginia practice—provision being made for transfers from the equity to the law court, or *vice versa.*[29]

VII. PRESUMPTION OF JURISDICTION.

§ 35. Jurisdiction—confusion in use of term.—Some of the confusion of thought resulting from the use of the term *jurisdiction* to represent many different situations, has already been adverted to. Courts and commentators have utilized it to designate the general powers of the court under its constitution (*i. e.* its potential jurisdiction) ; again, as including the methods by which the court has proceeded in acquiring and exercising its conceded jurisdiction in a particular case (*i. e.* the *active* jurisdiction) ; again, as importing *venue;* again, as applicable to judgments and decrees of the court, *in excess of its conferred powers;* and, finally, as embracing the right, as between a *court of equity and a court of law,* to try a particular case.

---

[28] Stuart *v.* Coalter, 4 Rand. 78; Boston Blower Co. *v.* Carman Lumber Co., 94 Va. 94; Oelrichs *v.* Williams, 15 Wall. 211.

[29] Equity Rule 22; Va. Code 1919, § 6084; Carle *v.* Corhan, 127 Va. 223.

Unless, therefore, attention is paid to the precise sense in which this overburdened expression is used in the particular statute or judicial opinion, or text, in which it is encountered, the student will find difficulty in groping his way through the medley of apparently conflicting statements of the principles involved.

§ 36. Presumption of jurisdiction—in general.—In view of what has been said in the preceding section, the statement, common in the authorities, that, nothing to the contrary appearing, a judgment or decree of a court of general jurisdiction will be presumed to have been within the jurisdiction, and that the jurisdiction has been regularly and validly exercised, needs qualification. The question can best be studied by distinguishing the senses in which the expression *jurisdiction* is used in the cases in which this presumption has been judicially expounded and applied.

Obviously the presumption, whatever it be, is appealed to, not while the case is *sub judice* in the court that rendered the judgment or decree, but when the validity of the judgment or decree is assailed on appeal, or in a collateral proceeding.

§ 37. Presumption of jurisdiction—(1) Potential. — Since the powers of a court of general jurisdiction are definitely fixed by its constitution—that is, by the unwritten law and enabling statutes—and since the question of jurisdiction here is one of law simply, to be determined from the nature of the case made in the plaintiff's declaration or bill—there is no need or room for presumption in aid of the jurisdiction, unless perhaps where the record has been lost or destroyed, or is otherwise not accessible. A simple inspection of the record determines the question. For example, as before shown, the circuit and corporation courts of Virginia, are courts of general jurisdiction, having cognizance of all cases at law or in equity. If the judgment or decree assailed, were entered by one of these courts, in a case at law or in chancery, in the exercise of law or chancery jurisdiction (that is, according to the course of the common law) the *potential jurisdiction appears*, and must appear, *from the nature of the cause, as shown on the record,* and no presumptions are needed or are to be indulged, in aid of such jurisdiction.

§ 38. The same—(2) Active jurisdiction.—It is in connection with the active jurisdiction that this presumption of the regularity of judicial proceedings, and the validity of judgments and decrees, is most frequently appealed to, and is most effective. Assuming the court to be one of general jurisdiction, and in the exercise of such general jurisdiction, its judgment or decree, when assailed, in another proceeding, or in the same case on appeal, and nothing appearing to the contrary, is presumed to be valid, and its procedure to have been regular. This is but the application of the familiar maxim *omnia praesumuntur rite esse acta.*[30]

§ 39. The same—(3) Statutory or limited jurisdiction. —But where the court, even though one of general jurisdiction, has entered a judgment, decree or other order, in a *summary or statutory proceeding,* and *not in the course of the common law* under its general jurisdiction, such judgment, decree or order, when assailed in another proceeding, or on appeal, will not be aided by the presumption of the court's having properly acquired and exercised the limited jurisdiction bestowed. Here the record must itself show that the conditions of fact essential to the jurisdiction were established, (this, tantamount to potential jurisdiction); and, further, that all specially required forms of procedure, *not in the course of the common law,* were observed.

But, the potential jurisdiction established, and having properly proceeded to acquire the active jurisdiction in the particular cause, and to exercise it according to the prescribed statutory requirement, all of which must affirmatively appear, the court's further action in so far as strictly judicial and not ministerial,

---

[30] See authorities *supra, passim;* Baker *v.* Vorhees, 10 Pet. 472; Applegate *v.* Lexington Min. Co., 117 U. S. 255; Shelton *v.* Sydnor, 126 Va. 625, 632; 15 C. J. 827 *et seq.*

will be entitled to the benefit of the maxim *omnia praesumuntur*.[31]

§ 40. Decree reciting jurisdictional facts.—As already indicated, the facts essential to invest the court with complete potential jurisdiction must, *ex necessitate,* appear on the record, and generally, if not always, on the face of the bill.

But in other cases, as on the question whether process was duly served, whether there was appearance by the defendant, or of other proper steps in maturing and trying the cause (*i. e.* questions of the active jurisdiction), a recital of such facts in the decree is held, as a general rule, to be as binding on the parties as any other fact adjudicated in the cause.[32]

---

[31] See Galpin *v.* Page, 18 Wall 370; Dinwiddie County *v.* Stuart, 28 Gratt. 526; Pulaski County *v.* Stuart, 28 Gratt. 782; *supra,* § 18, and authorities cited.

[32] See Craig *v.* Sebrell, 9 Gratt. 131; Moore *v.* Holt, 10 Gratt. 284, 291; Shelton *v.* Sydnor, 126 Va. 625; Barrey *v.* Saunders, 14 How. 535; Baker *v.* Voorhees, 10 Pet. 472; cases collected 15 C. J. 831 *et seq.* Compare Cooper *v.* Newell, 173 U. S. 555. As to conclusiveness of sheriff's return on the process, see Preston *v.* Kindrick, 94 Va. 760; Miedrick *v.* Lovenstein, 232 U. S. 236; 3 Va. Law Reg. 435; 54 Am. St. Rep. 245, n; Lile's Notes on Equity Jurisp. 244-245; *post,* §§ 65-67.

CHAPTER III.

Jurisdiction, continued.

II. IN PERSONAM—IN REM.

C. *Jurisdiction in Personam.*

§ 41. Jurisdiction in personam.—By this phrase is meant jurisdiction of the *person* of the defendant, as distinguished from the *thing* which constitutes the subject-matter of the controversy. We have already seen that active jurisdiction cannot be exercised unless one or the other of these is within the reach of the court's process; and that, in the absence of express restrictions, the process of every court of general jurisdiction is effective throughout the territorial limits of the state whose authority it exercises, but not beyond.

Thus, in the absence of express statutory restrictions, process from a Virginia court is effective throughout Virginia, but cannot be effective in any other state without the latter's consent; and no state is likely to consent to such an invasion of its sovereignty. Hence process from a Virginia court cannot operate as personal service when served on a defendant in another state. But when properly served on the defendant *within the home state,* the court acquires jurisdiction *in personam.* It is a fundamental principle that without such jurisdiction *in personam* no valid personal judgment or decree can be entered against any defendant. Such a proceeding would be without due process of law.[1]

---

[1] Pennoyer *v.* Neff, 95 U. S. 714; Baker *v.* Baker, Eccles & Co., 242 U. S. 394; Johnson *v.* Merritt, 125 Va. 162; DeArman *v.* Massey, 150 Ala. 639, 44 So. 688. *Divorce proceedings* are regarded as directed rather against the civil status of the parties than against the defendant personally, and are hence *quasi in rem.* 2 Bishop. Mar. Div. and Sep. §§ 23-27. Mere ownership of property within the state does not confer personal jurisdiction over the owner. And the question is one

D. *Jurisdiction in Rem.*

§ 42. Jurisdiction in rem.—Where jurisdiction of the person is thus lacking, but the *subject matter* of the litigation is within the state, and therefore subject to the process of the court, the court is then said to have jurisdiction *in rem*, or *quasi in rem*.

In order that this jurisdiction *in rem* may be effectively exercised, it is essential to due process of law that the proceeding be primarily *in rem* or *quasi in rem*, and not merely against the defendant personally. Such a proceeding must be directed specifically against the *property itself*, with the purpose of having the *res* directly affected by the decree of the court.

Examples of such proceedings are: suits to enforce subsisting liens, such as mortgages, mechanics' liens or judgments; suits to remove clouds from title to property; suits to recover possession of property, or to establish or enforce a trust therein; attachment proceedings; creditors' bills, divorce proceedings, etc.[2]

§ 43. The same—order of publication.—In cases such as these (i. e. *in rem*), where there can be no personal service by reason of the defendant's non-residence, the statutes of all the states permit citation of the defendant by publication of the summons in a prescribed newspaper, or (in Virginia as an alternative) by personal service in the foreign state.[3]

§ 44. Order of publication—effect of the decree.—It has long been settled that no personal judgment or decree can be had against a non-resident, or against any defendant beyond the

---

of *jurisdiction*, not of *notice*, so that it is immaterial that the non-resident defendant had notice of the proceeding and an opportunity to make defense. DeArman *v.* Massey, *supra;* Harkness *v.* Hyde, 98 U. S. 476; Scott *v.* Streepy, 73 Tex. 547, 11 S. W. 534.

In addition to *in rem* proceedings against the property of non-residents, similar *in rem* or *quasi in rem* proceedings are common against resident defendants, though in such cases the proceedings are normally *in personam* as well—so that personal service of process substitutes the service by publication. See *infra*, n. 4.

[2] Roller *v.* Holley, 176 U. S. 398, and cases *supra*.

[3] Va. Code 1919, §§ 6069-6071.

territorial jurisdiction of the court, on summons served by publication, or personally served beyond the limits of the home state, unless the defendant voluntarily appears and submits to the jurisdiction. It is an equally settled principle that in a proceeding *in rem,* or *quasi in rem,* as described above, properly brought and conducted in accordance with the local statutes, the decree will effectually bind the *res* against which the proceeding is, but no further.

It follows that if a non-resident own property in Virginia encumbered by a mortgage or other lien, the creditor may enforce his lien against such property, on a summons by publication against the debtor. So, where there is no lien, but the creditor institutes proper attachment proceedings against his debtor's property within the jurisdiction, he may subject the attached property to his debt. But it is important to observe that the judgment or decree in such proceeding binds only the property actually proceeded against, and no other, and never the person of the defendant who has not voluntarily appeared in response to the published summons. The owner of property is presumed to be in possession of it, in person or by agent, and when such proceedings are taken against his property the defendant is presumed, for the purposes of that suit, *and so far (and so far only) as that particular property is concerned,* to have notice of the proceedings when summoned by order of publication.[4] The proceeding partakes somewhat of the nature of condemnation proceedings.

The statute makes provision for two years of grace within which defendants summoned by publication and not appearing, may have the cause reheard, and any resulting injustice corrected.

------

[4] Pennoyer *v.* Neff, 95 U. S. 714; Roller *v.* Holley, 176 U. S. 398. "Can the Island of Tobago pass a law to bind the rights of the whole world? Would the world submit to such an accursed jurisdiction?" —Lord Ellenborough, in Buchanan *v.* Rucker, 9 East R. 191. See Johnson *v.* Merritt, *supra;* 32 Harvard Law Review, 870. If the defendant is a resident, and within the state—or a domestic corporation— an order of publication, under statutory authority, is much more effective. See A. S. White & Co. *v.* Jordan, 124 Va. 465.

E. Exterritorial Jurisdiction.

§ 45. Exterritorial jurisdiction. — The familiar maxim that equity deals with the individual is in a large measure the key to the principles by which equity is governed in dealing with an exterritorial *res*. The general rule is that if equity has personal jurisdiction of the parties, it may exercise jurisdiction of controversies between them though concerning exterritorial property, real or personal. Since the decree in such case is binding on the conscience of the defendant and since the defendant is within the range of the court's process, he may be compelled, by the process of contempt, to obey the decretal mandate of the court, even though that require the delivery or conveyance of exterritorial property, real or personal.[5]

§ 46. The same—exception.—The rule just stated, that it is sufficient for the purpose of adjusting controversies concerning exterritorial property, that equity has jurisdiction of the individual, is subject to an exception where the nature of the controversy requires that the court deal directly with the *res* itself. In such cases equity will usually decline the jurisdiction. Examples of such instances are suits for partition [6], sales of infants' land [7], and injunctions against trespass on lands, nuisances, etc.[8]

---

[5] Vaught *v.* Meador, 99 Va. 569, 7 Va. Law Reg. 341, n; Hotchkiss *v.* Middlekauf, 96 Va. 649, n. 23 L. R. A. 294; Newton *v.* Bronson, 13 N. Y. 587, 67 Am. Dec. 89, monographic note.

[6] Poindexter *v.* Burrell, 82 Va. 507.

[7] Hotchkiss *v.* Middlekauf, *supra.* See Am. Banking Co. *v.* Am. Surety Co., 127 Va. 209.

[8] Northern, etc., R. Co. *v.* Michigan Central, etc., R. Co., 15 How. (U. S.) 233; 2 L. C. E. 1817-1832.

CHAPTER IV.

Venue, or Place of Suit.

§ 47. Venue statutory.—The venue or place of suit, within a particular state, is always a matter of statute law.

In Virginia detailed provision is made with reference to the particular county or corporation in which suits may be brought.

§ 48. Venue of chancery suits in Virginia—We cannot here go into the detailed provisions of the statute, but must be content with a bare outline. The statute [1] provides that "any action at law or suit in equity," except where it is otherwise specially provided, may be brought in any county or corporation:

(1) Wherein any of the defendants may reside.

(2) If a corporation be a defendant, (a) where its principal office is; or (b) wherein the mayor, rector, president or other chief officer resides.

(3) If it be to recover land, or to subject it to a debt, then the proceeding may be in the county or corporation wherein such land, or any part thereof, may be.

(4) Special provision is made for suits against insurance companies, foreign corporations, non-residents, and suits in which the commonwealth or certain public officers are parties defendant.

(5) It is further provided that an action or suit may be brought in any county or corporation wherein the cause of action, or any part thereof, arose, although none of the defendants reside therein.[2]

§ 49. The same—provisions cumulative.—It is important to observe that the several provisions of this statute are, in the main, cumulative, and not exclusive of each other. For ex-

---

[1] Va. Code 1919, § 6049.
[2] Id. § 6050.

ample, a suit to subject land to the lien of a judgment may be brought under provision (1) "where any of the defendants reside," or under provisions (3) "where the land may be." [3]

§ 50. Mistake in venue.—If suit be instituted in any county or corporation contrary to the foregoing regulations, the objection will be, in general, not that the court in which the suit is thus erroneously brought is without *jurisdiction*, but merely that there is an error of *venue*—that is, that the defendant is sought to be deprived of the personal privilege of having the suit brought and tried in some other locality. It is an objection that may be waived, as already shown,[4] and, is waived unless the defendant pleads in abatement at an early stage of the proceeding.[5]

Numerous other special provisions with reference to venue of particular suits will be noticed as these suits are encountered in later sections of the volume.[6]

§ 51. Venue continued—in the Federal courts.—The particular locality in which suits in the Federal courts are to be brought is fixed by the Federal statutes. For the details of these statutory provisions, reference must be had to the statutes themselves.

For general purposes of venue, however, it may be said that the Federal Judicial Code distinguishes between cases in which the jurisdiction is based on the ground (1) of diverse citizenship, and (2) not on grounds of diverse citizenship. In the former case (subject to numerous exceptions) the suit may be brought either in the district where the defendant resides or that

---

[3] Harrison *v.* Wissler, 98 Va. 597; 6 Va. Law Reg. 471.

[4] *Supra,* §§ 22-30.

[5] Va. Code 1919, § 6105; Moore *v.* N. & W. R. Co., 124 Va. 528; *In re* Moore, 209 U. S. 490. A different principle applies where a *new right* is given by statute, and a *particular court* or a *limited venue*, or a specific remedy or procedure, is prescribed for the enforcement of the right. Here the right and the remedy go together, and the question of *venue* becomes one of *jurisdiction. Supra,* § 18.

[6] See *post,* chapters on *Divorce, Injunctions, Sales of Infant's Lands, Partition,* etc.

in which the plaintiff resides. In the latter case the proper venue is the district in which the defendant resides.[7]

CHAPTER V.

Process to Commence the Suit.

§ 52. Process in equity courts—its nature. — In the common law courts the process to begin the action varies with the nature of the action. If this be debt, or *assumpsit,* or covenant, the process or writ is likewise in debt, *assumpsit,* or covenant, as the case may be.

In equity, however, the process is uniformly a *subpœna,* or summons, requiring the defendant to appear and make defense "to a bill in chancery filed against him," with no further indication of the nature of the suit.[1]

§ 53. The same—when issued.—Under the original equity practice the *subpœna* could be had only on the filing the bill of complaint, in which were set forth the demands of the plaintiff, and in which was a prayer for the issuance of the writ.

In Virginia, while the writ *may* issue after the bill is filed, it is common practice, sanctioned by statute,[2] to issue the process in advance of the filing of the bill—the latter being filed only at the return day of the process.

In the Federal courts, the process cannot be had until after the filing of the bill.[3]

§ 54. The same—injunction suits.—Where preliminary action by the court is required, as in the case of applications for preliminary injunctions or appointment of receivers, of course the bill, even in ʻVirginia, must be filed before such

---

[1] Judicial Code, § 51. For an instructive exposition see Prof. Dobie, *Venue in the United States District Court,* 2 Va. Law Review, 1.
[2] See form, *infra,* § 63.
[3] Va. Code 1919, §§ 6061, 6078.
[4] Equity Rule 12.

preliminary action can be had, since the court or judge could not grant the injunction, or take other preliminary action desired, without knowledge of the case made in the bill. And as the injunction order is usually endorsed on or attached to, and served along with, the *subpœna*, it follows that in such suits the bill is always filed before issuance of the process.

§ 55. Process continued—how and by whom issued.— The subpoena is issued by the clerk of the court in which the suit is instituted, on the written order of plaintiff's counsel.

§ 56. The same—the memorandum or præcipe.—For his own protection, the clerk requires that counsel who apply for the issuance of process shall enter a written order for the desired process, in a book kept for the purpose. This order is known as the *"memorandum"* or *"praecipe,"* and the book (in Virginia) as the *"memorandum book."*

This memorandum is only for the guidance of the clerk, and is no part of the record in the cause. It should contain all data necessary for making out the desired process—such as the names of all the parties plaintiff and defendant; the rule-day or other day to which the process is to be made returnable; the county or corporation in which the several defendants reside, so that the clerk may be able to direct the process to the proper officers for service; who, if any, of the defendants are infants, or lunatics, or non-residents, with proper directions for the appointment of a guardian ad litem for those under disability; and for an order of publication against the non-residents. If the suit is to be accompanied by an attachment or injunction, directions should be given as to the property to be attached, and as to the service of the injunction. The memorandum should contain such other details and directions as the particular case may demand, and should be signed by counsel.

The following form will serve as a specimen:

Form of Memorandum.

Hiram Higgins, in his own right and as executor of Joseph M. Higgins, deceased, *v.* Sallie T. Higgins; Mary H. Smith (who was Higgins) and James R. Smith, her husband; Ann C. Rose (who was Higgins) and Samuel L. Rose, her husband; the Richmond Trust Company, a domestic corporation whose chief office is in Richmond; Mariah E., William Q. and Thomas W. Brooks, infant children of Ella H. and John B. Brooks, both deceased; Joshua S. Thompson, administrator of Robert H. Simpson, deceased, and Philip W. Simpson, a non-resident of Virginia, whose post-office address is 321 Chestnut Street, Philadelphia, Pa.

Issue *subpœna* in chancery against all defendants (omitting infants) to the sheriff of Albemarle county, with the following exceptions: Richmond Trust Company to the sergeant of the city of Richmond; order of publication [4] against Philip W. Simpson, a non-resident, in Charlottesville Progress. Appoint Albert S. Bolling, guardian *ad litem* for the infant defendants.

December 1, 1921.

WALKER & PLATT,
For plaintiff.

§ 57. Process continued—how served. — In Virginia, service of process is made by the sheriff of the county or sergeant of the corporation in which the service is made; or (save in divorce suits) service may be made by a private individual if verified by affidavit.[5]

The method of service is by delivering a copy of the process to the defendant in person. Further provision is made for constructive service, as by delivery to defendant's wife, etc., as in the case of process from a common law court.

In the Federal courts service is made by the marshal or his deputy or by a private individual appointed by the court for the purpose.[6]

§ 58. The same—when and where returnable.—In Virginia, process in chancery suits is placed by the statute, and

---

[4] Counsel should himself prepare the order of publication, to assure himself that it conforms strictly to the provisions of the statute, instead of delegating this important document to the clerk as is commonly done.

[5] Va. Code 1919, §§ 6041-6042, 6062.

[6] Equity Rules 13, 15.

by the prevailing practice, on all fours with process in actions at law, as well to issuance and service as to the return thereof.[7]

§ 59. Process continued — infant or insane defendants.—The rule denying infants or insane defendants the privilege of appearing in a court of law in person, or by attorney, is equally applicable to courts of equity. Hence, while such defendants are sued in the same manner as persons *sui juris*, yet after the bill is filed no further proceedings can be had against them until a guardian *ad litem* is appointed to represent their interests in the suit.

In Virginia the appointment may be made by the court or the clerk, and the appointee must be a competent and discreet attorney at law, if one can be found willing to serve. In the Federal courts the appointment is made by the judge or court.[8]

§ 60. The same—service on infants and lunatics.—In the absence of statute declaring otherwise, it is always safer (perhaps necessary) to serve process on infant and lunatic defendants.

In Virginia, the statute declares in terms that where a guardian *ad litem* is regularly appointed, there need be no service of process on either infant or insane defendants.[9]

But in order that the infant or lunatic may thus become, constructively, a party to the suit, and bound by the proceedings, it is essential that the guardian *ad litem* enter his appearance by answer or otherwise. On the failure of the guardian *ad litem* thus to enter appearance, the infant or lunatic is not properly a party to the suit, and hence the proceedings are invalid as to him.[10]

§ 61. The same—personal judgment. — Where a *personal* judgment or decree is desired, as distinguished from a decree disposing of the incompetent's property (*in rem*), per-

---

[7] See Va. Code 1919, §§ 6055-6056. As to the method of summoning defendants, resident or non-resident, by publication, see Va. Code 1919, § 6068. As to return of process in the Federal Courts, see Equity Rule 12.

[8] Va. Code 1919, § 6098; Fed. Equity Rule 70. See *Suits against Infants, infra.*

[9] Va. Code 1919, § 6098.

[10] Jeffries *v.* Jeffries, 123 Va. 147.

sonal service seems essential, in spite of statutory provisions to the contrary.[11] Though the infant or lunatic be incapable of understanding the import of process so served, service will at least apprise his friends, or others in whose charge or custody he may be.

§ 62. Writ tax.—In Virginia there is a writ tax of $1.50 on every chancery suit instituted, which must be paid to the clerk at the time of institution of the suit.[12]

§ 63. Process continued—variance between the writ and the bill.—According to common law practice, the writ must conform to the declaration, and its failing to so conform is ground for a plea in abatement. An illustration of such a variance would be a writ in debt and a declaration in *assumpsit*, or *vice versa*—or a writ in which A. is named as plaintiff and B. and C. as defendants, followed by a declaration in which B. alone is named as defendant.[13]

No such plea is known in the equity practice for the very good reason that there is *no requirement that the writ and the bill shall conform*. At law there is but a single writ, each defendant being entitled to the service of a copy, and the original is retained by the sheriff for the purpose of making his return thereon. Hence all the copies must conform to the original; and by a technical rule of practice the original must conform to the declaration.

On the other hand, in equity a separate *subpœna* may be issued for each defendant, *without naming any of the other defendants;* and whether a single writ is issued against several defendants, or separate writs against each defendant, the plaintiff may file his bill against but one of them, or against any number less than the whole—the effect being simply to exclude those

---

[11] N. Y., etc., Ins. Co. *v.* Bangs, 103 U. S. 435. See generally, Parker *v.* McCoy, 10 Gratt. 606; Strayer *v.* Long, 83 'Va. 715; Hess *v.* Gayle, 93 Va. 469; Simon *v.* Craft, 102 U. S. 427; Evans *v.* Johnson, 39 W. Va. 299; note 26 L. R. A. 739; Chavannes *v.* Priestly (Iowa), 9 L. R. A. 191.

[12] Va. Code, 1919, § 2401.

[13] Id. § 6103.

not named in the bill as defendants.[14]

The statute cited above, making provision for pleas in abatement for variance, in terms applies only to *actions* at law.

THE SUBPOENA.

The Commonwealth of Virginia,
To the Sheriff of Albemarle County greeting:

We command you that you summon *Peter Quinby* to appear before the judge of our Circuit Court for the County of Albemarle, at the clerk's office of our said court, at rules to be holden therefor, on the *first Monday in January next,* to answer *a bill in chancery* exhibited against him in our said court by *John A. Kendrick.* And have then there this writ.

Witness William L. Maupin, the clerk of our said county, at the courthouse thereof, this the 18th day of December, in the year of our Lord 1921, and of our foundation the one hundred and forty-fifth.

(signed) William L. Maupin,
Clerk.
By CHAS. E. MORAN,
Deputy Clerk.

§ 64. The sheriff's return.—The officer who serves the writ is required to endorse thereon his certificate of service—usually termed his 'return.' When served on the defendant personally, the usual form of the return is "executed on the ———— day of ———— 19 —," with the signature and official title of the officer.

Where the service is a substituted or constructive one, under special statutory provisions, the return must show on its face that the service was made under the conditions and in the mode prescribed by the statute,[15] else it will be quashed on motion—or, in Virginia, in certain cases, on plea in abatement.[16]

———

[14] See Equity Rule 12—declaratory of the unwritten rule.

[15] For details, see Burks' Pl. and Pr. (2nd ed.) § 181.

[16] "A defendant on whom a valid process summoning him to answer *appears to have been served,* shall not take advantage of any defect in the writ or *return* * * * unless the same be pleaded in abatement." Va. Code 1919, § 6103.

§ 65. The same—conclusiveness.—There is a wide diversity of view as to whether the truth of the sheriff's return of service may be controverted by the defendant—especially after judgment by default, followed by effort on the part of the defendant to enjoin the judgment on the ground that the return is false, and that in fact the defendant was never served with process, and therefore had no opportunity of making his defense.

The authorities seem almost equally divided on the question—save that all agree that if defendant can show *collusion* between the plaintiff and the officer, he will be entitled to an injunction against the judgment.

The Virginia court and the United States Supreme Court, together with the courts of a large number of the States, have adopted the negative side of the question, leaving the defendant to his remedy at law against the officer and his sureties.[17]

§ 66. The same—arguments pro and con.—There is much to be said on both sides of the question. In favor of the *affirmative* view, it may be said that to hold the defendant bound on a judgment in a proceeding of which he had no notice, seems to violate the fundamental doctrine that *every man is entitled to his day in court*—that is, due process of law under the United States Constitution.

The argument for the *negative* view is, that since the sheriff is a sworn and bonded officer, the court has a right to presume that his official return is true; and to permit a judgment entered

---

[17] See Preston *v.* Kindrick, 94 Va. 760; Knox County *v.* Harshman, 133 U. S. 152; Miedrick *v.* Lovenstein, 232 U. S. 236. The authorities are collected in a learned note to 19 Am. Dec. 135. See editorial note, 3 Va. Law Reg. 435-9; note 54 'Am. St. Rep. 245. The Virginia Court has carried the doctrine to an extreme and probably unwarranted length, by holding that even where the defendant appears in the case *before final judgment*, and offers to controvert the truth of the return, he will not be permitted to do so, unless fraudulent collusion with the plaintiff be alleged and proved. Sutherland *v.* Peoples Bank, 111 Va. 515; *contra* Fowler *v.* Mosher, 85 Va. 421. Notwithstanding the fact that the Supreme Court of the United States is committed to the negative view, it has approved an injunction in just such a case. Earle *v.* McVeigh, 91 U. S. 503. Recital of service in the decree is sufficient proof thereof. Sergeant *v.* State, 12 How. (U. S.) 371; Chesapeake, etc., R. Co. *v.* Washington, etc., R. Co., 99 Va. 715.

on such return to be afterwards set aside on mere oral testimony would *open the door to fraud,* and render judgments far less secure than the law regards them. The contrary rule would practically require the sheriff to take witnesses with him in every case to establish the fact of service.

§ 67. The same—foreign judgment.—The right thus to assail the truth of the return seems to be settled in all the courts, where the judgment in question is the judgment of a foreign state or country.[18]

CHAPTER VI.

Proceedings in the Clerk's Office.

§ 68. Maturing the suit.—As the proceedings in a chancery suit in Virginia, from the issuance of the original process to the maturity of the suit for hearing, are quite similar to the procedure at law, the student is referred for further details in this connection to the scholarly treatment of such proceedings by Professor Graves, in his course on Pleading and Practice at Law.[1]

Certain differences between the procedure at law and in equity, in maturing the cause for hearing, will be pointed out in connection with the particular pleadings to be noticed hereafter.

§ 69. Brief outline of proceedings.—In briefest outline, the proceedings in the clerk's office for the maturing of a suit in chancery are as follows: (1) Issue of process, returnable to a specified rule-day, or first day of a term; (2) return of the process by the sheriff on the day named, and on the same day filing of plaintiff's bill; (3) entry by the clerk of *decree nisi* [the translation of which barbarous phrase is that unless (*nisi*) defendant shall file his answer, or other pleading, by the next rules, two weeks off, the bill will be taken for confessed]; (4)

---

[18] Knowles *v.* Gas Light Co., 19 Wall. 58.
[1] And to Professor Burks' admirable treatise on the Pleading and Practice in Virginia.

filing of defendant's pleading at the next rule day as required in the decree *nisi*—or, in case of default, the clerk enters an order taking the bill for confessed (*pro confesso*); (5) if answer is filed, the plaintiff enters a general replication thereto, which, under the new Code, is required to be done by the clerk without special directions; and (6) whether answer be filed or not at the rule day mentioned, the clerk is required, as soon as the suit is matured, to set the same for hearing; and no further proceedings are had in the clerk's office; except to put the case upon the docket.

The case now passes from the control of the clerk into that of the court.[2]

§ 70. The same—in the Federal courts.—The new Equity Rules have made radical changes in the former practice. Among other notable changes the following may be mentioned here: Rule-days are abolished;[3] process is returnable within twenty days from the date of its issuance, and the answer must be filed within *twenty days* after process served;[4] in default of answer so filed the bill may be taken *pro confesso* (unless for cause shown) and thereafter the cause proceeds *ex parte*.[5]

§ 71. Proceedings on default of appearance.—In probably all systems of pleading in civil cases, the failure of the defendant to appear and make defense, after due notice, is taken as a *confession* of the truth of the matters alleged against him in the plaintiff's pleading. But it will frequently happen that, in spite of such implied confession, further proof is necessary before the plaintiff may have a final judgment or decree for the specific amount or thing to which he is entitled.

Thus, in the common law system of pleading (slightly modified in this respect by the Virginia statute),[6] if the action sound in damages, judgment by default of appearance is final only as to the validity of the *cause of action*, whereas the *amount of*

---

[3] See Va. Code 1919, §§ 6138-6139, containing sundry provisions for speeding the cause.
[3] Equity Rule 19.
[4] Equity Rule 12.
[5] Id. 16, 17.
[6] Va. Code 1919, §§ 6132, 6133.

damages must be ascertained on a writ of inquiry. If, however, the action does not sound in damages, but is brought for recovery of a specific thing or a definite amount due by contract, no writ of inquiry is required, and, after the expiration of the grace fixed by the statute, the office judgment is final, without evidence *aliunde*.

§ 72. The same—bill taken pro confesso.—In equity suits, under the Virginia practice, as indicated, where the defendant fails to plead at the rules, a decree *pro confesso* is entered againt him in the clerk's office. When the order is so entered, and the cause is on the docket at the beginning of the next term, the question of further procedure is naturally one of interest and importance to the plaintiff. Is he entitled, then and there, to a decree on the merits, or is the defendant entitled to further grace?

§ 73. Effect of bill taken for confessed.—Where the bill is thus confessed, and the cause is matured and on the docket, the procedure is assimilated to that in the law courts, in that the character of the decree to which the plaintiff is entitled, depends upon the nature of the case. The confession is sufficient proof of *all matters of fact properly and specifically pleaded in the bill.* If these allegations of fact be sufficiently definite to base a final decree thereon, the plaintiff may have such a decree at once without further grace to the defendant;[7] if not thus sufficiently definite, further proceedings may be required.

For example, where process has been duly served in a suit to set aside an alleged fraudulent conveyance, a confession by default is sufficient proof of the fraud.[8] But while sufficient proof of the *fraud,* yet if the bill in such case should fail to allege distinctly the *amount of the plaintiff's debt,*—describing it, for example, as a "large sum"; or where a trustee or other fiduciary is sued for a settlement of his accounts; or the bill

---

[7] See *infra,* next section.

[8] See Price *v.* Thrash, 30 Gratt. 515, 522; Fischer *v.* Lee, 98 Va. 159; Thompson *v.* Wooster, 114 U. S. 104; Hefner *v.* Ins. Co., 123 U. S. 747; 1 Va. Law Reg. 546.

seeks to enforce the lien of a judgment without indicating specifically the lands to be subjected—in all such cases, manifestly no final decree can be entered on the confessed bill, and further proof is required.

§ 74. Setting aside a decree pro confesso.—The statute with reference to setting aside office *judgments* by a plea to the merits within the first fifteen days of the next term [9] is in terms applicable to *judgments* (at law) only, and not to *decrees* in equity. So, it would seem that in a case proper for a decree on the merits, the plaintiff may take such a decree as the confession warrants, forthwith, on the opening of the term.[10]

§ 75. Filing of belated answer.—Under the former practice in Virginia, sanctioned by statute, the defendant was permitted to file his answer at *any time before final decree,* although the filing of the belated answer did not entitle him to have the cause continued or sent back to rules.[11] Leave to file the delayed answer was usually granted on condition that the trial of the cause should not be thereby delayed.

The present statutory rule requires that the defendant shall file his answer *within six months* from the date of service of process on him, unless such time be lessened or increased by the court. If his answer or defense is not filed within such time, it is declared that the same shall not be allowed to be filed *except for good cause shown,* and upon payment of certain costs, and upon certain terms prescribed by the court.[12]

It will be noted that this section of the Code is largely based on Federal Equity Rules 16 and 17, though much less severe.

---

[9] Va. Code 1919, §§ 6134-6135.
[10] See Equity Rule 16.
[11] Va. Code 1887, § 3275.
[12] Va. Code 1919, § 6122. See the statute for details. It is an interesting question, not known to have been judicially settled in Virginia, whether, on a bill taken for confessed, the cause may thereafter proceed *ex parte,* as required by the Federal Equity Rules, or whether the defendant, notwithstanding his default and confession, is entitled to notice of further proceedings, as the taking of depositions or proceedings before the master. The latter is believed to be the practice in Virginia—though probably not justified on principle.

§ 76. The same—grace for filing answer.—It is quite clear that the new provision mentioned in the last section, requiring the defendant to file his answer *within six months,* is not meant as requiring a stay of proceedings in the cause for six months, awaiting the answer. This section (6122) is to be construed with § 6131, requiring filing of the answer *at the rules following the filing of the bill;* and, in default of answer *at that time,* requiring the clerk to enter the bill *as taken for confessed*—which result, under § 6138, makes it the duty of the clerk to *set the cause for hearing,* and place it *on the court docket.*

It follows, then, that the new provision providing that the answer shall be filed within six months from the service of the process, is intended merely as a substitute for the former provision that answer might be filed at any time before final decree. If this be true, then the new six months' rule is a statute limiting a privilege rather than enlarging it—and in no wise stays the hand of the plaintiff or of the court in the meanwhile.[13]

§ 77. Bill pro confesso, continued—exceptions.—While the general rule, as stated, is that in default of appearance by the defendant a decree *pro confesso* will be entered as a matter of course, there are certain exceptions which it may be well to notice here—exceptions based on soundest principles; namely: (1) Where defendant has not been personally served with process, but has been summoned by *order of publication;* [14] (2) In *divorce* proceedings[15]—for obvious reasons; (3) In proceedings against *infants and lunatics.*[16] In these cases, in default of appearance, the cause is simply "set for hearing."

---

[13] The revisors say in their note to § 6122 that the provision was enacted in the interest of expediting the hearing of chancery causes, and in lieu of the old section permitting the filing of the answer at any time before final decree.

[14] See Va. Code 1919, § 6132.

[15] Id., § 5106.

[16] Id., § 6098.

CHAPTER VII.

Parties to Equity Suits.

§ 78. Preliminary.—Before passing to the consideration of the pleadings in detail, it will be well at this point to consider briefly the question of *proper* or *necessary parties* to chancery suits.

§ 79. Parties at law and in equity contrasted.—The difference in the practice at law and in equity with respect to parties is marked, and should receive the careful attention of the student.

The variance springs from the essential difference in the functions of the two courts. These functions cannot here be contrasted in detail, but for present purposes may be briefly summarized.

§ 80. Basis of rules as to parties in both courts.—The rules governing the question of parties defendant, at law as well as in equity, depend upon the fundamental principle that proceedings in a suit bind *only those persons who are parties* thereto. The justice of this principle is obvious. Persons not parties have had no opportunity to be heard, and it is contrary to first principles that one should be bound, in his person or his property, by a proceeding to which he was a stranger.

§ 81. Functions of law and equity courts contrasted.—Courts of law sit rather as triers of a disputed right between the plaintiff asserting legal title to such right, and the defendant who is alleged to be infringing or denying that right. Such courts ignore merely equitable rights—whether as between the parties to the action, or as between one or more of these and third persons. The circumstance that the judgment does not settle the whole controversy, or the certainty that, as the result of the liability fixed upon him by the judgment, or satisfied by him under the execution, a particular defendant must undertake other litigation with the plaintiff, or with his co-defendants, or with strangers, before the entire subject-matter of the controversy is beyond dispute, plays no part in the proceeding at law.

On the other hand, courts of equity sit not merely to decide disputed questions of legal right and legal liability, but, in large measure, as *administrative* tribunals, whose duty and pleasure it is to make a *complete disposition* of the property or other subject-matter of the litigation; and, to that end, to settle, once for all, the equitable as well as legal rights of *every person who has an interest in the subject-matter,* so that every such person shall be bound by the decree, and no further litigation among the parties will be necessary or permissible.

§ 82. The same—contrast continued.—Upon judgment had, the court of law, as a rule, takes no part in securing to the plaintiff the fruition of his judgment. The successful plaintiff must, in general, rely on the assistance of the sheriff to put him in possession of the money or property to which the judgment entitles him.

Courts of equity, however, possess proper machinery for specifically securing to the successful party the benefit of the decree, under the very eye of the court.

If the judgment be against several defendants, equally and jointly bound, the plaintiff may levy his execution on the property of any one of them, (even on that of a surety) for the full amount thereof, and wholly ignore the equities of exoneration or contribution among them. And the court of law is powerless, in that proceeding, to interpose and adjust the burden among the several defendants.

On the other hand, a court of equity is astute to see that the person who is to bear the burden at the end, shall assume it at the beginning.

§ 83. The same—contrast continued.—There can be but *two sides* to an action at law, and all parties on either side must be *jointly interested, in precisely the same way.* In short, the parties on either side, howsoever numerous, are regarded as a *unit.* All actions at law, therefore, are *bilateral* only.

In equity, on the other hand, a merely bilateral controversy may almost be said to be exceptional. Here there is no fixed limit to the number of sides that may be represented—and it is a familiar spectacle to find that the main contest is not between the plaintiff and one or more of the defendants, but between one or more defendants on one side, and one or more on the other. Of this, we shall see numerous examples later.

Again, the purpose of every action at law is to fix a legal liability, and the *same liability, on every defendant, and in favor of every plaintiff,* where there are more than one of either— as there may not be, except in case of partners or others in joint liability. That one should be made party defendant at law, for any other purpose than to assert a hostile claim against him, is inconceivable to the common law court, and therefore unknown in its practice.

In equity the situation is wholly different, and for the reason that the policies of the two courts are as dissimilar as are their origin and practice. As already indicated the policy of the equity court is to make a complete disposition of the entire controversy in all of its ramifications, and to award the subject matter of the litigation to him or them of the claimants to whom in equity and good conscience it rightfully belongs. In order, therefore, that the decree in equity may stand forever binding on all claimants, and the controversy rendered completely *res judicata,* all persons who are in any wise interested, and who might again litigate the question thus settled, are required to be made parties to the suit—whether as privileged to participate in the benefits to be adjudged, or liable to share in the burdens to be decreed, or whether impleaded simply to erect an estoppel against them.

§ 84. The same—friendly suits.—It is, therefore, not at all essential nor, indeed, common, for the bill to seek affirmative relief against every defendant named—and, therefore, the same relief need not be sought of every defendant; nor for the several defendants to form a single unit, as at law. Nor need the bill assert any hostile claim whatsoever against any defendant— in which case the proceeding is known as a friendly suit. Suits for partition, for the sale of infants' lands, for the aid of the court in the administration of trust estates, etc., are illustrations of suits that are, or may be, friendly.

It is hoped that this brief contrast between the judicial conception of the functions of courts of law and of equity, respectively, may make clear to the student why the rule as to parties is so widely variant in the two systems; and may, in a measure, prepare the student to understand the reason and application of the rule as to parties in equity, now to be mentioned.

§ 85. Condensed rule as to parties in equity.—It is not possible to formulate a rule full enough, and accurate enough, to determine the question of parties for every case in equity. This often becomes a difficult problem for even the most experienced practitioner. Nor are the courts always in harmony on the question of parties. But, save here and there in an unusual or complicated case, well-informed practitioners find the question of parties in equity comparatively simple. In case of doubt, the safe practice is to resolve the doubt affirmatively, by including the doubtful party as a defendant—since, on objection made, the result of the erroneous inclusion is merely the dismissal of the improper party from the cause.[1]

Now, as to our rule—sufficient, it is hoped, for present purposes: *All persons in being, and within reach of the process of the court, who are in anywise interested, legally or equitably, in the subject-matter of the litigation, and whose interests may be directly affected by the proceedings, whether beneficially or detrimentally, or who might again litigate the precise matter adjudicated, should be made parties to the suit.*

§ 86. Parties in equity—illustrations.—A few examples may serve to illustrate the rule as to parties in equity. Thus,

---

[1] The revisors of the new Virginia Code have wisely provided that no action or suit shall abate, or be defeated, by non-joinder or misjoinder of parties, plaintiff or defendant; but, on affidavit made, new parties may be added, or improper parties dropped, by order of the court at any stage of the cause—Code 1919, § 6102. See the statute for particulars. The statute substantially embodies the provisions of the New Jersey Practice Act of 1912, § 9. See also Va. Code 1919, § 6139.

where a trustee invokes the advice of the court in the administration of the trust, all the *cestuis* must be made parties. Not that any relief is prayed against them, but that they may be bound by whatever action the trustee may take in pursuance of the court's advice and direction.

So where the mortgagee files a bill to foreclose, after death of the mortgagor, he is required to bring in the heirs (or devisees) and the personal representative of the deceased mortgagor.

So where one legatee or distributee seeks an accounting from the personal representative, and a distribution of the estate, not only must the personal representative be a party, but all other legatees or distributees are necessary parties.

So where one or more shareholders institute a derivative suit in equity (as they may under proper conditions) against directors, to assert a liability for negligent or corrupt mismanagement of the corporate affairs, the corporation is a necessary party, since any recovery in the proceeding will be corporate assets, to be converted into the corporate treasury for the benefit of all shareholders.

These are but a few illustrations of the practically universal rule governing the question of parties to equity suits—but a rule which, like most administrative rules, will not be applied *strictissime,* when to do so, in a particular case, would sacrifice justice to form.

§ 87. Classification of parties—"necessary" parties.— Courts and commentators usually classify parties in equity as either *necessary* or *proper* parties.

Those whose presence is essential to a complete determination of the controversy or disposition of the subject-matter, are termed *necessary* parties—since without their presence in the suit there can be no effective decree.

Illustrations of necessary parties are: In a partition proceeding, or in any proceeding by which the joint estate is sought to be affected, as by a judgment, mortgage, mechanic's or other lien —all the co-tenants are necessary parties; the personal representative, and all legatees or distributees of an estate, on a bill filed for distribution of the estate; the corporation, in a derivative suit by shareholders; the grantor as well as the grantee in a suit by creditors to set aside a fraudulent conveyance; all persons against whom an injunction is sought; in a surety's suit for subrogation, the satisfied creditor, as well as the principal—the security being held by, or standing in the name of, the former.

Wherever, in these cases, the suit is *in rem*, or *quasi in rem*, any necessary party who is a non-resident may be summoned by order of publication.[2]

§ 88. The same—"proper" parties.—On the other hand, *proper* parties are those without whose presence in the suit a substantial decree may be made, but not a decree which shall completely settle all questions and conclude all rights involved in the litigation.[3]

For example, a suit to subject the surety's estate, where the principal is a non-resident, and both his estate and his person are out of the reach of the court's process; or a suit on a joint contract, where all the joint contractors cannot be reached. In these and similar cases the suit may proceed without the absentees.

§ 89. The same—in the Federal courts.—A somewhat less strict rule as to parties is made in the Federal courts of equity, consequent upon the limitation imposed upon their jurisdiction by the requirement of *diverse citizenship,* and by their inability to bring in parties who are without the district. In these courts the rule is somewhat more liberal than in the state courts.[4]

§ 89. Parties plaintiff.—The technical rule of the law courts that only those having *legal* title to the subject-matter of the controversy may sue, and that all those holding the legal title *must* unite as plaintiffs, howsoever numerous, is unknown to the equity practice.

On the contrary, where the case is otherwise proper for a

---

[2] *Qu. vid., supra,* §§ 42 *et seq.*
[3] Fletcher, Eq. Pl. & Pr. 40.
[4] See Equity Rules, 37-44; Minnesota *v.* Northern Securities Co.,. 184 U. S. 199; Fletcher, Eq. Pl. & Pr. 40.

court of equity, any person who has an interest, legal or equitable, may, as sole plaintiff—whether others be interested with him or not—file a bill for the protection and enforcement of his rights. If others with whom he is jointly interested refuse to unite as plaintiffs, they may, and should, be made parties defendant, with an explanation of the reasons why they are not parties plaintiff.[5]

§ 90. The same—real party in interest.—At law, in a limited class of cases, it is common practice to permit the equitable owner of a right to assert it by an action in the name of the holder of the legal title. Indeed, in absence of an enabling statute, this is the only way in which the equitable owner can, in any case, assert his rights at law. A once familiar instance of this practice was that of the assignee of a *chose in action* suing at law in the name of the assignor.

In equity, on the other hand, the rule is invariable that the suit must be brought in the name of the *real party in interest*, and not in the name of another.[6] The error here is fatal to the bill—as it is in all cases where the plaintiff has no real interest in the suit.[7]

The Doctrine of Representation of Parties.

§ 91. Parties by representation—(1) as plaintiffs.—Notwithstanding the general rule stated, in certain familiar cases where numerous persons are interested (though not necessarily jointly) in identically the same right, a few as representing the rest are allowed, for convenience, and to avoid an undue multiplication of parties, to prosecute the suit in behalf of themselves and the others concerned. This happens notably in case of shareholders in a corporation, taxpayers of a municipality, and members of a voluntary society, seeking a common purpose, where one or more may sue in behalf of all.[8]

---

[5] See Equity Rule 37—in this respect merely declaratory.
[6] Kane *v.* Mann, 93 Va. 239; Penn *v.* Hearon, 94 Va. 733.
[7] Keyser *v.* Renner, 87 Va. 249.
[8] Coffman *v.* Sangston, 21 Gratt. 263; Lynchburg *v.* Dameron, 95 Va. 545; Siegfried *v.* Perkins, 97 Va. 444; Johnson *v.* Black, 103 Va. 477; The Liberty Bell, 23 Fed. 843; State *v.* Cape May (N. J.), 49 Atl. 584; Crompton *v.* Zabriskie, 101 U. S. 601.

§ 92. Parties by representation—(2) as defendants.—
The general doctrine has already been emphasized that no man
is bound, in his person or property, by a judicial proceeding to
which he was not a party, by lawful process duly served upon
him. It has also been shown that in certain cases [9] one may be
made a party by publication duly authorized and duly executed,
and thus become bound as to a particular *res* against which the
proceeding is directed, without personal process served.

So far as concerns judgments or decrees against the *person,*
there is probably no single exception to the first mentioned
rule.[10] But under the doctrine of representation of parties, (or
'virtual representation') now under consideration, an exception
(actual or apparent) is made, in the interest of convenience, in
order to avoid either a multiplicity of parties, or, in the case of
unknown or unborn persons in interest, an indefinite delay of
proceedings to await the discovery of the unknown or the birth
of the unborn.

The necessities of the situation here have forced courts of
equity to recognize some relaxation of the general rules not
however as to decrees against the *person,* but only those affecting a particular *res,* the subject of the litigation.

**§ 93. Virtual representation, continued — multiplicity
of parties defendant.—**Thus where the plaintiff proceeds
against a voluntary, unincorporated society, composed of many
members, he may sue a few on behalf of the rest, if the purpose
of the suit be, not to fix a personal liability on the members
omitted as parties, but *to subject property interests* of the society.[11]

§ 94. The same—unknown parties.—Again, where a
particular *res* is brought under the administration of the court,
by plaintiffs who, as creditors, or claimants of the whole or
some part thereof, are seeking to assert their rights therein, and
it is known or suspected that other unidentified persons have a
claim to the *res,* or some part of it—as where a former person

---

[9] See *supra.* § 42 *et seq.*

[10] Hitchman, etc., Co. *v.* Mitchell, 245 U. S. 255; *supra,* § 42 *et seq.*

[11] A suit to enforce a debt against an unincorporated church is a
typical example. Linn *v.* Carson, 32 Gratt. 170.

in interest (actual or apparent) has died and his heirs are un-known—the rules of the equity practice permit such unknown persons to be made parties by the general description of "unknown parties." [12]

§ 95. The same—unborn persons.—It not infrequently becomes necessary for courts of equity to dispose of estates which are subject to contingent remainders, or other future interests, which, under the terms of the deed or devise, are limited to persons not yet *in esse*.

The Virginia Code,[13] and statutes of most of the states make provision for the sale of such contingent estates, under the particular conditions and for the purposes set out in the statutes.

But aside from the statutory situation mentioned, the creditors of the donor under whose deed or will the contingent estate has been created, have the right to subject the estate to the payment of their debts in priority to the claims of the donees or devisees, whether vested or contingent. In all such cases, the question of binding the unborn beneficiaries, so that if, and when, they come into being, they may not assail the action of the court, nor the title of the purchaser at the judicial sale, becomes one of prime importance.

§ 96. The same—under statutory proceedings.—Where the proceeding for the purpose of disposing of contingent estates is brought under the statute, and all persons in being who are interested are made parties, the statute itself declares that all persons thereafter born and becoming interested, shall be bound by the proceedings though not parties.[14]

§ 97. The same—not under the statute.—Where, however, the sale of such contingent interests is required, not under nor for the purposes contemplated by the statute, but under a

---

[12] With such marks of identity as can be adduced, such as "the unknown heirs of John Doe, deceased, a former resident of Albemarle County, Virginia, who is believed to have removed to the State of California in the year 1849." See declaratory statute, Va. Code 1919, § 6069.

[13] § 5161.

[14] Va. Code 1919, § 5161. For authorities construing such statutes, see n. 8 L. R. A. (N. S.) 62; Carneal *v.* Lynch, 91 Va 114.

paramount incumbrance executed or suffered by the original donor, such as a mortgage, judgment or other lien—or again where a court of equity is proceeding under its general equity jurisdiction to dispose of a *trust estate* for the general interests of the trust—the question of unborn beneficiaries must, in the absence of statutory aid, be otherwise provided for.

The rule here seems to be that if the holder of the *first estate of inheritance* be made a party, the proceeding will bind all remote interests of claimants not yet born or not yet identified, who would claim in privity of estate.

And where the limitation is so contingent that as yet there is *no vested estate of inheritance* (as "to A for life, remainder to such of her children as may survive her," and A is still living), then it is sufficient that the *life tenant* be treated as virtually representing contingent claimants not *in esse*.[15]

§ 98. The same.—Broadly speaking, the test of the sufficiency of the representation in a particular case is: Was the party, or were the parties, or the class, actually impleaded, *fairly representative* of the persons or class not *in esse*, considering the circumstances of the particular case, and viewed from the standpoint not of the absent and unborn only, but of *the living parties to the suit* in pursuit of their legal and equitable rights.

In such cases, while the court is anxious to guard the rights of the unidentified and absent parties, it must with equal care do justice to the living. It follows that a life tenant who asserts a title hostile to, or occupies a position of indifference to the title under which those not *in esse* must claim, is not a proper representative.[16]

---

[15] See opinion of Moncure, J., in Faulkner *v.* Davis, 18 Gratt. 651, 683-691, where the subject is discussed at length.

[16] Downey *v.* Seib, 185 N. Y. 427, 78 N. E. 66, 8 L. R. A. (N. S.) 1, and monographic note; Baylor *v.* De Jarnette, 13 Gratt. 152: Devise to E for life, remainder to her eldest son living at her death. E had no son at testator's death. Suit by creditors of testator to subject the estate, the life tenant and administrator alone being made parties. Pending the suit, a son was born to E, but not brought in as a party. Held, under the rule of virtual representation, the son is nevertheless bound by the proceedings.

Faulkner *v.* Davis, 18 Gratt. 651: To T in trust for W for life, remainder to her surviving children, and to the descendants of any deceased child, living at her death. Suit by W, life tenant, for sale

§ 99. The same—Federal court rule—trustee as representative of creditors.—By the ordinary rules of chancery practice, both the trustee and the *cestui que trust* are necessary parties to a suit involving the disposition of the trust estate. In the Federal courts, however, and particularly in the case of foreclosure of mortgages or deeds of trust made by corporations to secure an issue of bonds, it is the settled rule that the trustee is the proper representative of the interests of the bondholders, and the latter will not be admitted as parties, save under special circumstances.

The rule rests in the inconveniences and delays likely to result from the presence of numerous litigants. The rule also avoids difficulties of maintaining the federal jurisdiction when resting on diverse citizenship.[17]

§ 100. Parties in several characters. — The student should observe here the striking difference between the practice at law and in chancery in this particular. At law, one cannot sue or be sued in several characters, *e. g.*, in his own right and as administrator. In equity, however, one may, in a proper case, be plaintiff or defendant in as many characters as he represents, *e. g.*, "John Smith, in his own right, and as executor of Hiram Smith, deceased, and as trustee under the will of Mary Smith, deceased," may sue "William Brown, in his own right, and as committee of Anna Brown, a lunatic, and as guardian of Robert Brown, an infant, and as executor of Henry Jones, deceased."

And where it is doubtful whether the right claimed by the plaintiff, or against the defendant, be in one character or an-

---

and reinvestment. The trustee and five living children of W were made parties. Held, after-born contingent remaindermen are bound by the sale.

Harrison *v.* Walton, 95 Va. 221: Devise to H for life, remainder to her children surviving her, and the heirs of such as may be dead. Suit by life tenant for settlement of testator's estate and payment of debts, to which suit all of her living children are made parties defendant. Held, afterborn children of H are bound by the proceedings, as sufficiently represented by those who were actually parties.

[17] See Bates, Fed. Eq. Pr. 55; Corcoran *v.* C. & O. Canal Co., 94 U. S. 741; Va. Pass. & Power Co. *v.* Fisher, 104 Va. 121—approving the rule; 30 Am. Law Review 161; Kent *v.* Lake Superior, etc., Co., 144 U. S. 75. See further, Equity Rules, 37, 41.

other, the plaintiff may sue, or the defendant be sued, in both characters, and a decree may be rendered in the plaintiff's favor in that character in which he appears to be rightfully entitled, or against the defendant in that character in which he appears liable.[18]

§ 101. Defect of parties—how objection made.— Where the defect appears on the face of the bill, the proper course, as in every other case of a pleading defective on its face, is to *demur*. Where the absence of parties does not appear on the face of the bill, the proper course, as in every other case of new facts in avoidance, is to set up the defect by *plea* or *answer.*

§ 102. The same—objection by court ex mero motu. —But if it appear to the court in any manner, that *no proper decree can be entered until necessary parties are brought in,* the court will itself decline to proceed until such absentees are properly made parties. And, in a case of this kind, objection may be made for the first time in the appellate court—for the very good reason that the objection is one that cannot be waived, since the appellate court can no more proceed without necessary parties than can the lower court.

Where, for example, it distinctly appears that the real property of which *partition* is sought, belongs to *five* persons, but that only *four* of them are parties to the suit, the court will not stultify itself by dividing the property among the four, well knowing that the absent party will not be bound by the decree, and may later, in a new suit, render vain the entire proceedings in the first suit. Clearly, in such case, the circumstance that none of the four makes objection to the absence of the fifth co-owner will not prevent the court itself, *ex mero motu,* from raising the objection.[19]

§ 103. The same—waiver of objection.— But where the absent party's presence is *not essential to an effective decree* in the plaintiff's favor, the objection may be waived, and is waived

---

[18] Brent *v.* Washington, 18 Gratt. 526.
[19] The principle is too elementary to require citation of authority. See Sillings *v.* Bumgardner, 9 Gratt. 273.

unless the defendant raises the objection at the proper time; and the same principle applies where the objection is that one or more plaintiffs have been improperly joined.[20]

§ 104. Parties continued—suits by infants and insane persons.—Infants sue in their own names [21] by a *prochein ami,* or next friend,[22] and not by their guardians. Lunatics who have been so adjudged, and for whom a committee has been appointed, should sue in their own names by the committee, who may (as mere surplusage) be styled also as next friend. In the absence of the committee, suit may be by next friend.[23]

----

[20] Vaiden *v.* Stubblefield, 28 Gratt. 153. See illustrations of necessary and proper parties, *supra,* §§ 87-88.

[21] This means that the suit must be the *infant's suit,* and *not that of the next friend.* If in the name of the next friend *"on behalf of the infant"* it cannnot be maintained. No party, infant or adult, may sue by deputy. Morgan *v.* Potter, 157 U. S. 195.

[22] Va. Code 1919, § 5331.

[23] Jackson *v.* Counts, 106 Va. 7; Wheeler *v.* Thomas, 116 Va. 259, 270; Lake *v.* Hope, 116 Va. 687; Equity Rule 70. There is usually *no formal appointment* of the next friend of an infant or lunatic; his being named as such in the bill, and the suit proceeding without objection, is a tacit recognition of him as such by the court. Indeed, it seems to be the settled rule of the unwritten law that any person, though a stranger, may file a bill in the name of any incompetent (infant or lunatic) for the purpose of enforcing a supposed right belonging to such incompetent, even against the latter's will. On objection made, the court will order a proper inquiry, by a master or otherwise, to determine whether the suit shall proceed, and will make such other orders as may seem proper for the protection of the interests involved. Story, Eq. Pl. 60; Klaus *v.* State, 54 Miss. 644; Bethea *v.* Call, 3 Ala. 449; Judson *v.* Blanchard, 3 Conn. 579; Fulton *v.* Rosevelt, 1 Paige 178, 19 Am. Dec. 409; Kingsbury *v.* Buckner, 134 U. S. 650—the opinion in which, by Harlan, J., contains a learned discussion of suits by *procheins amis,* and the powers of the latter.

The statement that there need be no special appointment of the *prochein ami* seems questioned, without noticing the leading authorities, and on what appears to be a mistaken view of the authorities cited, in Lake *v.* Hope, 116 Va. 687, 707-709. It is not quite clear from the opinion whether the fatal error was in the omission of the usual phrase "admitted by the court to prosecute the interests of the lunatic (or infant) in this cause," which, in the absence of specific objection, is taken to be an implied appointment, or whether the court meant to assert the necessity of *a formal appointment in every case.* If the former were meant, the ruling, though highly technical and out of keeping with the liberal spirit of equity pleading in Virginia, is not otherwise objectionable. But if the court meant to declare that an *express and formal appointment of the prochein ami is necessary,* the conclusion is not believed to be supported by approved authority. Since the real point of the decision was that as

§ 105. Suits by infants, continued—by guardian.—
That an infant should sue by his *prochein ami* (or next friend),
and not by his guardian has been the approved practice, at law
as well as in equity, since the early English Statutes of Westminster I, c. 48 (3 Edward I) and Westminster II, c. 15 (13
Edward I). But in some of the states, probably as the result of
statute, the guardian is permitted to sue on the infant's behalf.
In either case, however, whether the suit be by the *prochein ami*
or by the guardian, (in absence of statutory provision to the
contrary), the suit (with an exception to be noted later) is the
infant's suit (not the guardian's) and must be in the *infant's*
name, *by the guardian.*

The guardian, (unlike the executor) has *neither legal nor
equitable title* to the ward's estate; whereas the executor has
such title to the personal estate of the testator, and not infrequently, by the terms of the will, to the realty as well. Neither
of these, normally, has title to the realty of the ward or testator, respectively. The guardian is, therefore, in a sense, an
agent only, with comparatively limited powers—and his agency
does not embrace authority to sue in that character on behalf
of the infant.

Thus he may not file a bill for an accounting on behalf of the
ward against a former guardian [24] nor to recover a distributive
share, in a decedent's estate [25]; nor in any case, it seems, to obtain possession of the ward's property *in the first instance.* If
once in the possession of the guardian, he may, of course, sue

---

the affairs of the lunatic were already in the hands of a regularly
appointed committee, the suit could not be maintained by the next
friend, there was no occasion to pass upon the regularity of the
appointment of the next friend, and the discussion of that question
was *obiter.*

The powers of the prochein ami are extremely limited. While he
has control of the suit, under the immediate supervision of the court,
he has no authority to receive funds payable to the incompetent, nor to
make admissions to the prejudice of the infant, nor to compromise
the suit. He is a mere *quasi* officer of the court, and subject to its
directions. Morgan *v.* Thorne, 7 M. & W. 400, 406; Miles *v.* Kaigler,
10 Yerg. (Tenn.) 10, 30 Am. Dec. 426; Cratty *v.* Eagle (W. Va.), 18
S. E. 59; Bernard *v.* Merrill (Me.), 40 Atl. 136; Burwell *v.* Corbin, 1
Rand. 152, 10 Am. Dec. 494.

[24] Lemon *v.* Harnsbarger, 6 Gratt. 301; Bradley *v.* Amidon, 10
Paige 235.

[25] Sillings *v.* Bumgardner, 9 Gratt. 273.

in his own name to recover possession of that of which he has been ousted; and, by parity of reason, damages for injury to the ward's property in his possession [26]; and of course he may sue on a contract made by himself as guardian.

§ 106. The same—suits against infants and insane persons.—These are brought and conducted as other suits in chancery—against the infant or lunatic personally—but the defendant's appearance and defense are made by a guardian *ad litem* [27] specially appointed to represent the incompetent.[28] Here again the answer or plea must be *in the name of the incompetent,* by the guardian *ad litem,* and not in the name of the latter on behalf of the former.

---

[26] See Burdett *v.* Cain, 8 W. Va. 282; authorities *supra.* There seems to be much confusion in the authorities on the question when the guardian may maintain a suit against a stranger to recover original possession of the ward's estate. See 21 Cyc. 188.

[27] The powers of the guardian *ad litem* are quite similar to those of the *prochein ami. qu. vid. supra.* While he may not, by his admissions or stipulations, prejudice the rights of the incompetent, he may consent to or waive mere matters of procedure not affecting the substantial rights of the ward; for example, he may consent to a hearing in vacation, or to a continuance of the cause, etc. Thompson *v.* Maxwell, etc., Co., 168 U. S. 451; Waterman *v.* Lawrence, 19 Cal. 210, 79 Am. Dec. 212; Lemmon *v.* Herbert, 92 Va. 653; Va. Code 1919, § 6308. See *Sale of Infants' Lands, post.*

[28] Where the affairs of the lunatic defendant are in the hands of a regularly appointed committee, whose interests are not in conflict with those of the lunatic, the committee may make defense, and no guardian *ad litem* is necessary. Hinton *v.* Bland, 81 Va. 588 (*per* Lewis, P.).

CHAPTER VIII.

Outline of the Pleadings.

§ 107. Preliminary.—The pleadings and the practice in chancery are much less technical and complex than those at law. Framed only for the administration of justice between litigants, they are, in the main, based on practical convenience and ·common sense, unincumbered, as are the pleadings at law, by hard and fast rules that owe their origin to an outgrown *regime*. In these respects the equity procedure is in striking contrast with the procedure at common law, which, in many aspects, has elevated questions of form and of adherence to technical rules above considerations of justice to litigants. In the former, the question is rather, Which party has the better right? In the latter, unmodified, Which counsel has the better wit?

§ 108. The pleadings—continued.—That the student may obtain a bird's-eye view of the pleadings which he is to encounter in his subsequent study of them, the more important pleadings in chancery are here listed, with a very brief statement of the general function of each—leaving a more detailed explanation of these functions for later treatment.

1. AGGRESSIVE PLEADINGS.

(1) *The Original Bill.*

A more or less formal statement of the material facts out of which arise the equities which it is the purpose of the suit to protect or enforce. It is the only method of obtaining the ear of the court in an original proceeding.

(2) *The Amended Bill.*

A second bill filed by the plaintiff to correct some defect, or supply some omission, *inherent in the Original Bill*—and used also to take the place of a special replication.

(3) *The Supplemental Bill.*

Substantially the same as the Amended Bill, except that the defect to be corrected, or the matter to be supplied, is due to some occurrence happening *since the Original Bill was filed.*

(4) *The Cross-Bill.*

A bill filed in a pending suit by a *defendant,* against the plaintiff, or against a co-defendant, or both, for the purpose of obtaining either discovery or affirmative relief, or both, and not merely for defense. It inaugurates a cross-suit in connection with the subject-matter of the original suit. The student must observe that a cross-bill may be filed only by a *defendant.*

(5) *The Petition.*

An aggressive pleading, filed in a pending suit, usually by a *stranger* to the suit (that is, one not a party), with the purpose of being made a party, in order to assert some right involved in the litigation—whence the term "intervention proceedings."

(6) *The Bill of Revivor.*

A bill filed in a pending suit, which, by reason of death of a party (or, at common law, the marriage of a *feme*) has abated, and the interests of the decedent have been transmitted to others as his successors in title. The purpose of the Bill of Revivor is to set up the rights of the successor or successors of the decedent, and to revive the original suit, so that it may continue, in its changed form, to a final decree.

(7) *The Bill of Review.*

A bill filed in the trial court, and after a final decree, by any party to a pending suit, plaintiff or defendant, for either of two purposes: (a) To call the attention of the court to some *error of law* committed by the court in previous proceedings in the cause, apparent on the record, and detrimental to the party filing the Bill of Review; and praying the same court to review the decree and correct the error; or (b) To bring to the attention of the court *new and material* evidence discovered since the final decree, which evidence could not have previously been discovered by reasonable diligence—and praying for a rehearing on such newly discovered testimony.

The circumstances under which such a bill may be filed, as well as the rehearing of interlocutory decrees, will be considered later.

2. DEFENSIVE PLEADINGS.

(1) *The Demurrer.*

A pleading which raises an issue of *law,* and not of fact. Its purpose is to test the sufficiency of the adversary's case *as made by the pleading demurred to.* It admits, for purposes of the demurrer, all the facts properly pleaded by the adversary, and submits to the court the question whether these facts entitle the adversary to the relief sought. It may be filed only to an aggressive pleading.

(2) *The Plea.*

A pleading by which the defendant offers a single fact, or a combination of circumstances all tending to *one point,* as a complete defense to the whole bill, or to some distinct and material portion thereof—*e. g.,* the statute of limitations, the statute of parol agreements, a denial of the contract alleged, payment, etc.

(3) *The Answer.*

The most common method of making defense to a suit in equity. By the answer, the defendant enters into a defense at large of all the equities asserted in the bill. The answer makes the discovery called for, if any, or explains why it cannot be made—and sets out at length the circumstances relied upon to repel the plaintiff's claim. A striking peculiarity of the answer, as we shall see later, is that it is not only a *pleading,* but, by the unwritten law, it is a *self-serving instrument of evidence* as well.

(4) *The Disclaimer.*

A rather unusual pleading, by which one who has been impleaded in a chancery suit, but against whom no claim is asserted, denies having, or ever having had, any claim, title or interest, or any pretense thereof, in or to the subject-matter of the litigation, and disclaiming any interest in such litigation. Such a pleading cannot, therefore, be resorted to by one against whom the plaintiff asserts a claim, or of whom discovery is sought. One may disclaim a right but not an obligation or duty.

3. PLEADING COMPLETING THE ISSUE.

The Replication.

The very brief pleading by which the plaintiff takes issue on the facts set up in defendant's plea or answer. It is a bare denial of such facts, and its purpose is simply to put the defendant on notice that his defensive allegations of fact are not admitted, but must be established by evidence. On the filing of the replication, the parties are supposed to be at issue, and the cause matured and ready for the taking of testimony.

Reminder.—The student is again reminded that the foregoing list presents the principal pleadings in equity only in barest outline, and that a more minute study of them must be made in the following pages.

We are now ready to take up a consideration of the several pleadings in somewhat greater detail.

CHAPTER IX.

The Bill.

§ 109. No forms of action in equity.—In the equity procedure one encounters no bewildering rules as to the name or classification of the particular suit, or, according to the nomenclature at law, *"form of action."* When from an investigation of the law and facts, counsel has determined that the client has a good cause for equitable relief, he is saved the problem of wasting brain-sweat in deciding whether he shall sue in debt, *assumpsit,* or covenant, in trover or replevin, in trespass *vi et armis* or trespass on the case. He simply decides to file a "bill in equity."

Naturally, however, as a guide to clear thinking, intelligent counsel will always mentally classify the particular equity suit that he proposes to institute—as a bill for specific performance, for injunction and relief, to trace trust funds, etc.

§ 110. Bills continued—classification.—While a scientific classification of bills is of no practical importance, it may be well to indicate the classes into which they naturally fall, and into which courts and text-writers divide them. These are (1) *Original Bills, and* (2) *Bills not Original.*

These terms of themselves indicate the difference between the two classes. The *Original Bill* is the first pleading filed by the plaintiff. In it the case is stated, and the desired relief prayed for. In the later development of the case, it frequently becomes necessary for the plaintiff to amend or supplement his first statement, whence we have an "amended" or "supplemental" bill; or to revive the suit which has abated by the death of a party, whence the "bill of revivor"; or for a defendant to set up a counter-claim against the plaintiff or some other defendant, which is done by "cross-bill"; in all of which cases the bills are *not original,* and hence are so classified.

(1) *Original Bills.*

§ 111. Classification.—The classification of original bills is extremely simple, namely, (a) Those praying for relief; (b) Those not praying for relief. Here, again, no explanation of terms seems necessary.

§ 112. (a) Bills praying relief.—A bill praying for relief is one that calls upon the court by its decree to protect or enforce some equitable right of the plaintiff—as, for example, a bill for an injunction, or for the specific performance of a contract. Most bills filed in equity are of this nature.

§ 113. (b) Bills not praying relief.—These are comparatively rare. They are filed either to *obtain evidence* for use in another forum ("discovery" only), or to *preserve evidence* which is likely to be needed in future litigation, and is in danger of being lost by reason of the apprehended death or removal of witnesses ("perpetuation of testimony"). Such bills will be more particularly noticed hereafter.

(2) *Bills Not Original.*

§ 114. Bills not original.—As already indicated, all bills filed subsequent to the original bill, are classified as *Bills not original*—for example, amended bills, cross-bills, bills of review, etc.

Following the foregoing classification, we shall now take up, in order, the several classes of bills mentioned in this chapter.

CHAPTER X.

The Bill in Detail.

(a) ORIGINAL BILLS PRAYING RELIEF.

§ 115. The purpose of the bill.—The purpose of the bill is twofold: (1) To state the plaintiff's case for the information of the defendant in the preparation of his defense; and (2) for the information of the court in the trial of the cause, and to fix the issues.

The defendant is supposed to know the plaintiff's grievances *only from his statement of them in the bill;* and it is to the *precise case thus stated,* and to that case only, that the *defendant can be required to answer;* to the case so made the *evidence must be confined;* and no relief will be granted that *does not substantially accord with the case as made in the bill.*[1] Hence the importance of accurate knowledge, by counsel, of the facts of his case, and of the law applicable thereto, before he undertakes to present his case in the form of the bill.

It is true that courts of equity are liberal in permitting amendments for the purpose of patching up a rickety pleading, or to meet unexpected phases of the proofs, so that a serious defect in the bill is not necessarily fatal to the plaintiff's case; but such amendments, when the necessity therefor is due to his fault, reflect upon counsel's professional skill, and cause delay and expense.

§ 116. The bill continued—several parts.—Commentators usually divide original bills into nine parts. The statement that such bills consist of so great a number of parts, is not meant to convey the idea that the rules of chancery pleading require any specific division into parts, or that counsel should

---

[1] Fulton *v.* Cox, 117 Va. 669; Fleenor *v.* Hensley, 121 Va. 367. *Allegata* and *probata* must "jump together": Boston Blower Co. *v.* Carman Lumber Co., 94 Va. 94.

consciously have these parts in mind in drawing the bill; but rather that in the orderly setting out of an equitable claim, the statement naturally resolves itself into these, or some of these, parts.

The emphasis usually laid upon these several parts or divisions of the bill may create the erroneous and discouraging impression upon the mind of the student that a bill in equity is a quite technical and complicated pleading.[2]

1. *The Several Parts of the Bill.*[3]

117. (1) The address.—Bills are addressed to the chancellor, by his official designation. The name of the chancellor may be used or not at the discretion of the draughtsman. Thus: "To the Honorable Archibald D. Dabney, Judge of the Corporation Court of the City of Charlottesville;" or "To the Honorable the Judge of the Corporation Court," etc.; "To the Judges of the District Court of the United States for the Western District of Virginia."

§ 118. Names of plaintiffs.—After the address to the chancellor or court, the bill should open with a statement of the name of the plaintiff, or names of the several plaintiffs, with his or their respective places of abode. In the bill they designate themselves as "your orators," or "your complainants." In all legal procedure, at law and in equity, the several parties always speak in the third person, and never in the first.

§ 119. The same—pleading by initials.—In the interest

---

[2] The same impression would arise if the student endeavored to learn from a printed book, and for recitation thereon in the lecture room, the several divisions of his weekly home-letter. He would learn that his letter should consist of many parts, namely, (1) the date and post-office address in the righthand corner, and not in the left; (2) the complimentary address, as "Dear Mother;" (3) acknowledgment of the last letter from home, with check (if any) enclosed; (4) comments on the late home news; (5) information as to the writer's health; (6) assurances that he is learning much law—especially Equity Pleading; (7) results of his last examinations; (8) prayer for additional check. Number (9) and others may be supplied by the student himself. Perhaps this comparison may induce us to approach the consideration of the nine parts of the bill with courage. A simple form of bill appears in the Appendix, *post.*

[3] See Equity Rule 20, the purpose of which is to simplify and shorten bills in the Federal courts.

of the certainty required by the rules of good pleading, and especially for the purpose of more certain identification of the parties litigant, then and thereafter, the names of the parties, both plaintiff and defendant, should be stated with the surname and at least one Christian name written at large, and not by initials merely. Married women should, of course, be designated by their own Christian names, and not by the names of their husbands. Thus "Mary Jane Smith" (omitting "Mrs.") and not "Mrs. John Smith."

Pleading by initials violates the rules of scientific pleading, whether at law or in equity, as introducing inaccuracy and uncertainty into pleadings and decrees, and is forbidden by the rules of practice in many states. Under the loose practice obtaining in Virginia, and in the Southern and Western States, such method of pleading is believed to be the rule rather than the exception. A recent *dictum,* however, by the Virginia court, in Richmond *v.* Gardner,[4] should bring the undesirable habit sharply to the attention of the Virginia bar, and to the profession of the South, where the practice most widely prevails.[5]

---

[4] 128 Va. 676. The court's language here declares that a judgment docketed and indexed (it does not appear in what form the judgment was originally entered) against "Moon, Hawley & Co.," without more, is invalid as notice to subsequent purchasers, because of the omission of the *"Christian"* names of the parties. In absence of statute permitting a partnership to be sued as a legal entity, and therefore in the firm name only, such a judgment as described is void for uncertainty, even *between the parties*—as much so as a judgment against "Smith", simply. And if a *judgment* in that form be invalid, it is clear that a *docketing* in that form is wholly ineffective as notice to subsequent purchasers. But there seems to have been no necessity in the principal case for the court to declare that the *"Christian"* names of the judgment debtors must appear, and that *initials are insufficient.* The court has obviously used the term *Christian* names inadvertently for *individual* names—the form in which the rule as to partners as defendants is usually expressed. If every judgment in Virginia, docketed only in the initialed surname of the defendant, instead of the Christian name, is to be regarded as undocketed, as the court declares, the situation is indeed a serious one, and calls for prompt legislative intervention.

[5] An editorial in the American Law Review (reproduced in 4 Virginia Law Reg. 782), denounces this practice as slovenly, and unworthy of a profession that prides itself on the accuracy of its phraseology. The Virginia lawyer should be interested to learn that this loose practice does not prevail in the Northern and Eastern States, and that "the practice seems to have originated in Virginia (although it does not prevail in Maryland), and to have extended thence over

§ 120. The same—statement of residence.—Good pleading requires not only that the names of the complainants be thus stated with certainty, but that, for similar reasons, their places of abode be likewise stated. This good practice does not, however, prevail generally among Virginia pleaders.

It is needless to add that where the jurisdiction of the court depends on questions of residence or of citizenship, such residence or citizenship is an essential allegation.[7]

§ 121. The same—Federal court rule.—By equity Rule 25, it is provided that every bill, "shall contain the full name when known, of each plaintiff and defendant, and the citizenship and residence of each party."

§ 122. (3) Statement of plaintiff's case — "stating part."—This is naturally and essentially the most important part of the bill. It is here that the plaintiff sets out, *in extenso*, the ultimate facts constituting his case against the defendant or defendants.

These facts should be stated with certainty, directness and clearness, and not by way of inference, and always according to

---

the Southern States. It never seems to have obtained the sanction of the courts, and so far as they have spoken upon the subject, both North and South, they have expressed their condemnation. Wilson *v.* Shannon, 6 Ark. 196; Norris *v.* Graves, 4 Strobh. Law (S. C.) 32; Seely *v.* Boon, Coxe (N. J.) 1, 1 N. J. Law 138; Chappel *v.* Proctor, Harp. Law (S. C.) 49; Miller *v.* Hay, 3 Exch. 14; Kinnersley *v.* Knott, 7 C. B. 980; Turner *v.* Fitt, 3 C. B. 701; Oakley *v.* Pegler, 46 N. W. 920; Beggs *v.* Wellman, 82 Ala. 391; Tweedy *v.* Jones, 37 Conn. 42; Nash *v.* Collier, 5 Dowl. and L. 341; Fewlass *v.* Abbott, 28 Mich. 270; Monroe Cattle Co. *v.* Becker, 147 U. S. 47. * * *. Nor is the usage confined to men alone. In the case of married women an additional complication is introduced. Under this peculiar practice, married women are sued, not by their Christian names, not even by their own initials, but by the initials of their husbands, with the prefix 'Mrs.' * * *"

Pleading by initials is not permitted in the Federal Court.[6]

[6] "The description of him" [one of the parties] "by initials," says the Supreme Court of the United States, per Gray, J., "is but an illustration of a loose and careless practice which this court does not countenance." Walton *v.* Marietta Chair Co., 157 U. S. 342. See also 31 Cyc. 96; Equity Rule 25 (1).

[7] See *Jurisdiction, ante*, ch. ii.

their logical sequence.[8]

Wherever the plaintiff's case depends in whole or in part on documentary evidence, such documents should be here briefly described according to their legal effect, and incorporated into the bill by reference—as "the original (or an exemplified) copy of the said deed (or other document) is herewith filed as a part of this bill, marked Exhibit No. 1 and prayed to be read as a part of this bill as if herein set out at large;" and the document in question should be filed along with the bill.

In drawing this portion of the bill, the draughtsman should assure himself that the facts stated constitute a proper case for equitable relief; and he should test his final draught by himself interposing, mentally, a demurrer to his own pleading. If the statement will withstand a demurrer, and is susceptible of proof by available testimony the young pleader may feel well satisfied with his work, and confident of a favorable result.

§ 123. (4) The common confederacy clause.—The use of this clause is now practically obsolete, and mention of the clause is only for its historical interest. One of the original grounds of equity jurisdiction was the existence of a combination and confederacy of the powerful to overawe the weak, and to resist or pervert the administration of justice in the ordinary common law courts—a situation, in general, long since passed away, and with it the necessity and the use of the clause. Of course if a conspiracy in fact is believed to exist, this clause of the bill will be retained.

§ 124. (5) The charging part.—This part of the bill (when used) contains a statement of the *anticipated defense* (other than a mere denial), followed by an allegation (or "charge") showing the futility of such defense.

In many cases there is no occasion to use this clause, and in none is it essential. Occasions arise, however, where it may be useful.

---

[8] "A short and simple statement of the ultimate facts upon which the plaintiff asks relief, omitting any mere statement of evidence." Equity Rule 25 (3).

§ 125. The same—advantages.—While, as stated, the clause may be omitted, it possesses, when proper circumstances concur, at least one important advantage, namely, in obviating the necessity for a further pleading by the plaintiff (in former times a special replication, now superseded by the amended bill) in reply· to the defense thus anticipated, when actually set up.

For example, if the plaintiff, suing for specific performance of a contract, anticipates that the defendant will set up the defense of *infancy*, or the statute of *parol agreements*, which defense the plaintiff expects to meet by proof, in the first case, of ratification after full age, or, in the second case, of part-performance, it is natural and proper to anticipate such defense, and to meet it by counter-allegations in avoidance. If such defense be not anticipated, and the ratification or part-performance be not charged in the bill, the result will be that when the defendant sets up the defense, the plaintiff will be obliged *to file a new pleading in reply,* in order properly to put the question of ratification or of part-performance in issue. This, as stated, in modern practice, calls for an amended bill. But by anticipating the defense, and charging the defendant with the ratification or the part-performance *in the original bill itself,* the question of ratification or of part-performance is presented as a part of the issue *at the outset,* without the further delay and expense of amending the bill; and the defendant, if required, must make discovery, or take issue, as the case may be, in the first instance, as to the truth of the charge of ratification or part-performance.

§ 126 (6) The jurisdiction clause.—This clause consists of a general averment of jurisdiction in equity—the usual form being that the plaintiff is "without remedy save in a court of equity, where matters of this kind are only and properly cognizable."

The clause is of no importance, and probably never was. Where the case made by the bill is not one for equitable relief, the presence of this clause does not cure the defect; nor does its omission affect the jurisdiction where the bill otherwise states a case proper for the cognizance of a court of equity.

Inasmuch, however, as the clause is still found in practically all bills, the student is advised to follow general custom by inserting the averment.

§ 127. The same—special jurisdictional facts.—Should the court be one of limited jurisdiction, or should there be special statutory requirements operating as conditions precedent to jurisdiction, the existence of such conditions must of course be alleged.

Thus, the jurisdiction conferred by statute on the chancery courts of Virginia to entertain suits for divorce, prohibits the exercise of this jurisdiction unless one of the parties has been domiciled in this state for at least one year preceding the commencement of the suit.[9] The bill in such a case should, therefore, make proper allegations of domicile in this state. And so, in a suit in the Federal courts, if the ground of jurisdiction be diverse citizenship of the parties, the bill must specifically allege such diversity of citizenship.[10]

§ 128. (7) Prayer for answer—interrogating clause.—This is commonly called the "interrogating clause," since it is here that the plaintiff, if he desires to search the conscience of the defendant, calls upon him to make answer under oath, to all matters and things alleged against him in the bill.

And, in order to prevent evasion, and more carefully to search the defendant's conscience, it is here that the plaintiff propounds, or may propound, specific and searching interrogatories, framed with such particularity and such variations as will compel a full answer.

§ 129. The same—waiver of answer under oath.—As we shall see later, the answer of a defendant, when responsive to the bill, is evidence in his behalf, and, by the rules of the forum, the defendant cannot be deprived of this advantage by a waiver in the bill of an answer under oath. In modern times, however, by statute, in most of the states the plaintiff may waive an oath to the defendant's answer, and thus reduce the answer

---

[9] Va. Code 1919, § 5105. See *Jurisdiction, ante*, ch. ii; *Divorce Suits*, ch. xxix.

[10] "A short and plain statement of the grounds upon which the court's jurisdiction depends." Equity Rule 25 (2).

to a mere pleading possessing no evidentiary value.[11] If such waiver is to be inserted in the bill, it should be done under this seventh clause.

130. The same—in Virginia—prayer for parties.— According to established practice in Virginia, this seventh clause consists not only of a prayer for answers from the defendants (with or without waiver of the oath), but, in addition, a prayer that the adversaries, by name, be made parties defendant to the bill.[12]

In Virginia, therefore, this clause becomes not only a prayer for answers but a prayer "for parties defendant."

§ 131. (8) Prayer for relief.—This is one of the most important parts of the bill, and should receive the thougthful attention of the draughtsman. Prayers for relief are of two kinds: (a) For *special relief—which may be in the alternative;* and (b) for *general relief.*

§ 132. The same—prayer for special relief. — After having made a full statement of his grievances, and demanded answers to his charges from the defendants by name, the bill would necessarily be incomplete did it not round out the complaint by asking for certain specific relief—as that the contract set up in the bill be enforced, or rescinded, or reformed; that the wrong complained of be enjoined; that the mortgage asserted in the bill be foreclosed, etc.[13]

§ 133. The same—prayer for alternative relief.—A fundamental rule of pleading at law is that "pleadings must not be in the alternative." This rule is not insisted on in equity pleading, and may be wholly ignored in the prayer for relief.

---

[11] See *The Answer, post,* ch. xvi.

[12] "In tender consideration whereof, and being without remedy save in a court of equity where matters of this kind are only and properly cognizable" (jurisdictional clause), "your orator prays that the said A., B., C. and D., be made parties defendant to this bill, and may answer the same, and every allegation thereof, on oath, as fully and particularly as if the same were here repeated, and they were thereunto particularly interrogated"—(or, if answers under oath are not desired, "may answer the same, but not under oath—the plaintiff expressly waiving answers under oath").

[13] See Equity Rule 25 (5).

That is to say, where the plaintiff, in the stating part of his bill, has made a case proper for equitable relief, 'but is *uncertain as to the specific relief to which he may be entitled* on the case made in the bill, and to be made in the proofs, his prayer for relief may be in the *alternative*. By this is meant, that the plaintiff may pray that one kind of relief be granted, or, that if his right to that particular relief should fail to be established under the law and the evidence, then that the court may grant other consistent relief, naming it.[14]

§ 134. The same—prayer for general relief.—It sometimes happens that after having stated a case proper for equity cognizance, the bill either fails to ask for all the specific relief to which the plaintiff is entitled, or else mistakes the nature of the relief properly applicable to the case made in the bill—or, again, that while the proofs fail to establish plaintiff's right to specific relief prayed, they yet establish the right to some other consistent relief.

To meet such a situation, it is customary for the plaintiff, immediately following the prayer for *specific* relief, to insert a prayer for *general* relief—"and for such other relief as to equity may seem meet and the nature of the case require."

Under the prayer for general relief the court may grant any relief to which the material facts and circumstances put in issue by the bill, and sustained by the proofs, entitle the plaintiff. But such relief must be consistent with the case made.[15]

---

[14] Tenant *v.* Dunlop, 97 Va. 235; Baker *v.* Berry Hill Co., 109 Va. 776; Equity Rule 25 (5). Thus, in a suit for specific performance of a contract to convey real property, wherein the bill sets up an apparent deficiency of acreage, the prayer may be for specific performance as to the whole acreage if to be had, or, if not, that the contract be enforced to the extent of defendant's ability, and compensation be made for the deficiency. So, relief may be asked against A., if he authorized B. to collect certain money, or against B., if he collected it without A.'s authority. Thomason *v.* Smithson, 7 Port. (Ala.) 144.

[15] See McGowan *v.* Parish, 237 U. S. 285; Hurt *v.* Jones, 75 Va. 341, 352; Woolfolk *v.* Graves, 113 Va. 1039. "This principle is so well known to the profession that it is difficult to believe that a lawyer of any experience would prepare a bill omitting the prayer for general relief"—Burks. J., in Steinman *v.* Clinchfield Coal Corp., 121 Va. 611, 639-40, in holding that where the bill has been lost after suit

§ 135. The same—illustrations. — Thus, under a bill brought to *rescind* a contract for fraud, the plaintiff cannot have *specific enforcement*, under the prayer for general relief—because of the inconsistency of the two kinds of relief.[16]

In Smith *v.* Smith [17] the bill, though stating a good case, *failed to ask for any relief*, general or special. It was held that by filing an answer to the merits, without objection, the defendant waived the irregularity, and appropriate relief was granted.

In Beall *v.* Silver[18] the prayer for special relief omitted to ask for *interest* on the principal of the debt asserted. Interest was allowed under the prayer for general relief.

In Evans *v.* Roanoke Savings Bank [19] the prayer for specific relief sought the setting up and *enforcement of a deed of trust*, which the grantor had fraudulently procured to be released. But as the rights of a *bona fide* holder had, in the meantime, attached, so that the specific relief prayed for could not be granted, a *personal decree* for the debt was entered against the fraudulent debtor, under the prayer for general relief.

In Beach *v.* Bellwood [20] the bill made out a case for reformation of a written agreement, but failed to pray for that relief specifically. Reformation was decreed under the prayer for general relief.

So where the wife's bill for divorce fails to ask for alimony, if the proofs establish a proper case for alimony it will be granted under the prayer for general relief.[21]

In Johnson *v.* Merritt,[22] plaintiffs who sued as heirs of a *husband*, were held not entitled, under the prayer for general relief, to assert inconsistent claims under the will of the *wife*.

---

ended, the court will presume that it contained a prayer for general relief. Here, in a suit to enforce the lien of a judgment, removal of a cloud from the title was held proper under the prayer for general relief.

[16] James *v.* Bird, 8 Rand. 510.
[17] 4 Rand. 95.
[18] 2 Rand. 401.
[19] 95 Va. 294.
[20] 104 Va. 170.
[21] Haven *v.* Trammell (Okla.), 193 Pac. 631; Lynde *v.* Lynde, 162 N. Y. 405, 56 N. E. 979, 76 Am. St. Rep. 332, 48 L. R. A. 679; 7 Va. Law Reg. 557.
[22] 125 Va. 162.

§ 136. The same—prayer for process.—By the original practice of the High Court of Chancery in England, and inferentially by rule of the Federal courts,[23] the bill must contain a prayer for process.

§ 137. The same—in Virginia.—We have already seen that according to the practice in Virginia, original process is usually issued *before filing of the bill*. Hence the prayer for such process is useless, and rarely found in bills filed in the Virginia courts.

§ 138. (9) Bills continued—the conclusion.—By long custom, bills conclude with the enigmatic phrase "And your orator will ever pray, etc." [24]

§ 139. (10) Bills continued—signature of counsel.—The rule of the chancery courts requires bills, as all other pleadings, to be signed by counsel. Such signature identifies the counsel with the cause, for the information of the court and its officials, and of adversary counsel. The signature is also taken to be, in a sense, a pledge of counsel's *good faith in bringing the suit*, or filing the pleading, and is supposed to be a safeguard against scandalous or other impertinent matter in the pleadings.

§ 140. The same—Federal court rule.—In the Federal courts the rule is that all pleadings shall be signed *"individually by one or more solicitors of record"*—that is, by counsel who have been admitted to practice in the court in which the plead-

---

[23] Equity Rule 12.

[24] The modern phrase is an evolution from ancient forms, some of which are subjoined. See IX Notes and Queries, 184:

"And your said almoner shall pray unto Almighty God for the prosperous state of your Majestie, according to his most bounden duty, in most high honor and felicity long to reign over us."

"And your said suppliant shall daily pray unto God for your Highness' prosperous estate in royaltie long to reign."

"And your said subject shall daily pray to God for the prosperous estate of your Majestie's Rayne."

"And your said humble subject shall duly pray to God for the preservation of your Highnesse in all felicitie most happily long to reigne."

"And your said supplyant shall daily pray for your honor."

"And your supplyant as nevertheless by duetie bounden shall daily pray to God for the increase of your Honour."

It is evident, as suggested by the compiler, that the "etc." may be filled up according to individual fancy.

ing is filed—"and such signatures shall be considered as a certificate by each solicitor that he has *read the pleading* so signed by him; that upon the instructions laid before him regarding the case there is *good ground for the same;* that no scandalous matter is inserted in the pleading; and that it is *not interposed for delay.*" [25]

§ 141. (11) **The same—affidavit to bill.**—The general rule is that save where required by statute in certain statutory proceedings, bills in chancery are not required to be sworn to.

§ 142. **Affidavit to bills—exceptions.**—Two prominent exceptions to this rule obtain, namely, (a) *Bills seeking ex parte action* by the court (*e. g.* a preliminary injunction), where the allegations of the bill are not *prima facie* established by documentary or other evidence accompanying the bill. The reason for requiring an affidavit in this instance, is obvious; and (b) *Bills for discovery and legal relief*—that is, where the . sole ground of equity jurisdiction is the needed discovery from the defendant—the controversy being one otherwise remediable at law—and the court of equity is asked to retain the cause and administer *legal relief.* Here the affidavit is required as a pledge of good faith on the part of the plaintiff, and to prevent a fraud on the equity jurisdiction. [26]

We shall see something more of these two classes of bills hereafter, as well of certain statutory proceedings in which the bill is required to be verified by affidavit.

2. General Characteristics of Bills.

§ 143. **General features.**—In addition to the characteristics of the bill already mentioned, looking chiefly to the statement, in substance, of a proper case for the interposition of equity, there are numerous rules and customs observed by careful and informed lawyers in draughting bills—some of which rules are of mandatory character, and for the breach of which a demurrer may be interposed. Most of these rest in common sense,

---

[25] Equity Rule 24.
[26] Affidavit seems also proper in the case of bills to perpetuate testimony (*post,* Ch. xi), and bills of interpleader.

and the young practitioner possessed of this saving grace would follow them intuitively.

§ 144. The same—facts, not mere legal conclusions, should be stated.—It is improper to allege *legal conclusions* instead of the *facts* from which such conclusions are drawn. For example, if defendant is sought to be charged as trustee for the plaintiff, the circumstances giving rise to the trust must be alleged; so, if the purpose of the bill is to have a deed set aside for the fraud of the defendant, or because the contract was tainted with usury or illegality, a mere allegation that the transaction was fraudulent, or usurious, or illegal, *without the facts constituting the fraud*, or usury, or illegality, would be insufficient.[27]

§ 145. The same—arguing the case in the bill—reciting evidence, etc.—It is bad form to anticipate the argument at the hearing, by making use of the bill for that purpose. It is an established rule of equity pleading that *"the case must not be argued in the bill."* Nor should the allegations be in argumentative form,[28] or include recitals of mere matters of evidence. But where the evidence is of a documentary character, and the documents are filed with the bill, it is often proper, and sometimes necessary for purposes of a clear statement, to make specific reference to such evidence. But if plaintiff charge defendant with fraudulent representations, and ask rescission of the contract, it would be highly improper to allege in the bill that A, a third party, was present and heard the misrepresentation. The proper method is simply to change the misrepresentation, with the accompanying facts, and to establish the allegation by introducing A as a witness at the proper time.[29]

---

[27] Ambler *v.* Choteau, 107 U. S. 586; Ritchie *v.* McMullen, 159 U. S. 235; First Nat. Bank *v.* Chehalis Co., 166 U. S. 440. "The defendant says that the claim asserted in the bill is barred by the statute of limitations", is a good illustration of pleading a legal conclusion.

[28] Bassett *v.* Cunningham, 7 Leigh 402, 408.

[29] See Equity Rule 25—"a short and simple statement of the *ultimate facts* * * * omitting any mere statement of evidence." An interesting collection of copies of early bills will be found in 31 Harvard Law Review, 844. See copy of a modern bill, *post, Appendix.*

CHAPTER XI.

The Bill—Continued.

ORIGINAL BILLS NOT PRAYING RELIEF.

§ 146. Bills not praying relief.—Examples of such bills are few. The leading instances are:
(1) Bills to Perpetuate Testimony, and
(2) Pure Bills of Discovery.

§ 147. (1) The purpose of the first is to seek the aid of the court in taking and preserving the testimony of certain witnesses for use in future litigation should it arise—the plaintiff fearing the loss of the testimony by death of the witnesses or otherwise.[1]

§ 148. (2) The object of the second—the pure bill of discovery—is to compel the adversary to disclose facts material to the plaintiff's case in an *action at law*, pending or contemplated between the same parties; such a resort to equity being necessary by reason of the common law disqualification, as a witness, of any party to the action—a rule which was enforced in equity as well as at law, save in the case of an answer in chancery.

The removal by statute, in all the states, of this disqualification, aided by statutes permitting interrogatories to be filed by either party, at law, has rendered practically obsolete the use of the pure bill of discovery.[2]

In neither of these proceedings, it will be observed, does the bill call upon the court to adjudicate any controversy between the parties—the purpose, in either case, being merely to *secure evidence* to be used at some future time, or in some other court.

---

[1] For a statutory substitute, see Va. Code 1919, § 6235.
[2] Id. §§ 6208, 6236-6238.

Hence the propriety of classifying these as bills *Not Praying Relief*.[3]

§ 149. Pure bill of discovery—continued.—A pure bill of discovery seeks no relief in consequence of the discovery. It is used in aid of the jurisdiction of some other court; as to enable the plaintiff to prosecute or defend an action at law, or any other legal proceeding of a merely civil nature, before a tribunal unable to compel a discovery on oath.[4]

The necessity for bills of this character grew out of the common law rule that a party to a judicial proceeding was not a competent witness. To prevent a failure of justice, equity permitted either party to an action at law to secure the testimony of his adversary by a bill of this character.

§ 150. The same—continued.—A bill of this nature must state the matter touching which a discovery is sought, the interest of both plaintiff and defendant in the subject matter and the right of the former to require the discovery from the latter.

Such a bill requires no affidavit, nor is it needful that the discovery be indispensable to the party's case. He is entitled to discovery if he shows that information or documents in the defendant's possession constitute material evidence in his behalf, although merely cumulative.[5]

If, however, the bill is not a pure bill of discovery, but asks for *legal* (as distinguished from *equitable*) *relief*, it must appear by affidavit that the discovery is essential to the plaintiff's case.[6]

§ 151. The same—discovery from corporation.—As a corporation cannot answer under oath, a pure bill of discovery cannot be maintained against a corporation as sole defendant. The proper practice is to make some officer of the corporation, supposed to be familiar with the facts, a co-defendant, and ask

---

[3] For further details, see Story, Eq. Pl. 300 *et seq.*

[4] Story, Eq. Pl. §§ 311 *et seq.;* article by Judge Lamb, 7 Va. Law Reg. 107.

[5] McFarland *v.* Hunter, 8 Leigh 489, 492-494; 1 Story, Eq. Jurisp. 64k-74e; 2 Id. 1483.

[6] *Infra*, n. 11.

for discovery from him.[7]

§ 152. The same—modern disuse of such bills—statutory substitutes.—Bills of discovery are now, with us, in large measure, superseded in practice by two statutory provisions, one allowing a *court of law* to compel a discovery upon oath, in answer to interrogatories filed, wherever it would be compelled upon a bill of discovery, if the interrogatories have not been unreasonably delayed;[8] and the other declaring *parties to suits competent to give evidence* on their own behalf, and to be competent and compellable to attend and give evidence on behalf of any other party to the proceeding.[9]

The statute, however, still preserves the right of any party to file a bill of discovery, instead of interrogatories.[10]

§ 153. Bill for discovery and legal relief.—After equity had assumed jurisdiction of pure bills of discovery, as explained in the foregoing sections, it went a step further, and in pursuance of its policy to give complete relief, assumed jurisdiction to retain the case and dispose of the whole controversy, even to the administering of *legal relief*.

This jurisdiction is not exercised in every case, but chiefly in those cases where the *discovery is essential to prove* the case, or establish the defense, of the plaintiff in the bill, and where equitable remedies are appropriate for the relief sought. Inasmuch as the plaintiff is driven into equity by the necessity for discovery, equity, in accordance with its custom of giving complete relief when once it has assumed jurisdiction for any purpose, may retain the bill, not only for purpose of *discovery* but for *relief* as well—though the case otherwise involve legal rights only.[11]

---

[7] Roanoke Street R. Co. *v.* Hicks, 96 Va. 510. But if the corporation answers, and the answer is verified, as of his personal knowledge, by an officer of the corporation, the answer is entitled to all the weight of a verified answer by an individual defendant: Carle *v.* Corhan; 127 Va. 223; 7 Va. Law Reg. 145; *infra*, §§ 252-254.

[8] Va. Code 1919, §§ 6236-6238.

[9] Id. §§ 6208-6214.

[10] Id. § 6238; Smith *v.* Smith, 92 Va. 696.

[11] Few questions of equity practice have evoked a greater divergency of views than the circumstances under which equity will administer legal relief because of having jurisdiction for purposes

§ 154. The same—affidavit to bill.—In a bill of this nature, the plaintiff must allege the necessity for the discovery, and, as an earnest of good faith, and to prevent a fraud on the equity jurisdiction—since the case is one otherwise proper only for a court of law—the plaintiff must make affidavit to the bill.[12]

CHAPTER XII.

Bills Not Original.

1. SUPPLEMENTAL AND AMENDED BILLS.

§ 155. Supplemental bills.—A supplemental bill, as its name indicates, is a bill filed to supplement the original bill, where, by reason of facts occurring *since the original bill was filed,* new allegations, or new parties, or a new form of prayer for relief, are made necessary.

Thus, where, subsequent to the filing of the original bill, inchoate or contingent interests involved in the suit have, by death or otherwise, become vested—or, where such interests have, by the occurence of new facts, devolved upon other persons—such enlarged interests or new parties should be brought before the court by a supplemental bill. In short, a supplemental bill is one serving to supplement an original bill which was *sufficient at the time of its filing,* but which has since become insufficient by the occurrence of *new facts* materially altering the original situation.[1]

§ 156. Amended bills—two functions. — An amended

---

of discovery. Hence the bare outline here is offered with diffidence. The question has received an elaborate, if inconclusive, examination in 1 Story, Eq. Jurisp. 64k-74e; 2 Id. 1480-1504; Story. Eq. Pl. (10th ed) 288; *infra,* §§ 197-201.

[12] 3 Pomeroy, Eq. Jurisp. 1415; Fletcher, Eq. Pl. & Pr. 811; Story, Eq. Pl. 288.

[1] Fletcher, Eq. Pl. & Pr. 385, 825; Story, Eq. Pl. 33; 1 Barton, Ch. Pract. 106; Wilson *v.* Wilson, 93 Va. 546; Glenn *v.* Brown, 99 Va. 322, 326-327; Bibb *v.* American, etc., Co., 109 Va. 261.

bill (closely akin to, but not to be confounded with, the supple
mental bill) has two functions in the equity procedure. One of
these is to correct *inherent imperfections in the original bill*, not
due to subsequent occurrences; and the other, to serve the
purposes of a *special replication* to the plea or answer. These
functions are more fully explained in the sections following.

§ 157. The same—first function.—As indicated, one of
the uses of the amended bill is to correct imperfections in the
original bill (in this aspect performing practically the office of
the supplemental bill, except that the former has relation to imperfections inherent in the bill when filed), or to introduce essential additional facts which were then in existence.

In brief, an amended bill is one whose purpose is to incorporate some change in an original bill insufficient for *complete relief in its original structure.*[2]

§ 158. The same—second function.—A second important office performed by the amended bill is as the modern substitute for the *special replication* to the plea or answer— special
replications being no longer used in the equity practice. This
happens when it becomes necessary for the plaintiff to set up
new matter in response to a defense asserted in the plea or answer. That is to say, under the modern practice the replication
may only *traverse* or *deny*, and may not *confess and avoid*, as at
law. If the plaintiff proposes to meet the allegations of the defendant's plea or answer by confession and avoidance, he must
file an amended bill confessing the allegations and offering the
new matter in avoidance.

For example: If the defendant should in his answer set up
the defense of infancy, and the plaintiff means to deny the fact
of infancy, he must file the general *replication;* but if the plaintiff relies upon a ratification after full age (which he might
have alleged in his original bill but did not), instead of filing a
special replication setting upon such ratification (as he would
do at law), the plaintiff would be driven to file an *amended bill,*

---

[2] Authorities *supra.*

with this allegation inserted.[3]

§ 159. Amendment of bills—freely allowed.—Courts of equity are extremely liberal in permitting the plaintiff to amend his bill, whenever this seems necessary to bring the substantial merits of the case properly before the court. The granting of leave to amend is in the discretion of the court, and ·is not demandable as a matter of right—but the practice of the courts is so liberal in this respect that instances of unjust decrees flowing from mere slips in pleading are as rare in equity as they are common at law.[4]

§ 160. The same.—The circumstances under which amendments are allowed or disallowed, are well stated in the case of Hardin v. Boyd.[5]

"In reference to the amendments of equity pleadings," says Mr. Justice Harlan, in that case, "the courts have found it impracticable to lay down a rule that would govern all cases. This allowance must, at every stage of the cause, rest in the discretion of the court; and that discretion must depend largely on the special circumstancs of each case. It may be said generally that in passing upon applications to amend, the ends of justice should never be sacrificed to mere form, or by too rigid an adherence to technical rules of practice. Undoubtedly great caution should be exercised where the application comes after the litigation has continued for some time, or when the granting of it would cause serious inconvenience or expense to the opposite side. And an amendment should rarely, if ever, be permitted where it would *materially change the very substance of the case made by the bill,* and to which the parties have directed their proofs."

§ 161. The same—in the Federal courts.—The new Equity Rules make most liberal provision for amendment of any

---

[3] Simmons v. Simmons, 33 Gratt. 451, 458. The reason for the newer practice seems to be based on the policy of requiring the bill, in its final form, to exhibit the complete case upon which the decree is entered.

[4] See Kelly v. Gwatkins, 108 Va. 6; Equity Rules 19, 28; Va. Code 1919, § 6084, permitting transformation of a bill in equity into a declaration at law, or *vice versa. Supra,* § 34.

[5] 113 U. S. 756.

pleading or record—the language of the rule being that "the court may at any time in furtherance of justice, upon such terms as may be just, permit *any process, proceeding, pleading* or *record* to be amended, or material supplementary matter to be set forth in an amended or supplemental pleading. The court, at every stage of the proceeding, must disregard any error or defect in the proceeding which does not affect the substantial rights of the parties." [6]

§ 162. The same—making new case by amendment.— In amending his bill, the plaintiff must be careful not so to alter the frame of his bill as to make an *entirely new case*—that is, a case which cannot be made to harmonize with that made in the original bill.

The test, as stated by Keith, P., in Pettyjohn *v.* Burson,[7] by which to determine whether the proposed amendment is proper, is to consider whether its purpose is to supplement some mistake or omission *"connected with the substance of the case, but not forming the substance itself,"* or whether there is an abandonment of the entire case made by the original bill, and the assertion of a new and different case by amendment.

The decisions on the subject, however, involve distinctions so nice that the student must be content with the general principle, and study its application as need arises.[8]

---

[6] Rule 19. See also Rules 28 and 34, both adopted in furtherance of the policy of liberality in the amendment of pleadings. Rule 22 authorizes transfer of cases 'from the equity side to the law side, and *vice versa*, as in Virginia—with the necessary amendment of the pleadings.

[7] (Va.), 22 S. E. 508.

[8] See 5 Va. Law Reg. 411; 8 id. 437; n. 50 Am. St. Rep. 737; n. 16 C. C. A. 508; Whalen *v.* Gordon, 95 Fed. 305; Belton *v.* Apperson, 26 Gratt. 207; Ewing *v.* Ferguson, 33 Gratt. 548; Straughn *v.* Hallwood, 30 W. Va. 274, 8 Am. St. Rep. 29. The ruling of the majority in Watson *v.* Brunner, 128 Va. 600 (Burks, J., dissenting), carries the privilege of amendment to the extreme limit. The bill was by a sub-contractor to enforce either the personal liability of the owner, or a mechanic's lien. After a decree denying both of these prayers, an amendment was permitted, asserting an assignment, or equitable lien, by virtue of an order on the owner from the general contractor. As pointed out in the dissenting opinion, the inconsistency between the original claims and the claim asserted in the amendment, seems to violate the rule that an entirely new case may not be set up by amendment.

§ 163. The same—leave to file.—As already stated, regularly an amended or supplemental bill can only be filed by leave of court. But in Virginia it is provided by statute,[9] that the plaintiff "may of *right* amend his bill before the defendant's appearance; and, notwithstanding such appearance, a plaintiff in equity may, at any time *in the vacation of the court* wherein the suit is pending, file in the clerk's office an amended or supplemental bill, or bill of revivor; whereupon the same proceedings may be had as if leave to file it had been previously obtained in court; but the court, on motion of a defendant, made at the term to which process to answer the same is returned executed on him, or, if it be returnable to rules, at the first term after it is so returned, may dismiss such amended or supplemental bill, or bill of revivor."

§ 164. Process on amended bill.—It is a general principle of the equity practice that the parties who have personally appeared in the suit must keep themselves informed of the subsequent proceedings without special notice—or, if inequity has resulted to such a party by reason of lack of notice, he must complain to the court before final decree.[10]

By the unwritten rule, this principle seems applicable to the amended bill, the filing of which does not require the service of process anew, *except as to new parties* made by the amendment, or as to parties *who have not appeared.*[11]

According to the usual practice, however, in Virginia, unless waived by consent (express or implied)—or where the new matter merely supplements or rounds out an allegation, or allegations, already understood by the defendant and already traversed or admitted in the answer, or otherwise requires no further answer—process on the amended bill is issued thereon against all the defendants named therein whose interests are in

---

[9] Va. Code 1919, § 6095; Holland *v.* Trotter, 22 Gratt. 139. See Equity Rule 28.

[10] Martin *v.* South Salem Land Co., 94 Va. 526, 553; Gills *v.* Gills, 126 Va. 526 (master's report).

[11] See Lawrence *v.* Bolton, 3 Pai. 294; Beekman *v.* Waters, 3 Johns. Ch. 410; Equitable Life Association *v.* Laird, 24 N. J. Eq. 319. Compare the case of the cross-bill: Perrow *v.* Webster, 124 Va. 321; *infra*, § 169.

anywise sought to be affected by the amendment; and the cause on the amended bill is matured, by plea or answer and general replication, much in the same manner as on the original bill. This practice seems recognized (if not required) by that provision of the Virginia Code quoted in the preceding section, namely, that "the court, on motion of a defendant, made *at the term to which process to answer the same is returned executed on him, or, if it be returnable to rules, at the first term after it is so returned,* may dismiss such amended . . . bill." [12]

§ 165. Error in naming a pleading.—In connection with the close distinction between the amended and the supplemental bill, it may be well to point out that in equity pleading, the name or designation of a particular pleading plays a much less important part than at law. In equity, substance is regarded rather than form. Hence, though a pleader may mistake the *name* of his pleading, yet, if it be proper in substance, the court will disregard the error and treat the pleading as if it were rightly named. For example: If a supplemental bill be proper, but the plaintiff files what he terms an "amended" bill, or a "bill of revivor," or a "cross-bill;" or if he term his pleading a "petition" when it should be an "answer," or *vice versa*—and the pleading be sufficient in substance,—the court will treat it as if it had been properly designated.[13]

2. The Cross-Bill.

§ 166. The cross-bill.—The cross-bill, as its name indicates, is a bill filed by one or more *defendants* against one or more of the *plaintiffs* in the original bill, or against one or more *co-defendants,* or against some or all of both *plaintiffs and co-defendants.*

The purpose of such a bill is not, in general, to repel the

---

[12] As to new parties by amendment, see Coffman *v.* Sangston, 21 Gratt. 263. As to answer to amended bill, see Equity Rule, 32.

[13] See Kendrick *v.* Whitney, 28 Gratt. 646, 654-655; Simmons *v.* Simmons, 33 Gratt. 451, 458; Whitten *v.* Saunders, 75 Va. 563, 572; Glenn *v.* Brown, 99 Va. 322; Matney *v.* Yates, 121 Va. 506; Sayre *v.* Elyton Land Co., 73 Ala. 85.

The new Federal Equity Rule in terms declares that "unless otherwise prescribed by statute or these rules, *the technical forms of pleading in equity are abolished.*" Rule 18.

plaintiff's claim, but is rather to obtain *affirmative relief* on behalf of the defendant filing the cross-bill. In short, it is rather a sword than a shield—and is the method by which the defendant asserts all available counterclaims.

A simple illustration of the function of such a bill may be taken from a divorce suit, where the defendant consort, not content with a mere defense of the charges made in the bill—a defense which, if established, would call for a dismissal of the bill—files a cross-bill setting up matrimonial delinquencies on the part of the plaintiff consort, and asking a divorce to the defendant on the grounds so set up.

So, where one co-tenant files a bill for partition against his co-tenants, any of the latter may file a cross-bill against him, or any co-defendant, or against both, asking for an account of rents and profits received by the latter.

Again, in a suit for specific performance, if defendant desired to have the contract rescinded, (as for fraud, or mistake, or defect of title) he would file a cross-bill, setting up the grounds relied on for rescission.

So, when discovery was an important branch of the equity jurisdiction, a defendant might (as he still may) obtain discovery from the plaintiff or a co-defendant by means of a cross-bill.[14]

§ 167. The same—new matter—new parties.—As the cross-bill is auxiliary to the proceeding in the original suit, and to a large extent a branch or dependency of that suit, so that the two constitute practically a single suit, it is not permissible, as a general rule, to introduce new parties, or new and distinct matter not germane to the matter embraced in the original suit —unless the new matter has arisen since the filing of the original bill.

If new parties are essential to doing complete justice in the case they should be introduced rather by *objection to the orig-*

---

[14] See generally on the subject of the cross-bill: Hudson *v.* Hudson, 3 Rand. 117; Moorman *v.* Smoot, 28 Gratt. 80; Derbyshire *v.* Jones, 94 Va. 140. The filing of the cross-bill does not in anywise relieve the defendant (plaintiff in the cross-bill) from filing an answer to the original bill—the functions of the two pleadings being wholly distinct.

inal bill for defect of parties, thus compelling the plaintiff to amend his bill and bring in the new parties. If, however, the pleadings and proofs indicate the necessity of a new party, and the introduction of such party by amendment of the original bill be impracticable, such new party may be introduced by making him a party to the cross-bill;[15] though the better practice would be for the defendant, in such case, to file a new and independent original bill, and ask that it be heard along with the pending cause.

§ 168. The same—effect of dismissal of original bill. —Whether the dismissal of the original bill will carry with it the dismissal of the cross-bill depends on the particular circumstances of the case.

Thus, where the original bill is dismissed as to a *particular defendant* on the ground that he is *not a proper party*, the dismissal of the cross-bill as to him necessarily follows, since the latter bill can be maintained only against a proper party to the original bill.[16]

But where the cross-bill asserts an affirmative right in opposition to the plaintiff in the original bill, and not merely by way of defense—a right not adjudicated in the dismissal of the original bill,—the court may retain the cross-bill and proceed to a final decree thereon, regardless of the dismissal of the original bill.[17]

§ 168½. The same—leave to file.—By the better practice, leave of court to file the cross-bill should first be obtained,[18] though in many jurisdictions previous leave is not considered necessary, and an objecting party may assert his objection to

---

[15] Derbyshire *v*. Jones, 94 Va. 140; Crockett *v*. Woods, 97 Va. 391; Shields *v*. Barrow, 17 How. (U. S.) 145; McMullen *v*. Eagan, 21 W. Va. 250.

[16] Derbyshire *v*. Jones, 94 Va. 140; Sulphur Mines Co. *v*. Boswell, 94 Va. 480.

[17] Ragland *v*. Brodnax, 29 Gratt. 401; Equitable Life Soc. *v*. Wilson, 110 Va. 571; Abels *v*. Planters, etc., Inc. Co., 92 Ala. 382, 9 So. 423; Pethtel *v*. McCullough, 49 W. Va. 520, 39 S. E. 199; Sigman *v*. Lundy, 66 Miss. 522, 6 So. 245; Fletcher, Eq. Pl. Pr. 918.

[18] Bronson *v*. La Crosse R. Co., 2 Wall. 283; Finlayson *v*. Lipscombe, 16 Fla. 751; Baker *v*. Oil Trust Co., 7 W. Va. 454.

the case made in the cross-bill by demurrer.[19]

§ 169. The same—process and procedure.—On the filing of a cross-bill, process is usually issued against the defendants named therein, and the suit is matured as if it were an original proceeding. Defense may be made by demurrer, plea or answer. It is not clear, however, that process is essential as to those parties to the original bill who have appeared in the cause—and who, therefore are held to take notice of the various steps taken in the course of the proceedings.[20] Service of process is necessary, however, on defendants as to whom the original bill has been taken for confessed and who have not entered appearance,[21] and of course as to new parties.

As a rule, defendants in the original bill are required to answer the original bill before the defendants in the cross-bill can be required to answer the latter—a practice sanctioned by statute in Virginia.[22]

§ 170. Answer treated as a cross-bill.—It not infrequently happens that a defendant has in his *answer* set up a claim which regularly should have been asserted by *cross-bill*. In such case the court may in its discretion treat the answer as a cross-bill, in order to do complete justice between the parties.[23] Of course in such case the adverse parties to the cross-claim would have the same right to answer the new matter set up in defendant's answer, as if the latter were in fact a technical cross-bill.

So where process would be required on a technical cross-bill,[24] it is equally necessary in the case of the answer treated as a cross-bill.[25]

§ 171. The cross-bill—abolished in the Federal courts.

---

[19] Neal *v.* Foster, 34 Fed. 496; Davis *v.* American, etc., Union, 100 Ill. 313; Story, Eq. Pl. 632; Fletcher, Eq. Pl. & Pr. 899.
[20] See Gills *v.* Gills, 126 Va. 526.
[21] Perrow *v.* Webster, 124 Va. 321; *supra*, n. 17a.
[22] Va. Code 1919, § 6097.
[23] Mettert *v.* Hagan, 18 Gratt. 231; Tate *v.* Vance, 27 Gratt. 571; Martin *v.* Kester, 46 W. Va. 438, 33 S. E. 238.
[24] See § 169, *supra*.
[25] Perrow *v.* Webster, *supra*.

—The new Equity Rules seem to have *abolished cross-bills*. Rule 30 declares that the answer "must state in short and simple form any *counter-claim* arising out of the transaction which is the subject-matter of the suit, and may *without cross-bill* set out any set-off or counter-claim against the plaintiff which might be the subject of an independent suit in equity against him, and such set-off or counter-claim so set up shall have the same effect as a cross-suit, so as to enable the court to pronounce a final judgment in the same suit both on the original and the cross-claims." [26]

3. The Petition—Intervention.

§ 172. The petition.—While strictly speaking a petition is not a bill, the two pleadings are of a sufficiently kindred nature to justify the classification of the petition with Bills Not Original.

§ 173. The same—by whom filed.—While the books on equity pleading usually assert that a petition may be filed either by one who is a party to the cause,[27] or by a stranger who desires to become a party by intervention, the cases in which petitions are filed by a party to the suit are so rare as not to need our special attention here.

The petition, as the term is used in ordinary practice, is a pleading, framed much like an original bill, *filed in a pending suit by one not a party to the proceeding, but who desires to become a party, in order to assert some right involved in the suit.*

Thus, where the estate of a decedent is being wound up in a chancery suit, the creditors of the estate who are not otherwise parties to the suit, may come in by petition, setting up their respective claims and asking that their claims be allowed and paid. So, if one of the legatees or distributees of the decedent should have assigned his interest, in whole or part, to a stranger, such stranger would come into the suit by petition, with the prayer that the assignment be recognized, and the claim paid to him.[27a]

---

[26] Rule 31 provides for an answer by the adverse parties to the cross-claim asserted in the defendant's answer.

[27] Fletcher, Eq. Pl. & Pr. 423. Petitions *to rehear* a cause are *sui generis*, and will be considered hereafter.

[27a] Equity Rule 37 provides for petition by intervenors.

§ 174. The same—leave to file—Virginia statute.—A petition in a pending suit may be filed only by leave of court.

By statute [28] in Virginia, however, such leave may be granted by the judge in vacation, and the petition may then be filed and matured in the clerk's office, as if it were an original bill. The process may be made returnable either to rules in the clerk's office or to a term of court; and new parties defendant may be named in the petition. After maturity of the proceedings depositions may be taken. But at the next term after maturity, defendant parties may make any objection or defense that they might have made had the petition been filed in court and process awarded by the court thereon.

§ 175. Process on filing the petition.—Aside from the statute just mentioned, regularly the petition is filed in court, on motion for leave to file; such leave being given, an order or *rule* is entered requiring the defendant or defendants therein named to appear on a day named, or within a designated time, *"to show cause, if any they have or can show, why the prayer of the said petition shall not be granted."*

A copy of this order is officially served on the defendants, and thereupon the case made by the petition is matured in court, by plea, answer, or demurrer of the defendant, and general replication by the plaintiff, as in the case of an original bill.[29]

Where, as is sometimes the case, the petition is of such a nature that it may be granted as of course,—where, for example, its purpose is not hostile to the rights of any party to the suit, or where, in a creditors' bill, the petition sets up a debt that must later be proved before the master—process thereon may be dispensed with.[30]

176. The petition to rehear.—The petition by an intervenor, just discussed, is not to be confused with the *petition to*

---

[28] Va. Code 1919, § 6096. An attachment may be had in a pending suit on petition therein. Id § 6410.

[29] Keys Planing Mill Co. *v.* Kirkbridge, 114 Va. 58.

[30] See generally on the subject of process on petitions, 8 Va. Law Reg. 96; Fletcher, Eq. Pl. & Pr. 425. See form of rule, in *Appendix, post.*

rehear. As its name indicated, the purpose of a *petition to re-hear* is to seek the rehearing of some decree previously entered in the cause, and the correction of supposed errors therein. It is filed by some party to the suit, and is addressed, not to a higher court, but to the court in which the suit is pending. This proceeding will be noticed more at length hereafter.

4. Bills of Revivor.

§ 177. Bills of revivor.—The purpose of such bills is, as indicated by their title, to revive suits which by reason of death or other disability of a party have abated—and the purpose of the bill of revivor is to bring the legal representatives of the deceased or disabled party before the court. By the original equity practice, the circumstances essential to its maintenance were prescribed with some strictness, and the proceeding was somewhat technical.[31] However, under modern statutes, or rules of court, the bill of revivor has to a large extent been rendered obsolete by the substitution of simpler methods.[32]

---

[31] See these bills elaborately treated in Story, Eq. Pl. (10th ed.) 354-387.

[32] Va. Code 1919, § 6168; Wilson *v.* Smith, 22 Gratt. 493; Equity Rules 35, 45.

CHAPTER XIII.

Bills Not Original.—Continued.

5. BILL OF REVIEW.[1]

§ 178. The bill of review.—The bill of review is a bill filed by some party to an *ended* chancery suit, for the purpose of having the trial court reinstate the cause on the docket, with the object of re-examining and correcting or annulling some previous decree in the cause, prejudicial to the rights of the plaintiff in the bill of review. Its purpose is somewhat similar to the writ of error *coram nobis* in the common law court.

§ 179. The same—grounds on which filed.—A bill of review may be filed on two grounds only, viz: 1. *Error of law on face of the record; or 2. Newly discovered evidence*—and, in either case, *only after a final decree in the cause.*[2]

§ 180. The same—(1) error of law on face of the record.—A bill of review does not lie to review or correct errors of judgment in the determination of *facts*. If there be error in this particular. it may be corrected, after a final decree, only by

---

[1] Discussed at large, Story, Eq. Pl. (10th ed.) 403-425.

[2] The books on equity pleading add the further essential that before a defendant is entitled to file a bill of review he must have *performed the decree*, or must allege his inability to do so. Story, Eq. Pl. 406; Fletcher, Eq. Pl. & Pr. 930. It is confidently believed that such practice does not prevail in Virginia, nor in America generally. It seems never to have been suggested in any of the numerous Virginia cases in which the bill of review has been under judicial investigation. On the contrary, it is common practice in this state to enjoin the enforcement of the decree sought to be reviewed until a hearing can be had on the bill of review—a practice expressly sanctioned by statute: Va. Code 1919, § 6316. The practice in the Federal courts seems, however, to be to the contrary, unless the plaintiff alleges inability to perform the decree: Davis *v.* Speiden, 104 U. S. 83; Ricker *v.* Powell, 100 U. S. 104. As satisfaction of the decree is not required as a condition of a review by the *appellate* court, no reason is perceived why a different rule should apply where the appeal for a review is made to the *trial* court.

an appellate court. But if error of *law* be apparent from an inspection of the record in the cause, and a final decree has been entered, a proper case for a bill of review is *prima facie* presented.

Thus, on a bill to have an absolute conveyance declared a mortgage, or to establish a trust in real property, and the court erroneously refuses to permit the introduction of parol testimony to establish the fact of the mortgage or the trust; in a suit by the surety for subrogation to securities held by the creditor whom the surety has satisfied, and the proof establishes a proper case for subrogation, but the relief is denied by the court; or, in any case, where the facts proved entitle the plaintiff, as a *matter of law*, to the particular relief sought by the bill—or, *per contra*, entitle the defendant to a dismissal of the bill—but the court mistakes the rule of law applicable to the facts proved and denies the relief in the one case or grants it in the other, the plaintiff, or the defendant, as the case may be, (assuming the decree final) would be entitled to a bill of review based on error of law apparent on the face of the record.

§ 181. The same—in findings of fact.—As already stated, on a bill of review brought under this head, the sufficiency or insufficiency of the *proofs* cannot be considered. The finding of the court upon the *facts*, howsoever erroneous, is conclusive on bill of review, and cannot be questioned on the testimony before the court.

As was said by Christian, J., in Thompson *v.* Brooks,[3] quoted with approval in Valz *v.* Coiner,[4] "It is well settled that a bill of review can only be brought upon two grounds—first upon newly discovered evidence, and second upon errors of law apparent upon the face of the record.[5] * * * As to errors of law, they must be such as appear on the face of the decrees, orders and proceedings in the cause, arising on facts either *admitted in the pleadings or stated as facts in the decrees*. Such

---

[3] 76 Va. 160, 163.
[4] 110 Va. 467, 469.
[5] As to what is meant by errors of law "on the face of the record," see Whiting *v.* Bank of U. S., 13 Pet. 6, 13-14; Story, Eq. Pl. 407.

errors of law, and such only, may be corrected by a bill of review. But if the errors complained of be errors of *judgment in the determination of the facts,* these can only be corrected by appeal."

§ 182. The same—negligence of party or counsel.— Negligence, or mistake, or forgetfulness, or unskillfulness, of counsel in failing to introduce proper testimony, or properly to except to the master's report, are not sufficient grounds for filing a bill of review. In the footnote [6] will be found cases illustrating various grounds on which bills of review have been rejected.

§ 183. Bill of Review continued — (2) newly discovered evidence.— The second ground on which a bill of review may be filed, is the discovery of *new evidence* since the decree complained of was entered,—evidence which *could not with reasonable diligence have been discovered before,* and of so material a nature that if previously brought to the attention of the court its introduction *would probably have altered the result.* Evidence which is merely cumulative is not sufficient.[7]

§ 184. The same—after-discovered evidence continued—practice.— A bill of review on the ground of the discovery of new evidence must distinctly and specifically state the character of the new evidence, and be accompanied by some *prima facie* proof that *such evidence exists*—either in the form of evidentiary documents or of affidavits of witnesses.

The rule here, based on the elementary principle that pleadings must not state legal conclusions merely, is well stated in Whitten *v.* Saunders:[8] "The rule," says Judge Staples, "is that the court must, upon a mere inspection of the bill [of review],

---

[6] Ellzey *v.* Lane, 2 H. & M. 593; Jones *v.* Pilcher, 6 Munf. 425; Rawlings *v.* Rawlings, 75 Va. 76; Beatty *v.* Barley, 97 Va. 11; Sharp *v.* Shenandoah Furnace Co., 100 Va. 27; Valz *v.* Coiner, 110 Va. 467; Phipps *v.* Wise Hotel Co., 116 Va. 739.
[7] Connolly *v.* Connolly, 32 Gratt. 657; Whitten *v.* Saunders, 75 Va. 563; Durbin *v.* Roanoke Building Co., 108 Va. 468; Sutherland *v.* Gent, 111 Va. 511; Goode *v.* Bryant, 118 Va. 314.
[8] 75 Va. 563, 573.

be able to see that the new matter discovered is of such a character that if brought forward in the suit it would have probably altered the decree; and it   must be so   stated that the defendant can answer understandingly, and thus present a direct issue to the court. It is not sufficient to allege that the party expects to prove certain facts. He must   *state the evidence distinctly upon which he relies, and must file the   affidavit of witnesses in support of his averments.*" [9]

§ 185. Bill of review continued—leave to file. — No leave of court is required where such a bill is filed to review a decree for *error of law*—but such leave is necessary where relief is sought on the ground of *after-discovered evidence.*[10]

§ 186. The same—why only after final decree?—Until a final decree and adjournment of the court for the term at which such decree was entered,[11] all the proceedings had in an equity suit are, in a measure, inchoate and interlocutory—or, in professional phrase, "in the breast of the court." By this statement is meant, not only that the proceedings in the suit *at that term* are thus interlocutory, but that *all the proceedings, from the first decree onward,* though had or entered at former terms of the court, are likewise interlocutory and in the breast of the court. It is only after a *final decree and adjournment* that the proceedings in the cause   crystallize, as it were, and

---

[9] See also Becker *v.* Johnson, 111 Va. 245. The bill should also be accompanied by an affidavit of the plaintiff that the newly discovered evidence could not have been discovered earlier by the exercise of due diligence. Story, Eq. Pl. 412-413.

Where a bill seeks on this ground to review a decree entered by the lower court by the direction of the appellate court, see U. S. *v.* Moorhead, 1 Black 488; National Brake, etc., Co. *v.* Christensen, 254 U. S. 425; Re Gamewell Fire Alarm, etc., Co., 73 Fed. 908.

[10] This is the unwritten rule (2 Daniell, Ch. Pr. 1577), and is affirmed by the Virginia statute. . Va. Code 1919, § 6316.

[11] It is common to find the statement in the books that the "enrollment" of the decree is the test of its finality. The term enrollment is derived from the ancient English practice which is explained in Story, Eq. Pl. (10th ed.) 403n (a), 421n (a). In the American practice decrees are never enrolled in the English sense. But for the purpose of determining the finality of decrees they are treated as enrolled (in the English sense) only *after final decree and adjournment of the term.* See *Enrollment of Decrees, post,* §§ 241-253.

present the elements of finality and rigidity characteristic of a judgment at law.

Where, therefore, *before final decree and adjournment,* a material error is discovered in any decree in the cause—whether of law or of fact—or where, in like case, new evidence is discovered—the court, on having its attention properly directed to the error or to the newly-discovered evidence, is free to hear the parties and to make such correction as justice demands. This is done by means of a *petition to rehear,* of which we shall see something hereafter.[12] But where the proceedings have ceased to be interlocutory, by the entry of a final decree and adjournment of the court, then under the influence of the maxim *interest reipublicae ut sit finis litium,* the court feels less disposed to open up the litigation for the purpose of re-trial of the whole or any part thereof. Hence the establishment of the somewhat narrow and technical rules applicable to the bill of review already noticed.

§ 187. The same—effect of final decree in a chancery cause.

—The entry of a final decree in a chancery cause and adjournment of the court, put an end to any further proceedings in the cause—save proceedings to compel the performance of the court's mandate, or an appeal to a higher court. The court cannot on motion reinstate the cause for further proceedings; and, on the other hand, all decrees and orders therein, howsoever erroneous must stand, until altered or reversed by proper proceedings, either by *bill of review* in the same court, or by *appeal* to a higher court.

As said by Burks, J., in Battaille *v.* Maryland Hospital,[12a] "there are but two ways known to the law by which such a decree" [i. e. a final decree] "could be set aside—by bill of review in the court which rendered it, or appeal to this" [the appellate] "court."[13]

---

[12] Richardson *v.* Gardner, 128 Va. 676, 685—quoting the text (inaccurately).

[12a] 76 Va. 63, 67.   ·

[13] In this connection see Va. Code 1919, § 6333, authorizing the correction of decrees *pro confesso*, and of certain clerical errors, by motion. See also id. § 6297, permitting reinstatement on the docket

§ 188. The same—what is a final decree.—It is not always an easy matter to determine whether a particular decree is final or not—nor are the courts fully in accord as to the true characteristics of such a decree.

The following criterion, laid down by Baldwin, J., in Cocke *v.* Gilpin,[14] has been approved in many cases:

"Where the further action of the court in the cause is necessary to give completely the relief contemplated by the court, there the decree upon which the question arises is to be regarded not as final but interlocutory. I say further action *in the cause,* to distinguish it from that action of the court which is common to both final and interlocutory decrees, to wit, those measures which are necessary for the *execution* of a decree that has been pronounced, and which are properly to be regarded as adopted not *in* but *beyond* the cause, and as founded on the decree or mandate of the court, without respect to the relief to which the party was previously entitled upon the merits of his case."

"A decree is not less final in its nature," says Burks, J., in Rawlings *v.* Rawlings,[15] "because measures may be necessary to compel parties to obey it."

§ 189. The same—final decrees continued.—Prof. Minor[16] describes a final decree as one "which disposes of the whole subject, gives all the relief that was contemplated, provides with reasonable completeness for giving effect to the sen-

---

for appointment of a commissioner to execute a deed under certain circumstances. The latter provision should be extended so as to cover all proceedings necessary to the complete execution of the decree.

[14] 1 Rob. (Va.) 20, 28, quoted with approval by Burks, J., in Rawlings *v.* Rawlings, 75 Va. 76, 84. See elaborate discussion by Staples, J., in Ryan *v.* McLeod, 32 Gratt. 367, 376-381; Johnson *v.* Merritt, 125 Va. 162; Richardson *v.* Gardner. 128 Va. 676—decree adjudicating principles of the cause, ascertaining debts, and ordering a sale of defendant's property, is not a final decree. A decree of the court of appeals is always final (after lapse of the time permitted by its rules for a rehearing), whether the original decree appealed from were in itself interlocutory or final. Mathews Co. *v.* Progress Co., 108 Va. 777.

[15] *Supra.*

[16] 4 Minor's Inst. 1066, 1506.

tence, and leaves nothing to be done in the cause save to superintend ministerially the execution of the decree." [17]

§ 190. The same—decrees final as to one party and interlocutory as to another.—A decree may be final as to one of the parties to the suit and yet interlocutory as to another—since, so far as the one party is concerned, his interest may be completely ascertained and the case disposed of as to him, and the cause be retained for further action as to the other.[18]

§ 191. Bill of review continued—time limitation.—In keeping with the sound policy of putting an end to litigation, as exemplified in the strict rules governing the filing of bills of review, already noticed, the Virginia statute [19] declares that "no bill of review shall be allowed to a final decree, unless it be exhibited within *one year* next·after such decree," with a saving clause in favor of infants and lunatics.

The bill should show on its face that it is brought within the tii..e prescribed by law, and it is not necessary that the defendants shall set up a plea of the statute of limitations thereto.[20]

§ 192. Process and procedure on bill of review.—The practice as to process and subsequent proceedings on a bill of review are substantially the same as in the case of the amended bill and the cross-bill heretofore considered.

---

[17] See also Repass *v.* Moore, 96 Va. 147; Gills *v.* Gills, 126 Va. 526. The Federal courts, as well as many state courts, are somewhat more liberal in construing decrees as final. See McGourkey *v.* Toledo, etc., R. Co., 146 U. S. 536; Fletcher, Eq. Pl. & Pr. 700. A (final) vacation decree under Va. Code 1919, § 6308, is not within the provisions of § 6140 giving the court control of proceedings in the clerk's office during the previous vacation. Matney *v.* Yates, 121 Va. 506, 513.

[18] Royall *v.* Johnson, 1 Rand. 421; Ryan *v.* McLeod, 32 Gratt. 367, 377; Bradley *v.* Bradley, 83 Va. 75; Battaille *v.* Maryland Hospital, 76 Va. 63, 71; Jones *v.* Buckingham Slate Co., 116 Va. 120; Gills *v.* Gills, 126 Va. 526; Johnson *v.* Merritt, 125 Va. 162.

[19] Va. Code 1919, § 6316; Johnson *v.* Merritt, 125 Va. 162.

[20] Shepperd *v.* Larue, 6 Munf. 529. The considerations which should induce the court to grant or deny a rehearing or review, are stated at large by Story, J. in Jenkins *v.* Eldredge, 3 Story 299, quoted in Story, Eq. Pl. (10th ed.) 421n (a).

§ 193. Bills of review in the Federal courts.—The Equity Rules do not in terms mention bills of review, but the language of Rule 69 ostensibly providing for petitions for rehearing, clearly contemplates bills of review as well. Reference must be made to the rule itself for particulars.[21]

§ 194. Injunction with bill of review.—Where the bill of review is filed by a party whose rights may suffer detriment unless the execution or enforcement of the decree be stayed or suspended until a hearing can be had on the bill of review, an injunction may be awarded suspending the decree accordingly.[22]

6. PETITION FOR REHEARING.

§ 195. Petition to rehear.—The purpose of a petition to rehear is much the same as that of the bill of review—namely, to have the trial court rehear the cause in the particulars set out by the party complaining of error, and to correct the errors alleged.

§ 196. The same—contrasted with bill of review.—While the purpose of these two pleadings is substantially similar, there is wide variance in the scope of the two and in the circumstances under which they may be filed, respectively.

We have just seen that the bill of review lies only after a final decree, and only for the correction of errors of law apparent on the face of the record, or to introduce newly discovered and material evidence, and must be filed within one year from the date of the final decree.

On the other hand, a petition to rehear is the appropriate method of bringing errors to the attention of the trial court (1) *before* final decree; (2) whether the errors be of *law or of fact;* or (3) for the introduction of *newly discovered evidence;* nor, in Virginia, (4) is there any *statutory limitation* applicable to such petitions.[23]

It thus appears that the courts are much more liberal in entertaining complaints of error in previous proceedings *before*

---

[21] See *infra*, § 195; Equity Rule 72.
[22] By declaratory statute in Virginia. Virginia Code 1919, § 6316.
[23] See *infra*, § 199.

final decree, presented by petition to rehear, than *after* the final decree, set up by bill of review.[24]

§ 197. The same—interlocutory decrees in the breast of the court.—As already shown, so long as no final decree has been entered, all the orders and decrees in a chancery suit are interlocutory, and remain *in the breast of the court,* regardless of any adjournment of the term—herein presenting a striking contrast with the practice at law.

Being thus in the breast of the court, such decrees do not constitute final records; and hence they are subject to alteration and amendment, in the sound discretion of the court, at any future term and until adjournment after entry of the final decree. Hence, where considerations of justice require it, there is not the same reason for judicial reluctance to grant relief under a petition to rehear as in the case of the bill of review.[25]

§ 198. Misnaming the petition to rehear as bill of review—or vice versa.—As pointed out,[26] mere error in naming a pleading is immaterial in equity. Hence, where a pleading termed a "bill of review" is filed before final decree, it may be treated as a "petition to rehear," or *vice versa.*[27]

§199. Petition to rehear continued—time limit.—In the absence of a special statute, there is no prescribed limit of time within which such petition must be filed,[28] although, as in the case of a bill of review, the complaining party may be denied

---

[24] Where the error complained of is merely one of figures, or merely clerical, or of form, or otherwise of a simple nature, it may be corrected on mere *motion.* Banks *v.* Anderson, 2 Hen. & Munf. 20; Kendrick *v.* Whitney, 28 Gratt. 646, 652; 2 Daniell, Ch. Pr. 244. See Equity Rule 72.

[25] Gardner *v.* Richardson, 128 Va. 676—quoting the text. See *Decrees, post,* Ch. xxi.

[26] Ante, § 165; Barger *v.* Buckland, 28 Gratt. 851.

[27] Kendrick *v.* Whitney, 28 Gratt. 646, 654; Laidley *v.* Merrifield, 7 Leigh 346; Whitten *v.* Saunders, 75 Va. 563, 572; Matney *v.* Yates, 121 Va. 506.

[28] Kendrick *v.* Whitney, 28 Gratt. 646, 651-654—a case in which it was held proper to entertain a petition to rehear a decree entered *thirteen years before,* and in which Judge Staples, who delivered the opinion, mentions cases in which rehearings were granted to correct errors occurring twenty-five years before petition filed—the suits, of course being still on the docket, and no final decree entered.

relief where he has been guilty of laches in not bringing the error to the attention of the court at an earlier stage of the proceeding, and particularly where, in the meantime, other persons have changed their position in reliance on the correctness of the proceedings, and the parties cannot be placed *in statu quo*.[29]

§ 200. The same—frame of the petition.—The petition should set forth specifically the errors complained of, and should conform, in its general structure, to the bill of review.[30] Indeed the petition to rehear appears to be the modern substitute for the practice of the English chancery of correcting errors in interlocutory decrees by "bill in the nature of a bill of a review"—though Judge Story suggests that the petition for rehearing cannot be resorted to where it is necessary to introduce supplementary matter, in which case, the new matter should be brought to the attention of the court by supplemental bill in the nature of a bill of review, and not by petition.[31]

§ 201. The same—in the Federal courts.—Rehearing in the Federal courts is provided for by Rules 67 and 72. Neither of these rules refers in terms to bills of review, but only to petitions to rehear. It is evident, however, from the language of Rule 69 that the term "petition to rehear" is not used in its technical sense, but is meant to include bills of review as well.

---

[29] See Phipps *v.* Wise, 116 Va. 739—a case involving a bill of review, but equally applicable to the petition to rehear.
[30] See also McLeod *v.* New Albany, 66 Fed. 378.
[31] Story, Eq. Pl. 421, *et seq.*

CHAPTER XIV.

Defensive Pleadings.

1. THE DEMURRER.

§ 202. The function of a demurrer.—The function of a demurrer in modern practice is to *test the sufficiency in law of the plaintiff's case as stated in the bill, or other pleading demurred to.* Its effect is much the same as at .law, in that it admits the truth of all the facts sufficiently pleaded in the pleading demurred to, and submits to the court the decision of the issue whether the pleading *on its face,* is legally sufficient, in form and substance.[1]

§ 203. Failing to demur to a defective bill—effect.—In equity, the failure to demur is nothing like so serious as at law, since, even though the defendant omits to demur, the court will not grant relief upon the hearing unless there be a proper case made by the bill and the proofs.[2] In short, where it appears that the case is without equity on its merits, the defendant may generally take advantage of the situation at the hearing, orally, or the court will *ex mero motu* raise the objection.[3]

§ 204. The same—aided by proofs.—But if the defective case made by the bill be afterwards supplemented by the proofs, so that at the hearing the record discloses a meritorious case, consistent with that made in the bill, and one proper for relief in equity, the court may administer proper relief, and the defendant who has failed to demur to the bill cannot complain of such action.[4]

lies.—Contrary to the rule at law, in the equity practice, a de-

---

[1] Watson *v.* Brunner, 128 Va. 600.
[2] Green *v.* Massie, 21 Gratt. 356.
[3] Stuart *v.* Coalter, 4 Rand. 74, 78; Salamone *v.* Keily, 80 Va. 86; Poindexter *v.* Burwell, 82 Va. 507.
[4] Salamone *v.* Keily, *supra.*

§ 205. The demurrer continued — to what pleading it murrer lies *only to a bill, bill of review, cross-bill,* or other aggressive pleading, and not to an answer or plea.[5] As we shall see later, if the *answer* is insufficient in not responding fully, the proper form of objection is to enter exceptions, or, if insufficient in *substance* as a defense to the bill, the cause is *set down for hearing on bill and answer;* and if the *plea* be deemed insufficient it is *set down for argument.*

§ 206. The same—effect if demurrer sustained.—Ordinarily, where a demurrer is sustained to the plaintiff's bill, he obtains leave, as of course, to amend his bill, and does amend accordingly, unless he has already put his best foot foremost and stated the case as strongly as the proofs at his command enable him to do; in which latter case, equally of course, an amendment would not serve his purpose, and his bill must be dismissed.

Formerly. if the plaintiff desired to test the validity of the court's ruling by an appeal, he must have refused to amend, and at once have taken an appeal, since, if even under protest he accepted the ruling as proper by amending his bill to conform thereto, he was held to have waived his privilege, and could not avail himself of it in the higher court.[6] But by recent statute this rather harsh rule no longer exists, provided the demurree gives notice that he does not accept the ruling as correct.[7]

§ 207. The same—objections that may be taken by demurrer.—As stated in a previous section, the purpose of a demurrer is to test the sufficiency *in law* of the adversary pleading as it stands on the record.

It follows that *any objection, of form or substance, apparent on the face of the pleading* (and no other) may be thus taken.

It is impossible to enumerate the manifold errors that an ig-

---

[5] See Story, Eq. Pl. 456; Kelly *v.* Hamblen, 98 Va. 383, 6 Va. Law Reg. 178, note; Langdell, Eq. Pl. 83, 94; 2 Barton, Ch. Pr. (2nd ed.) 370-371; Banks *v.* Manchester, 128 U. S. 244.

[6] See Fudge *v.* Payne, 86 Va. 303; Birckhead *v.* C. & O. Ry. Co., 95 Va. 648, 6 Va. Law Reg. 44; Tidewater Railway Co. *v.* Hurt, 109 Va. 204. Compare N. & W. Ry. Co. *v.* Old Dom. Bag. Co., 97 Va. 90.

[7] Va. Code 1919, § 6116.

norant and muddle-headed draughtsman may inject into his pleadings, hence a few practical illustrations of the more common grounds of demurrer must suffice.

§ 208. The same—illustrations of the demurrer.—Thus (hypothetically) if the plaintiff's bill for specific performance of a contract for the sale of personal property should fail to allege that the property is of a unique character, not readily obtainable in the market, or such other circumstance as under established rules should induce a court of equity to decree specific performance of a contract for the sale of personal property; or where the bill sets up a trust for an illegal or unrecognized purpose; or seeks an injunction on improper grounds; or in a suit by creditors to set aside a fraudulent conveyance, made for value, omits to allege notice of the fraud by the grantee—or to allege that the plaintiffs have recovered judgments at law (the rule is otherwise in Virginia);[8] or, in a divorce suit, the bill fails to allege a valid marriage between the parties, or proper domicil within the state, or sufficient grounds for divorce; or in any other case where, *assuming all the facts stated in the bill to be true,* yet these facts do not constitute a case for the cognizance of equity—in all of such cases the objection is properly taken by demurrer.

§ 209. Further illustrations of use of the demurrer.—The illustrations given in the preceding section are rather objections of *substance*—where the bill failed in substance to make out a case entitling the plaintiff to equitable relief.

But there are many other objections besides those going to the substance of the case. Thus if the bill shows on its face that *necessary parties* have been omitted—that the plaintiff has *no real interest* in the matter he is attempting to litigate (as where an administrator sues for partition of the real estate of his decedent—or for a sale of such real estate for payment of debts) —that the bill Improperly joins two independent causes of action, resulting in multifariousness [9]—that though a good cause of action is stated, it is not a case proper for equity cognizance

---

[8] See *Creditors' Bills, post,* ch. 31.
[9] *Post,* ch. xxiv.

because of a plain, adequate and complete remedy at law—that the plaintiff, though having an interest, is yet not entitled to sue alone, by reason of some legal disability, as infancy or lunacy, shown in the bill—in all of which cases, *if the objection appear on the face of the bill* (but not otherwise), a demurrer is the proper method of bringing the objection to the attention of the court.

§ 210. Questioning the jurisdiction by demurrer.—If it appear on the face of the bill that the case is not a proper one for equity jurisdiction—that is, that *no court of equity* would have jurisdiction on the facts stated—or if the jurisdiction invoked by the bill be a special statutory one (as a suit for the sale of infants' land) and the bill fails to show the proper jurisdiction—the question may be raised by demurrer; or, as we have already seen,[10] the demurrer may be omitted and the attention of the court brought to the defect orally at the hearing, since no court of equity will assume jurisdiction of a suit of which it has not proper cognizance, even though no objection be made by the defendant. Neither waiver nor consent can confer jurisdiction.

§ 211. Defense of statute of limitations by demurrer.— (1) remedy only affected.—While in a few states the statute of limitations may be availed of by demurrer, (that is, where the claim appears *from the face of the bill* to be time-barred), it is settled in Virginia and in most of the states, that even though the lapse of the prescribed period appear *from the face of the bill*, the statute *cannot be availed of by demurrer,* but must be set up by plea or answer—the reason being that the plaintiff would not, on demurrer, have the opportunity of replying a new promise or other facts which repel the defense of limitation[11]—as well as for the further reason that even though the claim be time-barred, and though this appear from the face of the bill, the bill yet states a valid cause of action, to be defeated only by the defendant's asserting his personal privilege of pleading the statute.

---

[10] *Ante,* §§ 12-15.
[11] Hubble *v.* Poff, 98 Va. 646, 6 Va. Law Reg. 557, note.

§ 212. The same—(2) right affected.—The statute of limitations, normally, does not bar the *right* but the *remedy* only —and the defense of the statute is a personal privilege of the defendant. The statute merely authorizes the defendant to shut the doors of the court-house, as it were, upon the plaintiff when he seeks to enforce the right. The cause of action itself still exists, and is a valuable consideration for a new promise.

The preceding section, in which is stated the rule that the statute of limitations cannot be set up by demurrer, contemplates a statute thus operating on the *remedy* only. But now and then is met with a statute which, in terms or by construction, bars not the remedy only but the *right as well*—for example, where the right sought to be enforced is not one of the common law but is given by statute, and by the terms of the same statute there is prescribed a limit of time within which the right must be enforced. In such cases it is usually held that *time is the essence of the right*, and that the *right itself* is barred after expiration of the limit fixed.

The action for wrongful death under Lord Campbell's Act, which the statute[12] requires to be asserted within one year—and mechanics' liens on real property to secure payment for improvements erected thereon, suits to enforce which are (in Virginia) limited to twelve months[13]— are illustrations of statutory *rights* to which a time limit is attached. In such cases, unless it affirmatively appear from the plaintiff's declaration or bill that the suit was instituted within the prescribed time-limit, the defendant may avail himself of the defense by demurrer[14]—and *a fortiori* where the reverse affirmatively appears.

§ 213. Demurrer—defense of statute of parol agreements—(1) where bill shows oral contract.—Where the bill shows on its face that the contract sued on is not in writing, with no allegations to take the case out of the statute, the defendant may, according to the apparent weight of authority, avail

---

[12] Va. Code 1919, § 5787.

[13] Id., § 6433.

[14] See The Harrisburg, 119 U. S. 199; Taylor *v.* Cranberry Iron Co., 94 N. C. 525; Manuel *v.* N. & W. R. Co., 99 Va. 188, 6 Val Law Reg. 776, note; Lambert *v.* Ensign M'f'g. Co. (W. Va.), 26 S. E. 451; 3 Va. Law Reg. 63; 6 id. 411, 558; 25 Cyc. 1398.

himself of the defense of the statute of frauds by demurrer.[15] Here the plaintiff admits, in most solemn form, that he lacks the statutory evidence, and that he is not entitled to enforce the contract against the unwilling defendant.[16]

§ 214. The same—(2) where the bill sets up the contract in general terms.—Where, however, the bill sets out the contract in general terms, *without showing whether it is in writing or not,* a demurrer will not lie. Inasmuch as the statute of frauds does not render the parol contract void, but merely excludes the *evidence* of its existence, it is generally held that the plaintiff need not allege the writing in his bill or declaration. Here the question is one rather of *evidence* than of *pleading.* Hence it follows that the omission of such allegation does not render the pleading insufficient on its face.

In such case, the defendant (by the weight of authority) must deny the existence of the writing, in his plea or answer. In some jurisdictions, however, including Virginia, it is held that the defendant, instead of specifically pleading the statute, may avail himself of it by *objecting to the parol testimony* when offered— and in the absence of objection, either in his pleading or when the evidence is offered, he is held to have waived the defense.[17]

§ 215. The demurrer in the Federal courts.—Along with other technical forms of pleading, the new Equity Rules have abolished the demurrer, in terms—and defenses formerly made by demurrer are required to be made by *motion* or in the *answer.*[17a]

§ 216. Demurring and answering simultaneously.—In the ancient equity practice, as at law, it was not permissible to answer and demur at the same time. By answering the bill on the

---

[15] 3 Cyc. 312.

[16] And yet where the plaintiff, in equally solemn form, on the face of his bill, admits that the right he asserts is barred by the statute of limitations, the rule, as has just been pointed out, is the reverse. The inconsistency here is obvious—since in neither case does the statute affect the validity of the contract, until specially invoked by the defendant.

[17] Eaves v. Vial, 98 Va. 104. The authorities are collected in 20 Cyc. 308-311; 9 Enc. Pl. & Pr. 705-709. See 5 Va. Law Reg. 794.

[17a] Rule 29.

merits the defendant was held to have waived any objection that he might have raised by the demurrer. But, in Virginia, and in the States generally, it is common practice,[18] thus to demur and

[18] See Bassett *v.* Cunningham, 7 Leigh 402.

answer simultaneously.

CHAPTER XV.

Defensive Pleadings—Continued.

2. THE PLEA.

§ 217. The plea.—Defense by plea, in modern times at least, is comparatively rare, although, where available, this form of defense has many advantages over that by way of answer— especially since the answer, by the operation of modern statutes, has been largely shorn of its old-time value as an instrument of evidence.

The defense by plea is used where the defendant desires to present a *single state of facts* (although possibly made up of numerous circumstances), as a defense to the plaintiff's suit. The advantage which the plea presents over the answer is that it shortens the litigation—reducing the issue, as it does, to a *single point*. It also saves the defendant from making discovery—the rule being that 'one who answers at all must answer fully'—although this immunity is now of little advantage.

Familiar illustrations of the use of the plea would be: The statute of limitations; absence of proper parties (where this does not appear from the bill itself); *res judicata;* usury; a release; an award; infancy; bankruptcy; denial of partnership; *bona fide* purchaser; denial of an essential jurisdictional fact alleged in the bill, etc.[1]

§ 218. Several pleas—duplicity.—Under the general equity practice, the defendant is permitted, as a matter of course, to file

[1] See form of plea, *post, Appendix.*

different pleas to *separate parts* of the same bill, but he will ordinarily not be permitted to file several pleas to the *whole bill*, or to the same part thereof. This, however, the court may in its discretion permit.[2]

The Virginia courts are quite liberal in this connection, and are disposed to extend the statutory relaxation of the rule against duplicity in pleas at law, to proceedings in equity, by analogy.[3] Thus it is common practice in Virginia to demur and answer at the same time.[4] Inasmuch, however, as the purpose of the plea is to shorten the litigation by reducing the issue to a single point, and since the defense by plea is not the only defense open to the defendant, instances are rare in which occasion arises for the use of more than a single plea to the whole bill or to the same part thereof.

1. Issue of Law on the Plea.

§ 219. Legal sufficiency of plea—how tested.—In a court of law the proper method of testing the legal sufficiency of any pleading is, of course, by demurrer, or by motion to exclude. But, as already pointed out, in equity procedure the demurrer lies only to an aggressive pleading. Hence objection to a plea cannot be taken by demurrer—nor is the motion to exclude proper.

Practically the same result is accomplished, however, by *"seting down the plea for argument"*—which means that before replying thereto the plaintiff invokes the opinion of the court whether the plea, *assuming its allegations to be true,* is sufficient in form and substance as a defense to the bill, or to any specific part thereof. Substantially, therefore, the only difference between a demurrer and a setting down for argument is one of terms only.[5]

§ 220. The same—result of hearing of the argument.—The result of this hearing will be, of course, a ruling either that the plea *is* or *is not* legally sufficient as a defense to the bill, or to

---

[2] See Fletcher's Eq. Pl. & Pr. 244-5; Shipman's Eq. Pl. 492; Bassett *v.* Cunningham, 7 Leigh 402.

[3] Va. Code 1919, §§ 6107, 6373.

[4] Bassett *v.* Cunningham, 7 Leigh 402.

[5] See Va. Code 1919, § 6120, which seems declaratory of the unwritten rule.

that portion of the bill to which it purports to be a defense—
with the results following:

§ 221. The same—(a) plea held insufficient.—If the plea
(assuming it true in fact), is held to offer *no valid defense,* it will
be rejected by the court, or, in the language of the order, *"disallowed"*—and the defendant, both by the unwritten rule and by
the statute, will be ordered to file an answer.[6]

§ 222. The same—(b) plea held legally sufficient.—If,
on the other hand, the defense set up by the plea is held to be
sufficient in law, then an order is entered *"allowing the plea"*—
that is, in substance, that the facts alleged in the plea constitute a
valid defense, provided they are capable of proof at the hearing.
The plaintiff must then decide whether he can afford to *take issue* on it by filing a general replication, denying the truth of the
allegations of the plea—as he must do if the plea merely denies
the allegations of the bill, and is not by way of confession and
avoidance—or whether he must not himself set up in reply *new
matter* by confession and avoidance. In the latter case, by the
ancient practice, the plaintiff filed a *special replication.* But, as
already shown,[7] special replications have long since become obsolete in the equity practice, and have been substituted by the
amended bill.

§ 223. The same—illustrations.—Thus, in a suit for divorce on the ground of the defendant's unjustifiable desertion
of the plaintiff, continued during the statutory period, if the defendant by plea simply *denies the desertion,* the plaintiff has no
other course open than to file a general replication, and thus take
issue on the truth or falsity of the plea.

But if the defendant plead by way of confession and avoidance, by *admitting the desertion* and justifying it on the ground
of the *plaintiff's adultery,* here the plaintiff must decide whether
he will deny the adultery (which he would naturally do if innocent, and which he would do by a general replication), or
whether (if guilty) he must admit the adultery and avoid the

---

[6] Ibid.
[7] *Infra,* § 258.

effect of the admission by setting up *condonation* on the part of
the defendant. If the latter alternative be adopted, he must file
an *amended bill*, reiterating the charge of desertion, admitting
his own adultery, and setting up condonation by the defendant.
Whether he shall adopt the one or the other method of defense
will, of course, depend upon the proofs at his command, or the
lack of proof available to the defendant.

2. *Issue of Fact on the Plea.*

§ 224. The same—issue of fact on plea.—Where the
plaintiff takes issue on the plea, by a general replication, either
party is entitled by the Virginia statute to have such issue tried
by a jury—this being one of the few examples of a jury trial in
a court of equity.[8]

§ 225. The same—issue of fact—(a) for defendant.—
If such issue be found in favor of the *defendant*—that is, that
the plea is *true*—and the plea is to the whole bill, an order is
entered *dismissing the bill*, with the result, of course, that the
defendant wins the suit. If, however, the plea goes to a particular portion of the bill—as, for example, to only one of several
claims—then such claim is adjudged in defendant's favor, and
is eliminated from the controversy.

Thus, if the purpose of the bill be to enjoin defendant from
cutting timber from a particular tract, and defendant by plea
sets up a fee-simple title in himself, with general replication by
the plaintiff, issue found for the *defendant* would necessarily call
for ending the entire controversy by dismissal of the bill, since
the whole foundation of the plaintiff's suit has failed.

If, on the other hand, the bill had included *two tracts*, and defendant had pleaded title in himself as to *one* of the tracts only,
issue found in defendant's favor would have eliminated that
tract from the controversy, without touching the question as to
the other.

§ 226. The same—issue of fact—(b) for plaintiff.—
The rule very generally prevailing in the original equity practice,

---

[8] Va. Code 1919, § 6121. Another instance occurs in an issue out of
chancery noticed hereafter. See Towson *v.* Towson, 126 Va. 640.

and in the Federal courts before the abolition of pleas by the new Equity Rules, was that where the defendant filed a plea to the merits, and the plea was found not true in fact, the plaintiff was entitled to a decree *pro confesso,* and defendant had not the privilege of making further defense (howsoever valid and available) by answer *(respondens ouster)*—though the plaintiff was entitled to insist, if he desired, upon such *discovery* by answer as his bill called for.[9]

§ 227. The same—in Virginia.—In conceding this to be the prevailing practice elsewhere, and in the absence of any known authority in Virginia, where the use of the plea is extremely rare, it is yet questionable whether, under the very liberal equity practice in this State, and under the influence of statutes modifying the stringent rules against duplicity in the common law courts, an issue of fact found in the plaintiff's favor on a plea in equity, (*e. g.* the statute of frauds or of limitations), would debar the defendant from the right of filing an answer setting up other available defenses.

Thus, in Virginia, even in the courts of law, the defendant may plead in abatment and in bar at the same time—he may file as many pleas in bar as he desires—he may demur and plead or answer simultaneously—he may withdraw his motion to exclude a replication after a ruling of sufficiency, and take issue in fact, etc.—these relaxations of the ancient prejudice against duplicity in pleading, all indicative of a policy of permitting a defendant to avail himself of every meritorious defense that he may have, without regard to technical rules against duplicity.

For instance, where a defendant, impleaded as a constructive trustee, believes that he is protected by the statute of limitations, and accordingly so pleads, the circumstance that his plea

---

[9] Story, Eq. Pl. 98, 697; Langdell, Eq. Pl. 98, 147; Fletcher, Eq. Pl. and Pr. 290; Adriaans v. Lyon, 8 App. (D. C.) 532; Dows v. McMichael, 2 Pai. Ch. 345 (*per* Walworth, Ch.); Kennedy v. Creswell, 101 U. S. 641; Farley v. Kittson, 120 U. S. 303. In the case last cited it was held that the defendant might answer over, under authority of (old) Equity Rule 34—a view which is vigorously assailed in a luminous paper, on this precise question, by Ro. S. Taylor, in 36 Am. Bar Association Reports 361. The rule in Alabama accords with the original practice: Sims, Ch. Practice 452; and so in Tennessee: See Gibson, Equity Practice.

is not sustained in fact, should not debar him from setting up by answer the further defense that he has *fully accounted* for the trust fund, or that he holds a *release* from the plaintiff, or that the fund in controversy was originally *his own,* or has become his own under a *bona fide purchase* thereof for value. True, all of these defenses he might originally have set up by *answer;* but the circumstance that, from motives of economy of time and expense, (for which the plea was devised) he has asserted one of his available defenses by plea, should not operate to shut out other honest defenses, of the existence of which he is full-handed with proof. If the rule in question should debar these other defenses in such case in this state, then we should have the rare (if not unique) spectacle of a Virginia chancellor consciously entering an unrighteous decree because of a highly technical rule of equity procedure—a rule resting in no statute, but originating in the unwritten practice adopted by equity courts in the interest of just judgments, unhampered by technical considerations.

In such case, of course the finding that the plea is untrue becomes *res judicata,* and the same defense cannot again be asserted in the answer.

3. *Defense by Plea Generally.*

§ 228. Plea supported by answer.—It is possible for the plaintiff so to frame the allegations of his bill as to compel the defendant to file *an answer along with his plea*—the result being, in the language of the books, 'a plea supported by an answer.' This somewhat rare specimen of pleading occurs where the plaintiff *anticipates the defense to be set up by the defendant,* and in the bill alleges matter in avoidance of such defense—or alleges special circumstances in corroboration of the allegations of the bill—and *prays discovery* from the defendant as to the truth of such allegations.

It will be noticed that the answer here is *no part of the defense.* The real defense is set up in the *plea.* The answer is insisted upon merely to supply *evidence* upon which the plaintiff relies *to overcome the defensive allegations of the plea.*[10]

---

[10] Story, Eq. Pl. 671.

For instance, if the bill charges a partnership between the plaintiff and defendant, evidence of which, in the form of written articles and books of account, are alleged to be in the defendant's possession, and discovery of the facts establishing the partnership, with production of books and documents, is demanded, a plea of no partnership would obviously be insufficient without an answer in support, making the required discovery.[11]

§ 229. Defense by plea—optional not obligatory.—Before passing from the plea it may be well to point out that, save as to matters *in abatement*, defense by plea is a privilege to be exercised by the defendant or not at his option. Any meritorious defense available by *plea* may be made by *answer* as well. In other words, there is no rule of equity procedure that certain defenses must be made by plea and certain others by answer. Hence, if he choose, the defendant may utilize his answer for every meritorious defense open to him.[12]

§ 230. Pleas in the Federal courts—abolished.—By the New Equity Rules, pleas, whether in bar or in abatement, are abolished, and defenses formerly presentable by plea are required to be made by *motion* or *answer*.[13]

· § 231. Plea of another suit pending—(1) in the same state—(a) in another court of equity.—The plaintiff is not permitted to harass the defendant by two suits concerning the same subject-matter, whether both be in equity or both at law, or one in each court.[14]

---

[11] See numerous illustrations, Story, Eq. Pl. 671-679.

[12] A single (possible) exception to the rule thus broadly stated exists in the case where defendant desires to set up a privilege *in avoidance of discovery* sought in the bill. He cannot set up the privilege by *answer*, because of the rule that a defendant who answers *must answer fully*. Hence in such case he is driven to his plea. Thus, if discovery is sought of privileged communications, or of matters the discovery of which would subject him to a penalty or forfeiture, the defendant must set up the privilege of non-disclosure by his plea (or demurrer if appearing on the face of the bill)—since if he answers at all he must answer fully. See Story, Eq. Pl. 847.

[13] Rules 29, 45, 52.

[14] The case of a mortgagee proceeding at law for a personal judgment for the debt, and in equity to foreclose the mortgage, is a striking exception. Jones *v.* Conde, 6 Johns. Ch. 77; Priddy *v.* Hartsook, 81 Va. 67.

Hence where *both suits are pending in equity,* in the same state, objection is properly made by filing, in the later case, a *plea of former suit pending.* If the plea is sustained an order follows, dismissing the later suit.[15]

§ 232. The same—(b) another action pending in a court of law.—It is clear that since a court of law does not recognize even the existence of a court of equity, no plea of a pending equity suit could be set up in abatement of an action at law. So that where there are two suits being prosecuted by the same plaintiff, against the same defendant, involving the same subject-matter, *one at law and the other in equity, the* objection must be made *in the equity suit.* This is done by motion for a rule against the plaintiff to show cause why he should not be put to an *election between the two suits.* If he fail to elect within the time prescribed in the order requiring an election, the suit in equity will be dismissed.[16]

§ 233. The same—(2) in a foreign state.—The general rule is that the courts of one state will take no notice of suits pending in another state. Hence a plea alleging the pendency of such a suit in not a valid plea, and will be disallowed.[17]

----

[15] Fletcher, Eq. Pl. & Pr. 258, 365; Hatch v. Spofford, 22 Conn. 485, 58 Am. Dec. 433; Story, Eq. Pl. 736-744. In case of dispute as to whether the two suits are for substantially the same purpose, the question is generally referred to a master for investigation and report. Id. 700, 742-743.

[16] Fletcher, Eq. Pl. & Pr. 365; Gibbs v. Perkinson, 4 H. & M. 415; Williamson v. Paxton, 18 Gratt. 475, 504; Priddy v. Hartsook, 81 Va. 64, 69; Keys Planing Mill Co. v. Kirkbridge, 114 Va. 58. The reason why the objection is made here by a *rule to elect,* rather than by a *plea* of the pending action at law, probably rests on the consideration that if set up by a plea, a decision on the plea in favor of the defendant would necessarily call for a dismissal of the plaintiff's bill, and force him to stake his entire reliance on the action at law—a result in conflict with the more gracious policy of the equity courts, which is not arbitrarily to dismiss the bill for this cause, but to permit the plaintiff to exercise his own option as to which of the suits he will abandon. The same option should be permitted under § 231, *supra.*

[17] Davis v. Morriss, 76 Va. 21; Staunton v. Embrey, 93 U. S. 548; Hatch v. Spofford, 22 Conn. 485, 58 Am. Dec. 433—a case *at law,* in which a plea of a former suit in equity, pending in another state, was offered in abatement, but the opinion in which, by Ellsworth, J., contains a luminous exposition of the general topic of pleas of former suits pending, both at law and in equity. See also Story, Eq. Pl. 741.

§ 233½. Plea to the jurisdiction—in abatement.—The plea to the jurisdiction has been considered in a previous chapter,[18] as has also the plea in abatement on other grounds.[19]

CHAPTER XVI.

Defensive Pleadings—Continued.

3. THE ANSWER.

§ 234. The Answer in chancery.—The Answer is the pleading by which the defendant sets up his defense, or defenses, at large, and in somewhat circumstantial detail. It is the most common method of making defense in chancery suits. The answer (with immaterial exceptions) may be used for any defense or defenses available to the defendant.[1]

§ 235. The same—both a pleading and an instrument of evidence.—The answer is unique in being the only pleading, at law or in equity, possessing *evidentiary value* in favor of the pleader. At law, the allegations of a declaration, or of a plea, or a replication, or other pleading—or those of the bill, or of the plea in chancery—have no value whatsoever as evidence in the pleader's favor, but are mere statements of the plaintiff's claim, or of the defendant's defense, to be supported later by such evidence as the parties may be able to produce at the trial.

But from earliest days it has been the settled rule of equity practice that the answer of the defendant must be *under oath,* and being under oath it is to be treated as of high evidentiary value.

1. *The Answer As an Instrument of Evidence.*

§ 236. Value of answer as an instrument of evidence—

---

[18] See *ante,* §§ 13-15, 25-29n, 50.
[19] *Ante,* § 64.
[1] See *supra,* § 220. For form of answer, see *post, Appendix.*

(1) in ordinary chancery cases.—The uniform rule of the chancery courts, unmodified by statute, is that the sworn answer of the defendant, *so far as it is responsive to the allegations of the bill* (and no further) is evidence in behalf of the respondent (but not of a co-defendant),[1a] of such weight that it may be overcome *only by the testimony of two witnesses,* or of one witness and corroborative circumstances, or other equivalent testimony.[2]

§ 237. The same—reason for the rule stated.—Commentators are not agreed as to the reason on which the rule stated rests; but that suggested by Chief Justice Marshall[3] seems quite satisfactory, namely, that "the plaintiff calls upon the defendant to answer an allegation he makes, and thereby admits the answer to be *evidence.* If it is testimony it is equal to the testimony of any other witness; and as the plaintiff cannot prevail if the balance of proof be not in his favor, he must have circumstances in addition to his single witness, in order to turn the balance."

§ 238. The same—waiver of the oath—the equity rule. —While there is some lack of harmony among the authorities, the better rule is that, in the absence of an enabling statute, the plaintiff *cannot deprive the defendant's answer of this evidentiary force, by waiving the oath in his bill.*[4]

[1a] Save under exceptional circumstances. Carle *v.* Corhan, 127 Va. 223.

[2] Story, Eq. Pl. (10th ed.) 849a, 875a; Thornton *v.* Gordon, 2 Rob. (Va.) 719; Seitz *v.* Mitchell, 94 U. S. 580. The rule does not apply where the statements of the answer are merely made on information and belief; nor where they are manifestly absurd, contradictory or impossible; nor where the answer is not direct and positive in its denials and explanations; nor where it appears that the defendant could have had no personal knowledge of the matters to which he swears; nor as to new matters stated in avoidance. 1 Story, Eq. Pl. (10th ed.) 849a (n); Banks *v.* Manchester, 128 U. S. 244; East India Co. *v.* Donald, 9 Ves. 275; Town *v.* Needham, 3 Paige 545; Fant *v.* Miller, 17 Gratt. 187. For rules governing the answer in the Federal Court, see *infra,* § 240.

[3] In Clark *v.* Van Riemsdyk, 9 Cranch 158, 160. See footnote to the section following.

[4] Thornton *v.* Gordon, 2 Rob (Va.) 719. "It has been argued," says Allen, J., in this case, "that the rule giving to the answer the weight of evidence arises from the right of the plaintiff to call for a discovery; that this is a right of the plaintiff and he may waive it.

§ 239. The same—statutory waiver.—But in Virginia, and probably in most of the states of the Union, the plaintiff is now permitted by statute [5] to waive the oath in his bill, and thus deprive the answer of its ancient force—and, indeed, of all force, as self-serving evidence. Where the plaintiff thus avails himself of the statutory privilege and waives answer under oath, the answer, whether sworn to or not, loses its evidentiary character and is relegated to the lower rank of a mere pleading.[6]

---

* * *" (But) "if this were the sole foundation of the rule, it would seem to follow that if, by calling upon the defendant to answer, the answer when made is admitted to be evidence of the fact, the plaintiff would be concluded by it.

"Perhaps the origin of the rule is to be found in the civil law, which required the evidence of two witnesses as the foundation of a decree. * * * To whatever source the rule is traced, it is firmly established as one of the fundamental principles of a court of equity. It is the *law of the forum*, and all who apply to it for relief must submit to have their causes tried according to its established modes of procedure." Jones *v*. Abraham, 75 Va. 466; Clements *v*. Moore, 6 Wall 299; Carle *v*. Corhan, 127 Va. 223; Farrell *v*. Forest Investment Co. (Fla.), 74 So. 216, 1 A. L. R. 25, and monographic note. The case last cited indicates that the Florida practice conforms substantially to the Federal Equity Rules; and the opinion is held that under the new Equity Rules the defendant cannot, by waiver, be deprived of the ancient advantage of answering under oath. The monographic note cited contains a full collection of authorities on the subject of the answer as evidence, both under the original practice, and under statutes authorizing waiver of the oath.

[5] Va. Code 1919, § 6128. By the terms of the statute, the plaintiff may either waive oath as to the *entire answer*, or he may require oath only as to certain *specific interrogatories* of the bill—in which latter case, the answer to these interrogatories would retain its former force as evidence.

Question arose in Johnson *v*. Mundy, 123 Va. 730, whether, on a waiver of answer under oath, the plaintiff might insist, nevertheless, upon discovery called for in the bill. In an exhaustive opinion by Sims, J., it was held, (1) that the rule of equity practice requiring the defendant who answers at all to answer fully, is not abrogated by the statutory waiver of oath—that is, *as a rule of pleading*, the answer must still reply to all material allgations of the bill; but (2) the waiver of the verified answer deprives the plaintiff of the former right to *search the conscience of the defendant* and to compel disclosures not required by the rules of pleading, but intended to serve as *evidence* in behalf of the plaintiff. It follows that *waiver of the oath deprives the plaintiff of the right to demand discovery*.

In Blanchard *v*. Dominion Nat. Bank, 125 Va. 586, the court takes occasion to suggest to the bar a brief form of waiver, viz., that the defendants named "be made parties defendant to this bill, and waiving answer under oath" that they may answer the same, etc.

[6] This seems clear enough from the language of the statute, and the conclusion is confirmed in Millhizer *v*. McKinley, 98 Va. 207; Baker *v*. Cummings, 4 App. D. C. 230. The verified answer may of

§ 240. The answer in Federal courts of equity.—The radical changes in the equity practice of the Federal courts are especially conspicuous in the rule governing the answer, which now becomes practically the *only pleading available to the defendant*. It is provided that every defense in *point of law* which was formerly the subject of demurrer or plea shall be made by *motion to dismiss or by answer*—and that *every defense heretofore presentable by plea in bar or abatement shall be made in the the answer*.[7]

It is further provided that the answer may set up "as many defenses, *in the alternative*, regardless of consistency, as the defendant deems essential to his defense."[8]

§ 241. The same—continued.—In the Federal practice, the answer is also made to serve largely as a substitute for the *cross-bill*, by the provision that "the answer must state in short and simple form any counter-claim arising out of the transaction which is the subject-matter of the suit, and may, *without cross-bill*, set out any *set-off* or *counter-claim* against the plaintiff which might be the subject of an independent suit in equity against him."[9]

Provision is made for a reply by the plaintiff, where such set-off or counter-claim is asserted in the answer—but in the absence of such cross-claims, the filing of the answer makes up the issue, and *no replication is required*.[10] Provision is also made for amending the answer.[11]

§ 241½. The same—continued—oath.—Former Federal Equity Rule 41 provided for the waiver of the verified answer. This provision is omitted from the new Rules, leaving it somewhat doubtful whether the original equity practice with respect to answers under oath is, or is not, revived.

The unusual function now performed by the answer under

---

course still be used as an *affidavit*, wherever an affidavit is admissible as evidence—as, for example, on motion to dissolve a temporary injunction. Va. Code 1919, § 6128.

[7] Rule 29.
[8] Id. 30.
[9] Id. 30.
[10] Id. 31.
[11] Id. 19, 34.

the new Rules—substituting both demurrers and pleas—and
the language of the several Rules touching the answer, seem by
implication to eliminate the right of the defendant to make oath
to his answer, when not required by the bill, and thereby obtain
the advantages secured to him by the original equity practice.[12]

**§ 242. The answer as evidence, continued—(2) hearing
on bill and answer only.**—As will be explained later, where
the plaintiff conceives that the answer sets up *no valid defense*,
instead of demurring to it, as he would at law, the proper mode
of testing the sufficiency of the defense asserted is to have the
case *set down for hearing on bill and answer*—without any
replication, and of course without the taking of testimony. By
thus going to hearing on bill and answer, the plaintiff admits
as true *all the allegations of the answer*—not only those *responsive* to the allegations of the bill, but even *new matter in
avoidance* of the plaintiff's claims.[13]

This follows as a necessary consequence of the plaintiff's having elected not to file a replication, thus precluding the defendant from offering testimony *dehors* the record, in support of the
answer. In other words, where the plaintiff thus sets the cause
down for hearing *on bill and answer only*, he in effect admits all
matters of fact well pleaded in the answer, and asserts that notwithstanding their truth they constitute *no valid defense to the
bill*—thus substantially *demurring* to the answer.

**§ 243. The same—(3) in a court of law—in response
to a pure bill of discovery.**—Where the bill is filed merely to
secure discovery to be used in a *pending action at law*, and the
discovery is so used, the court of law applies its own rules; and
hence treats the answer, when introduced before the jury, as the
evidence of a *single witness*. That is, the question of the weight
to be given to the answer as evidence will be left to the discretion

---

[12] See Equity Rules 29-32, 58—the last making special provision
for discovery under oath *when required in the bill* on interrogatories.
But see Farrell *v.* Forrest Investment Co. (Fla.), 74 So. 216, 1 A.
L. R. 25, n.

[13] *Infra*, § 248; Kennedy *v.* Baylor, 1 Wash. 162; Day *v.* Smith, 6
Munf. 142; Perkins *v.* Nichols, 11 Allen 542; Fletcher, Eq. Pl. & Pr.
356; Story, Eq. Pl. (10th ed.) 456. See Tabb *v.* Cabell, 17 Gratt. 160;
Cocke *v.* Minor, 25 Gratt. 246.

of the jury.[14]

§ 244. The same—(4) answer to a bill of discovery, retained by the court of equity—(a) discovery had.—Where a bill of discovery is filed in aid of a pending action at law, and discovery is had, regularly this ends the proceeding in the equity court, and the answer may then be used in the law court, with the effect as shown in the preceding section.

But, particularly where the action in the law court is merely contemplated or threatened,[15] and the prospective plaintiff at law has filed his bill for discovery in aid of his action—or the defendant in aid of his defense, as he may do—the court of equity, in accordance with its policy of giving complete relief, and to prevent a multiplicity of suits, will generally *retain the bill,* and will proceed to give *complete relief,* though this be purely legal.[16] Having assumed jurisdiction for one purpose, certainty in the practice in such cases. jurisdiction attaches for all purposes.

Where the cause is thus retained, and the discovery sought is obtained, it seems that the court gives the answer the same weight as a court of law would have given it—namely, as the testimony of a *single witness.*[17]

§ 245. The same—(b) no discovery obtained.—Where the plaintiff's demand is properly enforceable only *at law,* but the *necessity of discovery drives him into equity,* the court of equity, as we have seen, may retain the bill and administer legal relief. Here, since the plaintiff must allege his inability to prove the allegations of his bill without discovery from the defendant, and must make oath to his bill—one of the few cases where the oath is required—it follows that if the defendant, by his testimony, in the form of his answer to the bill, should *deny the allegations of the bill,* of course the bill must be dismissed. The

---

[14] McFarland *v.* Hunter, 8 Leigh 489; Lyons *v.* Miller, 6 Gratt. 427; 7 Va. Law Reg. 108-110; Fletcher, Eq. Pl. & Pr. 820. But on an issue out of chancery, the verified answer is entitled to the same weight as if the issue were being tried before the chancellor. Powell *v.* Manson, 22 Gratt. 177.

[15] 2 Story, Eq. Jurisp. 1483.

[16] See *ante,* § 153, where reference is made to the distressing un-

[17] See following section, note.

question here is rather one of *jurisdiction*. If, in this situation, the plaintiff were allowed to dispute the truth of the answer, he would be *proving himself out of the court*—because he is in equity only on the ground that he is dependent upon the defendant's testimony, to prove his case. If he secures no such testimony from the answer, then the jurisdiction of the court of equity is ousted, and the bill must be dismissed.[18]

2. *How sufficiency of answer tested.*

§ 246.   The answer, continued—insufficiency.—As we have already seen,[19] a demurrer does not lie to an answer, but only to an aggressive pleading. But if an answer set up a counter-claim, and is treated as a cross-bill,[20] its sufficiency as to such counter-claim may be tested by a demurrer.

Objections to an answer may assume two forms: (1) That the answer *does not fully respond* to the charges made in the bill— or *does not make the discovery called for*, with the fullness and completeness required by the rules of the forum; and (2) That the defense, or defenses, set up in the answer are *not sufficient in law* as a bar to the relief sought in the bill.

§ 247.   (1) Answer not reponsive—exceptions. — By non-responsiveness here is meant the failure of the answer, in its actual content, to conform to the rules of the forum, because of *evasiveness*, or failure to answer fully the allegations or interrogatories of the bill.

Where such insufficiency appears, the plaintiff's objection is made by *excepting* to the answer, and in his exceptions distinctly stating the grounds of his objections.

It follows, then, that resort is had to exceptions *only when the plaintiff desires a more perfect answer*.[20a] If, on the other hand, the answer is merely *insufficient in law* as a defense to the bill, naturally the plaintiff will not desire a more perfect answer

---

[18] See this very much confused subject discussed by the late Judge Lamb, 7 Va. Law Reg. 107. See *supra*, § 153, note.

[19] *Ante, The Demurrer*, ch. xiv.

[20] *Ante, The Crossbill*, ch. xii.

[20a] Langdell, Eq. Pl. 84; Fletcher, Eq. Pl. & Pr. 333; Story, Eq. Pl. 864-866; 4 Minor's Inst. 1427-1428; Coleman *v*. Lyne, 4 Rand. 454, 456. See further, § 248, *infra*, n.

and thus give the defendant opportunity of setting up a better defense. In such case the plaintiff will proceed as indicated in the following section.

Exceptions to answers are abolished in the Federal court practice,[21] and in Virginia, by the revisal of 1919,[22] are substituted by *motion to strike out*.

§ 248. The same—Virginia statute.—It is not entirely clear from the section of the Virginia Code cited, whether, in abolishing "exceptions to answers for insufficiency" the revisors used the term *exceptions* in its accepted sense, as directed to the insufficiency of the answer *in failing to respond fully* to the allegations of the bill, or in the sense in which term has recently been (inadvertently and incorrectly) used by the Virginia court, as directed to the insufficiency of the answer as a *defense in law to the case made in the bill*—an objection heretofore asserted only by setting down the cause for *hearing on bill and answer*. Section 6123 provides that if, on exceptions sustained, the answer "be found amendable," the court may allow amendment. As an answer not properly responsive is *always amendable,* this legislation seems to be intended to substitute, by the motion to strike out, not only exceptions proper, to test the sufficiency of the answer in form,—that is, to require a better answer—but as a *defense* in law as well.[23] Doubt is cast on this conclusion, how-

------

[21] Equity Rule 33.

[22] Va. Code 1919, § 6123.

[23] That exceptions are only proper where the answer is 'not properly responsive, or is otherwise defective in form, is the settled practice, as shown by the authorities cited in the footnote 20 above. This especial function of exceptions is pointed out in Judge Carr's opinion in Coleman *v.* Lyne (*supra*), and is exemplified in Clark *v.* Tinsley, 4 Rand. 250; Craig *v.* Sebrell, 9 Gratt. 131, and Johnson *v.* Wilson, 29 Gratt. 390. But in Kelly *v.* Hamblen, 98 Va. 383, 391, the court, by an obvious inadvertence, confused *exceptions* to an answer with *hearing on bill and answer*—and this error was repeated in one or more subsequent cases. See Keys, etc., Co. *v.* Kirkbridge, 114 Va. 58. Possibly the confusion caused by these later cases, led to the ambiguous language of § 6123.

Federal Equity Rule 33, however, from which, as indicated in the revisors' note, a portion of § 6123 was borrowed, seems equally ambiguous. This rule reads as follows: "Exceptions for insufficiency of an answer are abolished. *But if an answer set up an affirmative defense, set-off or counter-claim, the plaintiff may, upon five days' notice, or such further time as the court may allow, test the sufficiency of the same by motion to strike out.* If found insufficient but amend-

ever, by a later section,[24] declaring that on waiver of oath in the
bill, the answer shall not be evidence in the respondent's favor,
"unless the cause be heard on bill and answer." The hearing on
bill and answer, therefore, seems preserved.

§ 249. The same—(2) answer insufficient in law.—As
just mentioned, objections by way of *exception* to the answer,
are not to fulfill the office of a demurrer, in raising the question
of the sufficiency *in law* of the answer as an affirmative defense
to the bill. If plaintiff desires to submit to the court the sufficiency of the answer *as a defense to the case asserted in the bill,*
the proper method is to *"set down the case for hearing on the
bill and answer."* Here there is no replication filed, and therefore no opportunity for either party to take depositions—since
until replication filed there is no issue of fact to be sustained by
testimony. The effect of this is, of course, *to admit the truth of
all matters of fact sufficiently pleaded in the answer,* whether responsive to the bill or whether in confession and avoidance; and
to submit to the court the decision of the question whether
on the facts as they appear from the answer, the decree should

---

able, the court may allow an amendment upon terms, or strike out the
matter."

Virginia Code, § 6123 reads thus: "Exceptions to answers for insufficiency are abolished. The test of sufficiency shall be made by a
motion to strike out; if found insufficient, but amendable, the court
may allow amendment on terms. If a second answer is adjudged
insufficient the defendant may be examined on interrogatories, and
committed until he answer them, or, on motion of the plaintiff, the
court may strike out the answer and take the bill for confessed."

It will be observed that the Code amendment omits that portion of
Rule 30 here italicized. It will be observed also that under Rule 30 the
motion to strike out is confined to the answer which *"sets up an affirmative defense, set-off or counterclaim."* The Code amendment is
not so restricted. The Federal rule seems clearly to authorize the
striking out of any affirmative defense, *not sufficient in law,* as a defense to the bill—as, for example, the statute of parol agreements
when the case presented in the bill is not within the statute. But it
seems to offer no substitute for exceptions to answer for evasiveness or non-responsiveness. The Code amendment, on the other
hand, seems meant to substitute the motion to strike out for every
form of insufficiency of answer—whether for insufficiency in law as a
defense or whether insufficient in not properly responding to the
charges, or the interrogatories of the bill. The form in which both
the Federal Rule and the Virginia Statute are expressed indicate
misconception of the true function of exceptions to answers.

[24] Va. Code 1919, § 6138.

not go in favor of the plaintiff.[25]

Jn short, going to hearing on the bill and answer is, for some purposes, practically the same as a *demurrer* at law to the plea.

Since this course on the part of the plaintiff excludes any opportunity on the part of either party to *take testimony*, there is good reason for the rule that the plaintiff thereby admits the truth of all facts set up in the answer relevant to the case stated in the bill.

§ 250. The same—hearing on bill and answer—continued.—It follows from the foregoing that going to hearing on bill and answer is a perilous proceeding, unless the plaintiff is sure that the admissions in the answer are sufficient to establish the material allegations of his bill—since, as already indicated, there is no opportunity in such a situation to introduce other evidence, and the entire answer, so far as relevant to the case made in the bill, is taken as true.

On such hearing, if the answer is held *insufficient in law* as a defense to the bill, the plaintiff is entitled to a decree. If, on the other hand, the answer is held sufficient, the bill is dismissed.[26] Hence the result is decisive for one or the other of the parties.

When the case is thus heard on bill and answer, it is immaterial *whether the answer is sworn to or not*—since, by so setting down the cause, the plaintiff admits the truth to the answer, to the extent stated.[27]
6128.

3. *Miscellaneous Rules Governing the Answer.*

§ 251. The answer continued — allegations not answered.—The contrast between the practice at law and that in equity is strikingly exhibited in the case where the defendant

---

[25] Story, Eq. Pl. 877; Fletcher, Eq. Pl. & Pr. 332, 677; Langdell, Eq. Pl. 83; 4 Minor's Inst. 1444; *supra*, § 242; Goodman *v.* Goodman, 124 Va. 249; authorities n. 12, *supra;* full note 1 A. L. R. 39.

[26] Langdell, Eq. Pl. 83; Daniell, Ch. Pr. 1189; Fletcher, Eq. Pl. & Pr. 677; Pickett *v.* Chilton, 5 Munf. 483; Cocke *v.* Minor, 25 Gratt. 246. *Quaere* as to how plaintiff should proceed where the answer is *insufficient* as a defense to one part of the bill and *sufficient* as to another part?

[27] Fletcher, Eq. Pl. & Pr. 677. The Virginia statute authorizing waiver of answer under oath makes express exception of the unverified answer in hearings on bill and answer only. Va. Code 1919, §

has failed to deny all the allegations of the plaintiff's declaration and of his bill, respectively.

The rule *at law* is that all allegations of the declaration not denied by the plea are *taken to be admitted*—while the rule in *equity* is precisely the reverse, namely, that allegations of the bill not denied nor noticed in the answer, are *not to be taken as admitted* by the defendant, but, if material to the plaintiff's case, must be proved by independent testimony. If the plaintiff desires to insist upon a response to such allegations he should except to the answer for insufficiency [28]—or, in Virginia, by motion to strike out.[29]

§ 252. The same—authentication of corporate answer.—The answer of the corporation itself, unsworn *ex necessitate*, and therefore not self-serving evidence in behalf of the corporation, is necessarily a mere pleading, whether by the unwritten rule or whether to a bill containing a statutory waiver of the oath. As a mere pleading then, there seems no reason why the corporate answer need be authenticated in any special form not required of natural persons, nor required of a corporation with respect to its other pleadings, at law or in equity.

Formerly, the signature of a corporation, not authenticated by its corporate seal, was an unthinkable proposition—whether in connection with contracts or pleadings—hence the rule, that the corporate signature should be authenticated by the corporate seal. Judges and lawyers of that by-gone day thought of corporate documents in terms of the corporate seal. It is not surprising, therefore, to find judges of that day laying down the rule that as corporations could not answer under oath, 'they must answer under their corporate seal.' Obviously, the thought in the judicial mind was, not the *necessity of the corporate seal,* but the *impossibility of the corporate oath.*[30]

---

[28] Coleman *v.* Lyne, 4 Rand. 454; Wright *v.* Wright, 124 Va. 114. The rule is otherwise in the Federal courts by Equity Rule 30; and is not applicable, in any case, on a motion by the defendant to dissolve a temporary injunction. Here failure to deny a material allegation is very properly taken as an admission of its truth, for the purposes of the motion to dissolve. B. & O. R. Co. *v.* Wheeling, 13 Gratt. 62.

[29] Va. Code 1919, § 6123; *supra;* § 248.

[30] See authorities n. 31, *infra.*

In spite of the circumstance that for almost a century the corporate seal has been relegated to the lower plane occupied by the seal of a natural person, the statement persists in extra-judicial opinions, and text books, that a corporation defendant must answer not under oath but under its corporate seal.

§ 253. The same, continued.—No case has been encountered in which a corporate answer has been rejected because not under the corporate seal. As the corporate answer is a mere pleading, there is no principle which would distinguish the corporate *answer* from the corporate *bill*, or *plea* in equity, or the *declaration*, or *plea*, or *replication*, at law. Nor is it believed to be customary in the practice in Virginia or elsewhere, to authenticate the pleadings of a corporation, whether plaintiff or defendant, or whether at law or in equity, by the corporate seal.

§ 254. Answer of corporation, continued—discovery. —Prior to modern statutes authorizing waiver of oath to the answer, as well as since, where the plaintiff desires discovery under oath from a corporation defendant, the approved method of procedure was, (and is, in the situation last stated), to make party defendant to the bill some officer of the corporation who is presumably familiar with the facts to which the discovery relates, and to pray discovery under oath from such officer. This procedure is justified by the circumstance that a corporation cannot be sworn, and therefore cannot, in its corporate capacity, answer under oath; and its answer under its corporate signature or seal, or both, is not evidence in its behalf, but a mere pleading.[31]

A bill of discovery, therefore, against a corporation, cannot be maintained, unless some officer thereof be made a co-defendant, and required to answer under oath.[32] But in case the bill calls for discovery, and yet fails to comply with the rule stated, if the corporation defendant waives the objection, and files its answer verified by one of its corporate officials, as of his personal knowledge, such answer is entitled to all the weight, as

---

[31] *Supra*, §§ 252-253; B. & O. R. Co. *v.* Wheeling, 13 Gratt. 62; Roanoke St. R. Co. *v.* Hicks, 96 Va. 510; Union Bank *v.* Geary, 5 Pet. 99; Lovell *v.* S. S. Mill Ass'n, 6 Pai. 54. See the following section.

[32] Roanoke St. R. Co. *v.* Hicks, *supra*.

evidence in behalf of the defendant corporation, as a verified answer of an individual defendant.[33]

§ 255. Amendment of answer.—Where the answer is sworn to, as it must have been under the former practice, there were sound reasons why the courts were reluctant to permit amendments—a privilege to be granted only in rare instances and for good cause shown, as in case of mistake or surprise.

But where, by reason of waiver of the oath in the bill, the answer is not sworn to, and hence is no longer the sworn testimony of the respondent, but a mere pleading, there is no reason why amendments should not be permitted as freely as in the case of any other pleading. Amendment of answers is provided for in the Federal practice.[34]

§ 256. Answer treated as cross-bill.—In a previous chapter,[35] it was pointed out that, in the discretion of the court, a defendant may be permitted to assert an affirmative claim in his answer, and thus present the example of an answer serving the double function of an answer and a cross-bill at the same time. The practice in such cases has been already explained.

---

[33] Carle v. Corhan, 127 Va. 223, citing with approval 7 Va. Law Reg. 145; Kane v. Schuylkill Fire Ins. Co. (Pa.), 48 Atl. 989.
[34] Equity Rules 19, 33.
[35] *Ante*, ch. xii.

CHAPTER XVII.

The Replication.

§ 257. The replication in equity.—This very simple pleading requires but little explanation. As already indicated in our treatment of the amended bill,[1] *special* replications are obsolete in equity pleading, and have been substituted by the amended bill; so that under modern equity practice the complete case of the plaintiff must *be shown in his bill,* original or amended.[2]

§ 258. Replication always general.—In modern times, therefore, the replication in equity is *general* only—that is, it is a mere traverse, (or denial) in general terms, of the defensive allegations of the plea or answer, and, by implication, a reassertion of the allegations of the bill. The replication may not, therefore, confess and avoid, but may merely *deny* the defensive allegations of the adversary pleading. If the plaintiff desires to confess the truth of the defendant's pleading and to avoid such confession by adducing new matter, he must resort to an amended bill.[3]

If, on the other hand, the plaintiff means to admit the truth of the defensive allegations in the answer, and to contest their legal sufficiency as a defense, he will omit the replication, with the effect shown in the following section.

§ 259. The same—function of the general replication.—

---

[1] *Supra,* § 158.

[2] The special replication was abandoned because of the delay and expense entailed. Story, Eq. Pl. 878.

[3] Thus, under a general replication, plaintiff cannot confess a release set up by the defendant, and avoid the effect by proving that the release was executed during infancy, nor set up fraud in the inducement—but he is restricted to proof that he *did not execute* such release. It seems, however, that if the release, or other defense, set up in the plea or answer, is *absolutely void*, and not voidable only—as a release by a married woman under the common law disabilities of coverture—or, doubtless, under circumstances constituting fraud in the *factum*—such invalidity may be shown under a general replication. Stewart *v.* Conrad, 100 Va. 128, 7 Va. Law Reg. 767 (n).

The special function subserved by the general replication is to inform the defendant that the plaintiff *does not admit the truth of the plea or answer,* but, on the contrary, that the plaintiff means to controvert all the defensive assertions therein—thus warning the defendant that he must sustain his defensive allegations by testimony. Hence the rule of the forum is, not without reason, that failure on the part of the plaintiff to file a replication is *an admission of the truth of the adversary pleading.* The result is, that if the latter be a *plea,* the case must be heard on the bill and plea only—that is, in professional phrase, the plea is *"set down for argument."* If the adverse pleading be an *answer,* the juridical situation is that the case must be *"heard on bill and answer"*—a very dangerous situation for the plaintiff, as we have already seen.[4]

§ 260. The same—It appears, therefore, that only by filing the replication is an issue of fact raised—an issue that must be decided on testimony to be introduced by each party. Until the replication to the plea or answer is filed, therefore, there is *no issue of fact,* and hence, regularly, *no testimony can be taken.* So that, after all, the general replication serves a quite useful function in equity practice.[4a]

§ 261. The replication in Virginia.—But as (prior to the recent amendment requiring replications to be entered by the clerk[5]), the actual filing of replications in Virginia was extremely rare—counsel usually relying on the clerk of the court to enter on the rule-book a memorandum of such filing, based on fiction only; or else relying on the recitation, usually inserted in the first decree, that the cause was "heard on the bill and answer (or plea) *with general replication thereto"*—many cases formerly reached the court of appeals in which (by oversight of the clerk or of the counsel) there was no replication, either in fact or in fictitious recital; but the parties had pro-

---

[4] *Supra,* §§ 204-205; Cocke *v.* Minor, 25 Gratt. 246.

[4a] Where the bill makes material admissions in favor of the defendant, in which admissions the answer concurs, a general replication by the plaintiff does not destroy the value to the defendant of these admissions, nor place their truth in issue. Blanchard *v.* Dominion Bank, 125 Va. 586.

[5] Va. Code 1919, § 6138.

ceeded, notwithstanding, *to take testimony as if there had in fact been a replication.* In such cases the court was accustomed, somewhat unreasonably, to reverse the case for want of a replication. To remedy this a statute [6] was enacted, providing, in substance, that the absence of a replication shall be immaterial where the defendant has *taken depositions as if there had been a replication;* or where, even though defendant has not taken depositions, substantial justice has been done.

§ 262. Replication in the Federal courts.—Under the new Rules,[7] replications are practically abolished, save where the answer asserts a set-off or counter-claim, or where a reply is specially ordered by the court or judge. The cause is regarded as at issue as soon as the answer is filed; and any new or affirmative matter therein shall be "deemed to be denied by the plaintiff."

If the cross-claim affect other *defendants,* provision is made for service of a copy of the claim on such defendants or their counsel, who are entitled to ten days within which to reply.

This brings us to an end of our consideration of the Pleadings in Equity, proper. Our subsequent studies in the volume will be devoted to what may be loosely termed Equity Practice.

---

[6] Va. Code 1919, § 6332.
[7] Rule 31.

CHAPTER XVIII.

The Testimony.

1. DEPOSITIONS.

§ 263. Oath—affidavit—deposition.—An *oath* is an oral statement of fact, duly sworn before an official authorized by law to administer oaths.

Affidavit is a *written* statement of fact, made in an *ex parte* proceeding, usually signed by the person ('affiant') making the statement, duly signed and sworn to before an authorized official, and duly certified by him. The certificate of the officer is termed the jurat.[1]

Deposition is the written, sworn and certified testimony of a witness, taken before an authorized official, in *inter partes* proceedings, in which adverse parties in interest are given opportunity to appear and cross-examine the witness ('deponent').

Both the *affidavit* and the *deposition,* therefore, necessarily connote a precedent or accompanying oath—though the term *oath* alone implies neither of these.

§ 264. The same—use of the affidavit.—Affidavits and depositions are both written and certified statements under oath —the difference being that the former are taken in a summary manner, without notice to the adverse party (*ex parte*), while the latter are taken on notice to all adverse parties, who thus have the opportunity of appearing and cross-examining the witness (*inter partes*). It follows that affidavits are incompetent testimony on the *merits* of the cause. They are only admissible to establish *prima facie* the truth of the allegations offered, for the purpose of procuring *preliminary* or *collateral action* by the court touching some *procedural step* in the cause, not affecting the merits of the controversy—as, for example, on a motion for a

---

[1] In Virginia, by long custom, affidavits are not signed by the affiant—the language being wholly that of the official before whom the affidavit is made. See forms in *Appendix.*

preliminary injunction; for the dissolution of such an injunction; to obtain an order of publication, or an attachment, against a non-resident; or a continuance of the cause because of the absence of a material witness; to establish an uncontested claim before a master, on an order of reference; to obtain an attachment against the person of the defendant in contempt proceedings, etc.

§ 265. The use of the deposition.—In the common law courts, regularly the testimony is presented to the jury by the witnesses in person, who testify orally (*ore tenus*) before the court and jury, and in the presence of the parties and their counsel. At law, it is only in exceptional cases that depositions may be substituted for oral testimony. Statutes generally provide that the deposition of a witness may be taken where he is beyond the state, so that compulsory process may not reach him—or where he resides at a considerable distance from the place of trial, or where too ill to appear, etc.[2]

As indicated in the following section, in equity depositions are regularly resorted to in lieu of testimony *ore tenus*. But whether used at law or in equity, testimony by deposition is used for the same purpose as that presented *ore tenus*, namely, to prove or disprove facts in issue in the cause, whether on the merits or otherwise.

§ 266. The testimony in chancery.—After the cause is at issue, the next step is the taking of the testimony of witnesses. In the equity practice the testimony is not taken in the presence of the chancellor at the trial of the case, but the depositions of the witnesses are taken in writing before a notary, or other authorized officer, prior to the hearing.[3]

------

[2] Va. Code 1919, § 6231.

[3] Formerly depositions were taken under a *commission* expressly issued for the purpose by the court (no longer required in Virginia —Va. Code 1919, § 6227), and were taken secretly by the examiner, on written interrogatories filed by the respective counsel. Neither counsel nor parties were permitted to be present, and hence until the taking of all testimony was closed and the result made public— which was done only by order of the court, technically known as "passing publication"—counsel had knowledge neither of the nature of the interrogatories filed by his adversary, nor of the answers of the witnesses thereto. It was only by special leave of court, and for cause shown, that further testimony could be taken after publication passed. The purpose of this secrecy was to avoid the temptation to procure perjured testimony in defense or rebuttal.

Reasonable notice, in writing, to the adversary is required of the time and place of the taking of the depositions, in order that he may appear and cross-examine the witness, if desired. After a deposition is taken, it is subscribed by the witness, certified by the officer, and then transmitted by the officer to the clerk of the court where the suit is pending.[3a]

§ 267. Depositions—dispensing with notice.—Where the
defendant has been summoned by *publication,* and has not appeared, in person or by counsel, no notice of the taking of depositions is required unless ordered by the court.[4]

It is a quite common custom in Virginia to take depositions, by stipulation between counsel, without service of notice.

§ 268. The same—rules of evidence.—The rules of evidence are practically the same in equity as at law—and so as to the competency of witnesses.[5]

§ 269. Exceptions to evidence.—In equity, as at law, objections to evidence, or to the competency of a witness offered by the opposite party, are considered as waived, unless the objection be seasonably made. These objections in equity are expressed in the form of *exceptions,* taken in writing, and entered in the body of the deposition. Such exceptions should distinctly point out the ground upon which they are based. Since the officer before whom depositions are taken has no power to pass upon the exceptions, the practice is, after exception entered, to permit the contested evidence to go in, subject to be excluded on argument of the exceptions before the court.

We cannot here go into the details of the practice in taking testimony,—and must content ourselves with a general reference to treatises on evidence, and to certain statutory provisions in Virginia.[6]

§ 270. Time within which depositions may be taken—

[3a] See Va. Code, §§ 6228-6234.

[4] Va. Code 1919, § 6071. See §§ 6223-6226.

[5] The right of discovery from either party was formerly a conspicuous exception, already noticed.

[6] Va. Code 1919, §§ 6223-6232, and revisors' annotations. For form of deposition, see *post, Appendix.*

(1) earliest period.—The question as to how early in the progress of the cause the parties may begin the taking of testimony, seems not to have been definitely resolved. Custom, however, seems to permit the plaintiff to begin the taking of testimony as soon as the cause is *matured and set for hearing,* though the defendant has not appeared. In the Federal courts[7] the rule contemplates that depositions (when permissible at all) may be taken after the cause is *"at issue"*—which, where the defendant has not appeared and pleaded, and evidence supplementary to the decree *pro confesso* is required, probably means after the cause is matured and set for hearing.

In Virginia, by the recent revisal,[8] it seems that the taking of depositions may be begun (by the plaintiff) *as soon as the bill is filed,* and therefore before any issue whatever is made up.

§ 271. The same—(2) latest period.—Where not regulated by statute or rule of court, as it is not in Virginia,[9] there is no fixed period within which the parties, plaintiff and defendant, must complete the taking of their testimony. So far as there appears to be any rule on the subject in the Virginia practice, the parties have a *reasonable time* within which to take testimony. In practice, this reasonable time is construed by professional comity to mean all the time either party desires—with the result that there is much inexcusable delay in the trial of chancery causes. The court has the power to rule either party to greater diligence, and to fix a limit of time beyond which no further testimony may be taken; but counsel in Virginia who would resort to such harsh and unaccustomed measures in a chancery suit, except under very unusual circumstances, would be regarded by his professional brethren as a disturber of ancient traditions and as encroaching upon one of the cherished privileges of the profession.

§ 272. Testimony continued — ore tenus in Federal

---

[7] See *infra,* § 272, n.

[8] Va. Code 1919, § 6225.

[9] See Goode *v.* Bryant, 118 Va. 314, 87 S. E. 588. The only known statutory provision on the subject in Virginia, is the provision that a deposition may be read, if returned *before the hearing of the cause,* or, though after an interlocutory decree, if it be as to a matter not thereby adjudged, and be returned before a final decree. Va. Code 1919, § 6328.

courts.—The method of taking testimony in the equity practice of the Federal courts has been revolutionized by the new Equity Rules, by the provision that "in all trials in equity the testimony of witnesses shall be taken in *open court.*" [10] But provision is made for taking depositions, by special order of the court, wherever permitted by (Federal) statute, or "for good and exceptional cause, * * * to be shown by affidavit." [11] The depositions when permissible must be taken promptly, as indicated in the footnote.

§ 273. Depositions—in case of infant or insane parties.

—By the unwritten rules of equity practice, the presence of infant or insane parties in the suit does not alter the usual method of taking depositions. In such cases, notice is served on the guardian *ad litem,* and the circumstance that the latter was not actually present when the testimony was taken is immaterial to the competency of the testimony.[12]

The statutory rule in Virginia has long been otherwise, where the purpose of the suit was to sell the lands of infant or insane defendants. In such cases, depositions are not competent evidence against such defendants unless taken in the presence of the guardian *ad litem,* or upon interrogatories agreed upon by him. This provision, by the recent revisal, has been extended to all cases in which infant or insane defendants are parties.[13]

---

[10] Rule 46. The same rule makes provision for what is practically a *bill of exceptions* where evidence is offered and excluded over the objection of either party.

[11] Rule 47. Depositions for the plaintiff must be taken, unless otherwise ordered by the court for good cause, *within sixty days* from the time the cause is at issue; and those for the defendant within *thirty days* thereafter—with *twenty days* for rebuttal testimony.

As to evidence before examiners, or like officers, see Rules 49-54. Provision is made by Act of Congress for depositions in certain cases—as where the witness lives more than a hundred miles from the place of trial, or is sick, or infirm, or is about to go without the jurisdiction, etc. U. S. Rev. Stat., §§ 863-867. Rule 54 preserves this right. As to the construction of these statutory provisions, see Patapsco Ins. Co. *v.* Southgate, 5 Pet. 604; McLennan *v.* Railway Co., 22 Fed. 198; Giles *v.* Paxson, 36 Fed. 882; Thum *v.* Andrews, 53 Fed. 84; Am. Exchange Bank *v.* First Nat. Bank, 82 Fed. 961, 27 C. A. 274; Gormley *v.* Bunyan, 138 U. S. 623.

[12] Moore *v.* Triplett, 96 Va. 603.

[13] Va. Code 1919, § 5339.

2. Issue Out of Chancery—Or 'Feigned Issue.'

§ 274. Issue out of chancery—when proper.—Although regularly the testimony in chancery is not taken *ore tenus,* but is presented in the form of depositions of witnesses, yet where the testimony is so conflicting, or the circumstances of the case are otherwise such, that the chancellor is in doubt as to the truth of a particular issue of fact, he may refer the question to a jury for a verdict thereon, in aid of his conscience.[14]

Originally such issues were framed by the chancellor and sent out to a common law court for trial—the latter court through judicial comity certifying the verdict back to the chancery court. But in Virginia, where the same court exercises both law and equity jurisdiction, these issues are tried *before the chancellor himself*—and whether on the chancery or law side of the court is immaterial.[15] The Virginia statute [16] authorizes the court, in its discretion, to order such an issue even *before any evidence is taken,* where it is "shown by affidavit or affidavits, after reasonable notice, that the case will be rendered doubtful by the conflicting evidence of the opposing party."

§ 275. The same—waiver by the parties.—In a recent Virginia case,[17] the testimony on certain disputed questions of fact was so conflicting as to present a proper case for an issue to be tried by a jury, but as *neither party requested such a trial* the chancellor himself tried and decided the issue. On appeal, the appellate court found the testimony of so conflicting a nature that grave doubt was entertained whether the finding of the

---

[14] Though the directing of such an issue is a matter of judicial discretion, an error in the exercise of this discretion is ground of appeal, and the appellate court will itself determine whether the discretion has been rightly exercised. Catron *v.* Norton Hardware Co., 123 Va. 380.

[15] Lavell *v.* Gold, 25 Gratt. 473; Meade *v.* Meade, 111 Va. 451. See Powell *v.* Mason, 22 Gratt. 177, where Staples, J., explains the practice and procedure. See further: Michie's annotation to Lavell *v.* Gold, *ubi, supra;* Stevens *v.* Duckett, 107 Va. 17; Carter *v.* Jefferies, 110 Va. 735; Face *v.* Cherry, 117 Va. 41; Goode *v.* Bryant, 118 Va. 314. For *forms* of such issues, see Carter *v.* Jefferies, *supra,* and Jones *v.* Buckingham Slate Co., 116 Va. 120, 124. See Federal Equity Rule 23.

[16] Va. Code 1919, § 6246 and annotations; Bunkley *v.* Com. (Va.), 108 S. E. 1.

[17] Shoemaker *v.* Shoemaker, 112 Va. 798.

lower court was or was not in accordance with justice. There
upon the appellate court reversed the decree, and directed the
chancellor, in spite of the implied waiver of the parties, to submit the issue to a jury.

The decision has been criticized [18] on the ground that since
the parties had waived a jury trial, the decree could not be reversed for the failure of the lower court to direct such a trial
—in accordance with the maxim *consensus tollit errorem.* But
when it is recalled that in this state the erroneous exercise of
judicial discretion is ground for reversal; that the question of
directing the trial of an issue by jury is to be determined by
the court, according to the circumstances of the case, *regardless of the wishes of the parties;* and that on appeal in a chancery case it is the duty of the appellate court to consider the testimony and pass upon the issues of fact involved, in spite of the
findings of the chancellor below; and hence that it is as fully the
right and duty of the higher court, *ex mero motu,* to direct such
an issue, in aid of its judicial conscience, as it is the right and
duty of the chancellor below, in aid of *his* conscience, the criticism loses force. In short, if the parties cannot by their waiver,
or by their expressed protest, deprive the *chancellor* of the
power to call in the assistance of the jury, neither should such
waiver or protest deprive the *appellate court* of the power to insist that a jury pass upon the issue.[19]

§ 276. Effect of the verdict.—The effect of the verdict
on an issue out of chancery is quite different, in theory at least,
from that of a verdict in a plenary action at law—since the former is regarded as *merely advisory,* and in aid of the chancellor's conscience; and if the chancellor disagree with the jury,
he may not only reject the verdict, but may himself decide the
issue of fact *contrary to the view taken by the jury.* While
this is the theoretical situation, in practice the verdict will generally be accepted; and if rejected, unless there were material
errors committed on the trial, or the circumstances unusual, the
appellate court would be apt to accept the decision of the jury
rather than that of the chancellor.[20]

---

[18] 17 Va. Law Reg. 717.

[19] Catron *v.* Norton Hardware Co., 123 Va. 380; Hook *v.* Hook, 126
Va. 249; Whitaker *v.* Lane, 128 Va. 317, 104 S. E. 252.

[20] Authorities *supra;* Bunkley *v.* Com. (Va.), 107 S. E. 1; Basey *v.*
Gallagher, 20 Wall. 670. As to new trials of the issue, see Ruffners

CHAPTER XIX.

The Master's Report.[1]

§ 272. Notice to parties.—The parties interested in the execution of an order referring the cause to a master (usually termed an *"order of reference"*) are entitled to notice of the time and place fixed upon for the hearing, and a reasonable opportunity to present evidence of their claims or in their defense.

In Virginia this notice may be given by publication in a newspaper when so directed by the court.[2] The evidence introduced before the master is by depositions, which he must return with his report.[3]

§ 273. Exceptions to report.—By statute, as in Virginia,[4] or by rule of court as in the Federal practice,[5] the report of the master, after completion, is filed in the clerk's office, where it lies for a prescribed period for such exceptions to confirmation as any party may desire to file. The period in Virginia is *ten* days, and in the Federal *twenty* days. Failure to file exceptions will ordinarily operate as a waiver of objections—and in the Federal courts the rule declares that if no exceptions are filed within the period allowed the report shall *stand confirmed.*[6]

---

v. Barrett, 6 Munf. 207; Grigsby *v.* Weaver, 5 Leigh 197; Watt. *v.* Stark, 101 U. S. 247.

[1] For sundry provisions with reference to the appointment, powers and duties of masters, and the proceedings before them, see Va. Code 1919, ch. 260; Equity Rules 59-68.

[2] Va. Code 1919, § 6180. See Equity Rules 59-68 (order of reference in Federal Courts declared permissible only in exceptional cases).

[3] Va. Code 1919, § 6185.

[4] Id. § 6186.

[5] Equity Rule 66.

[6] Id. The rule in Virginia is not so strict. In practice it is construed as giving any party the right to demand a hearing on the report after it has been filed for ten days, but not as denying any party the right to file exceptions at any time before the report is heard by the court.

§ 274. Character of exceptions.—Exceptions to a master's report have been likened to special demurrers, in that they must *specifically point out the errors* complained of, otherwise they will not be considered.[7] After filing his exceptions counsel should see that they are brought to the attention of the court, and, if overruled, that the decree so recites, since on appeal if the court's ruling on the exceptions does not appear, the appellate court will presume a waiver.[8]

§ 275. Weight to which report entitled. — While the finding of the master, on a question of fact, is *prima facie* correct—because he has seen the witnesses (as the chancellor has not) and been able to observe their demeanor, and their disposition to speak the truth candidly or otherwise—nevertheless such report is not entitled to the weight of the verdict of a jury. That is to say, if upon reading the testimony, as it is the duty of the court to do, on exception made,[9] the court is satisfied that the finding should have been otherwise, it will overrule the finding of the master. This rule has been made statutory in Virginia.[10]

§ 276. Confirmation of master's report.—In the absence of statute or rule of court to the contrary, the master's report is inchoate and inoperative until it has been considered and confirmed by the court.

It was pointed out in the third section above that by Federal Equity Rule 66, the master's report will *stand confirmed* unless exceptions be filed within twenty days from the time the report is returned.

---

[7] Bank *v.* Trigg, 103 Va. 327, 340; Wilkes *v.* Rogers, 6 Johns. 566; Story *v.* Livingston, 13 Pet. 359. See form in *Appendix*. Where the objection to the report rests in *matters of law*, arising on the face of the report, exceptions before the master are not necessary—as questions of law are not for the master but for the court. Carle *v.* Corhan, 127 Va. 223.

[8] Mountain Lake Co. *v.* Blair, 109 Va. 147.

[9] Shipman *v.* Fletcher, 91 Va. 473; John Diebold Co. *v.* Tatterson, 115 Va. 766; Alexander *v.* Critchter, 121 Va. 723; Barton, *Rise and Fall of the Commissioner in Chancery*, 1 Va. Law Reg. 485; Kimberly *v.* Arms. 129 U. S. 512. As the master is a *quasi*-judicial officer, it goes without saying that he cannot delegate his functions or any part of them to another person. Mountain Lake Co. *v.* Blair, 109 Va. 147.

[10] Va. Code 1919, § 6179.

According to the Virginia practice, the report never stands confirmed because of failure to file exceptions within the ten day period during which the report must lie for exceptions, nor, indeed, at any other time *until an order of the court is entered expressing confirmation.*[11]

CHAPTER XX.

Orders and Decrees.

§ 277. Explanatory.—The term "order" is properly used to denote some action of the court not touching the merits of the case—for example, appointing a guardian *ad litem;* giving leave to file a pleading; referring certain inquiries to a master; continuing the cause, etc.

The term "decree" is more correctly applied to formal and decisive action by the court, touching the merits of the cause.

§ 278. Preparation of decrees. — Orders and decrees, while couched in the language of the court, and expressing its mandate, are always drawn by counsel—usually by him in whose favor, or on whose application, the order or decree is granted.

Skill in draughting decrees is an essential professional acquirement, and the student cannot too early, or too eagerly, begin to cultivate skill in this line of professional duty.

In practice, counsel takes (mental or written) notes of the chancellor's decision—unless the chancellor himself hands down written notes for the purpose, as is sometimes done in a complicated case. Then, at his leisure, and usually in his own office, counsel draws the form of the decree, conforming as nearly as possible to the chancellor's directions. This is called a "note for decree."

It is then submitted to adversary counsel for approval. In case of dispute whether the decree correctly expresses the court's views, counsel apply to the chancellor to settle it.

---

[11] *Supra*, n. 6. As to conveyances by the master, see *post*, §§ 309-310.

When in final shape, the note for decree is signed by the chancellor—in Virginia, endorsed "enter" and authenticated by the chancellor's initials—and is then copied by the clerk in the "chancery order book."

§ 279. Recording of decrees.—All orders and decrees granted each day, are entered in this book, under a general heading showing that date; and at the foot of the entries for that day, the chancellor, on the next or some future day, appends his signature. The order or decree as it appears in the order book, and not the note for decree, constitutes the original record of the court's action. That is to say, the decree is inchoate as a record, until so entered and signed.[1]

§ 280. "Enrollment" of decrees—English practice.—The term "enrollment" in connection with decrees is one of common use in reference to proceedings in the English chancery courts. It probably has no place, and certainly has not the same judicial significance, in the American practice. Under the former English procedure, interlocutory decrees in chancery appear to have been not always, nor generally, in writing, and hence were not in the record otherwise than in the form of memoranda, or notes, taken by the registrar. But the "definitive sentence" (*i. e.*, the *final* decree) was written out and signed by the chancellor, and then *enrolled*. And when thus enrolled, the decree was treated as *final*, and therefore to be reheard only on a bill of review, *without regard to whether the term of the court were ended or not.* Indeed the English court of chancery kept no terms, in the American sense of that expression, but was always open.[2] Hence *enrollment connoted finality of the decree.* A *definitive sentence enrolled* was, therefore, the test of finality for purposes of a bill of review. The enrollment of decrees under the English practice was an elaborate procedure, wholly unknown in the American practice.[3]

---

[1] And when a vacation decree, otherwise valid, is entered in the order book by the clerk on Sunday, it is inoperative as a decree of the court, and hence cannot be the foundation of an appeal. Lee *v.* Willis, 99 Va. 16, 6 Va. Law Reg. 691n

[2] See Brooke's Abr. "Jurisdiction," 74; 1 Spence, Eq. Jurisp. 383.

[3] See *infra,* n. 5.

§ 281. The same—American practice. — On the other hand, according to American practice, all orders and decrees in chancery, interlocutory as well as final, are reduced to writing and copied in the order book, and signed by the chancellor. But this is not technical *enrollment*, which, as stated, is a procedure unknown in the American courts. Hence, in the American courts, *enrollment*, even in the loose sense of *recordation, does not connote finality.* Thus, as we have already seen in connection with *Bills of Review*,[4] a final decree must not only be a definitive sentence (and in Virginia something more than merely definitive, or settling the principles of the cause), but it must be entered on the order book and signed by the chancellor, and *the term of the court must have ended.* Hence, in the American equity practice, in addition to (1) the quality of finality in substance, and (2) recordation, the decree is not final until (3) adjournment of the term.[5]

---

[4] *Ante,* §§ 188-189.

[5] This attempted explanation of the distinction between the English and the American practice, seems justified, though somewhat obscurely, by Mr. Gould's notes to Story, Eq. Pl. 403 n (a), and 421 n (a) (10th ed.). The explanation is here essayed because of difficulty the author has had in getting at the sense in which the term *"enrollment"* is used in American books on equity practice, in connection with the review or rehearing of decrees. The statement constantly recurs that "a petition to rehear cannot be filed after enrollment of the decree,"—or that "a bill of review will lie only to an enrolled decree"—statements intelligible enough when referred to the English procedure, but hopelessly confusing when applied to the American practice. See, for example, Story Eq. Pl. 421, and *passim;* Fletcher's Eq. Pl. & Pr. 724, 746; Van Zile's Eq. Pl. & Pr. 332-335. Mr. Shipman ventures the explanation that a rehearing may be granted only where "the decree has *not been enrolled—as it is termed—that is, before the close of the term in which it is rendered."* Shipman, Eq. Pl. 152. But, as we have already seen, enrollment (in the sense of recordation) and adjournment of the term do not, according to our practice, render final a decree interlocutory in its nature.

In the earlier editions of Daniell's Chancery Practice (*e. g.* 2nd English ed. by Headlam, 1st Am. ed. by Perkins, 1846) 1220-1232, will be found a full account of the highly technical proceedings which accompanied the enrollment of a decree, as well as of the legal effect of enrollment. See also *id* (6th Am. Ed.) 1023-1024. The earlier editions of this classical work more accurately portray the English equity practice as inherited by the American courts, than do the later editions, because of the marked changes produced in the English practice by the General Orders of Lords Cottenham and Langdale in 1841, and incorporated into Mr. Daniell's later editions. The student will find some estimate of the comparative values to the American lawyer, of these several editions of Daniell, in the opinion of Mr. Justice Bradley, in Thomson *v.* Wooster, 114 U. S. 104.

§ 282. Nature of final decree.—This question has already been discussed in connection with *Bills of Review*[6] a discussion which need not here be repeated.

§ 283. Form of decrees.—The form of the decree will depend largely on its purport. There is no rule of practice fixing a prescribed form; but, as in the case of most legal documents, custom has fixed the form of at least certain parts of the decree, from which it is not well for the young practitioner to depart.

§ 284. Formal recitals.—Under the usual equity practice, the first decree entered in the cause recites, in the title, the names of all the parties, plaintiff and defendant, as well as all the pleadings and other proceedings on which the cause was heard. Subsequent decrees indicate the abbreviated title of the cause, with the recital that the cause "came on to be heard this day on the papers formerly read," with a further recital of steps taken and papers filed since the last decree.[7]

§ 285. The same—in the Federal courts.—In the Federal courts recitation of the pleadings is prohibited, and it is de-

---

"From what has been said," this master of the English equity practice says, "it may be collected that all decrees which *are final in their nature, i. e.* which amount to a determination of the question in the cause, *may be enrolled* * * *. But mere interlocutory decrees, made upon motion or petition, which do not decide any of the merits of the cause, and only relate to the proceedings in it, *cannot be the subject of enrollment.*" Id. pp. 1224-1225. In Sands' Suit in Equity (2nd ed.) 497, will also be found a description of the process of enrolling a decree in the English court of chancery. As further indicating the American view that decrees, whether 'enrolled' or not, and howsoever final in their nature, continue in the breast of the court until *adjournment of the term*, see former Equity Rule 88, and the new Rule 72—the latter declaring that errors of a certain character "may at any time *before the close of the term at which final decree* is rendered, be corrected by order of the court or a judge thereof, upon petition," etc.

[6] *Ante*, §§ 188-189.

[7] This practice, borrowed from the early English practice, continues in Virginia, though by statute or custom obsolete in most of the states. The practice at least possesses the advantage of permanently recording, on the face of the decree, a list of the parties and of the pleadings, and other documents on which the case was submitted, and upon which the decree was based, instead of reliance upon the clerk's notation of them in his docket or rule-book, or upon a search for this information among the (sometimes lost) papers in the cause.

clared that none of the pleadings, nor any master's report "or other prior proceeding, shall be recited or stated in the decree or order; but the decree and order shall begin, in substance, as follows: "This cause came on to be heard (or to be further heard, as the case may be) at this term, and was argued by counsel; and thereupon, upon consideration thereof, it was ordered, adjudged and decreed as follows, viz.: (here insert the decree or order)."[8]

§ 286. Decrees against infants.—As a general rule, decrees are as binding upon infants as upon adults. By the unwritten rule, however, it was error not to reserve in final decrees the right to the infant to show cause against the decree *within six months* after attaining his majority. This right has been made statutory in Virginia, without the necessity of any provision therefor in the decree.[9]

Under this reservation in the decree, or that provided for in the statute, the infant may impeach a decree only on the ground on which an adult might do so—namely for fraud or collusion, or for error; and only for cause *existing when the decree was rendered,* and not for causes subsequently arising.[10]

§ 287. Dismissal from docket.—In entering a decree completely disposing of the whole subject-matter of the litigation, it is usual to insert at the end of the decree an order dismissing the cause—the usual form being: *"The object of this suit having been accomplished, it is ordered to be stricken from the docket."*

After such order of dismissal, and adjournment, the court has no power to re-instate the cause, except on a bill of review (which, in Virginia, must be filed within one year),[11] or by

---

[8] Equity Rule 71. For forms of decrees, and particularly of the "bringing on" clause, under the Virginia practice, see *post, Appendix.*

[9] Va. Code 1919, § 6305.

[10] Walker *v.* Page, 21 Gratt. 636; Lancaster *v.* Barton, 92 Va. 615; Harrison *v.* Walton, 95 Va. 721, 30 S. E. 372, 41 L. R. A. 703, 64 Am. St. Rep. 830; Asberry *v.* Mitchell, 121 Va. 276. Like provision for rehearing of decrees is made in the case of unknown parties, or parties summoned by publication and who have not appeared. These have two years of grace. Va. Code 1919, § 6072. See *post, Sale of Infants' Lands.*

[11] See *ante, Bill of Review,* ch. xiii.

mandate of the appellate court, on an appeal duly taken. But the absence of such order of dismissal, and the circumstance that the cause remains on the docket, have no determining effect on the question of the finality of the decree. That question, as already indicated, depends on the *nature* of the decree, and adjournment of the term. The order of dismissal, for whatever cause, is necessarily a final order; but the absence of such an order does not necessarily leave the decree interlocutory.

§ 288. Need for further relief after final decree—reserving right to reinstate.—If there be need for further orders in the cause after final decree and adjournment, and there be no grounds for a bill of review or an appeal, or these be time-barred, such relief may be secured (if at all) only by the institution of a new suit.[12] To avoid this inconvenience, it is common practice, where the circumstances warrant the precaution, to reserve, on the face of the final decree, *the right to reinstate the cause, on motion,* for the purpose of securing complete benefit of the decree.[13]

By Virginia statute,[14] the court is authorized to reinstate the cause after final decree, in order that a new commissioner may be appointed, where a commissioner dies or becomes incapacitated before conveying property as directed by the decree.

§ 289. Voluntary dismissal—"without prejudice." — As hereafter shown more at large in connection with creditors'

---

[12] *Post,* § 321; Battaile *v.* Maryland Hospital, 76 Va. 63; Echols *v.* Brennam, 99 Va. 150. Such new bill will necessarily be confined to relief already decreed in the original suit—and its purpose will be merely to secure performance of the former decree, or to obtain modification thereof, or relief therefrom, because of circumstances that have occurred since the former decree was rendered. All matters in controversy in the original suit have become res judicata, and may not be again litigated. As to modification 'of final decrees of divorce, see *post,* §§ 415 *et seq.*

[13] See Peters *v.* Peters, 121 Va. 559. In a recent case in the Federal courts, in which was a decree dissolving certain relations among the packing houses of Chicago, and prescribing elaborate rules to prevent restraint of trade by the defendants, the court entered an order *retaining perpetual jurisdiction of the cause,* for the purpose of taking such further action therein as might be found necessary in order to secure to the public the benefits of the main decree. U. S. *v.* Packers Ass'n. (1921), ——— Fed. ———.

[14] Va. Code 1919, § 5267.

bills, the plaintiff is *dominus litis*, and may dismiss his suit at any stage before *affirmative rights of others* have attached. This rule is not confined to creditors' bills, but applies to equity suits of every nature.

An order of reference in a creditors' suit, or the filing of a *cross-bill* by the defendant asserting a counter claim, is held to deprive the plaintiff of the right to dismiss his bill.[15]

Where the plaintiff thus voluntarily dismisses his suit, or wherever the suit is dismissed involuntarily for reasons *not affecting the merits of the case,* the order should recite that the dismissal is *"without prejudice* to plaintiff's right to institute such further suits concerning the same matter as he may be advised"—since, in the absence of such a saving clause—particularly where the order does not plainly indicate that the dismissal was not on the merits, or was voluntary—the plaintiff, in a future litigation over the same matter, may be confronted by a plea of *res judicata.*

§ 290. The same—"dismissed agreed."—This precaution against prejudice by reason of the dismissal, is especially important where the order shows that the dismissal was by *agreement of parties.* Such a dismissal—usually indicated in the brief phrase "by consent of parties this suit is dismissed agreed"—when not recited to be *'without prejudice,'* implies an adjustment of the litigation, and *prima facie* may be pleaded in bar of a new suit on the same cause of action. "It is a declaration of record," says Anderson, J., "sanctioned by the judgment of the court, that *the cause of action has been, adjusted by the parties themselves,* in their own way, and that the suit is dismissed agreed."[16]

§ 291. Dismissal under 'five-year rule.'—To prevent the dockets of the courts from being encumbered with cases which, from neglect of the parties, have become stale, and are not likely to be revived, statutes very generally provide that such cases may be dismissed from the docket, after they have lain

---

[15] See *Creditors' Bills, post,* ch. xxxi.

[16] Hoover *v.* Mitchell, 25 Gratt. 387. See also Siron *v.* Ruleman, 32 Gratt. 215, 223 (*per* Burks, J.); Wohlford *v.* Compton, 79 Va. 333. *Cf.* U. S. *v.* Parker, 120 U. S. 89; Story, Eq. Pl. 793, n. (a).

neglected for a prescribed number of years. In Virginia, this period is fixed at five years. The statute, quoted in the footnote,[17] prescribes the circumstances under which the court is authorized, *ex mero motu,* to enter an order of dismissal.

§ 292. Correction of errors in decrees.—We have already learned how errors in decrees may be corrected in the *trial court,* namely, (1) In the case of interlocutory decrees by *Petition to Rehear,*[18] (and in certain cases by motion [19]), and (2) in the case of final decrees by *Bill of Review.*[20] Where these remedies have been resorted to in vain, or where such resort is not required, the only remaining remedy is by *appeal to a higher court.* The subject of appeals is reserved for a later chapter.

§ 293. Enforcement of decrees.—The several methods by which courts of equity enforce obedience to their decrees are explained in a later chapter.[21]

---

[17] "Any court in which is pending a case wherein for more than five years there has been no order or proceeding except to continue it, may, in its discretion, order it to be struck from the docket; and it shall thereby be discontinued. A court making such order may direct it to be published in such newspaper as it may designate. Any such case may be reinstated, on motion, within one year from the date of such order, but not after." Va. Code 1919, § 6172. See Snead v. Atkinson, 121 Va. 182.

[18] *Ante,* ch. xiii, § 195 *et seq.*

[19] Id., § 176, note.

[20] Id. ch. xiii.

[21] Ch. xxii.

CHAPTER XXI.

Judicial Sales.[1]

§ 294. What is a judicial sale?—Properly speaking a *judicial sale* is a sale made on behalf of a court of competent jurisdiction, through an authorized agent, usually a master or commissioner, and inchoate until confirmed by the court.[2]

Thus a private contract of sale made *in pais,* which, for lack of authority in the agent-vendor to enter into such a contract—as a master under a decree directing a *'public'* sale,[3] or a trustee without authority to sell [4]—is inchoate without judicial sanction, becomes a judicial sale on confirmation by the court.

Ordinarily, the term does not include a sale made by a sheriff under a common law execution, which requires no confirmation by the court.[5]

§ 295. By whom made.—Sales under decrees of a chancery court are usually made by masters, or commissioners—either regular or specially appointed by the court for the purpose.

---

[1] See Va. Code 1919, §§ 6266-6278; Michie's Ann. 21 Gratt. 636; 24 Cyc. 1.

[2] McAllister *v.* Harman, 101 Va. 17—a sale privately made by a trustee of the interest of one cotenant, and personally by the remaining cotenant, during the pendency of a partition suit brought for partition in kind, and not for a sale for partition or other purpose, is not a judicial sale, though reported to and confirmed by the court in the partition proceedings, and though the purchase money was ordered to be paid to the general receiver of the court.

[3] Hess *v.* Rader, 26 Gratt. 746.

[4] Richardson *v.* Jones, 106 Va. 540. A sale by an executor, possessing testamentary power of sale, made by order of court, in a suit brought in aid of administration, and confirmed by the court, is a judicial sale. Sproul *v.* Hunter, 122 Va. 102. See also Johnson *v.* Merritt, 125 Va. 162.

[5] See 24 Cyc. 1. In Yazoo & Mississippi Valley R. Co. *v.* Clarksdale (U. S.—Oct. 1921), 66 L. ed. 000, *per* Taft, C. J., a Federal statute declaring that all property *sold under any order or decree of any court* of the United States shall be sold at public sale at the courthouse of the county or parish or city in which the property is located, or on the premises as the court may direct, was held inapplicable to a sale by the sheriff under a *fieri facias.*

In Virginia it is customary to name one or more of the counsel in the cause, as special commissioners of sale. They are required, in each case, to give bond, in such penalty as the court may prescribe, with good security; and, to avoid abuses which have occurred in the past, the commissioner is forbidden to advertise the sale until he has executed the required bond. It is further provided that the clerk's certificate that the bond has been executed shall be appended to the advertisement.[6]

§ 296. Terms of sale.—The terms of sale are largely in the discretion of the court, to be fixed as seems best in the interest of all parties—or, as declared by the statute,[7] "for cash, or on such credit and terms as it" (*i. e.*, the court) "may deem best."

The usual terms of sale of real property in Virginia, are from ten to twenty-five *per centum* of the purchase price *cash* (dependent on the particular circumstances); and the residue on a credit, in equal installments, of *six, twelve* and *eighteen months* (or *one, two* and *three* years, according to circumstances); in all cases with interest from the day of sale; the purchaser executing notes or bonds for deferred installments, payable to the commissioner of sale, or to the order of the court. The deferred installments are generally secured by retention of title until the purchase money is fully paid, and not infrequently the court will require sureties on the notes or bonds, and always the waiver of the homestead exemption.[8]

---

[6] Va. Code 1919, §§ 6266-6272; if no special commissioner is appointed, the sale is made by the *sheriff or sergeant:* id., § 6278. The commissioner or officer may receive not more than five *per centum* of the first $300, and two *per centum* of the residue of the proceeds, as his commissions: id., § 6271.

[7] Id. § 6266.

[8] In some of the circuits in Virginia, on a judicial sale of real property, it is not unusual to secure the deferred payments by deed of trust back. This seems a useless expense—though the extra expense may go 'heaven-directed,' in the form of fees to counsel. The executory contract of sale between the court and the purchaser leaves the legal title in the control of the court—even without the common decretal formula "title to be retained until payment of the whole purchase money"—since the title may not be conveyed without express order of the court. With the title thus in the hands of the court, a vendor's (legal) lien results, for the foreclosure of which, in a summary way, in case of the purchaser's default, ample provision is made by a simple rule to show cause why a re-sale shall not be ordered. *Infra*, § 305.

§ 297. The sale—how made.—While the court has authority, in its discretion, to accept private bids,[9] judicial sales are usually made at public auction, and on the premises, unless the court orders otherwise, and the property is knocked down to the highest bidder.

The decree of sale should prescribe with preciseness the terms and place of sale, and should give directions as to advertising the sale.

§ 298. Relations between the court and the successful bidder.—Acceptance of the bid by the master or commissioner creates a somewhat anomalous relation between the court and the bidder. As the bid is not made in the presence of the court, and as the commissioner is without authority to do more than to accept the bid *subject to the court's approval,* if the ordinary rules of contract were applied the bidder would not be bound by his bid, for lack of mutuality—and might, therefore, without assigning reasons, and without liability, withdraw his offer at any time before acceptance by the court. But to require mutuality of obligation in such case, and to permit the successful bidder to withdraw after the sale is over and the other bidders dispersed, would render the expense of the sale a total loss, and otherwise lead to intolerable inconvenience. If the confirmation of a judicial sale be subject to the whims, not only of the first successful bidder, but of an indefinite number of subsequent successful bidders, it is a supposable result, in a particular case, that the sale could never be consummated.

Hence equity has established its own rule on the subject, namely that the bidder is bound *from the moment of the conditional acceptance of his bid,* while the court, as vendor, may (not arbitrarily, but in the exercise of a proper discretion) either *accept or reject the bid.*[10]

[9] Benet *v.* Ford, 113 Va. 442; Johnson *v.* Merritt, 125 Va. 162; *supra,* n. 3-4.

[10] While this somewhat dogmatic statement is generally accepted by the profession, difficulty has been encountered in finding authority in which the question is distinctly raised and decided. Mr. Daniell asserts that the English rule is *contra,* and that the bidder is not bound, until acceptance by confirmation of the report. 2 Daniell, Ch. Pr. (6th Am. Ed.) 1275, 1281. No American case has been found where the question of the right of the bidder, before confirmation, to withdraw his bid was squarely presented and squarely decided. The case of Camden *v.* Mayhew, 129 U. S. 73,

Statute of frauds.—Another departure, in this connection, from accepted doctrines of the law courts, is the rule of the equity court that its sales are *not within the statute of faruds*—and hence that the bidder is bound by his parol offer, without a writing.[11] The reason is, of course, that it cannot be presumed that the court would perpetrate or permit the perpetration of a fraud in a transaction to which the court is itself a party.

§ 299. How sale confirmed—report of commissioner.—After sale made, the commissioner makes a report thereof, in writing, to the court, returning with his report a certificate of deposit for the cash payment, and the notes or bonds of the successful bidder, with an itemized statement of the expenses incurred.[12] The report usually contains a recommendation from the commissioner that the sale be, or be not, confirmed, with reasons.

After lying ten days in the clerk's office for exceptions (or for a shorter period by consent of parties) the report may be

---

is the nearest known approach to such a decision. In this case, the property was knocked out to Camden as the highest bidder, on terms requiring full payment in cash. He refused to comply with the terms of his bid, and the commissioner so reported to the court. On the hearing of the report, the bidder, being present in court, was offered the option of complying with the terms or of having the property resold at his risk. He refused to exercise the option, whereupon the court, *without in terms confirming the sale,* entered an order of *resale at the bidder's risk;* and the property having brought at the re-sale a considerably less sum, a decree was entered against the original bidder for the difference between the amount of his bid and that produced by the re-sale. The court, in an elaborate opinion by Mr. Justice Harlan, affirmed the decree. It does not distinctly appear, however, from the opinion that Camden, in terms, repudiated his bid before confirmation —though his refusal in open court, to abide by it, would seem to have been in fact a repudiation. If so, the decision appears directly in point—since the only ground on which the bidder could have been held liable for the deficiency, was that he was bound by his bid, though not formally accepted.

In Talley *v.* Stark, 6 Gratt. 340, and Thomas *v.* Davidson, 76 Va. 338, it seems to have been assumed by all parties, as well as by the court, that the bidder was thus bound before confirmation. Stout *v.* Philippi, etc., Co., 41 W. Va. 339, 23 S. E. 571 seems also authority for the proposition. Authorities discussing the relations generally between the purchaser and the court, are collected in Freeman's annotation to Mount *v.* Brown (Miss.), 69 Am. Dec. 365, 368-375. See *infra,* § 305.

[11] Robertson *v.* Smith, 92 Va. 450.

[12] In some jurisdictions, the expenses are paid out of the cash collections, without a special order, and vouchers are returned with the report, but this is not the better practice.

brought to the attention of the court for confirmation or rejection. On confirmation, the transaction for the first time assumes the nature of a completed contract, binding the court as well as the purchaser.[13] On rejection, a re-sale is directed, and an order is entered requiring. the cash payment and the notes or bonds to be returned to the bidder.

§ 300. Appreciation or depreciation in value before confirmation.—The rule of the English equity courts was that if the property materially appreciated in value before the confirmation—as by the falling in of lives, discovery of mines, etc.—the court would refuse confirmation and order a re-sale; and, *per contra,* in case of material depreciation, as by injury from fire or flood, the bidder would not be held to his bid.[14]

The American rule seems to be the same, in spite of the apparent difference between the English and American view as to the binding nature of the unconfirmed bid.[15]

§ 301. Re-sale by purchaser before confirmation.—If before confirmation of the sale it comes to the attention of the court that the purchaser has re-sold his inchoate contract at an enhanced price, the court will usually refuse to confirm the sale, and will order the property to be again put up for sale—since such resale is an indication that the property did not bring its full value at the court's first sale. Such re-sale by the purchaser is known as "trading behind the back of the court."[16]

---

[13] Johnson v. Merritt, 125 Va. 162. For an exposition of the principles which should guide the court in confirming or refusing to confirm the commissioner's report of sale, see Brock v. Rice, 27 Gratt. 812 (*per* Staples, J.); Berlin v. Melhorn, 75 Va. 639 (*per* Burks, J.); Watkins v. Jones, 107 Va. 6; Howell v. Morien, 109 Va. 200. See *Opening the Bidding, infra,* § 302.

[14] 2 Daniell, Ch. Pr. (6th Am. Ed.) 1275—results necessarily flowing from the English rule, as already noted, that until confirmation the bidder was not bound by his offer.

[15] The rule as to re-sales by bidders at an enhanced price, and the principle of opening the biddings, noticed in the sections following, seem to sustain the proposition stated as to the effect of *appreciation* in the value of the property before confirmation. And while the books abound in assumptions that the converse rule obtains in case of material *depreciation,* little or no direct authority can be cited. See Heywood v. Covington, 4 Leigh 373; Taylor v. Cooper, 10 Leigh 317, 319; Cocke v. Gilpin, 1 Rob. 39; Brock v. Rice, 27 Gratt. 812, 815; Berlin v. Melhorn, 75 Va. 623, 641; Va. F. & M. Insurance Co. v. Crabtree. 85 Va. 857, 861 all indicating that the rule operates equally in favor of the bidder or against him.

[16] Camp v. Bruce, 96 Va. 521; 4 Va. Law Reg. 743, and note by Prof. Burks.

§ 302. Opening the bidding—upset bids.—Where lano has been cried out at a judicial sale, the legal situation before confirmation, as already pointed out, is peculiar—the purchaser being bound by his bid, while the court, under whose decree the sale is had, is not bound to accept the bid; but, on the contrary, may refuse to confirm the sale, and may order a re-sale, if, in its opinion, the property did not bring its fair value.

The policy of the court, however, is to encourage prospective bidders to attend its sales and thus insure a fair price for the property that it administers. This policy is best subserved when bidders are encouraged to feel that if the property is cried out to them the court will confirm the sale. The practice of entertaining new bids from other parties who come in after the sale is over, with offers of a larger sum for the same property (known as "opening the biddings"), is not only unfair to the original successful bidder, but tends to discourage bidding at such sales. Hence, where the market has been fairly tested by an open and public sale, courts are averse to receiving upset bids, particularly where the new bidder attended, or had an opportunity to attend, the public sale.[17] Such a bidder may fairly be suspected of trading on the judgment of the successful bidder.

Nor, after such a test of the market, will the court regard with favor after-stated opinions, affidavits of inadequate price, and similar inducements to reject the bid accepted and re-open the biddings.[18]

---

[17] This subject is well discussed in a note by Prof. Burks in 4 Va. Law Reg. 690, 693. See Stortz *v.* Voss (Ky.), 205 S. W 610; 8 Am. & Eng. Enc. Pl. & Pr. 65; Watkins *v.* Jones, 107 Va. 6; Lillard *v.* Graves, 123 Va. 193; Hilliard *v.* Union Trust Co., id. 724; Graham *v.* Burgess, 117 U. S. 191; Pewabic Mining Co. *v.* Mason, 147 U. S. 367. Where, however, the biddings are opened to let in a new bidder the practice is not to accept the new bid as final, but to *order a re-sale* at what is known as an *"upset price"*—that is, on the second offering no bid less than the new bid will be received, and if no larger price be offered at the re-sale, the property is cried out to the person whose enhanced bid induced the opening of the biddings. The latter is generally required, as a condition of ordering a re-sale, to give security to insure that he will stand to his upset bid.

[18] Benet *v.* Ford, 113 Va. 442; Hardy *v.* Coley, 114 Va. 570; Litton *v.* Flanary, 116 Va. 710; Lillard *v.* Graves, 123 Va. 193—advanced bid of ten *per centum* rejected in the last three cases. Nor does the circumstance that infants are parties in interest alter the rule. Litton *v.* Flanary, *supra.*

§ 303. Title of purchaser—caveat emptor.—In judicial sales it is a settled rule that the court *does not guarantee the title or acreage* (unless the latter be stipulated), but the purchaser buys at his own risk.

Courts of equity, however, are usually careful to see that all interests and all adverse claims are represented in the suit, so that the sale may be made free of liens or other incumbrances, or clouds on the title, and that the purchaser may receive a good title to the property sold.[19] The purchaser is usually allowed time before the sale is confirmed to examine the title, and will not be required to take the property if the title turns out not to be a marketable one. He should object to the title, however, by excepting to the report of the commissioner of sale, *before the sale is confirmed to him;*[20] exception made thereafter is generally too late, except in case of fraud or mutual mistake or surprise, which, had the sale been a private one between individuals, would have justified a court of equity in rescinding the same for that cause.[21]

§ 304. Collection of purchase money—by whom.—Unless the court otherwise directs, the commissioner of sale, after execution of the required bond, is authorized to collect the required cash payment, and the deferred installments of purchase money as they fall due from time to time.[22] These collections he should promptly deposit in some bank approved by the court, and take therefor a certificate of deposit payable to the order of

---

[19] See *Account of Liens, post,* Ch. xxxi. Kirk *v.* Oakey, 110 Va. 67; Virginia Iron Co. *v.* Bond, 111 Va. 319; Steinman *v.* Clinchfield Coal Corp., 121 Va. 611; 2 Daniell, Ch. Pr. 1276.

[20] Long *v.* Weller, 29 Gratt. 347; Boyce *v.* Strother, 76 Va. 862; Sproul *v.* Hunter, 122 Va. 102; Ostenburg *v.* Union Trust Co., 93 U. S. 424; authorities *supra,* n. 19.

[21] Pechin *v.* Porterfield, 128 Va. 53; Traylor *v.* Atkinson (Va.), 108 S. E. 199; authorities *supra.*

[22] Va. Code 1919, § 6272.

the court in the designated cause, and should file this certificate with his report.

§ 305. The same—purchaser in default.—In case the purchaser makes default, either *in limine* in not complying with the terms of sale by making the cash payment and executing the required obligations for the deferred payments,[23] or in failing to meet the deferred payments as they fall due, the court may, after service of a rule to show cause, order a re-sale at his risk—this summary proceeding being justified by the fact that by purchasing at the judicial sale, *the bidder becomes a quasi party to the suit,* and submits himself to the jurisdiction of the court for all purposes connected with the sale and purchase.[24] In case the property brings less at the re-sale, the defaulting purchaser is personally liable for the deficiency.

§ 306. The same—grace to purchaser.—As an order of re-sale for default of the purchaser is in substance but a process for the enforcement of a vendor's (legal) lien, it is error if the decree fails to provide for a reasonable time, by way of grace, within which the purchaser may make good his default before sale made—in analogy to the grace usual in decrees for foreclosure of mortgages.[25]

§ 307. Purchaser's right of possession. — Where the terms of sale do not otherwise provide, the purchaser becomes entitled to possession as soon as the master's report is confirmed.[26] Before confirmation, as already shown, he has no right whatsoever in the property.[27]

If the person in actual possession wrongfully refuses to de-

---

[23] Camden *v.* Mayhew, 129 U. S. 73; Stout *v.* Philippi, etc., Co., 41 W. Va. 337, 25 S. E. 571.

[24] *Supra,* § 298; Clarkson *v.* Read, 15 Gratt. 288; Long *v.* Weller, 29 Gratt. 347; Thornton *v.* Fairfax, 29 Gratt. 669, 677; Hurt *v.* Jones, 75 Va. 341; Williams *v.* Blakey, 76 Va. 254. The Virginia statute makes special provision for summary proceedings in the cause for a personal decree against the purchaser and his sureties—or against the commissioners and his sureties where the principal fails to account for his collections. Va. Code 1919, § 6273-6277.

[25] Long *v.* Weller, 29 Gratt. 347.

[26] Hurt *v.* Jones, 75 Va. 341.

[27] Terry *v.* Cole, 80 Va. 695.

liver possession to the purchaser, the court will direct a *writ of assistance* [27a] to issue to the sheriff, directing the latter to deliver possession to the purchaser—or, as an alternative, the court may issue an attachment against the recalcitrant for contempt.

After confirmation, and possession delivered, or open, to the purchaser, the risk of depreciation, from whatever cause, rests with the purchaser—the situation being analogous to that between vendor and vendee in an ordinary executory contract of sale between individuals. In case, therefore, the purchaser desires to take out insurance against loss by fire, or other precautions against injury or spoliation, he should do so as soon as the sale is confirmed to him.

§ 308. Purchase money paid—conveyance of title.— As soon as the purchaser has completed payment of the purchase money, he becomes entitled to a conveyance. This is practically always made by a master, or commissioner, specially appointed by the court for the purpose. The master, or commissioner, who made the sale, and who collected the purchase money, is not *ex officio* competent to make the conveyance, without special judicial authority.

§ 309. Conveyance by proxy—the master's deed.— It is probable that under the original equity practice, a deed or other document required by decree, could only have been executed by the defendant or defendants in person; and involuntary performance could only have been enforced by the process of contempt, or, if this failed to move an obstinate, or non-resident or absconding defendant, the only recourse was the sequestration of his property.

Since the decree could operate only *in personam*—on the person or conscience of the defendant—it was (as it continues to be, in absence of a remedial statute) incapable, *ex proprio vigore,* of operating to transfer legal title.[28]

This difficulty is now quite generally obviated by statutory provision authorizing courts of equity to appoint a special mas-

---

[27a] *Post,* § 316.

[28] Lile, Notes on Eq. Jurisp. (ed. 1921) pp. 32-33; Proctor *v.* Ferebee, 1 Ired. Eq. 143, 36 Am. Dec. 34, and n. *Cf.* Jones *v.* Woodstock Iron Co., 95 Ala. 551.

ter to execute conveyances, or other writings, on behalf of any party to the cause; and imparting to such writings the same potency as if such party were *sui juris*, and had executed the same in person.[29]

Other statutes go even further, and declare that the *decree itself* shall, *ex proprio vigore*, operate to *transfer legal title* according to its terms, either in all cases or in certain instances named. The Virginia statutes are of restricted application—being confined to decrees in partition suits [30] and those filling vacancies in the office of trustee.[31]

§ 310. The master's deed, continued.—As already indicated, the master who conducted the sale and received payment of the purchase money, has no implied authority to make conveyance of title, but must await the express direction of the court. His deed should recite the title of the cause, the court, and the date of the decree under which he derives his authority. In absence of statutory requirement, it is not necessary that the deed be made in the name or names of the party or parties on behalf of whom the conveyance is made; nor need their names be recited. The master may be named (in his official capacity) as sole grantor, and the words of conveyance may likewise be his own; and he may sign, seal, and acknowledge the instrument in his official capacity.[32]

By a recent statute in Virginia,[33] however, it is provided that

---

[29] Va. Code 1919, § 6296; Hurt *v.* Jones, 75 Va. 341; Johnson *v.* Merritt, 125 Va. 162.

[30] Va. Code 1919, § 5282.

[31] Id. § 5303.

[32] For form, see *Appendix*. As to the effect of the master's deed generally, see Johnson *v.* Merritt, 125 Va. 162. There seems no necessity for a report from the master that he has executed the deed, though in some of the circuits in Virginia such a report is customary. See Johnson *v.* Merritt, *supra*.

[33] Acts 1918, p. 444. The Act is unskillfully drawn, and is likely to give rise to puzzling questions of interpretation. Nor is the purpose at all clear. The probable thought in the mind of the draughtsman was to facilitate the tracing of titles; but as there is no requirement that the conveyance shall *be made in the names of the parties,* nor that the conveyance, when recorded, *shall be indexed in any other name than that of the master,* as heretofore, the provision that the deed "shall specifically set out" the names, seems to fail of its purpose. Nor is it clear what is meant by names of all persons "on whose behalf the same is executed;" and even if this were made

every master's deed "shall specifically set out, as nearly as may be practicable," the name or names of the person or persons "on whose behalf the same is executed;" save that where made on behalf of heirs of a decedent, these may be described simply as heirs of such decedent.

§ 311. The same—conveyance by foreign master.— As the decree of the courts of one state cannot affect property in another state, it follows that where the court of the former directs a conveyance by its master, of property in the latter state, such conveyance is inoperative to transfer legal title [34]—though possibly binding the conscience of the parties to the suit, and hence passing equitable title.

§ 312. Payment to disqualified master.—As indicated in a former section, the master is not authorized to receive payment of any part of the purchase money until he has duly qualified by executing the required bond, with approved security, before the clerk of the court. It follows that if the purchaser pays any portion of the purchase money to an unqualified master, he does so at his own risk; and, in case the master fails to account for the fund, the loss falls upon the purchaser, who will be required to pay a second time [35]—unless the clerk, in pursuance of the statute,[36] has certified to the qualification, and the certificate has been published with the advertisement of sale.[37]

---

clear, the inconvenience of naming every party in interest ("as nearly as may be practicable"—whatever this may mean) should be sufficient to condemn the provision as unwise. In creditors' suits, and in administration proceedings in chancery, there are frequently convened scores of persons interested in the *res* (individual or corporate), all with liens, and the conveyance or conveyances required to consummate the sale or sales ordered, are necessarily made "on behalf of" every such claimant in the suit, in addition to the party or parties actually holding the legal title. A still more vital question is, the effect of the omission of one or more names (where their insertion is 'practicable'), on the *passage of title*. The author has in mind a recent partition suit to which there are sixty or more parties. This criticism suggests that the Code provision be restored, or that the amendment otherwise receive the intelligent attention of the legislature.

[34] Fall *v.* Eastin, 215 U. S. 1; extensive annotation (indicating some dissent) 69 L. R. A. 673; Lile. Notes on Eq. Jurisp. (ed. 1921) p. 33.

[35] Lloyd *v.* Erwin, 29 Gratt. 598; Tyler *v.* Toms, 75 Va. 116; Lee *v.* Swepson, 76 Va. 173.

[36] Va. Code 1919, § 6269.

[37] Whitehead *v.* Bradley, 87 Va. 676.

§ 313. Loss of funds in hands of the court.—Where the purchaser has properly paid over funds to the duly authorized representative of the court (master or receiver), and the fund is lost by the defalcation of the official custodian, the loss falls, not on the purchaser, but on the persons entitled to the funds.[88]

§ 314. Statutory protection of purchasers on reversal of decree.—In Virginia [89] there is a valuable statutory provision for protection of purchasers at judicial sales. This statute provides that "if a sale of property be made under a decree or order of a court, and such sale be confirmed, the title of the purchaser at such sale shall not be disturbed, unless within twelve months from such confirmation, the sale be set aside by the trial court, or an appeal be allowed by the Supreme Court of Appeals, and an order or decree be therein afterwards entered requiring such sale to be set aside; but there may be restitution of the proceeds to those entitled."

---

[88] Pulliam *v.* Thompkins, 99 Va. 602, 39 S. E. 221. See Gill *v.* Barbour, 80 Va. 11; Patterson *v.* Crawford, 97 Va. 661; 5 Va. Law Reg. 630, 728, 805—on the question how such loss is borne as among creditors with different degrees of priority.

[89] Va. Code 1919, § 6306. This section is a substitute for § 3425 of the Code of 1887, which declared that if the sale were made six months after the decree, and was confirmed, no subsequent reversal of the decree should affect the title of the purchaser. The statute was held inapplicable where the decree was void on jurisdictional grounds. Brenham *v.* Smith, 102 Va. 30. The revised statute is a marked improvement on the original. The advantages are pointed out in the revisor's notes to § 6306. The principle of Brenham *v.* Smith, *supra*, however, seems necessarily inherent in the amended section, as, indeed, properly it should be.

CHAPTER XXII.

Enforcement of Decrees.

§ 315. Enforcement of decrees. — There are several methods by which the decrees of a chancery court may be enforced—among the more important of which are (1) *Writ of Assistance;* (2) *Writ of Attachment;* (3)*Writ of Sequestration;* (4) *Writ of Execution;* (5) *Order of Sale;* (6) *Performance by Proxy;* (7) *A New Original Bill in. Equity.*

§ 316. (1) Writ of Assistance.—Where the decree directs the transfer of possession of specific property, real or personal, temporarily or permanently, a writ of assistance may be authorized by the court, directing the sheriff, or other ministerial officer of the court, *to place the designated person in possession.*

In the execution of the writ, the officer has all the power, and may exercise all the force, that he possesses and might exercise under an ordinary execution.[1]

§ 317. (2) Writ of Attachment — process of contempt.—This writ, like that mentioned in the preceding section, is grantable only by the court. But, unlike the writ of assistance, it is directed against the *person* of the recalcitrant. It is in substance an order to the sheriff to *attach the person* of the offending party, and to produce his body before the court at a time named in the writ, to show cause why he shall not be pun-
of the court.[2]

---

[1] Fletcher, Eq. Pl. & Pr. 736; Shipman, Eq. Pl. 161; Equity Rules 7-9, 11 (rule 9 permitting the clerk to issue). The writ is often resorted to in order to place the *purchaser at a judicial sale* in possession of the property purchased—and to enforce orders directing a *receiver* of the court to take possession of property in litigation.
ised for contempt in refusing or neglecting to obey the decree

[2] Shipman, Eq. Pl. 159; Fletcher, Eq. Pl. & Pr. 733; Foster, Fed. Pr. 339-349a; Equity Rules 7-8; Va. Code, §§ 6309, 4521-4524; Va. Const. §§ 63, 156. For a general discussion of contempt proceedings, see 9 Cyc. 1; 7 Am. & Eng. Enc. L. 25; 5 Va. Law Reg. 49, 281, 345, 392, 832; Carter's Case, 96 Va. 791; Yoder's Case, 107 Va. 823; Gompers *v.* Buck Stove, etc., Co., 221 U. S. 418, 34 L. R. A. (N. S.) 874, note.

The rigor of this proceeding is often mitigated by the issue of a mere rule (without attachment, or arrest,) against the person alleged to be in contempt, to appear and show cause why an attachment shall not issue.

§ 318. (3) Writ of sequestration.—This is a proceeding by means of which the *property* of a recalcitrant party is seized ("sequestered"), under order of the court, by the officer of the court, or by persons specially designated for the purpose ("sequestrators"), with the object of retaining the *corpus*, and the rents, issues and profits, until the obstinate owner obeys the order of the court.

Its use is comparatively rare in modern times, since courts of equity have assumed (generally by virtue of statutes) to issue executions similar to those of the common law courts. The writ is still useful, however, where the decree directs the performance of *some act other than the payment of money* or the delivery of property within the jurisdiction [3]—as where the defendant places himself or the subject-matter beyond the process of the court, but has other property within the jurisdiction, or is a corporation and therefore not subject to attachment or imprisonment under contempt proceedings.[4]

§ 319. (4) Writ of execution—fieri facias.—Writs of execution in equity are substantially the same as executions issued from courts of law, and are so declared by the Virginia Code.[5]

Thus where the plaintiff has secured a personal decree against the defendant for the payment of money, the former may sue out of the clerk's office a writ of *fieri facias*, requiring the sheriff to levy on the defendant's tangible chattels (and in some of the states real property, as well), and to sell the same for the satisfaction of the decree.

---

[3] The payment of money, or delivery of property located within the jurisdiction may generally be enforced by execution or writ of assistance, as already explained.

[4] Fletcher, Eq. Pl. & Pr. 735. Specific provision is made for the writ in the Federal courts by Equity Rules 7-8. See Foster, Fed. Pr. 339-349a.

[5] Va. Code 1919, § 6459; Fletcher, Eq. Pl. and Pr. 734.

§ 320. (5) Order of sale.—The jurisdiction to subject property by a sale thereof, in the foreclosure of mortgages and the enforcement of other liens or specific charges thereon, has been long established, and is one of the most common and useful forms in which the equity jurisdiction is exercised.[6]

§ 320a. (6) Performance by proxy—master's deeds. —It has already been pointed out in a previous chapter [7] that courts of equity possess the jurisdiction, wherever the occasion arises, to convey title to property, when properly brought within its control, through the medium of a master specially appointed for the purpose, without the active participation of the party or parties in whom is the legal title, or who may be otherwise interested therein.

§ 321. (7) Original bill to enforce, rescind, or interpret decree.—It sometimes happens that after the original suit has been completely ended, without leave to reinstate, so that no further proceedings may be had in that suit—and after the lapse of the grace allowed for filing a bill of review, or for an appeal —or the situation is one not thus relievable—new situations develop, calling for the intervention of the court.

Where, for instance, by the occurrence of subsequent events, the enforcement of the decree has become inequitable; or dispute has arisen as to its correct interpretation, or controversy as to whether defendant has or has not properly performed; or where, by neglect of the parties or otherwise, their rights have become embarrassed or uncertain; or, in any case, where manifestly the intervention of the court has become essential to the securing of complete justice to the parties—a bill in the nature of an original bill may be filed for such relief as equity and good conscience may demand.[7a]

§ 322. The same—right of defendant to contest former decree.—Of course on such a bill there can be no review or re-trial of the original cause, all the issues in which have become *res judicata*—but the relief will be confined to fixing and

---

[6] Ch. xxi. See *post, Creditors' Suits,* ch. xxxi.
[7] *Supra,* ch. xx, §§ 309-310.
[7a] *Supra,* § 288.

enforcing the rights of the parties under the former decree.[8]

It seems, however, that the *defendant* in the new bill may set up fraud, mistake or other lack of equity in the decree sought to be affected, and thus invoke the protection of the maxim that "he who wants equity must do equity;" and the plaintiff in the new bill may then be put on terms of doing equity as the price of the court's assistance.[9]

---

[8] Story, Eq. Pl. 429; Fletcher, Eq. Pl. & Pr. 958; Mitford, Eq. Pl. 95; Root *v.* Woolworth, 150 U. S. 401.

[9] Story, Eq. Pl. 641; 2 Daniell, Ch. Pr. (6th ed.) 1586; Wadhams *v.* Gay, 73 Ill. 415; Gay *v.* Parpart, 106 U. S. 679; Lawrence Mfg. Co. *v.* Janesville Cotton Mills, 138 U. S. 552; Hamilton *v.* Houghton, 2 Bligh (H. of L.) 169. "I do not understand the rule to be that this court is bound to carry into execution an erroneous decree. On the contrary. I apprehend that when a person comes into this court asking for the benefit of a former decree, he must be prepared to show, if the cases requires it, that such decree was right." Ld. Chancellor of Ireland. in O'Connell *v.* McNamara, 3 Dr. & War. 411.

CHAPTER XXIII.

Miscellaneous Proceedings.

1. Proceedings in Vacation.

§ 323. Vacation proceedings.—By reason of the peculiar remedies in equity—and especially preventive and administrative remedies—courts of chancery, as the result of statute, rules of court or inherent power, exercise a more extensive jurisdiction in vacation than courts of law.

§ 324. The same—in the Federal courts.—The district courts of the United States, as courts of equity, are deemed always open for the purpose of filing pleadings, issuing and returning mesne and final process, and for interlocutory proceedings preparatory to the hearing of causes on their merits. And the judges are given power, as well in vacation as in term, on reasonable notice, to make and direct all such interlocutory orders, etc., preparatory to the hearing of causes on their merits.[1]

§ 325. The same—in Virginia.—By statute in Virginia, the chancellor may exercise, among others, the following powers in vacation:

(a) To grant *temporary injunctions*,[2] and, as ancillary thereto, to appoint *receivers*.[3]

(b) To *dissolve* temporary injunctions, and, as ancillary thereto, to *discharge receivers*.[4]

(c) "Judges of courts exercising chancery jurisdiction shall have the *same jurisdictional powers over chancery causes in vacation, as is conferred upon such courts in term;* but such jurisdiction shall not be exercised except after ten days' notice to all parties to be affected thereby, or their counsel."[5]

---

[1] Equity Rules 1-6.
[2] Va. Code 1919, § 6326; *post,* chs. xxvii, xxxii.
[3] *Post,* ch. xxxii.
[4] Va. Code 1919, § 6326; *post,* chs. xxvii, xxxii.
[5] Id. § 6307.

(d) Chancery causes *submitted in term* may be *decided in vacation* without such notice; nor need notice be given to a defendant summoned by publication, and who has not appeared.

Decrees so entered are declared as valid as if made in term; but where they constitute a lien, the lien is effective only from the time of day when the decree is received by the clerk for recordation.[6]

(e) By *process of contempt* to "punish disobedience of, and compel obedience to, any decree or order made in a cause in his court."[7]

2. STIPULATIONS AND CONSENT PROCEEDINGS.[8]

§ 326. Nature and purpose.—For dispatch of business and to save expense and inconvenience to parties and counsel, certain of the formalities of procedure are frequently waived by stipulation between the respective counsel.   Such stipulations, when proper, are favorably regarded by the courts.

Thus it is not unusual for counsel to agree to a continuance of the cause—to consent to a hearing of the cause, or some part thereof, before the court or a master, on a designated day, or in vacation—to waive formal notice of the taking of depositions —to the admission of the genuineness of certain documents, or the truth of certain allegations of fact without proof—to the filing, withdrawal, or amendment of pleadings—to the extension of time to the adversary for the taking of certain steps in the cause—to the waiver of informalities or irregularities—and generally to waive rules of practice or procedure not affecting the substantial merits of the cause.

While counsel have implied authority thus to waive matters of *practice and procedure,* they may not without express sanction waive the substantial *rights* of the client.

§ 327. The   same—form—stipulations   in   pais—in court.—To prevent unseemly controversies between counsel as to the precise scope and meaning of stipulations into which they have entered, all important agreements of this character should

---

[6] Id.

[7] Id. § 6309; See *Contempts, ante.* ch. xxii.

[8] Fletcher, Equity Pl. & Pr. 447-454; Thompson on Trials. 193-202.

be reduced to writing, or if made in court should be entered of record.

In many jurisdictions, in order that such stipulations may be recognized and enforced by the court in spite of their repudiation by one of the parties thereto, statutes or rules of court require that they shall be in writing, or else entered of record.[9]

It is needless to add that all such stipulations, whether oral or written, should be regarded by counsel as of highly honorary obligation, and when fairly entered into should be scrupulously observed. Nothing detracts more from the standing of counsel at the bar than the reputation among his professional brethren of denying or evading agreements thus made.

3. Provision for Speedy Trials in Federal Courts.

§ 328. Continuances in the Federal courts.—To prevent the delays traditionally incident to equity proceedings, the new Equity Rules have prescribed stringent regulations to speed the trial of equity causes. One striking provision seeks to eradicate the former evil of indefinite continuances by consent of parties, or generally at the request of either party.

The rule [10] provides that a cause when placed on the trial calendar shall not be continued beyond the term, save in exceptional cases, and except on order of the court and for good cause shown by affidavit, on such terms as the court may impose.

Such continuance beyond the term by *consent of parties*, may be allowed "on condition only that a stipulation be signed by counsel for all the parties and that all costs incurred theretofore be paid. Thereupon an order shall be entered dropping the cause from the trial calendar, subject to reinstatement within one year upon application to the court by either party, in which event it shall be heard at the earliest convenient day. If not so reinstated within the year, the suit shall be dismissed without prejudice to a new one."

---

[9] Smith *v.* Smith, 119 N. C. 311, 25 S. E. 877; Morse *v.* State, 39 Tex. Cr. R. 566, 50 S. W. 342; Caldwell *v.* McWilliams, 65 Ga. 99; Citizens Bank of Wichita *v.* Farwell, 56 Fed. 570.
[10] Equity Rule 57.

CHAPTER XXIV.

Multifariousness.

§ 329. Multifariousness—definition.—Multifariousness in equity pleading means the *improper joinder of several causes of action* in the same suit—each capable of enforcement in separate proceedings. It is the correlative of *"misjoinder"* in courts of law, where counts in *debt* may not be joined with counts in *assumpsit,* nor counts in *trover* with those in covenant; nor, at law, may there be plaintiffs with separate interests, nor defendants not jointly liable.

§ 330. The same—policy of equity.—It is the policy of courts of equity to prevent a multiplicity of suits, and, so far as this can conveniently be accomplished, to settle, in a single suit, all controversies which, in their last analysis, affect a single subject matter. Thus, where the purpose of the bill is to clear the title to real property, or completely to dispose of a particular *res,* real or personal, the bill will ordinarily not be condemned for multifariousness though various conflicting interests may appear, and though every party defendant may not be interested in each of the numerous collateral controversies whose settlement the bill invokes.[1]

§ 331. Multifariousness—several kinds.—Several aspects of this serious fault in equity pleading are encountered in practice: (1) the joinder of two or more *independent claims* by *the same plaintiff against the same defendant;* (2) the joinder of *independent. claims by several plaintiffs,* each asserting separate claims against one or more defendants, whether the latter be jointly concerned or not; or conversely, (3) the joinder of two or more *distinct claims* by the plaintiff against *several defendants, all the defendants not being interested in all the claims* asserted.

§ 332. The same—the first class.—As shown in the pre-

---

ceding section, multifariousness of the first class occurs where two or more distinct and independent causes of action—each in itself sufficient for the jurisdiction of the court—are asserted by the plaintiff against a defendant or defendants, where every defendant is interested in all the claims asserted in the bill.

An illustration of a bill of this character would be a suit by A against B, C and D, for specific performance of a contract between the plaintiffs and the *three defendants* for the sale of Blackacre, and also for the partition of Whiteacre belonging to the *four parties*.

§ **333. The same—effect.**—It is quite clear that where the several claims asserted by the same plaintiff, in the same bill, *arise out of the same transaction,* no valid objection can be made on the ground of multifariousness.[2] Indeed, in such case, it is the plaintiff's duty to unite all such claims in the same suit.[3]

Even where the several equities asserted do not arise out of the same transaction, and are *wholly independent of each other,* as illustrated in the preceding section, it does not necessarily follow that the court will treat the bill as multifarious. The fault here is not so serious as the other forms of multifariousness; and the question whether or not such a bill will be sustained will depend largely on the circumstances of each case. If it seems to the court that both equities can conveniently be administered in a single suit, the court may, in its discretion, overrule the objection and permit the bill to stand.[4]

The consideration that courts of law are liberal in permitting innumerable claims, of the same general nature, and all against the same defendant or defendants, to be asserted under the guise of separate counts in a single declaration, suggests equal or greater liberality in courts of equity, wherever the several claims may be heard together, without inconvenience to the parties.

---

[2] Pack *v*. Whitaker, 110 Va. 122.

[3] Zetelle *v*. Myers, 19 Gratt. 62.

[4] See Story, Eq. Pl. 271 (n), 278 (n.), 280; 1 Daniell. Ch. Pr. 335; 5 Va. Law Reg. 840. In Seefried *v*. Clarke, 113 Va. 365, a bill to set aside a conveyance for fraud and for partition of the property involved was sustained. Such practice is expressly authorized by Equity Rule 26.

§ 334. The same—second class—distinct plaintiffs asserting distinct claims.—A more serious phase of multifariousness occurs where two separate and distinct claims are asserted, not by the same plaintiff, or plaintiffs in joint interest, as in the preceding section, but by *plaintiffs whose interests are separate and distinct,* and whether against the same or different defendants. Thus, where A sues C for specific performance of a contract to convey Blackacre, and B unites as plaintiff in the same bill, seeking specific performance of a separate contract with C for the conveyance of Whiteacre, the bill is clearly and hopelessly multifarious.[5]

§ 335. The same—third class—distinct and unrelated claims against several distinct defendants.—A third and equally hopeless form of multifariousness, closely akin to that just noticed, occurs where several distinct and disconnected claims (whether by one or several plaintiffs) are asserted against several defendants, but *all the defendants are not interested in all the matters litigated.* As a rule, this will not be permitted; and on demurrer the court will dismiss the bill.[6] Creditors' bills and administration suits, as we shall see, are notable exceptions (but more apparent than real) to this rule—the reason being that the purpose of such suits is to make a *complete disposition of a fund or estate,* and this can only be done in a single suit.

§ 336. The same—joinder of valid with invalid cause of action.—It is important, however, to observe that where one of the causes of action alleged cannot be maintained, (as, for example, for lack of jurisdiction, or for lack of equity), the attempt to connect it with the other cause of action will not render the bill multifarious; but the former will be regarded as mere surplusage. In short, in order to render a bill multifarious there must be *two complete, independent causes of action asserted—* the maxim being *utile per inutile non vitiatur.*[7]

---

[5] This form of multifariousness is condemned by Equity Rule 26.
[6] This is likewise condemned by Equity Rule 26.
[7] Matney *v.* Yates, 121 Va. 507; Appalachia *v.* Mainous, id. 666.

§ 337. The same—general observations.—While these general rules are comparatively simple of statement, the courts have much difficulty in applying them, and it is common to find it stated judicially that a determination of the question whether a bill is multifarious or not, depends largely upon the peculiarities of each case, and the enlightened discretion of the court.[8]

An illustration of a multifarious bill is presented in the case cited in the footnote.[9] In that case J, A and W had been partners; W withdrew, and a new partnership was formed between J and A, which was later dissolved. J then filed a bill against both of his former partners, A and W, for a settlement of the accounts of *both partnerships*. It was properly held, that inasmuch as W, who first withdrew, had no interest in the settlement of the accounts of the second partnership between J and A, it was improper that he should be united in the suit, and hence that the bill was multifarious.

§ 338. Multifariousness continued — how objection made—effect.—Since the objection of multifariousness must necessarily appear on the face of the bill, the proper method of making the objection is, of course, by demurrer. If held to be multifarious, the mispleading is fatal, and the bill will be dismissed.[10]

---

[8] See Brown *v.* Bedford, etc., Co., 91 Va. 31; Spooner *v.* Hilbish, 92 Va. 333; School Board *v.* Farish, 92 Va. 156; Saunders *v.* Bank, 113 Va. 656; Matney *v.* Yates, 121 Va. 506.

[9] Dunn *v.* Dunn, 26 Gratt. 291.

[10] Dennis *v.* Justus, 115 Va. 512, 515—*ex mero motu*—*per* Keith, P.

CHAPTER XXV.

Consolidation of Causes.

§ 339. Consolidation.—Where several suits are pending in the same court, by the same plaintiff, or, in proper case, by independent plaintiffs, against substantially the same defendants, and involving substantially the same subject-matter, it is often convenient and economical to have an order consolidating the several causes, and thereafter proceeding with them as a single suit.

§ 340. "Consolidation"—"hearing together"—distinction.—The terms *consolidation,* and *hearing together,* are not infrequently confused, and used as if they denoted the same thing. They are, however, distinct. Whenever causes are consolidated they are necessarily heard together, but "hearing together" does not necessarily imply "consolidation." It frequently happens, however, as appears from the reported cases, that an order of *consolidation* is treated throughout by counsel and court as a *mere order to hear together*—in other words, that the former term has not been used in its technical sense. It is in the latter sense that we shall use it in this brief study.

§ 341. "Consolidation"—general effect.[1]—Where several causes are technically *consolidated* they become in effect a *single suit,* at least in so far as the circumstances of the several causes permit complete unity. The evidence in one becomes evidence in the other (subject of course to the control of the court to prevent injustice); the parties to one become parties to the other;[2] and the cause proceeds for all purposes as if the several causes had been *originally asserted in a single bill.* It must be observed, however, that it is the *proceedings* that are consolidated and not the *claims asserted,* save where the latter belong to the same plaintiff.[3]

---

[1] As to the effect on the appellate jurisdiction, see *infra,* this chapter.
[2] Patterson *v.* Eakin, 87 Va. 49—noticed at length, *infra,* § 347 n.
[3] See Home Building Co. *v.* London, 98 Va. 52.

§ 342. "Hearing together"—effect.—On the other hand, where there is a mere order of *hearing together*, unmodified, the suits remain as several as before, the only effect being that for convenience and economy the several steps toward a final disposition. of the several causes are taken at the same time, and usually in the same decree.   The parties to one are not necessarily parties to the other, and the evidence in one is not necessarily evidence in the other.

These results may be, of course, and often are, enlarged more or less by express stipulation, or by conduct or acquiescence of the parties, or by the action of the court. Where such departure from the type occurs, the situation will present some, or all, of the features of a technical consolidation.   ·

§ 343. Consolidation—confusion in the authorities.— There has been a most unfortunate situation produced in Virginia by the apparently conflicting views expressed from time to time by our Court of Appeals in this connection—a confusion due largely to *dicta* originating in Claiborne *v.* Gross,[4] in which one of the judges suggested that consolidation of causes, without consent of parties, was *beyond the powers of a court of equity,* and consequently unknown in the equity practice—a doubt. more than once repeated in later cases. In a somewhat careful search, not a single Virginia case has been discovered in which there is a direct decision on the propriety of consolidating causes in equity. In all of the Virginia cases in which the question has appeared, however, it has been assumed that the effect of consolidation was to convert the several suits *into one suit for all purposes*—and in each of them the absence of this assumption would have eliminated the necessity of considering the question of the propriety of the consolidation.

The still unsettled condition of the Virginia authorities on the primary question of the propriety of consolidating equity causes, seems to justify the somewhat extended notice of the Virginia authorities in the sections that follow.

---

[4] 7 Leigh 331.

Outside of Virginia there are comparatively few authorities denying or doubting the power of courts of equity to order the consolidation of causes under proper circumstances discussed below, though in many jurisdictions the term seems to be used as connoting a mere *hearing together*.[5]

§ 344. Consolidation—without consent of parties.— Since *ex vi termini* technical consolidation connotes the complete conversion of several suits into one suit, it follows that where the several claims could not *originally* have been asserted in a single suit, they may not, when separately asserted, be *subsequently* united by consolidation, except by consent. If the joinder of the several claims in a single *original* bill would have rendered the bill *multifarious*, their *subsequent joinder by consolidation* would present the same vice.

The evil of multifariousness rests not alone in the inconvenience to the court of hearing dissimilar claims, asserted by different parties, but in the *wrong done to litigants* in compelling them to become parties to a litigation in one or more branches of which they have no interest.[6]

§ 345. The same—by consent.—But as the objection of multifariousness is not jurisdictional, and hence, under sanction of the court, may be waived by the parties, there would seem, on principle, to be no difficulty presented where the consolidation is *by consent* or *acquiescence* of all parties—a proposition apparently conceded by all the authorities.

§ 346. The same—several suits between the same parties.—So where the several suits are between the *same parties*, concerning substantially the *same subject-matter* [7]—as where

---

[5] The authorities from other jurisdictions, are collected in 8 Cyc. 589, 592, 608. See also, Fletcher, Eq. Pl. & Pr. 455; Rev. Stat. U. S., § 921; Toledo, etc., R. Co. v. Continental Trust Co., 95 Fed. 497; Beach v. Woodyard, 5 W. Va. 321; Wyatt v. Thompson, 10 W. Va. 645; Burnham v. Dalling, 16 N. J. Eq. 310; O'Bannon v. Roberts, 2 Dana (Ky.) 54; Bowles v. Schoenberger, 2 B. Mon. (Ky.) 372. The practice in Tennessee seems to be practically to compel the parties to consent, where the court thinks a consolidation proper, by taxing the extra costs against the party refusing. Gibson, Suits in Chancery §§ 754-755.

[6] See *Multifariousness, ante,* ch. xxiv.

[7] In such case there may be consolidation even *at law*. McRae v. Board, 3 Rand. 481.

the plaintiff has instituted several creditors' suits against the same defendant. Here all the claims might have been, and therefore more regularly should have been, originally asserted in a single suit; and consolidation is but a more convenient and more economical method of converting what are in fact but several branches of a single suit, into one suit.

§ 347. The same—different plaintiffs who might have united in a single suit.—Here again, on like considerations, there is no sound reason why the several suits may not be consolidated; and it is in this class of cases that consolidation is most common in practice—as in the case of several creditors' bills, or bills by legatees, shareholders, tax-payers and others representing members of a class similarly situated.[8] In such

---

[8] See *Creditors' Bills, post,* ch. xxxi. In Claiborne *v.* Gross, 7 Leigh 331, two separate creditors' bills by different plaintiffs against the same defendant were consolidated, without consent, by order of the trial court—one case involving an amount that made it appealable, while in the other the amount was below the required minimum. The consolidated suit was dismissed, and plaintiffs appealed. Opinions were delivered by two of the three judges participating in the decision— both discussing, with some elaboration, the power of the court to direct a consolidation without consent. Carr, J. (Brockenbrough, J., concurring) denied the power in any case, without consent, with Tucker, P., arguing *contra.* Both admitted, however, that the question was immaterial, since, in spite of the order of consolidation, the lower court in its decree had *treated the causes as separate,* and there had been separate petitions for appeal. All agreed in dismissing the appeal as to that one of the causes in which the amount involved was not within the jurisdictional minimum. Hence the entire discussion of the propriety of the consolidation was extra-judicial. This becomes the more apparent in the light of subsequent decisions establishing the principle that even where the several plaintiffs assert their claims in the *same bill, each claim on appeal must involve the jurisdictional amount.* White *v.* Building Fund Association, 96 Va. 270.

In Barger *v.* Buckland, 28 Gratt. 850, three creditors' bills, by different plaintiffs against the same defendant, were consolidated, apparently without express consent of all parties. No process had been served on the defendant in one of the cases, but he appeared and made defense to the entire cause as consolidated, without objection. Here again the court expresses a doubt (citing the *dictum* in Claiborne *v.* Gross, *supra*), whether the court might properly consolidate the causes without consent of parties, but concludes that by appearing and defending without objection, the defendant had waived the objection. The discussion of the question of the power to consolidate was therefore an obvious *dictum.* See an equally obvious *dictum* in Patterson *v.* Eakin, 87 Va. 49, overruling, so far as one *dictum* may overrule another, the *obiter* expressions noticed above. This case is again noticed in the footnote to the section following.

cases not only may the court direct a consolidation, but, as shown in a later chapter on creditors' bills,[9] the assumption of jurisdiction in one of the suits (as by an order of reference), demands either a consolidation or its equivalent, namely, a suspension of all the other suits, and a convention of all the creditors in the suit ripened by the order of reference. The consolidation, therefore, is but another method of securing the necessary convention of all parties in the single ripened suit.[10]

§ 348. The same—claims which could not have been united in a single suit.—On the contrary, where the claims asserted in the several suits are so diverse, either as to subject-matter or parties, that to have asserted them in a single original bill would have called for a *dismissal of the bill on demurrer for multifariousness*, it seems clear that it would be error to direct a *consolidation*, without consent of parties. If, as already shown, the effect of consolidation is to convert the several independent suits into a single suit, as fully and effectually as if all the claims had been asserted in a single original bill, then manifestly the question of the propriety of such joinder is the same in the one case as in the other. If it be error and an injustice to force an objecting party into a litigation multifarious *in its inception*, it is equally erroneous and unjust to compel him against his will to litigate his rights in a proceeding which *has become multifarious by subsequent consolidation*. If the proceeding be in fact multifarious, the question of *how the multifariousness was produced*, or when, is immaterial. The injustice to the protesting party is as obvious, and as serious, in the one case as in the other.[11]

---

[9] *Post*, ch. xxxi.

[10] In Barger *v.* Buckland, *supra*, the consolidation of several creditors' bills, by different plaintiffs, was held proper when acquiesced in by the parties, though the court was not quite clear (citing the *dictum* in Claiborne *v.* Gross, *supra*) whether consolidation, or whether an order for *"hearing together"*, were the proper procedure.

[11] See *Multifariousness, ante*, ch. xxiv. Wyatt *v.* Thompson, 10 W. Va. 645. Such a case was indirectly presented in Smith *v.* Pyrites Mining Co., 101 Va. 301, where what was termed a "supplemental bill" was dismissed by the lower court, and an appeal taken more than twelve months afterwards. On motion to dismiss the appeal as barred by limitation, the question involved was whether the decree of dismissal below was a final decree. Neither the parties to the supplemental bill nor its purposes were the same as in the original bill.

**§ 349. Effect of consolidation on the appellate juris-
tion—(1) Same plaintiff in each case.**—Where all the
claims asserted in the several suits are by the *same plaintiff*, or
by the *same plaintiffs jointly*, though each severally is less than
the jurisdictional amount required for an appeal, yet if in the

---

The court held the appeal barred, and took occasion to say that because the parties and objects were not the same, even treating the
new bill as an original bill, the two causes could not have been consolidated, but might have been *heard together*. But the point was not
involved in the decision.

At first glance, the case of Patterson *v.* Eakin, 87 Va. 49, seems at
last to afford authority on the lines of our present inquiry, but, as
in apparently all the other Virginia cases in which the subject of
consolidation is discussed, the question was not involved, and the
discussion *obiter*. In that case there were two suits by different plaintiffs, but both involving the administration of the estate of the same
testator—one by a creditor seeking enforcement of a vendor's lien on
a single parcel of real estate, and the other by devisees for a sale of
other real estate of the testator for payment of a single remaining
debt, and a reinvestment of the residue. After various proceedings
in each, including a sale to satisfy the vendor's lien, the two suits
were consolidated, apparently without consent. Subsequently a sale
of the property last mentioned, made under order of the court, to one
Patterson, was confirmed in vacation, without notice to one Figgatt,
who had in the meanwhile become assignee of both debts, as well as
assignee from the purchaser of the parcel affected by the vendor's
lien. The two judicial sales had produced an aggregate amount *far in
excess of all the debts*, so that in fact Figgatt had not the slightest
concern with the vacation order of confirmation. But his petition to
vacate the order of confirmation, because of lack of notice to him,
was sustained by the lower court, and Patterson, the purchaser, appealed. Instead of contenting itself with a declaration in the first
instance, that as Figgatt's debts were abundantly provided for, and
therefore no injury could result to him by the omission of notice
of the application for confirmation, the appellate court entered into
an extended discussion of the powers of courts of equity to consolidate
causes. It discarded doubts that had been expressed in the previous
cases noted above; declared that Figgatt, as assignee of the purchaser
in the first suit, thereby became a party to that suit, and that on consolidation he thereupon became a party to the second suit as well;
and hence that he was entitled to notice of the application for a confirmation of the sale involved in the second suit. Thus the court
seems to decide squarely that consolidation was a proper method of
procedure in the case at bar (as it probably was, since the two suits
involved substantially the same subject-matter, and the objects sought
in both might well have been accomplished in a single suit), and that
the effect was a complete conversion of the two causes into one. But
after this exhaustive study of the propriety and effect of consolidation, and a thorough vindication of the petitioner's right of notice, the
conclusion was announced that, after all, as Figgatt could not possibly have suffered detriment from lack of notice, the lower court
committed error in granting his petition, based on absence of notice—and hence the action of the lower court was *for that reason re-*

aggregate they are within the required amount, it seems clear that on consolidation of the suits, *the aggregate amount involved* would be the test of the *plaintiff's* right to appeal.[12] This is manifestly so in determining the right of the *defendant* to appeal, even though the several claims are asserted by different plaintiffs [13]—since, as to the defendant, the aggregate of the claims is the amount involved.

§ 350. The same—(2) different plaintiffs.—But where the claims are distinctly *several,* and are asserted by *different plaintiffs,* though against the same defendant, the consolidation can have no greater effect than if the several causes had been asserted in the same bill.[14] And the same rule must be applicable to both. That is, the combination of the several claims, whether in a single *original suit* or *by consolidation,* does not alter the several and distinct nature of the claims, and therefore adds nothing to their privileges of appeal. As already pointed out, in such case it is not the *claims* that are consolidated, but the

---

versed. In other words, the question of consolidation and its effect was immaterial. So that the case is not decisive authority for any proposition connected with the subject of consolidation.

The question was again mooted in Merritt *v.* Johnson, 125 Va. 162, and though the court declared the consolidation in that case improper, there was no necessity for passing upon the question, as the error was held to be harmless. The opinion on the point was therefore *obiter.*

[12] In Devries *v.* Johnston, 27 Gratt. 80, the precise question of the effect of a consolidation of such causes was directly presented. Here, three separate suits by the *same plaintiffs* (partners) against the *same defendants* (also partners), each suit involving *less* than the amount required for appellate jurisdiction, but aggregating more than the required jurisdictional amount, were consolidated; and the question was whether the consolidation had the effect of giving the appellate court jurisdiction of the *plaintiffs'* appeal. Anderson, J., who delivered the opinion, held that such was the effect—but unfortunately there were other questions involved, and two of the four judges sitting dissented, without assigning reasons, with the result that the decree below was *affirmed.* The case, therefore, settled nothing. But on principle Judge Anderson's ruling seems sound—since all the claims were due to the appellants as partners, and might have been united in one suit. And since, instead of dismissing the appeal (as must have been done had the court been without jurisdiction), the decree of the lower court was affirmed, the presumption is that the dissenting judges concurred on the question of jurisdiction.

[13] *Infra,* n. 15.

[14] As in the case of bills by members of a class similarly situated, discussed *supra,* § 347.

proceedings merely; and though there be a decree *joint* in form, it is in its nature *several,* and must, for purpose of appeal by the plaintiffs, be so regarded.[15]

§ 351. Resume.—From the foregoing, we conclude that equity causes may be consolidated only under the following circumstances:

1. *By consent of parties;* or
2. *Where the several claims asserted, whether by the same or by different plaintiffs, might originally have been asserted in a single suit.*

---

[15] Claiborne *v.* Gross, 7 Leigh 331—(a case of consolidation, noticed at length, *supra,* § 347, n. 8); Umbarger *v.* Watts, 25 Gratt. 167 (several creditors in the same bill); White *v.* Building Fund Association, 96 Va. 270 (another case of several creditors in the same bill). Where the *converse* situation is presented, and the *defendant,* against whom all the claims are asserted, becomes appellant, the *aggregate* of all the claims asserted, whether in a single or a consolidated suit, fixes the amount involved for the purpose of appellate jurisdiction. Craig *v.* Williams, 90 Va. 500 (a case of consolidation); Hicks *v.* Roanoke, etc., Co., 94 Va. 741.

CHAPTER XXVI.

Special Instances of Suits for Relief.

§ 352. Preliminary.—No attempt will be here made to catalogue, even if this were possible, the various equitable grounds on which suits in equity may be filed.

The student is presumed, from his studies of equity jurisprudence, to be familiar with the diversified field of rights and remedies over which courts of equity exercise either exclusive or concurrent jurisdiction. Nor need it be suggested that wherever there is an equitable right to be protected, or an equitable remedy to be sought, the plaintiff may have access to the ear of the court by a bill praying the desired relief—and (in an original proceeding) by *bill only*.

§ 353. The more common classes of suits.—Among the more common classes of suits in equity may be mentioned: Suits to foreclose or redeem a mortgage; to enforce a vendor's or a mechanic's or a judgment lien on real property; for specific performance of a contract; to establish and enforce a trust; for the construction of wills and trust instruments, and for advice to fiduciaries; for the settlement of fiduciary and other accounts; for the settlement of decedents' estates; to set aside conveyances fraudulent as between the parties, or as to creditors; for exoneration, contribution or marshalling; for divorce and alimony; for sale of lands of persons under disabilities; for the assignment of dower; to set up lost instruments; to correct mistakes; for injunctions; for partition; for relief from penalties and forfeitures; creditors' bills; bills for discovery, etc.

§ 354. Some of these more in detail.—A few of the suits named have been selected for a more or less detailed study of the proceedings, with special emphasis on related questions of practice likely to make difficulty for the young practitioner—namely:

I. Bills for Injunction.
II. Bills for Partition.
III. Bills for Divorce.
IV. Bills for Sale of Lands of Infants and Lunatics.
V. Creditors' Bills.

CHAPTER XXVII.

I. Injunction Suits.

§ 355. Grounds of injunction.—The circumstances under which relief by injunction will be granted, belong rather to the topic of equity jurisprudence than to that of equity procedure. The Virginia Code[1] enumerates a large number of instances in which injunctions may issue—most of these declaratory of the unwritten law.

1. *Venue of Injunction Suits.*

§ 356. Venue of injunction suits.—The Virginia statute[2] provides that "jurisdiction of a bill for an injunction of (1) any *judgment or judicial proceeding* shall be in the court in which the judgment was rendered, or such proceeding is pending"—with special provisions for injunctions against judgments of justices of the peace or proceedings before them; and (2) "jurisdiction of an injunction to *any other act or proceeding* shall be in the circuit court of the county, or the circuit, corporation or other court of the city having chancery jurisdiction, in which the act or proceeding is to be done, or is doing, or apprehended."

A later section[3] also provides that every order granting a temporary injunction, shall be directed to the clerk of the court *having jurisdiction under the section quoted.*

That is to say, the statute classifies bills for injunction into two categories, viz. (1) Those directed against *judgments or judicial proceedings;* and (2) Those directed against *some other act or proceeding.* By judicial interpretation[4] another class exists, viz.: (3) Bills for equitable relief, in which the injunction sought is *ancillary only* to the ultimate relief invoked.

§ 357. The same—statute applicable to pure bills only.—It is settled that where the injunction is not the only object

---

[1] *Passim*—see title *Injunctions* in index, and ch. 266.
[2] Va. Code 1919, § 6318.
[3] § 6321.
[4] See *infra*, next section.

of the suit, but is merely ancillary to other equitable relief (class 3 above)—*e. g.* to enjoin the negotiation of a promissory note, and to have the same cancelled for fraud; or in a divorce suit to prohibit the defendant from disposing of his estate, so that it may be forthcoming to satisfy a decree for alimony—the statute has no application. The court having acquired jurisdiction to administer the main equitable relief sought, has jurisdiction for all purposes necessary to complete relief, including the injunction as ancillary thereto. Here, it is not the prayer for *injunction* that confers the jurisdiction, but the *ultimate relief* sought.[5]

§ 358. The same—statute mandatory, or directory only?—Having eliminated the third class of injunction suits, as set out in the last section but one, and having determined, in the last preceding section, that the statute embraces *pure bills* of injunction only—*e. g.* to abate a nuisance, to enjoin trespass or waste, or picketing or other interference with plaintiff's employees by strikers, etc.—question arises whether the statute is *jurisdictional,* and therefore *mandatory,* or whether its provisions affect the *venue only,* and are therefore *directory,* and pleadable only in abatement.

As jurisdiction to award injunctions is one of the most ancient of the prerogatives of courts of equity, these courts are no more in need of special statutory authority to exercise that jurisdiction than they are of special authority to grant equitable relief in other instances under the general equity jurisdiction—as specific performance, enforcement and protection of trusts, and the multitude of other instances in which the equity jurisdiction is exercised — a jurisdiction confirmed to these courts by general jurisdictional statutes.[6] In thus designating the courts of particular localities for the trial and determination of injunction suits, it was scarcely the purpose of the statute to confer (an already inherent) jurisdiction, but rather, it would seem, in spite of its somewhat mandatory language, merely to conserve the convenience of the parties, in analogy to the gen-

---

[5] Winston *v.* Midlothian, etc., Co., 20 Gratt. 696; Muller *v.* Bayly, 21 Gratt. 521; *infra,* n. 8.

[6] Va. Code 1919, §§ 5890, 5910. See Moore *v.* N. & W. R. Co., 124 Va. 628.

eral statutes of venue.[7]   In other words, the specific localities
mentioned are merely cumulative, and are but extensions of the
general statutory provisions for venue of judicial proceedings.
This conclusion is strengthened by the familiar principle that
an additional remedy or mode of procedure for the exercise of
an already existing right or jurisdiction is, in absence of re-
strictive language, to be interpreted as cumulative, and not as
exclusive of existing remedies or practice.

These considerations warrant the conclusion that the statutory designation of specific localities in which suits for injunctions are to be instituted and heard, is directory and not mandatory—and is to be interpreted as authorizing an additional
venue, and not as conferring or limiting equitable *jurisdiction*
of injunction suits.

If this be true, then the objection that the suit is instituted in
some county or corporation beyond the venue specifically designated, may be raised, if at all, only by plea in abatement; and if
the venue be proper under the general statutes of venue, even a
plea in abatement will be ineffective.[8]

---

[7] Va. Code 1919, §§ 6049-6050.

[8] For observations on the confusion wrought by the numerous
senses in which the term "jurisdiction" has been used, as well as for
the distinction between *"jurisdiction"* and *"venue,"* see *ante*, chs. ii, iv.
The question discussed in this section has made difficulty for the Virginia courts for more than three-fourths of a century, and it is re-
grettable that the revisors of the Code of 1919 did not purge the
statute of the long-standing ambiguity. In Randolph's Ex'r *v.* Tucker,
10 Leigh 655 (interesting as involving the testamentary capacity of
John Randolph of Roanoke), the court held, practically without discussion, that the statute limited the jurisdiction to the county in which
the judgment sought to be enjoined had been entered—and therefore
that the statute was jurisdictional. The case was not one of a pure
bill of injunction, but the injunction was ancillary. This ruling, so
far as it applies to *ancillary* injunctions, has been over-ruled, in later
cases, as will appear. In Beckley *v.* Palmer, 11 Gratt. 625—another
case for injunction and relief—on full discussion, a similar ruling
was announced, with some dissent; but, apparently unwilling to rest
the decision on that ground, the court held that the bill was without
equity; and, instead of dismissing the bill, for lack of jurisdiction (as
must have been done if jurisdiction were absent) the decree of the
lower court was amended, with directions to dismiss. As the bill
was without equity, there was no occasion to pass upon the jurisdictional question, and the ruling may fairly be characterized as *obiter*.
This decision has likewise been disapproved, as will appear, so far
as it was applied to a suit for *injunction and relief*. Later in Winston
v. Midlothian, etc., Co., 20 Gratt. 686, it was held (without discussion)

2. *Temporary Injunctions.*

§ 359. Preliminary injunctions—"restraining orders."
—Distinction is sometimes made between a preliminary (or temporary) *injunction* and a *restraining order*—the latter contemplating a less extended stay than the former, and resorted to only in cases of great emergency. The *restraining order* is usually limited to a very brief period fixed in the order, and the plaintiff is required in the meantime to give notice to the defendant of his intention, within the period named in the order, to apply for a temporary injunction.[9]

§ 360. The same—notice.—By the unwritten law, the question whether the defendant is entitled to notice of the application for a preliminary injunction rests in the sound discretion of the court or judge to whom the application is made. Whether such notice should or should not be required depends on the special circumstances of each case. Justice requires that

---

that the statute was inapplicable where the injunction was *ancillary* to other relief. In Muller *v.* Bayly, 21 Gratt. 521—another case of *ancillary* injunction—the question was considered at some length by Moncure, P. (who had concurred in the opinion in Beckley *v.* Palmer, *supra*). It was held that as the injunction was ancillary only, the statute was inapplicable. The court was not content, however, to place the decision on the narrower ground, but proceeded to place it on the broad ground that whether the case was one of a *pure* bill or of an *ancillary* bill of injunction, the statutory provisions were subject to waiver by the parties—and hence were not jurisdictional, since jurisdiction, cannot be conferred by consent. The opinion clearly indicates disapproval of the ruling in Beckley *v.* Palmer (*supra*). In N. & W. R. Co. *v.* Postal Tel. Co., 88 Va. 932, 936 (2 cases), the question arose for the first time in connection with a *pure bill* of injunction, where the venue was not in accordance with the statute. But as both cases were disposed of on a motion to dissolve a temporary injunction, as *improvidently awarded*, the question neither of venue nor of jurisdiction was involved, though the court took occasion to say (without discussion) that the error in the selection of the court was fatal to the maintenance of the suit. In Statham *v.* Blackford, 89 Va. 771—a case of mandamus, under a somewhat similar statute— three of the five judges held that the statute was waived by failure to plead in abatement, and hence that the statute was one of *venue* only. In Baker *v.* Briggs, 99 Va. 360—a suit for injunction and relief— the statute is only quoted in sustaining the ruling that as the suit was brought in the county where the act to be enjoined was threatened, the venue was proper.

[9] Provision is made for such restraining orders (*sub nom. injunction*) by Va. Code 1919, § 6317, with sundry provisions for enlarging or vacating them. Equity Rule 73 makes like provision for such orders in the Federal courts. See next section.

notice should be given; if practicable, and the emergency permits; but if there be reason to apprehend that by being put on notice of the application the defendant will be able to defeat, and probably will defeat, the very purpose for which the injunction is sought, notice will not be required. The Federal Equity Rule, quoted in the section following, seems a concise and accurate statement of the unwritten rule.

The question of notice in such cases is regulated in many states by statute. In Virginia the statute is but declaratory of the unwritten law.[10]

§ 361. The same—in the Federal courts—notice.— The Federal courts are prohibited from granting a *'preliminary injunction'* without notice to the opposite party.[11] But a temporary *'restraining order'* may be granted without notice, where it "clearly appears from specific facts, shown by affidavit or by the verified bill, that immediate and irreparable loss or damage will result to the applicant before the matter can be heard on notice." In such case "the matter shall be made returnable at the earliest possible time, and *in no event later than ten days* from the date of the order." The opposite party, on two days' notice to the adversary, may appear and move the dissolution or modification of the order.[12]

§ 362. The same—affidavit to bill.— The Virginia statute,[13] which seems in this respect but declaratory of the unwritten law, forbids the awarding of an injunction in any case not ready for hearing, "unless the court or judge be satisfied, by *affidavit or otherwise,* of the plaintiff's equity." That is to say, the allegations of the bill must be sustained *prima facie,* either by affidavit or other sufficient evidence.

§ 363. The same—jurisdiction to award.— In Virginia, preliminary injunctions, even in vacation, may be awarded by the judge of any circuit or corporation court, or of a city court

---

[10] Notice may be required "if in the opinion of the court or judge it be proper that such notice shold be given." Va. Code 1919, § 6322.
[11] Equity Rule 73.
[12] Id.
[13] Va. Code 1919, § 6322.

having chancery jurisdiction, in the state—regardless of the locality of the controversy or the residence of the parties.[14]

But it should be observed that while the plaintiff in the bill may thus secure his temporary injunction, or restraining order, from any equity judge in any one of the more than one hundred counties and cities in the state, the *maturing and hearing of the cause on its merits,* is by the statute assigned to a *particular venue,* as shown in preceding sections. This means that the order awarding the temporary injunction by a judge beyond the circuit, is directed to the clerk of the court of the proper *venue,* where the suit is, or is to be, instituted, and where the case is eventually to be tried on its merits.[15]

§ 364. Original jurisdiction in judges of Court of Appeals to award injunctions.—The Virginia statute [16] provides that where a circuit or corporation court, or other court of chancery, or a judge thereof, shall refuse to award an injunction, or shall dissolve or refuse to enlarge it, application may be made on the original papers, with a copy of the proceedings in court and with the judge's order of refusal, to *a judge of the court of appeals,* who may thereupon award the injunction. Such order, when awarded by the appellate judge, is directed to *the clerk of the lower court,* of the proper *venue;* and thereafter "the proceedings thereupon shall be as if the order had been made by such (lower) court or the judge thereof." [17]

§ 365. The same—address of bill.—Before applying for the temporary injunction, counsel must consider and decide in

---

[14] Va. Code 1919, § 6319. See *Receivers, post,* ch. xxxii.

[15] Va. Code 1919, § 6321.

[16] Va. Code 1919. § 6320. This statute does not impair the ordinary course of appeals where injunctions are refused, or dissolved, in cases matured and heard on the merits. French *v.* Chapin-Sachs Mfg. Co., 118 Va. 117.

[17] Id. § 6321. The effect of this statute was the subject of a somewhat acrimonious discussion by the majority and minority of the judges in Wilder *v.* Kelley, 88 Va. 274. The dissenting opinion of Lewis, P. (concurred in by Fauntleroy, J.), seems the only possible interpretation, *viz.* that when the appellate judge grants the injunction he acts *not in an appellate capacity,* but as the judge of another court of co-ordinate jurisdiction; and therefore the preliminary injunction so awarded may be dissolved by the judge of the lower court, on preliminary motion in vacation. This seems plain from the language of the statute.

what particular court and *venue* the suit is to be instituted. Regardless of the circumstances that application for the order is to be made to a judge beyond the circuit, the bill should be addressed to the *judge of the court of the proper venue,* and not to the particular judge from whom, in the first instance, the injunction is sought. In the latter instance, as well as in that where application is to a resident judge, presentation of the bill in person, accompanied by an informal oral motion or request— or, if by mail, an informal letter accompanying the bill—is sufficient.

§ 366. The injunction order—preparation. — Counsel should not expect the judge or court to prepare the desired order, but should himself carefully frame the order desired, and should present the same, along with the bill, at the time of the application.[18]

§ 367. The same—indemnifying bond.—The practice of all chancery courts, as a condition precedent to the granting of a temporary injunction, is to require that the plaintiff, or some one for him, shall execute, before the clerk of the court, a bond, with good security, in a penalty fixed by the court, conditioned to indemnify the defendant against all loss or damage which may be incurred by the defendant in case the injunction shall be dissolved.[19]

§ 368. Preliminary injunction—how served. — Where the injunction is granted before service of the *subpœna,* as may be done in a proper case, a copy of the order is generally endorsed on or attached to the *subpœna,* and served by the sheriff along with the *subpœna,* the clerk certifying thereon that the required bond has been executed. If issued after *subpœna* served, the order is served like any other process.

3. Bill to Enjoin Legal Proceedings.

§ 369. Bill to enjoin proceedings at law—requiring confession of judgment.—Where defendant at law files a bill

---

[18] For form, see *Appendix.*

[19] This practice is confirmed by the Virginia statute (Code § 6324), except as to personal representatives or other persons from whom, in the opinion of the court, it may be improper to require bond.

in equity to enjoin proceedings at law, the court may put him on terms of *confessing judgment at law,* as the price of its assistance. This is largely a matter of judicial discretion.

§ 370. The same — (a) when such confession required.—In such case, if it appear from plaintiff's bill that the defendant (plaintiff at law) is entitled to a judgment at law, and that the equity-plaintiff (defendant at law) has a valid defense, but available *in equity only,* then on the latter's application for a preliminary injunction against the proceeding at law, fairness to the equity-defendant requires that the equity-plaintiff shall *confess judgment at law*—subject, of course, to the control of the court in the injunction proceedings.

Here, if the plaintiff in equity succeeds in making out his equitable defense at the equity-hearing, the court will enter a perpetual injunction against the judgment so confessed, and no harm will have resulted from the confession. If, on the other hand, the equity-plaintiff *fails to make out his equitable defense* at the hearing—thus calling for a dissolution of the injunction and a dismissal of the bill—the confession of judgment, previously required, saves the plaintiff at law from harm by reason of the injunction; since not only are further proceedings at law unnecessary, but the plaintiff at law is left where he would have been had the injunction not interfered, namely, with a judgment in his favor.

Here the court has merely applied the maxim that "he who wants equity must do equity." It has required the equity-plaintiff, as the price of its assistance, to put his adversary in a position where as little harm as possible will result from the preliminary injunction, in case it finally be dissolved.

§ 371. The same—(b) when confession not required.—But where the defense is *not equitable only*—where the plaintiff in equity *denies his adversary's right to recover in any forum, legal or equitable,* and the application for relief in equity is only because, under all the circumstances, equity is a more appropriate tribunal in which to conduct the litigation, then no such terms as a confession of judgment ought to be exacted of the equity-plaintiff as the price of the court's assistance; since this might *imperil his legal defense,* in case he should fail to make out his equitable defense at the hearing, and therefore be remitted to his legal defense. In other words, it "would not be safe," as the courts express it, to require a confession in such case.

§ 372. The same, continued.—The peril to the defendant at law here arises from the fact that by the confession at law, he waives his legal defense—the confessed judgment being a finality in the law court—and the defendant must, therefore, stake his *entire defense* on the *equitable* relief demanded. Should this fail, he is left without any defense, though he may have had a good defense at law. *Without* such confession of judgment, should the relief in equity fail, he is relegated to the legal defense, which is still open to him.

It is error, therefore, in such case, to require a confession of judgment. But where such confession has been erroneously required by the lower court, and the bill is subsequently dismissed and the injunction dissolved for want of equity, the court should dissolve the injunction only *on condition that the plaintiff at law withdraw his judgment and consent to re-open the case* and to reinstate it on the docket, so as to give the defendant at law opportunity to try the case in the law court, on its merits. And where the lower court refuses to do this, the decree will be reversed on appeal, and a proper decree to that effect entered by the appellate court. This was done in the case first cited.[20]

And even where the injunction order does not require a confession of judgment, yet, if the confession of judgment and the injunction are entered on the same day, the court of appeals will presume that the judgment was confessed, subject to the result of the equity proceeding.[21]

4. *Motions to Dissolve.*

§ 373. Motions to dissolve preliminary injunctions— in vacation.—As the plaintiff may, in a proper case, obtain a preliminary injunction in term or in vacation, so the *defendant* has the like privilege, after reasonable notice to the adverse

---

[20] Great Falls Mfg. Co. *v.* Henry, 25 Gratt. 575; Dudley *v.* Miner, 93 Va. 408.

[21] Staples *v.* Turner, 25 Gratt. 336. As to the jurisdiction in equity to enjoin a judgment at law on the ground of newly discovered evidence, and the practice in such cases, see Wynne *v.* Newman, 75 Va. 811; Pickford *v.* Talbott, 225 U. S. 651, 56 L. Ed. 1240, n; 21 L. R. A. 747 n: Llle, Notes on Eq. Jurisp. (ed. 1921). p. 246.

party, of moving to *dissolve,* in term or in vacation, and before the cause is matured for hearing.[22]

And, again, as the plaintiff may secure the injunction on *ex parte affidavits*—and may offer supplementary affidavits to sustain the allegations of his bill, in opposition to defendant's motion to dissolve—so the defendant, on his motion to dissolve, may be heard on *counter-affidavits.* In such case, the defendant may use his sworn answer as an affidavit—but *only as an affidavit,* since the cause not having been matured, the answer, on the motion to dissolve, whether oath be waived in the bill or not, is not read as a *pleading,* nor as having the evidentiary value of a sworn answer under the original equity practice.[23]

§ 374. The same—effect of dissolution on the pending suit.—Where the injunction is thus dissolved on a preliminary motion, the result is, of course, no more final than was the *granting* of the injunction *in limine.* A hearing at this stage, before the cause has matured, and before the parties have had opportunity of presenting the complete testimony in the form of depositions of witnesses, in nowise disposes of the question of the injunction *on its merits.* Hence, the order of dissolution, or the refusal to dissolve, may later, on a full hearing after the cause has ripened for trial, be rescinded by the court. The order, therefore, is not final; and though the bill be a pure bill of injunction, and the injunction be dissolved, the court or judge may not, at that stage of the proceeding, dismiss the bill.[24]

But, equally of course, where the injunction is dissolved after the cause is matured, and *after a hearing on the merits,* the order presents the same degree of finality as any other decree entered under similar circumstances. That is to say, if the case be a pure bill of injunction, an order dissolving the injunction will necessarily call for a dismissal of the bill.[25] If on the other hand, the injunction be *ancillary only,* the order will dispose of the injunction, but the suit will proceed in other aspects.[26] So here, a refusal to dissolve, will normally result in a decree either continuing, enlarging or perpetuating the injunction.

---

[22] Id. § 6326; Equity Rules 1, 73.

[23] But where the motion is heard on bill and answer only, the answer is conclusive. See *Answers as Evidence, ante,* ch. xvi.

[24] Mount *v.* Radford Trust Co., 93 Va. 427.

[25] See Va. Code 1919, § 6328.

[26] Pulliam *v.* Winston, 5 Leigh 324.

CHAPTER XXVIII.

II. Partition of Estates.

§ 375. Equitable jurisdiction.[1] — The more convenient remedy afforded in equity for making partition of real property[2] has practically superseded the former proceeding at law.

§ 376. Procedure.—The procedure in partition suits is by ordinary bill in equity, though to some extent regulated by statute.[3]

1. *Venue.*

§ 377. Venue of suit.—Suit may be brought in any court of general equity jurisdiction in the county or corporation *wherein the land or any part of it lies.*[4]

§ 378. The same—statutory venue mandatory or directory?—The question whether the provision of the statute[5] declaring that "any court having general jurisdiction of the county or corporation *wherein the estate, or any part thereof, is,* shall have jurisdiction in cases of partition," prescribes a *venue* that is *jurisdictional,* and therefore mandatory and of the essence of the proceeding, or is merely *auxiliary to the general statutes of venue,*[6] and therefore to be objected to only by plea in abatement, seems not to have been adjudicated. In preceding chapters[7] the distinction between technical *jurisdiction* and *venue* has been considered, and the confusion resulting from the use of these two expressions as if interchangeable, has been adverted to.

---

[1] Consult Virginia Code 1919, ch. 214, and revisors' valuable annotations; Freeman, Co-tenancy.

[2] The statute makes provision also for the partition in equity of *goods and chattels*—by sale if necessary. Va. Code 1919, § 5286.

[3] See Va. Code 1919, ch. 214.

[4] Id. § 5279. Equity will not take jurisdiction of suits for partition of lands *in another state.* Pillow *v.* Southwest, etc., Co., 92 Va. 144, reported, with note by Judge Burks, in 1 Va. Law Reg. 663.

[5] Va. Code 1919, § 5279.

[6] Id. §§ 6049-6050.

[7] Chs. ii, iv. See also *supra,* §§ 356-358, where the same question is discussed in connection with *Injunction Suits.*

§ 379. The same—venue continued. — As partition of real property *in kind* is an ancient heritage of equity, and exists independently of statute, a statute merely declaring the jurisdiction, and naming the particular locality in which it is to be exercised, would on principles heretofore considered [8] be declared directory only; and error in the *venue* could be availed of only by a plea in abatement.

But the Virginia statute quoted, very much enlarges the original equity jurisdiction here, and confers new powers—some of which were previously non-existent in any court, and others the exclusive prerogative of courts of law. The right of a co-tenant to an *enforced sale* for partition, where partition in kind is impracticable, is a new right created by the statute.[9] So the broad powers conferred to deal with *questions of legal title* in such proceedings, constitute a very radical extension of the equity jurisdiction.[10]

This being true, and according to the principle heretofore discussed,[11] that where new rights are created by statute, and a special procedure is prescribed for its exercise—thus constituting the jurisdiction a special and limited one—the *remedy* becomes an adjunct of the *right,* and is therefore of the essence of its enjoyment, the provision here with reference to the venue of suits for partition would seem to be jurisdictional; and therefore error in the venue will be fatal to the validity of the proceeding.

The court has practically so held, where the decree directed a *sale* for partition—as being a new statutory right.[12] But the same result should follow even where the suit does not contemplate the exercise of the extended jurisdiction, but is a simple suit for partition in kind, with no question of legal title presented. It would seem that the several provisions of the statute are too closely interwoven to enable the court to declare that a portion of the jurisdiction expressed therein may be ex-

---

[8] *Ante*, chs. ii, iv.
[9] See Roberts *v.* Hagan, 121 Va. 573.
[10] Stuart's Heirs *v.* Coalter, 4 Rand. 74, 15 Am. Dec. 731; Straughan *v.* Wright, 4 Rand. 493; Seefried *v.* Clark, 113 Va. 365; Phillips *v.* Dulaney, 114 Va. 681; Bailey *v.* Johnson, 118 Va. 505.
[11] *Ante*, chs. ii, iv.
[12] Roberts *v.* Hagan, 121 Va. 573.

ercised under the *general* statutes of *venue*, while other portions
are to be exercised only within the narrow *venue* prescribed by
the *special statute*.[13]

This conclusion is stengthened by the consideration that partition proceedings are peculiarly *in rem* and local in their nature; and by the further consideration that whether the proceedings will result in partition in kind (under the general equity jurisdiction), or in a sale of the whole or of a part of the *res* (under the statutory jurisdiction), with partition in kind of the residue, are normally questions to be judicially determined in the course of the proceedings, whereas the existence of *jurisdiction* confronts the court and litigants at the very inception of the suit, and, if challenged, must be decided *in limine*.

2. *Parties.*

§ 380. By whom suit brought.—The statute[14] declares that *"tenants in common, joint tenants* and *co-parceners* shall be compellable to make partition; and a *lien creditor* of any owner of undivided estate in real estate may also compel partition for the purpose of subjecting the estate of his debtor, or the rents and profits hereof, to the satisfaction of his lien."* A life-tenant of one moiety, with remainder over, may maintain a bill for partition of the entire estate,[15] and a guardian may maintain such a suit on behalf of his ward.[16]

§ 381. Partition in kind—necessary parties—consort of co-tenant.—The question of necessary parties to partition

---

[13] See *supra*, n. 10. The principle applicable to the special statutory and limited jurisdiction, are again considered in connection with *Suits for Divorce, post*, ch. xxix, and *Suits for Sale of Infants' Lands, post*, ch. xxx.

[14] Va. Code 1919, § 5279.

[15] Carneal *v.* Lynch, 91 Va. 114, 50 Am. St. Rep. 819.

[16] Zirkle *v.* McCue, 26 Gratt. 517. So plaintiff with legal title to the whole, but co-tenant of the equitable title with others, may have partition: Hogan *v.* Taylor, 110 Va. 9. And on a bill for dower by the widow of a testator, one of the devisees may by *cross-bill* assert the right to partition among the several devisees, and a sale if necessary, after assignment of dower: Kavanaugh *v.* Shacklett, 111 Va. 423. But where the plaintiff is not a co-tenant with the defendant—as where the defendant is in possession claiming the whole estate, and plaintiff claims an undivided interest through a wholly *different source of title* (a grant from the commonwealth)—a bill for partition will not lie, but the remedy is in ejectment. Preston *v.* Va. Mining Co., 107 Va. 245. See *post*, § 388.

suits will depend somewhat on the ultimate outcome contemplated. Of course every person having or claiming an interest in the estate is a necessary party. If the estate is to be *divided in kind,* clearly no interest of the consort of any co-tenant will be affected. On consummation of the partition, the contingent marital right of curtesy or dower, formerly attached to the *undivided* interest, will, by mere force of the partition, attach to the parcel in *severalty.*

§ 382. The same—lien creditors.—So, likewise, if there be *separate liens* or other charges on the undivided interest of any co-tenant, such lien or charge will *ex proprio vigore* follow the parcel assigned to the debtor-cotenant in severalty. Hence such lienors need not be made parties, unless their substantial interests are sought to be affected, in which case, if not made parties in the bill, they may intervene by petition.[16a]

On the other hand, if there be a *paramount* charge on the estate, or any part of it—as, for example, dower in the widow of the ancestor or grantor, or a mortgage by all the cotenants or their predecessor in title—the widow in the one case, or such paramount mortgagee in the other, should be made a party for the assignment of dower or the liquidation of the mortgage, as the case may be, and partition made of the residue.[17]

§ 383. Sale for partition—parties, continued—lienors.—Where, because of inconvenience or impossibility of making partition in kind, the estate is to be *sold,* the question of parties becomes more important, for courts of equity are averse in any case to selling real property otherwise than *free of liens;* and in order that there may be a sale free of liens, all lienors must become parties to the suit. Such lienors should therefore be made parties to the bill, or otherwise brought into the suit—as by rule, or voluntary petition, or under an order of reference to a master—before the decree of sale.[18]

§ 384. The same—consort of co-tenant.—On similar prinicples it would seem that where a sale is contemplated, the

---

[16a]. Wright *v.* Wright, 76 Va. 857.

[17] Custis *v.* Snead, 12 Gratt. 260.

[18] The statute makes provision for securing the rights of lien creditors: Va. Code 1919, § 5281. See Moon *v.* Highland Development Co., 104 Va. 551; *supra,* § 382.

consort of a co-tenant should be made a party, so as to bar the contingent marital right. But it appears to be a settled principle that where the statute permits a sale for partition, such contingent marital interests of dower and curtesy, *by mere force of the statute,* are divested by the sale, even though the consort be not a party to the proceeding [19]—and this rule is made statutory in Virginia.[20]

3. *Lessees and Alienees.*

§ 385. Leases or alienations by one co-tenant.—Where one co-tenant has aliened his own undivided interest, or any part of it, such alienee will, of course, be made a party to the suit, and proper allotment made.

So where there is a valid, *paramount lease* of all the interests, in the entire estate, or in some definite portion thereof, the partition or sale must be made subject to the lessee's rights.[21] But since no one co-tenant can, without a proper agency, by his sole act of lease or alienation of the whole, or any definite portion, by metes and bounds, affect either the substantial rights of his fellows or their right of partition (in kind or by sale), it follows that any alienee or lessee of such co-tenant can claim no greater right than his grantor or lessor; and although such alienee or lessee should properly be made a party to the suit, the partition or sale may be made as if such alienation or lease had not been made,[22] but subject to the qualification stated in the following section.

§ 386. The same—by metes and bounds.—Any co-tenant who is *sui juris* may, of course, alien his *undivided* interest, or any part thereof, as freely as if his portion had been allotted to him in severalty. But since one co-tenant may not, without consent of all, or without proper judicial sanction, claim any part of the common estate in severalty by metes and bounds,

---

[19] In analogy to condemnation proceedings. The question is well discussed in Lee *v.* Lindell, 22 Mo. 202, 64 Am. Dec. 262, and Weaver *v.* Gregg, 6 Ohio St. 547, 67 Am. Dec. 355. See Freeman, Co-tenancy 411, 474.

[20] Va. Code 1919, § 5281. The cases in the preceding foot note, apply the rule to the *wife* only—but, by analogy, it must be equally applicable to the husband's inchoate curtesy.

[21] Id. § 5285; Lucy *v.* Kelly, 117 Va. 318.

[22] Phillips *v.* Dulaney, 114 Va. 681; Stark *v.* Barrett, 15 Cal. 370.

manifestly he may not alien thus in severalty to another so as to pass to his grantee any greater rights in the premises than he himself had. It follows, therefore, that no such conveyance in severalty, by metes and bounds, will be recognized to the prejudice of the other co-tenants. But such a conveyance (according to the better authority) will pass an equity to the grantee, which a court of chancery will respect, so far as this can be done without infringing the other co-tenants' rights. Where such alienee (or one co-tenant himself) has in good faith taken possession of a separate portion and made improvements, the court, in estimating in partition proceedings the value of the entire tract, will exclude the value of the improvements made; and, further, with due precaution for justice to all parties, will assign the severed parcel, with the improvements thereon, to the improving co-tenant, or his grantee. This is eminently equitable, in that it prevents the unjust enrichment of one person at the expense of another.[23]

It necessarily follows that a suit for partition of the *aliened* parcel only, may not be maintained by the other co-tenants against the alienee in severalty, since the equities of the latter can only be worked out in partition proceedings affecting the entire original holding.[24]

4. *Other Relief—Questions of Legal Title.*

§ 387. Combining partition with other relief.—Under the liberal provisions of the Virginia statute, the appellate court has held that *assignment of dower* may properly be united with a prayer for *partition*, whether the two purposes be sought in

---

[23] Dennis *v.* Dennis, 116 Va. 619. Where such conveyances in severalty have been followed by sub-alienations, in parcels, of the portion thus attempted to be severed, the equities of the parties are apt to become highly complicated. See such a case in Highland Park Mfg. Co. *v.* Steele, 235 Fed. 465—the opinion in which, by Connor, J., will be found enlightening on the general subject of alienations in severalty by co-tenants. See further: Freeman, Co-tenancy, 199 *et seq;* id. 465; Boggess *v.* Meredith, 16 W. Va. 29; Young *v.* Edwards, 33 S. C. 404, 11 S. E. 1066, 10 L. R. A. 55, 26 Am. St. Rep. 689.

[24] Highland Park Mfg. Co. *v.* Steele, *supra;* Bigelow *v.* Littlefield, 52 Me. 24, 83 Am. Dec. 484; Barnes *v.* Lynch, 151 Mass. 510, 24 N. E. 783, 21 Am. St. Rep. 470. See 30 Harv. Law Rev. 403.

the original bill, or the prayer for partition be presented in the cross-bill.[25]

And in a bill for partition of a trust-estate rescission of a wrongful conveyance by the trustee to one of the co-tenants, may be decreed.[26]

§ 388. Trying questions of legal title in partition suit. —The Virginia statute [27] declares that the court "in the exercise of such jurisdiction may take cognizance of *all questions of law affecting the legal title* that may arise in any [such] proceedings, between such tenants in common, joint tenants, co-parceners and lien creditors."

This provision has been construed by the courts in most liberal spirit. While it is held that the right to a jury trial, on purely legal questions, cannot be taken away by extending the equitable jurisdiction, and hence that a partition suit may not be substituted for *ejectment* at law,[27a] yet that if the suit be *properly one for partition,* the court having jurisdiction for one purpose may proceed to give *complete relief,* even in matters of purely legal right. Thus, in Pillow *v.* Southwest, etc., Co.,[28] followed in Morgan *v.* Haley,[29] it is held that if defendant, though *in adverse possession of the whole estate,* is one who, in his own person or through his predecessors in title, was *once a joint owner with the plaintiff,* or with his predecessors in title, the whole question of the legal as well as the equitable rights of the parties may be threshed out in the partition proceeding.

Nor is jurisdiction of a suit in which the bill sets out a case proper for partition, ousted, and the suit subject to dismissal on a preliminary motion, by the filing of defendant's answer, setting up complete ownership and possession in himself, by title

---

[25] Kavanaugh *v.* Shacklett, 111 Va. 423. See Carneal *v.* Lynch, 91 Va. 114. *Supra,* § 306, n.

[26] Seefried *v.* Clarke, 113 Va. 365. See also Laurel Creek, etc., Co. *v.* Browning, 99 Va. 5—a suit for cancellation of lease and for partition.

[27] Code 1919, § 5279.

[27a] Preston *v.* Va. Mining Co., 107 Va. 245.

[28] 92 Va. 144—reported, with an instructive note by Judge Burks, in 1 Va. Law Reg. 663.

[29] 107 Va. 331.

hostile to that through which the plaintiff claims, and not derived from a common source.[30]

5. *Partition in Kind.*

§ 389. The partition—where divisible in kind.—If the property be divisible in kind, any co-owner has the right to insist that *the partition be so made.* The majority of the co-owners in such case may not insist on a sale against the will of any of their fellows.[31]

[31] Custis *v.* Snead, 12 Gratt. 260; Howery *v.* Helms, 20 Gratt. 1.

§390. Partition in kind—how made.—The primary question in every suit for partition is *whether a division in kind is practicable or not.* That such a division is, or is not, practicable may be apparent from the character of the property as described in the pleadings. But where the question is not thus settled, it is usual to have an order of reference to special commissioners named by the court—usually three or five,[32] and generally nominated by the parties—to ascertain whether a partition in kind be convenient and practicable, looking to the best interest of all the parties, or whether their interests will be promoted by a sale, in whole or in part; and if partition be found practicable, to report to the court a scheme for dividing the estate as equally as possible among the several owners, according to their respective

---

[30] Goodman *v.* Goodman, 124 Va. 579. The real point decided here is, that where the bill states a case proper for the jurisdiction of equity, the bill may not be dismissed *on preliminary motion* of defendant, on the filing of his answer, though the answer sets up facts which if true, ought to defeat the jurisdiction. The motion was clearly premature. Doubtless, if at the final hearing, the defendant had established the allegations of his answer by proof, the suit must have been dismissed, as clearly the plaintiff's remedy would be at law, in ejectment, and not in equity under the guise of relief in partition proceedings.

The cases of Litz *v.* Rowe, 117 Va. and Bailey *v.* Johnson, 118 Va. 505, are distinguishable, in that these represented efforts on the part of petitioners, not parties to the bill, to assert, by intervention in a partition suit, a hostile title, not derived from a common source. See in this connection, Preston *v.* Va. Mining Co., 107 Va. 245.

In setting out the title in a partition bill, under which the plaintiff asserts a relation of co-tenancy with the defendants, there need be no formal deraignment of title, provided the bill fairly indicates the relation and how produced. Goodman *v.* Goodman, *supra.*

[32] But this may be done through reference to a single master, if the court see fit, and no injustice appears. Phillips *v.* Dulany, 114 Va. 681. See Cummingham *v.* Johnson, 116 Va. 610.

interests. Equality here connotes not equality of *area,* or of acreage, but of *value.*

Subject to the approval of the court the commissioners may *assign* the designated parcels to the parties, respectively, or may fix the designation by *lot.*[33]

§ 391. The same—the commissioners—procedure. — The commissioners are generally required by the order to be first sworn to perform their duties impartially. They are required to go upon the lands to be divided, and are usually authorized by the court to employ a competent surveyor to lay off, by metes and bounds, the several parcels, making due provision, in the case of agricultural property, for wood and water, and for rights of way and other necessary easements and conveniences, and to prepare a plat accurately indicating the location and description of each parcel. On the coming in of the report, the court will enter such decree as seems best for the interests of all parties.

§ 392. The same continued—modified partition—owelty.—Where the property is not susceptible of partition into parcels of precisely equal value, the court may direct a sale of part and partition of the residue; or inequality in the values of the several shares may be compensated by charging the more valuable parcels with a lien for a designated sum (*"owelty of partition"*) in favor of those of less value.[34] The shares of two or more of the co-tenants may be laid off together if they so desire.[35]

6. *Making Title.*

§ 393. How title made to the several parcels in partition proceedings—(1) in case of co-parceners.—By the unwritten law, on partition by *co-parceners,* even by parol, legal title to the several parcels is said to vest in the parties *without mutual conveyances*—the effect of the partition being merely to designate the parcels, and upon such designation title flows direct from the ancestor. Hence, in partition proceedings in equity, the decree was, and still is, itself sufficient, without mutual conveyances.[36]

---

[33] Cox *v.* McMullin, 14 Gratt. 82.
[34] Va. Code 1919, § 5280.
[35] Id.
[36] Bolling *v.* Teel, 76 Va. 487; Wright *v.* Johnson, 108 Va. 855. See Freeman, Co-tenancy, 397-400.

§ 394. The same—(2) in case of other co-tenants.—
In order to vest legal title in severalty in the several co-tenants
who are *not co-parceners,* by the unwritten law voluntary partition must have been consummated by *mutual conveyances.*
And since the decree of a court of chancery cannot *ex proprio
vigore* vest or divest legal title, a decree for partition must have
been consummated by like conveyances, either by the parties
or by a master acting in that behalf.[37]

§ 395. The same—statutory title.—To avoid the expense and inconvenience of mutual conveyances, the Virginia
statute declares that the decree of partition shall vest in the respective co-owners, the titles to their shares "in like manner and
to the same extent as if the said decree ordered such title to be
conveyed to them and the conveyance was made accordingly." [38]
The statute is in terms retrospective.

7. Partition Impracticable—Sale.

§ 396. Partition by sale.—Where neither a complete nor
a modified partition in kind can conveniently be made, having
due regard to the circumstances of each parcel and the interest
of all parties, the court may, under statutory authority, as
shown, decree a sale of the entire estate, and a division of the
proceeds among the several co-owners.[39]

As already pointed out,[40] by the unwritten law a sale for partition could only be had by consent of parties, and courts were
without jurisdiction to compel an involuntary sale for purpose
of partition. In exercising the statutory power, therefore, the
court must proceed in substantial conformity to the statute, as
in all other cases of statutory and limited jurisdiction.[41]

---

[37] Id.

[38] Va. Code 1919, § 5282. Provision is made by § 5216, for the
recordation of the decree. Counsel should also see that the order
directs that the report and plat be recorded. In Wright *v.* Johnson,
108 Va. 855, where the wife's parcel had been erroneously assigned
by decree to her husband, not consummated by deed, it was properly
held that legal title did not, by virtue of the statute, vest in the
husband where the wife was a *co-parcener*—since the statute was not
intended to operate to defeat an existing legal title.

[39] Id. § 5281. The whole may be allotted to one, on equitable
terms. Id.

[40] *Ante,* § 379.

[41] Roberts *v.* Hagan, 121 Va. 573. See *ante,* § 18 *et seq.*

§ 397. Disposition of proceeds—infants.—As already mentioned, the statute[42] makes careful provision for the protection of lien-creditors, and of the rights of infants and lunatics.

If the dividend of an infant or lunatic exceed $500, and be not held in trust, it is to be invested under the supervision of the court, and not paid over to the guardian or committee—but if less than $500 it may be so paid over to the guardian or committee. If held in trust, the amount, whatever it be, is paid over to the trustee, but only on his giving proper security.[43]

§ 398. The same—when and to what extent conversion occurs.—As to those who are *sui juris*, the proceeds of the sale are regarded as *personal estate* from the time of confirmation of the sale.[44] In the case of infants and lunatics, their dividends are to be regarded as *real estate* as to so much as may remain at their death intestate and incapable of making a will—in short, until death or the removal of the disability.[45]

---

[42] Va. Code 1919, § 5281. See Roberts *v.* Hagan, 121 Va. 573.
[43] Id.
[44] Id. § 5283.
[45] Id. § 5347.

CHAPTER XXIX.

III. Suits for Nullity and Divorce.[1]

§ 399. General equity jurisdiction.—The jurisdiction of divorce and matrimonial causes, originally exercised by the English ecclesiastical courts, is now very generally exercised in America by courts of equity—in some particulars by inheritance, but chiefly by virtue of express statutory enactment.[2]

§ 400. The same—in Virginia.—In Virginia the circuit and corporation courts, on the chancery side thereof, and all other courts having chancery jurisdiction, are invested by statute[3] with complete jurisdiction of suits for annulling or affirming marriages, and for divorce.

§ 401. The venue of the suit.—The statute[4] provides that the suit, whether for divorce, nullity or for affirmation of the marriage, "shall be brought in the county or corporation in which the parties last cohabited, or (at the option of the plaintiff), in the county or corporation in which the defendant resides, if a resident of this state, and if not a resident, in the county or corporation in which the plaintiff resides."

That is to say:

(1) *Where the defendant is a resident of the state*: The suit may be instituted (at the plaintiff's option) either in the county or corporation (a) where the parties *last cohabited*, or (b) where the *defendant resides*.

(2) *Where the defendant is a non-resident*: Suit is to be brought in the county or corporation of the *plaintiff's residence*.

§ 402. The same—venue jurisdictional.—As the jurisdiction of the matrimonial causes mentioned is a special statutory and limited one,[5] it would seem that such jurisdiction must

---

[1] See Va. Code 1919, ch. 205.
[2] 1 Bishop, Mar. Div. & Sep. 801-807; Blankenship *v.* Blankenship, 125 Va. 595. See Ruge *v.* Ruge (Wash.), L. R. A. 1917F, 721.
[3] Va. Code 1919, § 5105.
[4] Va. Code 1919, § 5105.
[5] *Supra,* § 400. See *Jurisdiction, ante,* ch. ii; *Venue, ante,* ch. iv.

be exercised in conformity to the statute bestowing it. In such cases, as heretofore shown, the question of venue becomes jurisdictional; with the result that not only is no plea in abatement necessary to raise the question of venue, but the bill is demurrable unless it shows on its face that the suit is instituted in the proper statutory venue. It follows that the objection cannot be waived, and the court will *mero motu* dismiss the bill when defective in this respect.[6]

§ 403. Divorce suits, continued—essentials of jurisdiction in Virginia.—It is important to observe that Virginia does not (as probably does no other state) throw wide open the doors of her equity courts to all the world seeking relief from matrimonial bonds, as in cases where ordinary equitable relief is sought. But the statute[7] conferring equitable jurisdiction of nullity and divorce suits, in terms, provides that *no nullity or divorce* suit shall be maintained in the courts of this state *"unless one of the parties has been domiciled[8] in this state for at least one year preceding the commencement of the suit"*—and no suit for *affirming a marriage,* unless one of the parties be domiciled here at the time of suit brought.

It is clear that these requirements are *jurisdictional,* and must

---

[6] Yates *v.* Yates, 115 Va. 678; Blankenship *v.* Blankenship, 125 Va. 695. In Towson *v.* Towson, 126 Va. 640, 651, 654, there are *dicta* by Burks, J., indicating that the venue here is not jurisdictional. This seems to lose sight of the rule so frequently laid down by the court, before and since, that a statutory right may be exercised only in accordance with the prescribed statutory procedure. See *ante,* chs. ii and iv; *Sale of Infant's Lands, post,* ch. xxx.

As to venue of suits for alimony without divorce, see Lang *v.* Lang (W. Va.), 73 S. E. 716, 38 L. R. A. (N. S.) 950, where it is held that the venue of such suits is not dependent on special statutes regulating divorce proceedings, but on the general statutes of venue. On the general subject of such suits for separate maintenance, see Almond *v.* Almond, 4 Rand. 662, 15 Am. Dec. 781; Lang *v.* Lang, *supra,* n. 38 L. R. A. (N. S.) 950; 7 Va. Law Reg. 219; 1 Bish. Mar. Div. & Sep. 1386 *et seq.*

[7] Va. Code 1919, § 5105.

[8] As to what constitutes domicil and the distinction between "domicil" and "residence", see Cooper *v.* Commonwealth, 121 Va. 338; Towson *v.* Towson, 126 Va. 640, 651-654, where Burks, J., points out that the statute under consideration exacts "domicil" for purpose of *jurisdiction,* but fixes "residence" as the *venue.* As there shown, one may have but one domicil at a time, but may have several residences—the latter usually connoting a much less permanent abode. The topic is treated fully in 2 Bishop, Mar. Div. & Sep., chapters iv-v.

be alleged and proved as a condition precedent to the maintenance of the suit, or to the validity of the decree.[9]

§ 404. Suit money—preliminary orders for safeguarding wife's interests.—The statute [10] invests the court, or the judge in vacation, with ample power "at any time pending the suit, in the discretion of such court or judge" to "make any order that may be proper to compel the man to pay any sums necessary for the maintenance of the woman and to enable her to carry on the suit, or to prevent him from imposing any restraint on her personal liberty, or to provide for the custody and maintenance of the minor children of the parties during the pendency of the suit, or to preserve the estate of the man, so that it be forthcoming to meet any decree which may be made in the suit, or to compel him to give security to abide such decree."

These preliminary orders, or any of them, on a proper showing made, supported by affidavit, may be entered in vacation, and before the maturity of the suit—and, on like allegations and like verification, even before process served [11] and without notice to the defendant, in analogy to a preliminary injunction. Indeed, most of such orders would in fact be equivalent to an injunction, mandatory or prohibitory, if not so in form and substance.

§ 405. Institution and conduct of the suit.—In Vir-

---

[9] 2 Bishop, Mar. Div. & Sep. 766; Yates *v.* Yates, 115 Va. 678; Blankenship *v.* Blankenship, 125 Va. 695; Towson *v.* Towson, *supra.* Though the domicil of the husband usually fixes the domicil of the wife, yet where the husband has abandoned the wife, or the wife has for good cause separated from him, she may acquire a separate domicil of-her own for purposes of divorce. Steckel *v.* Steckel, 118 Va. 198.

[10] Va. Code 1919, § 5107. The statutory provisions here enumerated are largely declaratory of the unwritten practice. 2 Bishop, Mar. Div. & Sep. 462, 966-992, 1100-1113.

[11] But not, in Virginia, before *process issued*, since the statute authorizes the exercise of these powers by the court or judge only "pending the suit." § 5107. The provision for suit money for the wife "to enable her to carry on the suit" is not in practice interpreted as confined to a plaintiff-wife only—the generally accepted rule being to require the plaintiff-husband to provide suit money to the defendant-wife, to enable her to employ counsel and otherwise make proper defence, unless she be otherwise provided with funds. 2 Bishop, Mar. Div. & Sep. 965, 976. See the revisors' annotations to Va. Code 1919, § 5107, for citation of various cases construing the statute and adjudicating questions of alimony, temporary and permanent.

ginia the statute[12] declares that divorce suits shall be instituted and conducted as other suits in equity, with the following exceptions:

1. The bill is never to be taken for confessed—that is, in default of defendant's appearance after due service of process, the cause is simply *set for hearing*.

2. No decree of divorce may be granted on the uncorroborated testimony of the parties or either of them.

3. The cause is to be heard independently of the admissions of either party, in the pleadings or otherwise.

4. No process or notice in such proceedings may be served in this state, except by an officer authorized to serve the same.

§ 406. The same—summons by publication. — Where the plaintiff has acquired the prescribed one year's domicil in this state, the court of the proper venue has jurisdiction of the suit, notwithstanding the non-residence of the defendant. While the decree in a divorce suit is, in a sense, personal, it is yet in so far as concerns the divorce itself, in substance rather *in rem* —as affecting the *civil status* of the parties.[13] Having properly acquired jurisdiction of one of the parties (the plaintiff), the court has the power, in spite of the absence of personal jurisdiction of the other, to determine the civil status of the plaintiff, though the defendant has been summoned by publication only, and has not appeared.

§ 407. Summons by publication—how issued and published.—The order of publication is issued by the clerk on proper affidavit of the non-residence of the defendant, either in term or in vacation. In it must be stated "the object of the suit and the grounds thereof *as shown by said application*" (sic)[14],

---

[12] Va. Code 1919, § 5106. Acts 1920, p. 503.

[13] See generally 2 Bishop, Mar. Div. & Sep. 23-37, 140-158, 550-558; Atherton *v.* Atherton, 181 U. S. 155; 2 Va. Law Reg. 46; 7 Va. Reg. 118, 137; 8 Va. Law Reg. 826. Of course, in so far as the decree is *personal*—as requiring payment of alimony, surrendering control of children in the custody of the absent defendant, etc.—it is inoperative on a non-resident defendant not actually served with process within the state, and not appearing. De La Montanya *v.* De La Montanya, 112 Cal. 101, 53 Am. St. Rep. 165, n; Bishop, Mar. Div. & Sep. *ubi supra*.

[14] The italicized words are portions of a former statute amended in the revisal, and obviously remaining here through inadvertence.

and said order of publication shall be published as required by law.[15]

Constructive service is also authorized by personal service on the non-resident defendant in another state, by a private person not interested in the suit, verified by a proper return under oath. Such service is declared as having the same effect as an order of publication duly executed.[16]

§ 408. The bill.—The bill in a nullity or a divorce suit is drawn in much the same form as other bills in chancery. The features of special importance in such bills, to which the attention of the young practitioner should be directed, are:

(1) In divorce suits, an allegation of the *actual marriage* of the parties, with particulars as to the date, place, etc., together with the maiden, or prenuptial, name of the wife. Divorce is necessarily predicated on a previous valid marriage.

(2) The essential *jurisdictional allegations*, already noticed.[17]

(3) In case the wife is plaintiff and suit money or alimony' is desired, some account of the *estate and income* of the husband.

(4) The number, names, sex and ages of the living *infant children* of the marriage; and the general circumstances of the. parties, financial or otherwise.

(5) *The particulars of the matrimonial offense* with which the defendant is charged, and which are asserted as a ground of the divorce sought. It is important that the circumstances and nature of the offense or offenses be charged with sufficient particularity as to persons, time and places, to enable the defendant properly to prepare to meet the charges in his or her answer, and to secure proper testimony in defense. It is especially important here that the young practitioner should observe the familiar rule of pleading that allegations of legal conclusions, in the place of the facts from which such legal conclusions flow, are inadmissible in pleading.

(6) By special statutory provision in Virginia,[18] if the mar-

---

[15] Va. Code 1919, §§ 5108, 6069-6070.
[16] Id. § 6071.
[17] *Supra*, §§ 401-403.
[18] Acts 1920, p. 503.

riage occurred in this state, bills for divorce are required to be accompanied by a *certified copy of the marriage license,* with a copy of the celebrant's return thereon, indicating the time and place of the marriage, "except where it is alleged in said bill that such certified copy cannot be obtained, *unless the same shall have been lost or destroyed"* (sic).[18a]

§ 409. The same—how adultery charged.—Thus, for example, where the gravamen of the bill is the adultery of the defendant, the allegations of *time* and *place* should be as specific as possible, and the *name of the paramour* stated, if known, and if unknown the bill should so allege.[19] If the plaintiff is unable to allege these particulars, the bill is prematurely filed, since without them the bill is a mere "fishing bill." Ignorance of these particulars indicates that the plaintiff knows little or nothing of the facts of the case sought to be established against the defendant, and lacks the evidence to establish them.

§ 410. Further pleadings.—After bill filed, the further pleadings and procedure are the same as in other suits in chancery, with the exception, already noted,[20] that the bill is not taken for confessed in default of defendant's appearance.

The defendant may either plead or answer. In case of the an-

[18a] The italicized phrase is a typical illustration of modern statutory draughtsmanship.

[19] In justice to the defendant, naming the paramour, if known, seems clearly essential; and the soundness of the rule is not doubted, in spite of *dicta* to the contrary in Miller *v.* Miller, 92 Va. 196, and Farr *v.* Farr, 34 Miss. 597, 69 Am. Dec. 406, and perhaps a few other cases, based on the suggestion that as the alleged paramour is not a party to the suit, and has no opportunity to be heard, the reputation of an innocent person might thus be scandalized. But this suggestion was anticipated long before by Dr. Lushington in Croft *v.* Croft, 3 Hag. Ecc. 310 (5 Eng. Ecc. Rep. 120), in the statement that "justice must be done to suitors, so that it is impossible to exclude" [from the pleading] "matter which ought to be admitted in evidence, because incidentally it may affect the character and involve the conduct of those who are not parties to the suit." Mr. Bishop declares the name of the paramour, if known, "the very gist of the description" of the adulterous acts charged. 2 Bishop, Mar. Div. & Sep. 1333. See Id. 1326 (form of allegation), and 576. See Wood *v.* Wood, 2 Paige 113; Marsh *v.* Marsh, 6 N. J. Eq. 391, 84 Am. Dec. 164; Starke, 2 Va. Law Reg. 69. As the name of the paramour, if known, must necessarily be brought out in the *testimony,* the privilege of omitting it from the *bill* is, after all, an illusory protection to the paramour at the expense of the defendant—thus presenting the anomaly of the judicial sacrifice of the rights of a litigant, in a vain effort to protect the reputation of a stranger.

[20] *Supra,* § 405.

swer, the same rules are applicable as to answers in other equity suits,[21] except that no decree can be rendered on the uncorroborated admissions therein.[22]

§ 411. The testimony—parties as witnesses.—By the common law, neither husband nor wife were competent witnesses in a divorce suit brought by one against the other—nor, indeed, in any case in which either was interested. The rule has been altered in most of the states, though in Virginia it was retained in divorce suits until the revisal of 1919, when husband and wife were declared competent witnesses for or against each other in all cases,[23] with certain qualifications in criminal cases.[24] But neither may, without consent of the other, "be examined in any case as to any communication privately made by one to the other while married; nor shall either be permitted, without such consent, to reveal in testimony after the marriage relation ceases any such communication made while the marriage subsisted."[25]

§ 412. The testimony, continued—how taken. — In the absence of special provision to the contrary, the testimony in divorce suits in equity is taken by depositions, as in other chancery suits. And such was the practice in Virginia until altered in 1914, by an act reproduced in the Code of 1919,[26] providing that in any suit for divorce the trial court may require the whole or any part of the testimony to be given *orally in open court*—with the right of either party to require that such testimony, and the court's rulings on exceptions thereto, shall be reduced to writing. Such writing, when certified by the judge, is declared as standing on the same footing as a deposition regularly taken in the cause.

§ 413. The same—depositions in case matured by order of publication.—Where the defendant has been summoned

---

[21] Latham *v.* Latham, 30 Gratt. 307; Haynor *v.* Haynor, 112 Va. 123; 2 Bishop, Mar. Div. & Sep. 778.

[22] Va. Code 1919, § 5106.

[23] § 6210, and revisors' note.

[24] § 6211.

[25] § 6212. How far this provision would exclude communications, "privately made," by the husband, for example, in the way of abuse, insulting epithets, unfounded charges of infidelity, etc., is a question for future judicial construction.

[26] § 5109.

by publication, and has not appeared, the statute [27] provides that no depositions shall be commenced until at least fifteen days shall have elapsed after the order of publication shall have been duly published as required by law.

It is further provided that in no case in which the defendant has been summoned by publication and has not appeared, shall it be necessary to make other publication or give other notice in any proceeding in court, or before a commissioner, or for the purpose of taking depositions, unless specially ordered by the court—unless such defendant be represented by counsel residing in this state, of record or known to the plaintiff. In the latter case, reasonable notice of proceedings before the commissioner, or of the taking of depositions, shall be given to such counsel, or any of them, if more than one.[28]

§ 414. The decree.—The court has a wide discretion in the sentence of divorce, in making provision for alimony to the plaintiff-wife, and for the custody and maintenance of the children; and by the Virginia statute,[29] may make such further decree as it shall deem expedient concerning the estate, and maintenance of the parties or either of them.

It is also provided [30] that the court may from time to time afterwards, on petition of either of the parties, revise and alter such decree concerning the care, custody and maintenance of the children, and make a new decree concerning the same, as the circumstances of the parents and the benefit of the children may require.[31]

§ 415. Modification of final decree for alimony by reason of subsequent events.—Whether after final decree and dismissal of the cause from the docket, the court may re-assume jurisdiction of the case, and for good cause modify the

---

[27] Va. Code 1919, § 5108.

[28] Va. Code 1919, § 6071.

[29] Va. Code 1919, § 5111.

[30] Id.

[31] It seems there may be a decree for alimony though not specifically prayed in the bill, since alimony is but an incident of the main relief: 7 Va. Law Reg. 557; Haven v. Trammell (Okla.), 193 Pac. 631; Lynde v. Lynde, 162 N. Y. 405, 56 N. E. 979, 76 Am. St. Rep. 332, 48 L. R. A. 679.

provisions of the decree for alimony and for the custody and maintenance of the children of the marriage, is a question that has received the attention and vexed the deliberations of the courts in many cases. Efforts to secure such alteration arise from various causes, many of them strongly appealing to the sympathy of the court.

Where the circumstances of the parties have materially changed since the decree, in a manner not to be foreseen at the time of the decree—circumstances which, if they had existed at the time, would have called for a wholly different provision for alimony from that actually made—one or the other of the parties will naturally clamor for a modification to conform more equitably to the new situation.

Thus the husband's estate may subsequently have largely increased in value—or, on the other hand, may, by reverses of fortune, have been proportionately depleted. So the wife, by inheritance, or otherwise, may have become possessed of a large estate sufficient to provide a comfortable, or even luxurious, living, or the same result has followed by her re-marriage to a second husband; or, on the other hand, by reason of ill health or other misfortune, the alimony allowed is insufficient for her needs. Or, again, the wife may be living in unlawful relations with a paramour, or otherwise leading a notoriously immoral life.

Certainly in such changed circumstances there should be some principle justifying a modification of the decree, to meet the altered conditions, and some procedure by which this may be accomplished.

§ 416. The same technical difficulties.—But the rule of practice, both at law and in equity, that a final judgment or decree, from which no appeal has been taken, may not be altered except for errors of a limited class, and only within a very limited period of time, (as by bill of review in an equity case), while in most cases a most desirable rule, has operated to hamper efforts toward relief in the cases under consideration, and many judicial efforts have been made to relax or distinguish the rule in this class of cases.

§ 417. The same—situations distinguished—results.—
The most exhaustive and satisfactory treatment of the question
known to the author, is found in the scholarly opinion of Webster, J., in Ruge *v.* Ruge,[32] of the Supreme Court of Washington. The court here examines and analyzes most of the cases,
English and American; and by like analysis and criticism, dem-
onstrates that the views of Bishop[33] are not fully sustained by
the authorities cited by that distinguished author.

The conclusions announced by the court seem eminently sound
on principle, and, as demonstrated by the court, are sustained,
either consciously or unconsciously, by an overwhelming majority of the American cases.

These conclusions are, in brief:

(1) *Decree a mensa.*—Where the decree is one *a mensa,* or
for separate maintenance only—and hence not affecting the marriage status—the continuance of the marriage relation gives the
court a continuing jurisdiction to regulate the marital rights of
the parties; and hence to modify the decree as new circumstances may demand.

(2) *Decree for temporary alimony.* — Where the decree
awards *temporary alimony* only, or suit money, the power to
modify obviously exists *pendente lite.*

(3) *Alimony for support of children.*—So far as the alimony decreed is for the *benefit of the infant children* of the
marriage, the latter, in a sense, continue under the protection
of the court; and the relation of parent and child continuing,
unaffected by the decree, gives the court continued jurisdiction
to modify the decree, wherever the interests of the children
require it. This jurisdiction is expressly conferred by the Virginia statute.[34]

(4) *Reservation of further jurisdiction in decree.* — Obviously, the jurisdiction to modify the decree exists, as in every
other case, where the court in its decree expressly reserves to
itself the further jurisdiction of the cause for such alterations
and modifications as the court may thereafter deem proper.

---

[32] 165 Pac. 1063, L. R. A. 1917F, 721, annotated.
[33] 2 Mar. Div. & Sep. 872.
[34] Va. Code 1919, § 5111.

Such a reservation indicates "an unfinished determination of the judicial mind," and that the court has not completely and finally disposed of the case.[34a]

(5) *Statutory authority to modify.*—It is equally obvious that the power to modify exists when given by *express or implied statutory enactment,* as has been done in many states.

(6) *Decree not within any of the five classes foregoing.*—But where the divorce is absolute, and the alimony awarded is not temporary but permanent; where there are no infant children; nor express reservation in the decree; nor an enabling statute; nor question of fraud or mistake such as would justify modification in other cases—then the decree for alimony stands on the same footing as other final decrees, and is no more subject to modification than would a decree for a sum in gross, whether for alimony or for a debt due by express contract.[35]

§ 418. The costs.—The question of costs in divorce suits is largely a matter of statute or of local practice. The Virginia statute [36] declares that in such cases costs may be awarded to either party as justice and equity may require. Since, however, the husband is normally the chief or only source of the family income, he is, in practice, generally required to pay the costs, including fees of the wife's counsel, whether he be plaintiff or defendant, and whether the decree be in his favor or that of the wife. The court will however, take into consideration the suit-money allowed to the wife pending the cause; and if this was

---

[34a] See *ante,* § 288.

[35] No Virginia case is known to have considered the question. But assuming as we well may, that relief may be had in Virginia in classes 1 and 3 foregoing—as obviously it may under class 4, and may not under class 5 (the Virginia statute § 5111, giving the court authority thus to modify the decree, only as to custody and maintenance of the children), and as it may not under class 6—the question of procedure becomes important. Assuming the decree to have passed, by lapse of time, beyond the reach of a bill of review or of an appeal (even if either of these were otherwise available for the purpose indicated) the only practical relief would be by way of an original bill. See *ante,* § 288.

In Sperry *v.* Sperry (W. Va.), 92 S. E. 574, the court recognized the rule as stated, and reversed the decree because of the failure of the lower court to make proper reservation in the decree. Relief was granted in Emerson *v.* Emerson. 120 Md. 584, 87 Atl. 1033, but rather on the provisions of the Maryland statute.

[36] Va. Code 1919, § 5106; Acts 1920, p. 503.

clearly intended to cover costs, including attorney's fees, no further allowance will be made. The financial circumstances of the parties are important considerations, particularly where the wife's suit was not brought in good faith, or where the divorce is granted to the husband for the wife's matrimonial delinquency.[37]

§ 419. Causes for divorce—substantive law.—No effort has been made in this chapter to deal with the substantive law of divorce, but the chapter is confined to the outline of the pleading and practice only. For the substantive law, the student is referred to his studies of Domestic Relations, and particularly to Bishop's scholarly and exhaustive treatise on Marriage, Divorce and Separation—one of the few modern text-books that deserves such characterization.

---

[37] See generally on this subject, 2 Bishop, Mar. Div. & Sep. 810-820.

CHAPTER XXX.

IV. Sale of Lands of Persons under Disability.

§ 420. Equitable jurisdiction—statutory. — Whatever may be the rule in the case of lands of lunatics and persons *non compotes,* according to best authority courts of equity have not inherent jurisdiction to sell, exchange, or incumber the lands of infants, unless the same are held *in trust.* In the latter case, under its long established jurisdiction over trusts generally, there can be no doubt of the ample power of equity to sell or otherwise deal with the trust estate, whether belonging to infants or adults.[1]

Inasmuch, however, as the welfare of infant owners of land often requires a sale or other disposition, statutes conferring the necessary jurisdiction, and regulating its exercise, exist in all of the states.

As these proceedings are, in general, statutory, their nature depends in large measure on the terms of the particular statute under which they are brought. But as the purpose of these statutes is everywhere the same, and the temptation the same for dishonest persons to take advantage of these helpless persons, much similarity of procedure will be found to exist in the several states.

§ 421. The same—Virginia statutes — general purposes.—The Virginia statutes provide for the disposition of the estates of both infants and insane persons, and contemplate two main purposes:

1. A disposition of the real estate (1) by a sale thereof, for reinvestment of the proceeds; or (2) an exchange thereof for other real property; or (3) for a lease thereof; or (4) an incumbrance thereon for money borrowed for betterment purposes, etc.—none of which purposes contemplates expenditure of the *corpus*[2]*; and*

2. A sale for the purpose of *expending the proceeds,* or a

---

[1] Rhea *v.* Shields, 103 Va. 305; Shirkey *v.* Kirby, 110 Va. 455.
[2] Va. Code 1919, ch. 217.

portion thereof, for the *maintenance* of the lunatic [3] or his family, or for the *maintenance and education* of the infant.[4]

§ 422. Nature of estate.—The statute in express terms is applicable to estates of every character—the language being "whether the estate of the minor, insane person or of any of the persons interested, be absolute or limited, and whether there be or be not limited thereon any other estate, vested or contingent." [5]

§ 423. Limited estate in infant—absolute estate sold. —Where the estate of the infant in the subject-matter is a limited one, or is not a sole and absolute estate, the powers of the court are not confined to a sale simply of the *infant's interest* in the estate, but the court in such proceeding may sell the *absolute estate*, though it may thus be disposing of the estate of adults as well as that of the infants.[6]

1. *Outline of the Procedure.*

§ 424. Outline of the procedure.—The subjoined outline will indicate the chief features which must characterize the proceedings under these statutes. And as most of these provisions are mandatory, as presently to be shown, it behooves the young practitioner to give them his careful attention.

§ 425. Venue of suit.—The suit must be brought "in the circuit court of the county or the circuit or corporation court

---

[3] Id. §§ 1055-1057—a special proceeding, for details of which reference must be had to the sections cited.

[4] Id. § 5126—the proceedings in which are required to conform to those under chapter 217, considered in this chapter of the text.

Reference may be here made also to § 5161, authorizing the sale of *contingent estates*, whether of infants or adults; § 5281, with respect to *partition* of estates, whether of infants or of adults; § 6542, sale of *infant's homestead;* §§ 5344-5345, authorizing the wife of an infant or insane husband, whose lands have been sold by decree under chapter 46 or chapter 217 of the Code, *to unite in the master's conveyance to release dower* or other interest, with provisions for securing proper compensation for the interest so released; § 5346, giving jurisdiction to courts of equity to provide for *releasing curtesy of insane husband, or dower of insane wife*, where the sane consort desires to sell his or her real estate; § 5338, Acts 1920, p. 405, validating certain irregularities in proceedings under chapter 217.

[5] Va. Code 1919. § 5335.

[6] Faulkner *v.* Davis, 18 Gratt. 652; Rhea *v.* Shields, 103 Va. 305, 309-310.

of the corporation, in which the estate proposed to be sold exchanged, encumbered or leased, or some part thereof, may be." [7]

Since this is a purely statutory proceeding, under a statutory jurisdiction, and since, as will appear later, any material departure from the statutory requirements will oust the jurisdiction, it is clear that the jurisdiction here cannot be exercised by the court of any other county or corporation than as here prescribed. Here *venue* and *jurisdiction* are coterminous.[8]

§ 426. Proper plaintiff.[9] — In these cases suit may be brought only by (a) The *guardian* of any infant in interest, or (b) The *committee* of any insane person in interest—or (c) If the estate be held in trust, suit may be by (1) the *trustee or trustees,* or (2) any *beneficiary.*

§ 427. The bill—essential allegations and characteristics.[10]—The bill must show: (1) A plaintiff or plaintiffs with proper statutory authority, as explained in the preceding section; (2) the proper *venue,* as indicated above; (2) "plainly *all the estate, real or personal,* belonging to such infant or insane person, or so held in trust—that is, not only the estate sought to be sold, but all other estate belonging to the infant, or insane person;" (4) a description of the property to be sold, exchanged,

---

[7] Va. Code 1919, § 5335.
[8] See *Limited Statutory Jurisdiction, ante,* § 18 *et seq; infra* § 437.
[9] Va. Code 1919, § 5335.
[10] Va. Code 1919, § 5335. The reasons for requiring these details are obvious. The plain policy of the statute is that there shall be no conversion, complete or partial, of the real property of those who are under guardianship and unable to care for their own interests, except where such conversion is clearly to their advantage. In order to determine this vital question, the court must be advised of all the circumstances surrounding the infant or lunatic and his estate, so as to be able intelligently to consider the whole situation, and afford complete protection to all parties concerned. Hence the detailed information called for.

Since the infant is incapable of making a will of realty before majority, and the insane person is wholly *incapax testandi,* the prospective heirs and distributees have a special (if not anxious) interest in maintaining the integrity of the estate. It is eminently proper, therefore, for the safeguarding of their own interests, as well as those of the infant or insane person, that these kindred should be made parties and given opportunity to be heard.

Where father and mother, as trustees, are plaintiffs, they are properly in the suit as heirs and distributees of their infant children. Lancaster *v.* Barton, 92 Va. 615.

etc.; (5) the character of the infant's or insane person's holding—whether in trust or otherwise, and whether as sole owner or jointly with others named, and the nature of the estate, whether in absolute estate or otherwise; (6) "all the facts calculated to show the propriety of the sale, exchange, encumbrance or lease"—which would include the ages and general circumstances of the infant or insane parties; (7) the purposes to which the proceeds of the sale, encumbrance, etc., are to be devoted. (8) The infant or insane parties, or the beneficiaries of the trust, as well as the trustee or trustees when these are not parties plaintiff, and all other persons interested in the estate, must be made parties defendant, as well as (9) "all those who would be the heirs or distributees of the infant or insane defendants, if all such infant or insane defendants were dead." Further, the bill (10) should allege that by the proposed sale, exchange, etc., the interest of the infant or insane defendant or defendants, will be promoted, and that the rights of no person will be violated thereby; and, finally (11) the bill must be verified by the oath of the *plaintiff*.[11]

§ 428. Verification of bill.—Ordinary bills in chancery require no verification—or, in the few cases where required, the verification may usually be made by any person cognizant of the facts. Here, however, to indicate good faith on the part of the plaintiff in his capacity as representative of the infant or insane person, the bill must be verified by *oath of the plaintiff*, and no substitute is permissible.

§ 429. Guardian ad litem.—Before any steps are taken in the suit there must be a guardian *ad litem* appointed for each infant or insane defendant.[12]

---

[11] In Lancaster *v.* Barton, *supra*, it was held that an affidavit which failed to show that it was made by the plaintiff, might be supplemented by proof *aliunde*, in a collateral attack on the decree of sale. See also Durrett *v.* Davis, 24 Gratt. 302, 310-311.

[12] Va. Code 1919, § 5337—who must be "a discreet and competent attorney at law if one be found willing to act:" § 6098. As to his appointment, service of process, etc., see *ante*, § 106. He has no power to make admissions, whether *in pais* or of record, which will bind the infant. He may not consent to a decree on the merits, or waive proofs: *infra*, § 431; Dangerfield *v.* Smith, 83 Va. 81, 91; Waterman *v.* Lawrence (Cal.), 79 Am. Dec. 212. But he may consent to mere

§ 430. Required answers.—There must be the following answers, and *their presence in the record is mandatory*:[13]

(a) Answer of the guardian *ad litem, in proper person,* and *on oath.*[14]

(b) Answer of the *infant,* or *insane person,* by the guardian *ad litem,* and (by the safer practice) under oath of the latter.[15]

(c) If the infant be over fourteen years of age: Answer of the infant *in proper person,* and *on oath.*[16]

§ 431. The evidence—depositions.—The necessary facts must be proved by testimony of witnesses *independently of any admissions in the answers.* No depositions may be read unless

---

matters of procedure not affecting the substantial rights of the infant —as by consent to a hearing in vacation, etc.: Kingsbury *v.* Buckner, 134 U. S. 678, 681; Lemmon *v.* Herbert, 92 Va. 633.

[13] Va. Code 1919, § 5337; *infra,* § 437.

[14] Since various oaths required in these proceedings are demanded by the statute, they are not the subject of waiver. The purpose of requiring an answer *in proper person from the guardian ad litem* (an innovation in the equity practice) as to have an expression of his personal knowledge of the facts alleged in the bill, and of the circumstances surrounding the infant, and of his judgment as to the propriety or impropriety of the sale or other object sought by the bill. The statute evidently does not contemplate here a merely formal or perfunctory answer from the guardian *ad litem.*

The purpose of the oath is not to afford evidence (as the case must be proved independently of the pleadings) but to guarantee good faith on the part of the guardian *ad litem.*

[15] The statute does not in terms call for this answer, but as it is not usual or necessary, in this state to serve process on infants (see *ante,* § 60, *et seq.*), without such an answer the infant (particularly if he be under fourteen years of age, for whose appearance in the suit no other method is provided) would not properly be a party to the suit—since he becomes a party in such case only by the filing of an answer in his own name by his guardian *ad litem.* The oath here is not in terms required, but as the rules of the forum require all answers to be verified, caution suggests that it be not omitted. But such oath is not believed to be essential. It is vital, however, that the answer of the infant or lunatic should be *in his own name,* by guardian *ad litem,* and not in the name of the latter on behalf of the ward. See *ante,* § 104, *et seq.* See curative statute, (Va. Code 1919, § 5334, Acts 1920, p. 405) indicating the necessity for such answers in the future.

[16] This is a wise provision, giving the infant himself opportunity, after he has presumably reached some degree of mental maturity, to express his own judgment and wishes with respect to the proposed conversion of his property. If the infant be beyond the limits of the commonwealth, or insane, or confined in a reformatory or prison, the answer in proper person is not necessary. Va. Code 1919, § 5337.

taken *in the presence of the guardian ad litem,* or on interrogatories agreed upon by him.[17]

§ 432. The decree. — "If it be clearly shown," declares the statute, *"independently of any admissions in the answers,* that the *interests of the infant, insane person,* or beneficiaries in the trust, as the case may be, *will be promoted,* and the court is of opinion that the *rights of no person will.be violated thereby,* it may decree a sale of said estate, or any part thereof," etc.[18]

§ 433. The sale.—It is provided that neither the guardian, guardian *ad litem,* committee (of the insane person), the trustee, nor the lessee, shall become a purchaser directly or indirectly.[19]

---

[17] See Coleman *v.* Virginia Stave Co., 112 Va. 61, and Wheeler *v.* Thomas, 116 Va. 259, where the decrees were held void and subject to collateral attack, for a violation of the fundamental rule that the essential facts of a case, and particularly in these proceedings, may not be established by *ex parte* affidavits. Affidavits were rejected also in Smith *v.* White, 107 Va. 616.

The requirement of the guardian *ad litem's* presence here is an additional safeguard against wrong to the infant or lunatic, in that it at least brings home to the guardian *ad litem* the nature of the testimony to be submitted, and if he be faithful to his trust the testimony will be more thoroughly sifted.

[18] Va. Code 1919, § 5348. It is to these inquiries that the testimony will mainly be directed. The necessary facts may be established either by a reference to a master to ascertain and report them, or by depositions properly taken and read by the court. The statutory rule that a master's report must lie ten days for exceptions, is held (on not entirely satisfactory reasoning) to have no application to this proceeding. Lancaster *v.* Barton, 92 Va. 615. It is scarcely necessary to suggest that the decree should plainly indicate that the required conditions precedent were fulfilled—namely: "It being clearly shown, independently of any admissions in the answers, that the interests of the infant defendant will be promoted by what follows, and that the rights of no person will be violated thereby, the court doth adjudge, order and decree," etc. Indeed, the careful practitioner who appreciates the spirit of the statute, and its judicial interpretation, will be careful to recite in the decree, in detail, the observance of all the essential statutory requirements.

[19] Id. § 5341. As indicated in a previous section, though the interest of the incompetent be a partial or limited estate, the court may, and should ordinarily, decree a sale of the entire or *absolute estate.* The court in such proceeding has jurisdiction to confirm a conditional sale of the property *privately made* on behalf of the beneficiary or beneficiaries, if satisfied by testimony, taken as required by the statute, that such sale is to the interest of the incompetent parties. Smith *v.* White, 107 Va. 616.

§ 434. The proceeds.—Careful and minute provisions are made for the safe reinvestment or other proper disposition of the proceeds of sale, incumbrance, etc., under the supervision of the court. The proceeds, representing as they do the *corpus* of the infant's real property, do not pass into the hands of the *guardian,* but are managed by a receiver or other person appointed by the court for the purpose, who is required to give ample security for the faithful discharge of his duties.[20]

§ 435. The same—proceeds under $500. — In keeping with the wise policy of eliminating the necessity, and the accompanying expense, of a guardian, where the estate of the infant is small, the statute [21] further provides that "wherever it shall appear to a court having control of a fund, or supervision of its administration, *whether a suit be pending therefor or not,* that an infant is entitled to a fund arising from a sale of lands *for a division or otherwise,* or as distributee of any estate, and the amount to which said infant is entitled is less than $500.00, it shall be lawful for the said court, without the intervention of a guardian, upon its being made to appear to said court that the said infant is of sufficient age and discretion to use said fund judiciously, to cause said fund to be paid directly to said infant"—with further provision for payment to the parents for use of the infant where the latter is of tender years and incapable of handling the fund.[22]

---

[20] Va. Code 1919, § 5342—with the further provision that "nothing herein contained shall prevent the court having charge of any of such funds from applying at any time all or any portion thereof to the proper needs and requirements of any such ward or insane person." *Cf. id.* § 5326.

[21] *Id.*

[22] It will be observed that this provision applies not only to funds derived from a sale or other disposition of the infant's property *under this chapter,* but to any case in which any fund belonging to an infant, not exceeding the limited amount mentioned, is under the "control or supervision" of the court. Compare a kindred, but dissimilar, provision in § 5281, where the fund is derived from a sale for *partition.* As § 5242, quoted above, applies in express terms to a fund "arising from a sale of lands for a *division,* or otherwise," there seems a conflict between the two sections.

Should the infant die during non-age, or the insane person without recovering his sanity, so much of the fund received under this chapter (217), or as the result of a sale in partition proceedings under chapter 214, will pass to such persons as would have been entitled to the land if it had not been sold or divided: *id.* § 5347. In other

2. Interpretation of Statute—When Liberal—When Strict.

§ 436. (1) Liberal as to subject-matter. — As these provisions are meant to supply a need for which the unwritten law did not provide, and are highly remedial in their nature, they are to be liberally construed in support of a clearly defined legislative policy, so far as concerns the *subject-matter* of the several statutes.[23]

§ 437. (2) Strict as to procedure. — In supplying a right which the common law did not afford, the legislature, in providing the proper machinery for its exercise, has been careful to place every reasonable safeguard around the helpless persons whose inheritances are thus permitted to be aliened or encumbered without their concurrence, and who are without ability to protect their own interests.

As a purely statutory right, it must, in accordance with the settled rule of construction, be exercised in substantial compliance with the *statutory remedy*—and any material departure from the procedure as prescribed by the legislature will render the proceeding not only voidable but *void,* and therefore subject to collateral attack. The exercise of this jurisdiction by courts of chancery is not under their *general equitable jurisdiction,* but under a *special, statutory* and *limited* jurisdiction—and a failure to exercise the power substantially as given will be fatal to the proceedings.[24]

---

words, the fund derived from such sales, though in form personal estate, is treated, during the period of infancy or insanity, as realty, just as if conversion had not taken place.

The provisions of § 5340, with reference to mortgaging the estate of an incompetent for betterment purposes, seems to afford quite inadequate protection to the lender—whose lien is confined to the *increment of value produced by the improvements made,* and is made subordinate to the right of the infant to demand, out of the proceeds of sale, on foreclosure, an amount equal to the *original value of the estate,* anterior to the execution of the incumbrance. Such an investment will scarcely prove attractive to careful investors.

[23] Faulkner *v.* Davis, 18 Gratt. 651, 669-670; Rhea *v.* Shields, 103 Va. 305; Coleman *v.* Virginia Stave Co., 112 Va. 61.

[24] Williamson *v.* Berry, 8 How. (U. S.) 495; *In re* Valentine, 72 N. Y. 186; Battell *v.* Torrey, 65 N. Y. 296; Roche *v.* Nesters, 72 Md. 264, 7 L. R. A. 533; Coleman *v.* Virginia Stave Co., 112 Va. 61; Brenham *v.* Smith, 120 Va. 30; Roberts *v.* Hagan, 121 Va. 573; Watkins *v.* Ford, 123 Va. 268; Parker *v.* Stephenson, 127 Va. 431; Hoback *v.* Miller (W. Va.), 29 S. E. 1014. See *ante,* § 18 *et seq.* See Rhea *v.*

It should be observed, however, that these statutes have in no wise affected the ancient jurisdiction of equity over *trust estates,* even though held by infants. If, therefore, the estate be in trust, the jurisdiction to decree a sale when the interests of the beneficiaries require it, is not dependent on these statutes, which merely afford an additional remedy. Hence trust estates of infants or insane persons may be sold or encumbered under decree of the court of chancery without complying with the statutory proceedings.[25]

3. The Title of a Bona Fide Purchaser.

§ 438. The same—how far bona fide purchasers protected.—The principle here is well expressed by Buchanan, J., in Coleman *v.* Virginia Stave Co.:[26] "While the purchaser at such a sale is not bound to investigate the truth of the matters stated in the bill and deposed to by the witnesses, touching the estate owned by the infants, or as to the propriety or necessity of the sale, since his title cannot be affected because the case made by the record happens not to be warranted by the facts, (Durrett *v.* Davis, 24 Gratt. 302, 308), yet he is required to see to the *regularity of the proceedings* upon which the jurisdiction of the court is founded (s. c.); for he is presumed to know that the infant until six months after his maturity has the right to show cause against the decree of sale, for errors upon the face of the record, or to show that the court has no jurisdiction to enter the decree, or, if it had jurisdiction, that the proceedings were irregular and not binding upon the parties, or

---

Shields, 103 Va. 305, 313—a case in which the court found the trustee plaintiff and his counsel guilty of gross imposition upon the *cestui que trustent* under cover of these statutes, but was unable to give relief because the proceedings were substantially regular, and the property had passed into the hands of *bona fide* purchasers. "The developments in this case" said Whittle, J., "accentuate the necessity for the exercise of such vigilance on the part of trial courts, in dealing with this class of cases, as will render the recurrence of similar results impossible; otherwise a benign statute specially enacted for the protection of the unfortunate may be converted into an instrument for their destruction."

[25] Shirkey *v.* Kirby, 110 Va. 455, 457. *Sed quere.*

[26] 112 Va. 61, 77.

that the case made by the record did not warrant the decree."[27]

§ 439. Right of infant to show cause against the decree.—As heretofore indicated, under a long-settled rule of the chancery courts, infants have six months after attaining their majority within which to assail the validity of decrees affecting their rights—a privilege which formerly it was error not to reserve to them on the face of the decree, but now reserved to them by statute in Virginia, even though omitted from the decree.[28]

---

[27] In this case there was almost a comedy of errors—though to the purchaser, who lost both his purchase-money and the property purchased, it was more nearly a tragedy. The bill failed to mention what other property the infants owned, there was no answer by the guardian *ad litem* in proper person, and affidavits instead of depositions were resorted to to show the propriety of the sale. For these and other irregularities, the decree was successfully assailed by one of the infants, in an independent suit against the purchaser of the property—the court holding that the decree was void. The case of Wheeler *v.* Thomas, 116 Va. 259, illustrates even greater irregularities, with like fatal results. *Cf.* Rhea *v.* Shields, 103 Va. 305.

See authorities in n. 22 *supra*, for illustrations of similar fatal errors —most, if not all, of them set up in collateral attacks on the decree. In Parker *v.* Stephenson, *supra*, the infant plaintiff in equity, collaterally assailing a mortgage placed on his estate under defective proceedings, was required to account to the *bona fide* purchaser under foreclosure proceedings, for the purchase money, as a condition of equitable relief.

It is clear that irregularities in these proceedings cannot be waived by the incompetent or his representatives. He is presumed to be objecting at every point and no demurrer is needed to protect him from defective allegations of the bill. Parker *v.* Stephenson, *supra*.

As to the rights of a purchaser at a judicial sale, where the decree is subsequently reversed, see Va. Code 1919, § 6306; see *Judicial Sales, ante*, ch. xxi.

[28] Va. Code 1919, § 6305. The cause or causes which may thus be shown as against a *bona fide* purchaser of the property sold under the decree, are indicated in the foregoing section—and are confined, in the main, to matters affecting the *jurisdiction* of the court, the *regularity of the proceedings*, and the *good faith* of the purchaser, and always to matters existing at the time of the decree of sale, and do not extend to circumstances subsequently arising. See *Decrees, ante*, ch. xx; Durrett *v.* Davis, 24 Gratt. 302; Zirkle *v.* McCue, 26 Gratt. 517, 527; Lancaster *v.* Barton, 92 Va. 623; Coleman *v.* Virginia Stave Co., 112 Va. 161; Asberry *v.* Mitchell, 121 Va. 276.

CHAPTER XXXI.

V. Creditors' Bills.

§ 440. Creditors' bills—distinctive feature. — The distinctive feature of a creditors' bill is that its purpose is not, as in an action at law, to obtain a personal judgment or decree against the debtor, but *specifically to subject the debtor's property* to an already existing charge or lien thereon—as by judgment, mortgage, or other *in rem* claim—for the enforcement of which there is no adequate remedy at law.[1]

It is a settled principle both of law and equity (save where the rule is changed by statute, as has been done in a few cases), "that every debtor, until his property is *specifically bound* to the satisfaction of his debt by his own agreement or by some judicial or other legal proceeding, has an absolute right to dispose of it at pleasure; a power which no tribunal whatever has authority to control or limit. The *obligation of a debtor is purely personal,* and in no way affects his property or any portion of it. To this rule no solitary exception can be found, nor can one exist, until the principles of our law are so changed as to authorize courts of equity to administer the estates of living persons as if they were dead."[2]

§ 440½. The same—distinctive feature, continued.— Since, therefore, one's property can be charged only through his person, courts of equity refuse to entertain bills thus to charge a debtor's property, unless the debtor himself has already voluntarily charged it in favor of the creditor, or unless the charge grows out of a trust, or of a statute, or, in the absence of these, unless the creditor has proceeded against the person of the debtor at law, and has *exhausted all his legal remedies* against him. The usual proof required to establish the ex-

---

[1] In short, to subject what may be termed *equitable* assets.

[2] Green, J., in Tate *v.* Liggatt, 2 Leigh 84, 99-100. To the same effect, Carr, J., in Rhodes *v.* Cousins, 6 Rand. 209, 211. Attachment proceedings under statutory provisions, and proceedings in bankruptcy, are notable exceptions.

haustion of legal remedies is a judgment on which execution has been issued and returned no effects.

It follows, under the general rule, that if the claims asserted in the bill are not already specific charges upon the property of the debtor, there must be such judgment, execution and return, as a condition precedent to the maintenance of a creditors' bill

We may say, therefore, that the distinctive and essential feature of a creditors' bill is that its purpose is, in general, (1) to subject the debtor's estate, or some part of it, to a *specific and existing charge* thereon—for the enforcement of which charge there is no convenient remedy at law; or (2), to obtain the aid of the court in subjecting to the satisfaction of the plaintiff's *judgment,* upon which execution has been issued and returned no effects,[3] the whole or some part of the debtor's estate, which, because of its equitable nature or otherwise, *cannot be reached by execution at law.*[4]

1. *Bills by General* [5] *Creditors.*

§ 441. The same—bills by creditors at large—exceptional cases.—While the rule, as shown in preceding sections, is that creditors at large (also termed 'general creditors') cannot be entertained in equity for the subjection of their living debtor's estate to payment of debts, there are a few exceptions as the result of necessity or of statute.

Thus, as indicated more at large in a subsequent section, statutes in some of the states permit general creditors to assail

---

[3] By virtue of statute in Virginia (Code 1919, § 6472), the lien of a judgment on real property may be enforced in equity without issuance or return of the execution. Price *v.* Thrash, 30 Gratt. 315; Stovall *v.* Border Grange Bank, 78 Va. 188. In Virginia the creditor is not required to exhaust the debtor's personal estate before proceeding against the real property. Rush *v.* Dickenson County Bank, 128 Va. 114.

[4] See generally on the subject: Tate *v.* Liggatt, 2 Leigh 84; Spindle *v.* Fletcher, 93 Va. 186; Freedman's Bank *v.* Earl, 110 U. S. 710; Cates *v.* Allen, 149 U. S. 451; Guggenheimer *v.* Lockridge, 39 W. Va. 457; note to Suckley *v.* Rotchford, 12 Gratt. 72 (Va. Rep. Ann.); Flemming *v.* Grafton, 54 Miss. 79; 12 Cyc. 1; note 63 L. R. A. 673; note 90 Am. Dec. 288-300; Lile, Notes on Equity Jurisprudence (ed. 1921), p. 217, *et seq.;* cases *infra.*

[5] That is, creditors who have not reduced their claims to judgment, or who are not otherwise *in rem* creditors.

voluntary or *fraudulent* transfers of property by their debtor.

So it is held also that where a *corporation is insolvent,* and has been *abandoned by its officers and agents,* creditors at large may maintain a bill for the conservation of its assets and their application to payment of debts.[6]

It follows, save in exceptional cases, that general creditors of a living person,[7] or of an existing corporation,[8] cannot maintain a creditors' bill.

§ 442. The same—exception where no judgment possible.

—In spite of the general rule as indicated, exception is necessarily made where to insist upon the rule would amount to a denial of justice. Thus where by reason of peculiar circumstances no judgment at law can be obtained against the debtor—as where the latter has absconded, so that no process can be served on him, and the property sought to be subjected cannot be reached by attachment under the local statutes—equity will entertain a bill by a general creditor.[9]

§ 443. The same—assailing fraudulent conveyances.

—In the absence of an enabling statute, creditors at large cannot maintain a bill to assail conveyances made by their debtor in fraud of creditors. If the claims are not already specific charges

---

[6] Finney *v.* Bennett, 27 Gratt. 365; Nunnally *v.* Strauss, 94 Va. 255. And so, where, by reason of the dissolution of the corporation no action at law can be maintained against it (in absence of an enabling statute). Pullman *v.* Stebbins, 51 Fed. 20.

[7] Where the debtor is *dead,* all debts created in his lifetime necessarily become specific charges on his estate—that is, *in rem* claims —since, they can no longer be asserted *in personam.* The jurisdiction of equity, therefore, to maintain creditors' bills for an accounting from the personal representative and heirs, and the payment of the decedent's debts out of his estate, is unquestioned. See Catron *v.* Bostic, 123 Va. 355.

[8] Va. Pass. & Power Co. *v.* Fisher, 104 Va. 121; Hollins *v.* Brierfield Coal Co., 150 U. S. 371. But where the affairs of a corporation, or partnership, or other association, are being *wound up in an equity proceeding,* brought by lien creditors, shareholders, members or other parties in interest, general creditors may come in under an order of reference and prove their claims—since the winding up necessarily requires that *all liabilities* be represented. The latter may not orginate the proceeding, but are usually permitted to intervene in the special instances mentioned, and prove their respective claims. *Infra,* § 451.

[9] Merchants Bank *v.* Paine, 13 R. I. 592 (excellent discussion). See Peay *v.* Morrison, 10 Gratt. 149; *supra* n. 6.

on the property, there must be judgment and execution returned *nulla bona,* as a condition of maintaining a bill to assail the transaction.[10]

In some of the states (among them Virginia and Mississippi) statutes have been enacted expressly authorizing creditors at large to maintain such suits.

§ 444. The same—fraudulent conveyances — the Virginia statute.—By the Virginia Code [11] it is provided that creditors may file a bill to set aside voluntary or fraudulent conveyances by their debtor, not only before obtaining judgments at law, but *even before their debts have matured.*

The statute [12] further fixes the priorities of the different creditors by declaring that the plaintiff shall have a lien from the time of bringing his suit; and a petitioning creditor from the time of filing his petition (in court or in the clerk's office).

2. *Proper Parties.*

§ 445. Creditors' bills, continued—proper plaintiffs.—Any creditor whose claim presents the essential characteristics indicated in the preceding sections, may file a creditors' bill to subject any of the property of his debtor liable to be thus charged.

Such a bill may be filed by (1) a single creditor for his own benefit or (2) several creditors may unite in the same bill, howsoever disconnected their several claims, provided the claims are chargeable on the same estate; or, again, (3) one or more creditors may file the bill *"on behalf of themselves and all other creditors similarly situated,* who may come in and contribute to the costs of this suit."

§ 446. The same—general creditors' bill.—Where the bill is thus filed on behalf of the plaintiffs and others who may come in, it is known as a *general creditors' bill.* But although filed on behalf of the *plaintiffs only,* if it appear that there are

---

[10] Tate *v.* Laggatt, 2 Rand. 84 (full discussion); Cates *v.* Allen, 149 U. S. 449 (federal equity jurisdiction declined, though authorized by state statute); Fleming *v.* Grafton, 54 Miss. 79.

[11] § 5186.

[12] For a more detailed notice of this statute, see the author's Notes on Equity Jurisprudence (ed. 1921), ch. xix.

other creditors who are entitled to enforce specific charges upon the subject-matter, they will be permitted, and sometimes required, to come into the suit, which will then, so far as that proceeding is concerned, be treated as a *general creditors' bill*.[13]

The reason for thus sanctioning the assertion of diverse claims in the same suit, in apparent violation of the strict and salutary rule of equity pleading that bills must not be multifarious—tantamount to a misjoinder at law—is, not that such a proceeding obviates a multiplicity of suits (as the student is apt erroneously to assume) but that it enables the court *completely to administer the assets or estate against which the proceeding is directed;* and hence *all who are entitled to share in the distribution are proper, and in many instances necessary, parties to the suit.*[14]

§ 447. The same—parties defendant.—As a general rule, it is not necessary nor, indeed, proper, to make other creditors parties defendant; but the debtor himself, and all other persons having a legal or equitable interest in the estate sought to be subjected, other than creditors, are necessary or proper parties defendant. As we shall hereafter see, *creditors not named in the bill* may become parties *by petition,* or by proving their claims *under the order of reference.*

. Where, however, the *legal title* to the subject-matter is outstanding in one or more of such creditors, (*e. g.* as mortgagees) or in a trustee in his or their behalf, it is at least proper, and the better practice, to make such title-holder a party defendant —since the court must needs have control of the legal title, particularly where the subject-matter consists of real property.

§ 448. The same—how other creditors become parties.—Creditors, not otherwise appearing as parties plaintiff or defendant, may come into the suit either (1) by petition, or (2)

---

[13] The term "general" in connection with creditors' suits is used in two distinct senses. A *"general creditor"* is one whose claim is not in judgment, or not otherwise a lien, and who therefore may not maintain a creditors' bill—whereas, the expression "general creditors' bill" (or "general creditors' suit") denotes a bill or suit for the benefit of *all lien* creditors (and not "general" creditors) of the common debtor. See *Order of Reference, infra,* §§ 449-452.

[14] Almond *v.* Wilson, 75 Va. 613; McClannahan *v.* N. & W. R. Co., 118 Va. 388; Freedman's Savings Bank *v.* Earle, 110 U. S. 710.

by proving their claims before the master under the order of reference.

It seems scarcely necessary to add that the right thus to come into the suit, after bill filed, is confined to those creditors whose claims are of such a nature that they might have been asserted by original bill—that is, *in rem* creditors—save where under special circumstances the order of reference otherwise directs.[15]

Thus where judgment creditors of A, a living person, have instituted a creditors' suit to subject the debtor's real property, no creditor at large could assert his claim therein.

3. *Order of Reference—Priorities.*

§ 449. Creditors' bills continued—order of reference. —In a creditors' suit the court assumes the administration of the entire estate or fund on which the claims asserted are chargeable. For that purpose, if necessary, the cause is referred to a master for an account of the assets to be administered in the proceeding, the amount of the several claims charged or properly chargeable on such assets, and the respective priorities, if any, of such claims, together with such other facts and inquiries as the court may direct, or the master deem necessary, for a proper disposition of the cause. We shall see something more of the order of reference in later sections.[16]

§ 450. The same—distribution of proceeds—priorities. —So far as concerns creditors who have *existing liens* before bill filed (and, as before stated, cases are comparatively rare where the situation is otherwise), their priorities are in nowise affected as the result of the suit brought. Where, however, the plaintiff's liens arise only *by virtue of the suit,* (as by attachment, or proceedings to set aside fraudulent conveyances under the Virginia statute referred to above) such liens are necessarily inferior to prior valid incumbrances. That is to say, if A has first lien and B second, the priority of these liens is not affected by the circumstance that C takes the initiative by filing a

---

[15] See *supra,* § 441, n. 8.

[16] *Infra,* § 452 *et seq.* The Virginia statute requires the master to report delinquent taxes on the property of the debtor: Va. Code 1919, § 6267.

creditors' bill—whether C is already a lien creditor inferior to A and B, or whether his lien accrues by virtue of his suit.

This is but another way of saying that creditors must take their debtor's estate in the condition in which they find it—standing, as they must, in the debtor's shoes.[17]   Hence if there be a valid lien already existing at the time the plaintiff creditor brings his suit, the suit does not displace or otherwise affect the existing prior lien.

Nor, doubtless, would the result have been otherwise, in the case stated, had A, the superior lienor, instituted the suit on behalf of himself and other creditors similarly situated.[18]

But where there is *no existing lien*[19] before bill filed, and the lien arises only out of the equitable consideration of the plaintiff's vigilance and prior suit, as occasionally happens, then the question of priority becomes important.

§ 451. The same—priorities continued.—Where, as in the case last mentioned in the preceding section, the liens of the various creditors arise *only upon the filing of the bill* or of the bringing of the suit,[20] or otherwise asserting the liens, the rule

----

[17] Subject, of course, to the provisions of the registry statutes, statutes of fraudulent conveyances, and other statutory exceptions where they exist. Lile's Notes on Eq. Jurisp. (ed. 1921), pp. 60-61.

[18] Here A's invitation is in terms to other creditors "similarly situated"—and it would seem scarcely equitable to deem him to have waived any priority to which he was entitled, by an invitation in this form to other creditors.

[19] For example in attachment proceedings by general creditors of a non-resident—or, under the Virginia statute already noticed, *supra*, § 444, in suit by general creditors to assail a fraudulent conveyance of the debtor.

[20] These expressions are substantially synonymous under the general equity practice—since the filing of the bill and the issue of the *subpœna* are usually contemporaneous steps; the filing of the bill, with prayer for *subpœna*, being the only method of obtaining the *subpœna*. Hence the language of the books on equity procedure, and in the opinions of the courts, in declaring that the lien arises from the *filing of the bill* connotes the *bringing of the suit*. It happens that in Virginia the issuing of the *subpœna* may precede the filing of the bill. In Wallace *v.* Treakle, 27 Gratt. 479, the court described the lien of the plaintiff-creditors at large as arising from the "filing of the bill," (apparently overlooking the circumstance that the *subpœna* might have been issued months before) and thus, doubtless unintentionally, creating a departure in Virginia from the accepted rule.

To obviate any difficulty on this score, the Revisors have wisely provided by statute that the lien in suits to set aside fraudulent conveyances shall arise from the "bringing of the suit." Va. Code 1919, § 5186.

is that the plaintiffs in the bill, as a reward for their vigilance in the discovery of the equitable subject-matter, and their diligence in instituting the proceedings at their own expense and risk, are entitled to priority over all other creditors "similarly situated"—though still postponed, as before indicated, to cred-*itors with prior existing liens.* But if such plaintiffs (creditors at large) sue not for their own benefit only, but on behalf of other creditors *in simili casu,* thereby making the bill, at the outset, a *general* creditors' bill—then, having invited the other creditors to share the burden of the suit, the plaintiffs are held impliedly to have agreed to share the benefits also, with such creditors as accept the invitation so extended. Hence, in the latter case, all the general creditors who come in, whether as original plaintiffs, or by petition, or under the order of reference, should share *pari passu* in the proceeds.[21]

**In Wallace *v.* Treakle, 27 Gratt. 479—a case not clearly reported,—a single plaintiff appears to have sued on behalf of *himself and of several other creditors specifically named*—a very unusual proceeding, and one probably not warranted by rules of equity pleading. The court appears to have treated all four as plaintiffs in the case. The suit was not a general creditors' suit, and its object was to set aside several conveyances made by the common debtor as a fraud on creditors. It was held that the fund should be applied: (1) to prior judgment liens, in the order of their accrual; (2) to the claims of the plaintiffs, arising from the filing of the bill; and (3) to claims of other creditors asserted later, by petition or under the order of reference, and in the order in which such claims were filed.

The question whether the phrases "filing the bill" and "bringing the suit" are synonymous, is discussed in the preceding footnote.

In Freedmans' Bank *v.* Earle, 110 U. S. 710, the opinion by Mr. Justice Matthews contains a most instructive review of the history and present status of proceedings by creditors to reach the equitable estate of their debtor. In that case the bill was filed by a judgment creditor to subject the equity of the debtor in real property incumbered by a prior deed of trust. Under the existing law of the forum (the District of Columbia) *neither the judgment nor the execution was a lien, legal or equitable, on the equity of redemption;* but (as held) such equity constituted equitable estate which the judgment creditor might subject in equity. The bill was not in form a general creditors' bill, but was filed solely in the interest of the plaintiff. Other judgment creditors subsequently came into the suit, and sought to share the proceeds ratably with the plaintiff. It will be observed that this was a case where the lien arose *only upon the filing of the bill.* The court held that the proceeds of sale should be applied (1) to the existing lien under the deed of trust; and (2) to the plaintiff's judgment as a superior claim to the claims of those creditors who came later into the suit. "It is to be noted, therefore," said the court, in speaking of creditors' suits, "that the proceeding is one instituted by the judgment creditor *for his own*

On the other hand, while, as a general rule, no other than lien creditors can file a bill to wind up the affairs of an insolvent partnership, corporation or other associated enterprise, yet inasmuch as the defendant's affairs cannot be completely settled without payment of all the debts, so far as the assets are sufficient for that purpose, the order of reference will usually make provision for the proof of *all liabilities,* whether in judgment or not.[22] These exceptions obviously arise from the necessities of the case.

4. *Effect of the Order of Reference.*

§ 452. General effect of order of reference.—Usually the first important decree entered in a creditors' suit is one of *reference to a master* for an account of all property and assets properly chargeable with the claims asserted, and to be asserted, and of the respective amounts and priorities of such claims.

Such an order operates as a declaration on the part of the court that it will *assume the exclusive administration of the*

---

interest alone, unless he elects to file the bill also for others in a like situation, with whom he chooses to make common cause; and as no specific lien arises by virtue of the judgment and execution alone, the right to obtain satisfaction out of the specific property sought to be subjected to sale for that purpose, dates from the filing of the bill. 'The creditor' says Chancellor Walworth, in Edmeston *v.* Lyde, 1 Paige 637, 640, 'whose legal diligence has pursued the property into this court, is entitled to a preference as the reward of his vigilance,' and it would 'seem unjust that the creditor who has sustained all the risk and expense of bringing his suit to a successful termination, should in the end be obliged to divide the avails thereof with those who have slept upon their rights, or who have intentionally kept back that they might profit by his exertions when there could no longer be any risk in becoming parties to the suit.' As his lien begins with the filing of the bill, it is subject to all existing incumbrances, but is superior to all of subsequent date." See also the opinion of Chancellor Kent in McDermutt *v.* Strong, 4 Johns. Ch. 687, where the same doctrine is expounded.

The case of Johnson *v.* Waters, 111 U. S. 640, illustrates the converse situation. There the plaintiff sued on behalf of *himself and all other creditors similarly situated,* to set aside certain conveyances of the debtor's lands in fraud of creditors, and to subject the lands to the plaintiff's judgment. The judgment in question was *not a lien before suit brought.* It was held that by suing on behalf of himself and all other creditors, the plaintiff had *waived priority over other creditors* who should come in; and that in case of deficiency of assets the fund should be distributed *ratably* among all the creditors who came into the suit. Compare § 444, *supra.*

[22] See *supra,* § 441.

debtor's assets for the benefit of all creditors whose. debts are properly chargeable thereon, and who may come into the proceeding. Hence though the suit may originally have been solely for the purpose of asserting a single lien on behalf of the plaintiff, an order of reference for an account of liens *converts the suit into a general creditors' suit.*[23]

The effect of such an order is of more significance than appears on its face, namely: (1) It operates to convert the suit into a general creditors' suit, and thus to deprive the original plaintiff or plaintiffs of the further *dominion of the suit;* (2) It operates as an *injunction* against the institution of other creditors' suits against the same debtor to subject the same assets, and *suspends all other pending creditors' suits* of the same character; and, as a necessary consequence of the principle last stated, (3) It suspends the running of the *statute of limitations* against all claims provable in the suit, and thereafter actually asserted therein, as shown more at large below.

§ 453. Order of reference continued—(1) effect on dominion of suit.—For reasons indicated in the preceding section, the entry of an order of reference converts the suit—which up to that time is merely the suit of the plaintiff or plaintiffs in the original bill, over which they have complete dominion, and may dismiss at will—into a suit for the benefit of *all creditors similarly situated,* whether they have already come in or not, and transfers the dominion of the suit to the creditors as a whole, thus depriving the original plaintiff or plaintiffs of their original right to dismiss or otherwise control the suit.[24]

§ 454. The same—(2) effect on other creditors' suits. —Since it is impossible, in the nature of things, to administer a single estate or fund in several independent suits, and in view of the general effect, already indicated, of an order of reference as an assumption of the jurisdiction completely to administer

---

[23] Simmons *v.* Lyles, 27 Gratt. 922, 928, *per* Staples, J.; Shultz *v.* Hansbrough, 33 Gratt. 571, 578, *per* Burks, J.; McClannahan *v.* N. & W. R. Co., 118 Va. 388.

[24] Piedmont Life Ins. Co. *v.* Maury, 75 Va. 508; Hirshfield *v.* Fitzgerald, 157 N. Y. 166, 46 L. R. A. 839, note. The same result would follow where another creditor has intervened in advance of the order of reference.

the estate or fund, (in effect, a *quasi partition* among creditors) it follows that should any other court thereafter, although in an already pending suit, assume the same jurisdiction, there would necessarily be a conflict of jurisdiction, which could only be removed by the surrender of jurisdiction by one or the other of the courts. To prevent such a conflict, the rule has been established that the court *first entering the order of reference* retains the sole jurisdiction. It follows that no other proceedings can be maintained elsewhere. Hence the first order of reference operates as an *injunction against the institution of other creditors' suits against the same estate or fund, and suspends further proceedings in other pending creditors' suits, instituted for similar purposes,* whether in the same court or in different courts of the same state.

It follows also from this, that the general rule that as between conflicting jurisdictions in the same State, priority of jurisdiction is acquired by that court in which the proceeding is first instituted, is inapplicable to creditors' suits; and that *priority of jurisdiction here is acquired by that court which first enters the order of reference.*[25]

§ 455. The same—(3) effect on the statute of limitations.—As a natural consequence of the foregoing, such a decree has the further effect of suspending the statute of limitations as to all creditors *whose claims are properly provable in the suit,* and who *actually come into the suit.*[26]

This consequence results from the rule that an injunction against suit on a contract, or other claim, suspends the running of the statute of limitations—as does also the pendency of a suit for the enforcement of the claim. By the entry of the order of reference, as already indicated, other suits are, in effect, enjoined, and the main suit becomes, in theory, one for the enforcement of *all claims properly provable*—even those not as yet actually asserted.

---

[25] Kent *v.* Cloyd, 30 Gratt. 555; Bilmeyer *v.* Sherman, 23 W. Va. 657; Craig *v.* Hoge, 95 Va. 275; Buck *v.* Coldbath, 3 Wall. 334. The same effect follows the appointment of a receiver in a creditors' suit. *Post,* ch. xxxiii.

[26] Callaway *v.* Saunders, 99 Va. 350, 7 Va. Law Reg. 40, note. See Richmond *v.* Irons, 121 U. S. 27; Jackson *v.* Hull, 21 W. Va. 612; 1 Daniell, Ch. Pr. 643.

§ 456. Effect on statute of limitations, continued—Virginia statute.—By a quite recent statute in Virginia,[27] the effect on the statute of limitations of an order of reference in a creditors' suit, under the unwritten rule, has been somewhat altered—and not clearly for the better.

The statutory provision is, in substance, as follows:

1. *Where the suit is originally commenced as a general creditors' suit.*—Here, the running of the statute of limitations is declared to be suspended from the *commencement of the suit* (instead of from the date of the order of reference under the equity rule) as to (a) all debts provable in the cause, *and actually proved* under *the first order of reference* therein entered. But as to (b) debts *not* thus proved under the first order of reference, but which are proved under a later order in the same cause, the statute continues to run until such later order of reference is entered.

2. *Where the suit is not commenced as a general creditors' suit.*—Here the statute declares that if such suit becomes a general creditors' suit by subsequent proceedings in the cause, by entry of an order of reference, the statute of limitations is suspended, *from the time of the entry of the order,* but only as to creditors who come in under such order of reference. As to creditors coming in afterwards by petition, or under a second order of reference, the statute continues to run regardless of previous proceedings, until the filing of such petitions or the entry of the later order of reference.

§ 457. Statute of limitations, continued — right of competing creditor to plead.—The general rule that the statute of limitations is a personal plea, and may be set up by the debtor only, is firmly established. The rule rests on the principle that the effect of the statute is not to bar the *right* but the *remedy* only—and not even to bar the remedy unless the debtor asserts the bar as a personal privilege.[28]

---

[27] Acts 1920, p. 87.

[28] See 3 Va. Law Reg. 63; Clayton *v.* Tyson, 32 Gratt. 72; Smith *v.* Hutchinson, 78 Va. 683.

But a somewhat different principle is applicable, in certain cases, where the question is not one of securing a personal judgment against the debtor, but concerns competing claims of creditors and others in the distribution of a particular fund or estate under the administration of the court, and time-barred claims are being asserted against the *res,* to the detriment of other creditors or claimants. The several situations here presented are considered in the section following.

§ 458. The same, continued.—(1) Where the estate being administered is that of a *decedent,* it seems a settled rule that since it is the duty (and not merely privilege) of the personal representative to plead the statute in a proper case, any creditor of the estate, whose interest requires it, may set up the statute.[29]

(2) Again, where the claim is barred not by the ordinary statute of limitations but arises out of a statute, which, *along with the right, prescribes a time limitation* within which the right must be asserted, any creditor whose rights would be affected by enforcement of the time-barred claim, may set up the statute.[30]

(3) But where the several competing claims are being asserted against the estate of a *living defendant,* (as in a creditors' bill to enforce the lien of judgments), who himself refuses to interpose the plea of the statute against time-barred claims, and the participation of these claims will prejudice other creditors who are parties to the suit, the authorities are not harmonious on the question whether the latter class of creditors may interpose the plea of the statute. It seems settled in Virginia [31] that they may, while the rule in West Virginia is the reverse.[32]

---

[29] Tazewell *v.* Whittle, 13 Gratt. 345; Woodyard *v.* Polsley, 14 W. Va. 211; 6 Va. Law Reg. 852.

[30] McCartney *v.* Tyrer, 94 Va. 198 (mechanic's lien); 3 Va. Law Reg. 63; 6 Va. Law Reg. 852. Here the right itself, and not the remedy only, is affected by the statute.

[31] Ayres *v.* Burk, 82 Va. 338; McCartney *v.* Tyrer, 94 Va. 198— editorially discussed in 3 Va. Law Reg. 63 and 6 Va. Law Reg. 852. One may of course, plead the statute, in defense of his own *title to property*—as against a debt of a predecessor in title, asserted as a lien. See Walker *v.* Burgess (W. Va.), 30 S. E. 99.

[32] Welton *v.* Boggs (W. Va.), 32 S. E. 232; McClannahan *v.* N. & W. R. Co., 122 Va. 705—a case in which title by adverse pos-

§ 459. Several bills pending—practice.—The practice where there are several creditors' bills pending to subject the same *res* is explained in Stephenson *v.* Taverners: [33] "Where there are several such suits pending at the same time," says Moncure, J., "it seems the decree for an account of outstanding claims 'may be made in the cause which is first ripe for a decree, whether that cause was first commenced or not; and when the decree is made in the younger suit, then the proceedings in the elder suit must be stayed.' Ross *v.* Crary, 1 Paige 417, note (a)."

5. *Purpose and Necessity of Order of Reference.*

§ 460. Account of liens—purpose.—Before decreeing a sale of real property at the suit of lien-creditors, the policy of courts of equity is to convene all lien-holders; to ascertain definitely the amounts of the several liens, with their respective priorities; and to obtain precise information as to the location and description of the property or properties owned by the debtor and against which the proceeding is directed.

§ 461. The same—advantages—(1) sale free of liens. —The enforcement of this policy accomplishes several important and beneficial results, notably in that the convention of all lien-holders enables the court to sell the property *free of liens*— thus encouraging prospective purchasers to bid more freely than they would do if obliged to bid blindly, and to accept title subject to unknown and unascertained liens not represented in the suit. Thus both the debtor and his creditors are benefited by a more advantageous sale.

§ 462. The same—(2) enabling lien-holder to bid intelligently.—*The fixing of the priorities* enables each creditor to know precisely the aggregate of all liens superior to his own, and therefore, if he desires to become a bidder at the sale in order to save his own debt, he may do so intelligently. Here,

---

session was successfully maintained against a judgment lien creditor of a former owner.

[33] 9 Gratt. 398, 406-407. It is not unusual to consolidate such causes, or to order them heard together—with the necessary order of transfer, where the several causes are pending in separate courts.

again, by encouraging creditors to bid, the prospects of an advantageous sale are increased.

§ 463. The same—(3) defining the res.—*Precise knowledge of the location and description of the res* which the court is to administer is manifestly necessary in all judicial proceedings. The homely maxim of equity is that it "will never sell a pig in a bag."

§ 464. Order of reference continued—when essential. —In pursuance .of the policy referred to, the settled practice in equity is to refuse to decree a sale of real property where the record indicates that there are conflicting liens, or liens of unascertained or disputed amounts, or an absence of certainty in the location or description of the subject-matter, or other impediments to a fair sale. And for disregard of this rule the decree will be reversed on appeal. The rule does not depend on the *character* of the lien or liens asserted in the bill, but on the *uncertainty* in one or more of the particulars mentioned, namely, in the *amount or amounts due*, in the several *priorities*, or in the *subject-matter*, or in some other matter likely to operate as a clog upon the bidding.[34]

So far is this policy carried of requiring certainty in these several particulars, that where a creditor secured by a deed of trust is proceeding, with the co-operation of the trustee, to enforce his claim by a sale of the property *in pais*, the court will enjoin the sale and order a proper account to be taken, where it is made to appear by the debtor-plaintiff's bill, or that of any interested party, or otherwise, that the title to the trust subject is clouded, or the *res* is uncertain, or the amount of the debt is in dispute, or that there are other conflicting liens on the property. This means not only that the court will not itself decree a sale where these circumstances appear, but that it will *actively*

---

[34] See *Judicial Sales, ante,* ch. xxi; Coles *v.* McRae, 6 Rand. 718; Simmons *v.* Lyles, 27 Gratt. 922; Kendrick *v.* Whitney, 28 Gratt. 646; Shultz *v.* Hansbrough, 33 Gratt. 567; Bristol, etc., Co. *v.* Caldwell, 95 Va. 47; Sims *v.* Tyrer, 96 Va. 14; Rush *v.* Dickenson County Bank, 128 Va. 114.

The rule is generally not applicable to *personal property*—because of its perishable nature, and because personal chattels may usually be sold in detail, instead of in bulk. Coles *v.* McRae, *supra;* Bank *v.* Trigg, 106 Va. 327.

intervene by injunction, and forbid a sale in pais, until these uncertainties are cleared up.[35]

§ 465. The same—when not essential.—Where the reason of the rule ceases the rule itself ceases. Hence on a creditors' bill brought solely on behalf of the plaintiff or plaintiffs, whose claims are certain, or may be made certain by proofs in the cause, with like certainty or possible certainty as to the *res,* with nothing on the record to indicate the existence of other conflicting liens, the court will not assume the probability or possibility of other liens, and hence may order a sale without an account of liens.[36] And so, where it is evident that the non-enforcement of the rule would not produce the harmful results against which it is directed.[37]

§ 466. Attachment, injunction and receivership. — These ancillary processes of attachment, injunction and receivership are nowhere more commonly found, nor more beneficially administered, than in combination with creditors' suits.[38]

---

[35] Gay *v.* Hancock, 1 Rand. 72; Miller *v.* Argyle, 5 Leigh 460; Wilkins *v.* Gordon, 11 Leigh 547; Hudson *v.* Barham, 101 Va. 63; Dechert *v.* Chesapeake, etc., Co., 101 Va. 804.

[36] Repass *v.* Moore, 96 Va. 147; Shickel *v.* Berryville Land Co., 99 Va. 88.

[37] Bank *v.* Trigg, 106 Va. 327—where it appeared that the first lien amounted to several millions of dollars, largely in excess of the value of the property, and that the inferior liens were for such comparatively small amounts as to exclude the probability that the inferior lienors would desire to bid at the sale.

[38] See *Injunctions, ante,* ch. xxvii; *Receivers, post,* chs. xxxii-xxxiii.

CHAPTER XXXII.

Receivers.*

§ 467. Receiver—nature of the office.—A receiver is a disinterested executive officer appointed by a court of equity,[1] whose duty it is, under the direction and supervision of the court, to take possession of property, real or personal, involved in an equity suit, for the purpose of preserving it *pendente lite,* where for good reason it seems to the court that no party to the suit should have the custody of it.[2]

1. *Appointment of Receiver.*

§ 468. The same—purpose of his appointment.—While the main purpose of a receivership, as indicated, is to preserve the *res* during the litigation, and finally to dispose of it as the court may direct, the office is not always a passive one nor the receiver necessarily a mere custodian. Not infrequently the preservation of the *res* in controversy, because of its inherent nature, requires that it be actively used or operated, in which case the scope of the receivership becomes much wider than that of mere custodianship of the property.

Thus, where the *res* consists of the assets of a railway company, or other public utility, which, in the interest of the public as well as of its owners and creditors, must be operated— or where, though not of public concern, the value of the property would be seriously affected by ceasing the operations con-

---

*Consult: High on Receivers (4th ed.).

[1] *Statutory receivers*—that is, those designated directly by statute, or appointed by executive officials or boards, under authority of statute—are not within this definition. See Relfe *v.* Rundle, 103 U. S. 222; *post,* § 507 *et seq.*

[2] The nature of the office, and the purpose and effect of the appointment of a receiver, are lucidly explained by Baldwin, J., in Beverley *v.* Brooks, 4 Gratt. 187, 208. (Michie's Ed. Ann.).

In the selection of the receiver the court will consider the interests of all parties, as well as the fitness of the appointee for the particular office. Where the property is being administered by liquidating trustees, who are fit persons, the court will usually name one or more of such trustees as receivers. Dechert *v.* Chesapeake & Western Co.. 101 Và. 804; Martin *v.* Kester (W. Va.), 39 S. E. 598.

nected with it (as in the case of the plant of a newspaper, or of a manufacturing property with a large quantity of unfinished material on hand, or profitable unfilled contracts)—the receiver may be directed to operate the property as a *going concern*, so as to preserve the good-will and otherwise prevent serious loss to the owners and other parties in interest.

§ 469. Circumstances justifying appointment of receiver.—In order to call into exercise the extraordinary jurisdiction to seize the defendant's property, and to take it out of his possession before the plaintiff has established his right thereto, or the validity of his claim against it, by a trial on the merits, the court must be satisfied that there are good reasons why the property should be thus taken into its custody by the appoinment of a receiver.

There are two chief circumstances upon which the bill for a receiver must rest, namely, (1) The plaintiff must have an *equitable cause of action*, based on *a legal or equitable interest in the res itself,* and not a merely personal claim against the defendant owner; and (2) It must appear that the *rights of the plaintiff will or may be jeoparded if the property be left in the defendant's possession*—as by removal beyond the jurisdiction, misuse, misapplication, spoliation, wastage, or otherwise.

§ 470. The same.—"The exercise of the extraordinary power of a chancellor in appointing receivers," says Mr. High,[3] "as in granting writs of injunction or *ne exeat,* is an exceedingly delicate and responsible duty, to be discharged by the court with utmost caution, and only under such special or peculiar circumstanees as demand summary relief. Indeed the appointment of a receiver is regarded as one of the most difficult and embarrassing duties which a court of equity is called upon to perform. It is a peremptory measure whose effect, temporarily at least, is to deprive of his property a defendant in possession, before a final judgment or decree is reached by the court determining the rights of the parties. It is therefore not to be exercised doubtingly, but the court must be convinced that the relief is needful, and that it is the appropriate means of secur-

---

[3] High, Receivers 3.

ing an appropriate end. And since it is a serious interference
with the rights of the citizen, without the verdict of a jury, and
before a regular hearing, it should be granted only for the pre-
vention of manifest wrong and injury."

§ 471. The same—special circumstances to be shown.

—In view of the harshness of the proceeding as described in
the sections preceding, it is important for the student to observe
that to justify the appointment of a receiver the plaintiff must
disclose in his bill such a case as clearly to give him standing in a
court of equity to assert it; as well as the peculiar circumstances
that render a receivership essential to protect the right in question. It must be remembered that the appointment of the receiver is *not the primary object of the suit,* but is merely *ancillary* to some equitable right which it is the chief purpose of the
bill to protect and enforce. It is vital therefore that the application for the receivership be based on a valid equity sought
to be enforced—for the consideration and security of which the
appointment of the receiver is necessary.

Hence, in order to exhibit a case proper for the appointment
of a receiver, the plaintiff's bill must (1) assert a *valid equitable claim or right* (that is, one not remediable at law) *to, or
charged upon, the very property sought to be made the subject
of the receivership;* and (2) must allege the *special circumstances which make the appointment of a receiver essential for
the preservation of the property,* and for its forthcoming at the
proper time, in response to the decree of the court, on the final
determination of the controversy.[4]

§ 472. The same—(1) nature of the plaintiff's right.

—The plaintiff's right must rest on an equitable claim, or one for
the assertion of which there is no adequate legal remedy; and
must be in the nature of an *equity in the property,* (i. e. *in rem*)
so that the defendant's relation to the *res* is in the nature of a
trust for the plaintiff's benefit. Unless the right be *in rem* in
its original form, it must be converted into such a right, by
judgment or otherwise, before the plaintiff has a *locus standi*

---

[4] High, Receivers, 11-12. See Meyers Bros. *v.* Harman Bros. (W.
Va.), 89 S. E. 146; Beverley *v.* Brooks, 4 Gratt. 187, 208.

for the appointment of a receiver—on the kindred and familiar principle that a *general* creditor cannot maintain a creditors' bill, or interfere with the defendant's possession of his own estate.[5] Thus a creditor in position to maintain a creditor's bill;[6] a plaintiff asserting a trust in the *res*, express or implied;[7] suits by shareholders of a corporation seeking an accounting or a winding up of the corporate affairs;[8] partners seeking a dissolution and winding up of the firm business, or an accounting and winding up after dissolution;[9] and a mortgagee suing for foreclosure, afford illustrations of proper plaintiffs in an application for a receiver.

§ 473. The same—(2) necessity of receiver for preservation of the res.—Assuming that the bill contains proper allegations as to the plaintiff's right primarily to equitable relief, the second essential of a receivership is that there be a well grounded apprehension of immediate danger of serious loss to the plaintiff, unless the property be taken in the custody of the court.[10] Both the equitable *in rem* claim, and the jeopardy of the *res*, must concur.

§ 474. The same—special appointment. — While in many states courts of equity are served by a permanent official known as a *General Receiver*, the duties of such an official are usually no other than those of the financial agent of the court, to receive funds paid into court, and to preserve, invest or otherwise dispose of them as the court may order.[11]

The receiver to whom this brief discussion is confined is a temporary officer, named by special designation of the court in the cause in which he is appointed.

---

[5] High, Receivers, 9-11.

[6] For the essentials of which see *Creditors' Bills, ante*, § 439 *et seq.* High, Receivers, 399-471.

[7] High, Receivers, 9, 412, 694-699.

[8] After exhausting all means of redress within the corporation itself. Hawes *v.* Oakland, 104 U. S. 450; Passenger & Power Co. *v.* Fisher, 104 Va. 121; Saunders *v.* Bank of Mecklenburg, 113 Va. 656; Marshall on Corporations, § 304; Equity Rule 27; High, Receivers, 292 *et seq.*

[9] High, Receivers, 472-552.

[10] High, Receivers, 11.

[11] Va. Code 1919, §§ 6280-6294.

§ 475. The same—appointment in vacation.—The analogy between the preliminary injunction and the appointment of a receiver is both close and striking—an analogy to which we shall have occasion to recur again. Both are in their nature extraordinary and preventive proceedings; neither affects the merits of the controversy; the purpose of each is to preserve the *status quo;* and the one is frequently the complement of the other. In many cases the appointment of a receiver without the further protection of an injunction, or, *per contra,* the granting of the injunction without the precautionary measure of a receivership, would be fruitless. It follows, therefore, that *jurisdiction to grant injunctions draws with it, ex necessitate, jurisdiction to appoint a receiver.* Hence the question whether a particular court or judge has jurisdiction to appoint a receiver, and whether the appointment may be made in vacation (where there is no determining statutory provision) will depend on the juris-. diction of the court or judge with respect to the granting of injunctions. Power to grant the latter, in term or in vacation, includes the necessary incident of appointing the former.[12] And the power to appoint in vacation carries with it the power to discharge in vacation.[13]

2. *Notice of Application.*

§ 476. Appointment continued—notice of application. —While there is thus a strong analogy between the issuing of a preliminary injunction and the appointment of a receiver, the latter is yet a much more serious disturbance of the apparent rights of the defendant. The injunction is merely negative, and does not alter the immediate *status quo,* whereas the receivership is, in a sense, an anticipatory execution, (or, perhaps, more accurately, an equitable attachment), and for the time being deprives the defendant of the possession of his property at the very inception of the suit, before the plaintiff has established his claim by a trial on the merits, and before the defendant has had opportunity of making his defense.

---

[12] High, Receivers, 15-16; 105-106; Smith *v.* Butcher, 28 Gratt. 144; Harwell *v.* Potts, 80 Ala. 70; Rainey *v.* Freeport, etc., Co., 58 W. Va. 424. See *Injunctions, ante,* ch. xxvii.
[13] Crawford *v.* Ross, 39 Ga. 44; High, Receivers 824-826.

It is natural in such circumstances that courts should be more averse to the appointment of a receiver than to the granting of a preliminary injunction, and should proceed with greater caution in the one case than the other.

It is an imperative rule, therefore, (with the exceptions presently to be noted) that no application for the appointment of a receiver will be granted on a mere *ex parte* application, but that the defendant must have seasonable notice of the application, with opportunity to introduce counter-affidavits to meet those offered by the plaintiff in support of the allegations of his bill.[14]

§ 477. Notice of application—continued.—But this rule is not inflexible, nor carried further than justified by the reason on which it rests.   Hence the court will not insist upon notice to the defendant where it is impracticable—as where the defendant has absconded; or where he is beyond the jurisdiction and is not represented by counsel or other authorized representative, and the situation is urgent.   Nor will notice be required where it is clearly shown that notice to the defendant would probably *defeat the very object sought* in the application for the receivership—as that the defendant, in consequence of the notice, would probably remove the *res* from the jurisdiction, or otherwise attempt to defeat the main purpose of the bill.

In other words, the rule of notice gives way where its enforcement would threaten greater injustice to the plaintiff than its omission would probably cause to the defendant.[15]

---

[14] High. Receivers, 112 *et seq;* Freidenheim v. Rohr, 87 Va. 764; Ruffner v. Mairs, 32 W. Va. 655, 11 S. E. 5; Stockton v. Harmon, 32 Fla. 312, 13 So. 833; Ensley Devel. Co. v. Powell, 147 Ala. 300, 40 So. 137; Rogers v. Dougherty, 20 Ga. 271.   In Bristow v. Home Building Co., 91 Va. 18, 20 S. E. 946, it was held that where, on the subsequent appearance of the defendant, the court overruled his motion to discharge the receiver appointed without notice, this is equivalent to holding that the *ex parte* application for an injunction and receiver was properly granted without notice.

The appointment of a receiver, without notice, cannot be a more summary proceeding than the familiar proceeding under *attachment* statutes, which require no notice to the defendant prior to the seizure of his property.   So, while the requisites for the appointment of a receiver and for the issue of an attachment are not always identical, it would seem that where the plaintiff makes out such an equitable case as would justify an attachment at law if the claim were legal, he will at least have stated a proper case for the appointment of a receiver.

[15] High, Receivers, 113-117; Jacksonville, etc., Co. v. Stockton, 40

3. *Receiver's Bond.*

§ 478. Receiver's bond.—Unless dispensed with by consent of parties, or, in rare cases, where plainly unnecessary, before the receiver is competent to perform any official duty he is required to execute a bond, with sufficient sureties, conditioned on the faithful performance of his duties, including a due accounting for all funds or property coming into his hands officially. The order appointing him usually provides that he shall have no powers thereunder until he has executed the required bond, in the penalty prescribed in the order.

§ 479. The same—retroactive effect.—Where there is an interval between the appointment and the qualification of the receiver, the better rule is that the qualification operates retroactively, and the rights and title of the receiver will be reckoned as of the date of his appointment. Hence the receiver's title will take precedence over a hostile levy made in the interval between his appointment and his qualification.[16]

4. *Effect of Receiver's Appointment.*

§ 480. Effect of appointment.—The appointment of a receiver is in nowise the determination of the merits of the controversy. Indeed, as already indicated, such appointment is strikingly analogous to the *preliminary injunction* or to an *attachment*—to either of which proceedings the receivership is not infrequently ancillary. The purpose of the preliminary injunction is to preserve the *status quo;* the purpose of the *attachment,* to hold, preserve and to secure the forthcoming of the property attached; and so the object of the *receivership* is simply to safeguard the *status quo* the more securely, by removing the subject-matter of the controversy beyond the reach of any of the litigants, and placing it in the custody of the court, so that it

---

Fla. 141, 23 So. 557; Pollard *v.* Southern Fertilizer Co., 122 Ala. 409, 25 So. 169; Verplanck *v.* Mercantile Ins. Co., 2 Paige 438 (per Walworth, Chancellor).

[16] High, Receivers, 121a; *In re* Christian Jensen Co., 128 N. Y. 550, 28 N. E. 665; Temple *v.* Glasgow, 25 C. C. A. 540, 80 Fed. 441, distinguishing Frayser *v.* Railway Co., 81 Va. 388. Compare Woods *v.* Ellis, 85 Va. 471, where the contrary was assumed without discussion.

may be forthcoming to meet such final decree as may be made in the cause.[17]

§ 481. The same—the receiver's title.—It follows from what has been said, that the appointment of the receiver operates only as a temporary sequestration, and has *no effect on the title* to the property or the merits of the controversy; but the title, legal and equitable, remains undisturbed by the appointment—the right of *possession* alone being affected. The title of the receiver, therefore, is in no sense that of the *trustee* of an express trust, or of an *assignee.*

From this, it further follows, as we shall see later, that *actions at law* brought by the receiver under the direction of the court, for the purpose of reducing the *res* into his possession, must generally be asserted in the name of the *legal* owner, and cannot be maintained in the name of the receiver.[18]

§ 482. The same—property is in custodia legis.—The possession of the receiver is the possession of the court, of which the receiver is but the arm—and hence the effect of the receivership is to place the estate *in custodia legis,* for the benefit of such of the litigants as may be declared entitled to it or its proceeds on the final determination of the controversy.

§ 483. Interference with receiver's possession.—The important consequence of the taking of the *res* into the custody of the court, (*in custodia legis*) through the instrumentality of the receiver, is, that any interference with the receiver's possession, without consent of the court, *will be treated as a contempt*

---

[17] Beverley *v.* Brooke, 4 Gratt. 187, 208. The order directing a transfer of possession to the receiver is such a 'change of possession' as is contemplated by Va. Code 1919, § 6336, and is therefore appealable. Dechert *v.* Chesapeake, etc., Co., 101 Va. 804.

[18] Save of course where the receiver can *show title*—as by assignment, or by statute, or where he has possessory title and is asserting no other. See *post, Suit by Receivers,* §§ 498 *et seq.* This, on the familiar principle that equity acts *in personam* only, and hence its decrees cannot *ex proprio vigore* transfer legal title. Sterrett *v.* Second Nat. Bank, 246 Fed. 753, 3 A. L. R. 256 (annotated), affirmed 248 U. S. 52. Lile, Notes on Equity Jurisp. (ed. 1921), p. 32; Proctor *v.* Ferebee (N. C.), 36 Am. Dec. 34, n. In some of the states, the practice is to compel the holder of the title to convey it to the receiver. Fletcher, Eq. Pl. & Pr. 491; High, Receivers, 443-449.

of court and punished accordingly.[19] The court may also, of course, vindicate its authority by injunction.[20]

Not only is it such contempt for a private person thus to interfere with the receiver's possession, but it is equally so where such interference is in the form of *legal proceedings against the rceiver or the property under his control.* Thus an officer who levies an execution or a distress warrant on property in the possession of a receiver, without consent of the court, is guilty of contempt.[21]

5. *Familiar Instances of Receiverships.*

§ 484. Familiar instances of receiverships.—It is, of course, impossible to enumerate, in the form of concrete statement, the various circumstances justifying a receivership, but perhaps a few illustrations of the more common cases in which receivers are appointed—almost as a matter of course—may be helpful to the student:

(a) *Foreclosure of mortgages* and other liens on *real* property, where it is doubtful whether the proceeds of the mortgaged property will be sufficient to satisfy the debt, and, because of the insolvency of the debtor, the mortgagee desires to sequester the rents and profits. Here a receiver may be named to collect the rents and profits.[22]

(b) *Foreclosure of mortgages* or other liens on *personal or mixed* property, where good cause is shown for placing the property in the custody of a receiver. Under this head would come the foreclosure of mortgages on railways and other public service companies—or on the property of private corporations or of

---

[19] High, Receivers, 163 *et seq.*

[20] Id. 256.

[21] Id. 163 *et seq.* See Camden *v.* Va. Safe Deposit, etc., Co., 115 Va. 26. So where the estate of the debtor (an insolvent corporation) is in the hands of a receiver, creditors of the insolvent may not maintain a suit to assert claims in favor of the insolvent debtor (*e. g.* liability of directors of the insolvent corporation for negligent or fraudulent management), without first applying to the receiver to assert the liability. Saunders *v.* Bank of Mecklenburg, 113 Va. 656.

[22] High, Receivers, 639-691; Smith *v.* Butcher, 28 Gratt. 144; Freedman's Sav. Bank *v.* Shepperd, 127 U. S. 494; Shepperd *v.* Pepper, 133 U. S. 626.

individuals, where the mortgaged assets are of such a character as to be liable to spoliation or wastage.[23]

(c) In cases of *creditors' bills* generally—where the assets are of a character to need the special protection afforded by a receivership.[24] The receivership is particularly appropriate in creditors' suits to subject *personal* assets transferred in fraud of creditors.[25]

(d) *Shareholders' suits* [26] to wind up the affairs of the corporation, for insolvency or other proper cause; as well as derivative suits by shareholders or creditors of insolvent corporations against directors or other officials to recover corporate funds wrongfully appropriated or negligently lost.

(e) *Controversies between partners*, calling for a dissolution and winding up of the partnership affairs, where the partners cannot agree upon the terms of the dissolution, or on the custody, control and disposition of the assets after dissolution.[27]

(f) *Controversies between trustee and cestui que trust*, where the latter seeks a removal of the trustee for fraud, incompetency, or other cause indicating the propriety of placing the trust *res* in the custody of a receiver.[28]

§ 485. Putting the plaintiff on terms — doctrine of Fosdick v. Schall.—As has already been indicated, the appointment of a receiver in any case is not a matter of right, but rests in the sound discretion of the court. Hence wherever application is made for a receivership, the court may apply the maxim that he who wants equity must do equity,[29] and therefore may exact terms of the plaintiff as the price of the court's assistance.

A striking application of the maxim was made by the Supreme Court of the United States in Fosdick *v.* Schall,[30] and

---

[23] High, Receivers 376-389a, 647.

[24] High, Receivers, 399, *et seq.* The student will of course recall that in the absence of statute, *general* creditors cannot maintain such a bill. See *Creditors' Bills, ante,* ch. xxxi.

[25] By special statute in Virginia general creditors may have relief in such cases. *Ante,* § 444.

[26] High, Receivers, 292-295c.

[27] High, Receivers, 472-508.

[28] Id. 697, *et seq.*

[29] For an exposition of the scope of this maxim, see Lile's Notes on Equity Jurisprudence (ed. 1921), p. 26.

[30] 99 U. S. 235.

the principle there established has become the settled practice, particularly in connection with railroad receiverships.

In substance, the rule of Fosdick v. Schall is this: Where a railroad company is unable to meet its bonded indebtedness, or the annual interest payments thereon, and the bondholders, or their representative, the trustee in the mortgage or deed of trust securing the bonds, make application to a court of equity for a receivership looking to foreclosure proceedings, the court, as a condition of appointing a receiver and administering the assets in such proceedings, may require the bondholders to submit to a marshalling of the assets in behalf of unpaid employees and others who have furnished labor or materials for operation of the road since insolvency, and prior to the receivership. .

§ 486. Fosdick v. Schall, continued.—The theory upon which this doctrine is applied is that the income from the operation of the railroad should first be applied in payment of wages of employees and of persons supplying material and equipment to enable the railroad to continue operations as a going concern. And, until bill filed for foreclosure, the bond creditors have no lien on current income. Those persons supplying labor and materials, therefore, have first claim upon such income.

Where, however, this income has been *diverted to the payment of overhead charges, such as interest on the bonded indebtedness*, leaving wages of employees and debts for current supplies unpaid, the court, in assuming control of the road through a receivership, will, *out of the capital assets* covered by the mortgage, *restore to income account* so much of the income so diverted as may be necessary to liquidate claims for wages and current supplies. In other words, the court will require the bondholders, though secured by a first mortgage lien, to surrender their priority in the capital assets to the equitable claims for labor and supplies furnished *after insolvency, and prior to the receivership*.

This principle is justified not only on the right of the court to grant the receivership and administer the assets on equitable terms, under the maxim quoted, but on the further consideration that in permitting the railroad company to remain in possession and continue operations after insolvency, the company should be considered, in a sense, as operating the road *in the interest of the bondholders,* and as their *quasi trustee* or *agent;* and hence the superior lien of the bondholders must yield to the equities of those whose labor and materials have kept the company a going concern, and have thus conserved the mortgage security for the benefit of the first lien creditors.

§ 487. The same, continued.—Not all claims for labor and supplies are thus privileged under the rule; but, as heretofore applied by the United States Supreme Court where the principle originated, the labor and supply claims must be of *recent origin,* arising within a short period, usually not over six months anterior to the receivership—though in Southern R. Co. *v.* Carnegie Steel Co.,[31] the rule was extended to cover a period of eleven months.

---

[31] 176 U. S. 257. In Lackawanna, etc., Co. *v.* Farmers Loan & Trust Co., 176 U. S. 298, the claim was denied on the ground that the material supplied (steel rails) was in such quantity as to amount to a *reconstruction* of the road, or the construction of a new road, and therefore more properly chargeable to capital than to income account. The opinion of Mr. Justice Harlan in Southern Railway Co. *v.* Carnegie Steel Co., *supra,* contains a luminous discussion of the rule in its several aspects.

CHAPTER XXXIII.

Receivers—*Continued.*

6. *General Powers of Receiver.*

§ 488. General powers and duties of receiver. — As more than once heretofore indicated, the receiver is the mere arm of the court, and hence his powers and duties are necessarily dependent on the terms, express or implied, of the decree appointing him, and of such subsequent orders as the court may, from time to time, enter, enlarging, restricting or otherwise modifying the original order.

§ 489. Implied powers—duties passive.—Where his duties are merely passive, the implied powers of the receiver are somewhat similar to those of a special agent—and will not be extended by implication beyond those powers clearly incidental to those expressly conferred. But the order of appointment will be construed as conferring all powers reasonably incidental to the main powers.[1]

§ 490. Implied powers, continued—duties active. — Where, however, the duties of the receiver are not simply passive, but are active in their nature—as where they include the general management and operation of the *res*, as a going concern (*e. g.* a railway or other public utility, or a manufacturing plant, or the publication of a newspaper)—since, in the nature of the case, minute instructions as to the details of the management are impracticable, the receiver must of necessity be invested, by implication, with wide discretionary power. And in the conduct and management of such operations, where not otherwise restricted by the directions of the court, the receiver may exercise such incidental powers as under the circumstances necessarily or reasonably accompany the conduct of the business intrusted to his management.[2]

---

[1] See Thompson *v.* Phœnix Ins. Co., 136 U. S. 287; authorities in next footnote.

[2] State Bank of Virginia *v.* Domestic Sewing Machine Co., 99 Va. 411; High, Receivers 36, 175-180, 313-342, 390-394.

§ 491. Suits against receivers.—For the reasons already mentioned, the institution of a suit against the receiver, in his official capacity, without consent of the court, is a contempt—punishable in contempt proceedings, and remediable by injunction.[3] Many authorities go further, and hold that the question of consent is a jurisdictional one, and the absence of such consent is fatal to the jurisdiction,[4] even in a court of law in a foreign state.[5]

§ 492. The same — how rights against receiver asserted—intervention.—Creditors and others holding claims against the debtor, and seeking to subject the *res* in the receiver's hands—claims arising *anterior* to the receivership, or not out of any act of or transaction of the receiver or his agents—must, of course, *intervene in the equity suit* in which the *res* is being administered, unless such claims are already asserted in the original bill. Such claims are not against the *receiver* but against the *debtor*, and his assets under the control of the court. Such intervention may be either by a formal petition, or by proof under an order of reference. As stated, such claims are liabilities of the *main defendant* whose estate has been sequestered by means of receivership.

But where claims arise *against the receiver as such* (of course,

---

[3] High, Receivers, 254.

[4] Though the weight of authority is *contra*. Id. 254a. See Melendy *v.* Barbour, 78 Va. 544; Reed *v.* Axtell, 84 Va. 231; Barton *v.* Barbour, 104 U. S. 126. Where, however, the suit is against the receiver *personally*, as for a trespass committed under color of his receivership, but outside and in excess of his authority, the rule probably does not apply—since here the plaintiff is not seeking in any manner to assert a claim against the property *in custodia legis*. High, Receivers, 257.

[5] In Barton *v.* Barbour, *supra*, the court held that in the absence of an allegation of consent by the appointing court, an action *at law* could not be maintained in the District of Columbia, against a receiver of a Virginia court, for personal injuries suffered by the plaintiff, in Virginia, from the negligence of the receiver's servants. Mr. Justice Miller's dissenting opinion seems to present the sounder view. While the appointing court may protect its own receiver, and punish by contempt any persons who institute legal proceedings against the receiver without its consent, courts of other jurisdictions —and particularly courts of law—are under no obligation to recognize the representative character of the defendant, whose description as "receiver" is (in a court of law) merely *descriptio personae*. See *infra*, § 493, n. 7.

subsequent to his appointment), *out of his management* or operations connected with the sequestered property—claims which the receiver refuses to pay, or to audit for payment—the proper method of proceeding is to file (by consent of the court), a petition in the pending chancery suit, showing a valid *prima facie* claim against the receiver, and praying for permission to prosecute the claim, either by proceedings in the cause itself, or in an independent suit against the receiver, in such forum as the court may designate, at law or in equity, according to the nature of the demand.[5a]

§ 493. Judgment against receiver—nature—how enforced.

—Where the claim is thus against the receiver officially, and not for personal wrongs which he may have committed beyond the scope of his official duties,[6] a valid judgment recovered against him, in a proceeding so authorized, does not, in equity, bind the receiver *personally*—since in substance the proceeding is *against the receivership*, or the fund represented by it.[7]

The plaintiff's proper procedure, after judgment, is to petition the court administering the assets to allow and order the judgment paid out of the receivership funds, according to the priority to which it may be entitled. As previously pointed out, execution on such judgment cannot be levied on the assets in the hands of the receiver. To permit claimants thus to levy executions would seriously disarrange the priorities of the various claims, and would render the orderly administration of the assets impossible. Hence such a levy would be punishable as a contempt of the court.[8]

[5a] High, Receiver 254, 254a-255.

[6] High, Receivers 269, *et seq.*

[7] High, Receivers 255, 395, *et seq.*; McNulta *v.* Lochridge, 141 U. S. 327; Bartlett *v.* Cicero Light Co., 177 Ill. 68, 52 N. E. 339, 68 L. R. A. 78, 69 Am. St. Rep. 206. As to the conclusiveness of such judgment upon the interests represented by the receiver, see Painter *v.* Painter, 138 Cal. 231, 71 Pac. 90, 94 Am. St. Rep. 47, note. Doubtless, where the judgment is in a *court of law*, (which ignores equitable titles and proceedings), designation of the defendant as "receiver" would usually be treated by the law court simply as *descriptio personae*, and the judgment would be, in form and effect, against the receiver *personally*. But as the plaintiff in the judgment is a *quasi-party* to the suit in the equity court that appointed the receiver (by reason of his intervention for license to sue), that court will control the judgment at law, and treat it as affecting the *res only*.

[8] High, Receivers 141, 163; *supra*, § 483.

§ 494. Statutory license to sue receivers.—The manifest inconvenience of intervening in a chancery suit, pending perhaps at a point far removed from the locality in which the claim against the receiver arose, has resulted in statutes in many states, authorizing such suits to be brought *without previous leave of the court.*

§ 495. The same—scope of statutes.—These statutes vary in their scope, which, in some jurisdictions, is confined to suits against *receivers of corporations,* while in others, as in Virginia [9] and in the Federal jurisdiction,[10] it embraces receivers of both corporate and individual property.

Naturally these statutes do not throw the door wide open to litigants in such independent actions to contest with the receiver their claims against the insolvent defendant—claims properly justiciable only in the pending suit in which the receiver was appointed; but the license to sue the receiver without consent of the appointing court extends only to suits "in respect *of any act or transaction of his* in carrying on the business connected with such property." [11]

§ 496. The same—how judgment enforced.—To permit the successful plaintiff in such licensed action against the receiver to issue execution on his judgment, and to levy on the *res* in the hands of the receiver, or otherwise to proceed to enforce his judgment out of the assets of the insolvent, against which assets prior claimants have already proceeded by the very circumstance of the existing receivership—would seriously disarrange the priorities of the various claimants, and hamper the orderly administration of the assets in the hands of the court.

Hence, either by express provision of the statute,[12] or by judicial construction,[13] the successful plaintiff is not permitted to levy on the *res* in the receiver's hands; but, after securing his

---

[9] Va. Code 1919, § 6291.

[10] Judicial Code (Suppl. 1911), § 66.

[11] For a discussion of the cases construing the Act of Congress, see High, Receivers 395b.

[12] As in Virginia, § 6292.

[13] As in the Federal jurisdiction. St. Louis S. W. R. Co. *v.* Holbrook (C. C. A. 1896), 73 Fed. 112; Texas, etc., R. Co. *v.* Johnson, 151 U. S. 81. See High, Receivers, 395b.

judgment, he must *intervene by petition* in the main suit; whereupon "the court shall direct the payment of such judgment in the same manner as if the claim upon which the judgment is based had been proved and allowed in said case" [14]—that is, the court will give the judgment such relative priority as the claim upon which it is based would have been entitled to *had it been asserted and allowed in the main suit.* In other words, the judgment is enforced in the same manner as other judgments against receivers.[15]

§ 497. The same—the Federal statute.—The language of the Federal statute is: "Every receiver or manager of any property, appointed by any court of the United States, may be sued *in respect of any act or transaction of his in carrying on the business connected with such property,* without previous leave of the court in which such receiver or manager was appointed; but such suit shall be *subject to the general equity jurisdiction* of the court in which such receiver or manager was appointed, so far as the same may be necessary to the ends of justice." [16]

The proper construction of the final clause subjecting "such suit" to the "general equity jurisdiction" of the court appointing the receiver, does not authorize the court to *reopen the judgment* when offered in intervention proceedings by the judgment creditor, but merely to fix the *time and mode of payment,* and to adjust the competing rights of all claimants in the suit.[17]

The statutory license is broad enough to include, and does include, the right to sue the receiver in any court of competent jurisdiction, *state or federal.*[18]

8. Suits by Receivers.

§ 498. Suits by receivers—consent of court.—It has already been pointed out that in absence of statute conferring

---

[14] Va. Code, § 6292. See the statute for further details. For methods of service of process on receivers, see *id.* § 6065.

[15] See *Judgment against Receivers, ante,* § 493.

[16] Judicial Code (Suppl. 1911), § 66.

[17] St. Louis S. W. R. Co. *v.* Holbrook (C. C. A. 1896), 73 Fed. 112; Texas, etc., R. Co. *v.* Johnson, 151 U. S. 81.

[18] McNulta *v.* Lochridge, 141 U. S. 327; Texas, etc., R. Co. *v.* Johnson, *supra.*

other powers, the receiver, being a mere officer of the court, may exercise no other powers than those conferred. It follows that merely *by virtue of his office* he has no authority to institute suits on behalf of the interests which he represents. This rule is based on the logical and salutary principle that it is the province of the court itself (*i. e.* of the principal or appointing power) to determine whether it shall, through its receiver, become a litigant in a suit, at the risk of useless litigation and a waste of the funds which it is administering, rather than that the question should be left to the uncontrolled discretion of its agent or appointee.

Where, therefore, the receiver sues, as such, he must allege and prove his authority to do so from the court appointing him.[19]

§ 499. The same—(1) transactions prior to receivership.—Where the receiver sues *at law* to assert a right connected with his receivership, but which arose before his appointment—a right therefore, vested in the insolvent, and title to which is not divested by the receivership,[20]—on principle, and according to the better authority, he must assert the claim in *the name of the person to whom the right originally accrued,* and not in his own name.[21] This follows from the circumstance, already noted, that the receiver, normally, has not legal title.

---

[19] High, Receivers, 200-203. As to the necessary allegations in such case, see Taylor *v.* Canaday, 155 Ind. 671, 57 N. E. 524, 59 N. E. 20; Coddington *v.* Canaday, 157 Ind. 243, 61 N. E. 567; High, Receivers, 201; *infra,* § 500. Mere authority to "collect" debts due the insolvent, does not confer authority *to collect by suit.* McAllister *v.* Harman, 97 Va. 547; Screven *v.* Clark, 48 Ga. 41.

Where the debtor of the insolvent or of the receiver is already properly a party to the suit, the claim of the receiver against him may be tried in the main suit, even though the claim be otherwise triable only at law. N. Y. Life Ins. Co. *v.* Davis, 94 Va. 427. See Barton *v.* Barbour, 104 U. S. 126.

[20] See *supra,* § 481.

[21] This rule would seem of special force in courts of *law,* and in those jurisdictions (as in Virginia) were *legal title* alone is recognized in such courts. See Battle *v.* Davis, 66 N. C. 252; Freeman *v.* Winchester, 18 Winchester, 18 Miss. 577; Yeager *v.* Wallace, 44 Pa. St. 294, where the rule is especially well stated by Strong, J.; Homer *v.* Barr, etc., Co., 180 Mass. 163, 61 N. E. 883, 91 Am. St. Rep. 269; Murtey *v.* Allen, 71 Vt. 377, 45 Atl. 752, 76 Am. St. Rep. 779. Some of these authorities refer to *foreign* receivers, but the principle seems equally applicable to domestic receivers, except as indicated in the following section. High, Receivers, 209-210—indicating some conflict in the authorities. The practice is settled in some states by statute,

§ 500. Suits by receivers, continued—where receiver is assignee, or otherwise has title.—Where, however, the receiver's claim of title does not rest on the mere order of the court, but is derived through an *assignment* by the insolvent, or under a *statute* expressly or impliedly investing him with title,[22] since the reason for the rule denying him the right to sue in his own name no longer exists, the rule itself gives way.

In such case, having title, he may sue in his own name, and (in a court of law) without designating himself as receiver, since in a law court such designation is merely *descriptio personæ*.[23]

§ 501. The same—(2) transactions subsequent to receivership.—On a cause of action arising subsequent to the appointment of a receiver, *out of a transaction had with the receiver or his agents,* there is, on principle, no difficulty in his maintaining a suit thereon *in his own name,* in any court of contempt jurisdiction, foreign or domestic, at law or in equity, according to the nature of the case. As a party to the transaction he has *legal title* to the claim. In such case he might maintain an action at law without naming himself as receiver, since in a court of law such designation is merely *descriptio personæ,* as noted in the preceding section.

Thus he may maintain assumpsit in his own name for the purchase price of goods sold by him as receiver;[24] in trover for a chattel bailed by the receiver to the defendant;[25] to recover of a wrongdoer (even in a foreign jurisdiction) property of

---

as in New York. Id. 211-212, 447; Porter *v.* Williams, 5 Seld. 142. As shown in Mr. High's valuable treatise, so often cited in these notes, some of the adverse authorities hold that by having *lawful possession of documents*—as in the case of bills, notes or other *choses in action*—such possession gives the receiver a special title, so as to authorize suit in his own name. High, Receivers *ubi sup.* Nor, on principle, is the situation altered by the circumstance that express authority to sue in his own name *is conferred by the appointing court.* Id.

[22] See *infra, Foreign Receivers,* § 503 *et seq.*

[23] Boyle *v.* Townes, 9 Leigh 158; Wray *v.* Jamison, 10 Humph. (Tenn.) 186; High, Receivers 244.

[24] Singerly *v.* Fox, 75 Pa. St. 112.

[25] Boyle *v.* Townes, 9 Leigh 158.

which the receiver has once obtained possession in his own state, since such possession gives him a *special title* as against a wrong-doer;[26] and, of course, on all contracts or transactions made or had with him or his agents in connection with the affairs of the receivership.

§ 502. Conflicting receiverships—priority of jurisdiction.—As between courts of co-ordinate jurisdiction in the same state, it is the settled rule that the court first moving in the process of administering the *res* by appointing a receiver, will have priority of jurisdiction over another court subsequently appointing a receiver of the same property—and this whether the first receiver has taken actual possession of the *res* or not.[27] And this rule applies equally where one of the competing receivers is appointed by a State court and the other by a Federal court[28]—save, of course, where, under the Federal Constitution, the right of the Federal court is superior, as in bankruptcy proceeding, etc. The analogy between the effect of appointing a receiver as fixing priority of jurisdiction, and the effect of an order of reference in a creditors' suit,[28] seems complete.

9. *Conflict of Laws—Foreign Receivers.*

§ 503. Conflict of laws—appointment of receiver of property in another jurisdiction.—Where the court has personal jurisdiction of the defendant, it has full power by its decree to compel him to deliver the *res* over to the custody of the receiver, in whatever jurisdiction it may be located. If the defendant be not personally served with process within the jurisdiction, or is not otherwise within the control of the court, the jurisdiction is limited to the *res* within its control, and the court can enter no personal decree—nor exercise jurisdiction over property of the defendant located in another state. Nor does jurisdiction over the person make the decree *ipso facto* effective beyond the jurisdiction, as such decree operates *in personam*

---

[26] Caghill *v.* Woodbridge, 8 Baxt. (Tenn.) 580, 35 Am. Rep. 716; note 15 Am. St. Rep. 82; Kehr *v.* Hall, 117 Ind. 405, 20 N. E. 279.

[27] High, Receivers, 48.

[28] *Id.* 50-62a, 388. See *Foreign Receivers*, next section.

[29] See *Creditors' Suits, ante,* ch. xxxi.

only—on the conscience of the defendant. But operating thus on his conscience, the defendant may be compelled by proper process to obey the order of the court directing that the possession of the foreign *res* be delivered to its receiver [30]—or, as it seems, may compel an assignment or conveyance thereof to the receiver, in trust for the interests represented in the suit.[31]

In case the property be held adversely in the foreign state, or legal proceedings be otherwise necessary in the foreign state to obtain possession, the right of the receiver to maintain suit in the foreign court will depend on circumstances to be considered in the following sections.

§ 504. Foreign receivers.—It not infrequently happens, particularly in connection with receivers of insolvent corporations, that there are assets, tangible or intangible, widely scattered throughout different states. In such cases, the question how far the powers and rights of the receiver appointed in the home state will be recognized in other jurisdictions, becomes an important one.

§505. The same—suits by foreign receivers.—It is settled that the full faith and credit clause of the Federal Constitution does not require the courts of one state to recognize the official character and authority of a receiver appointed in another state. The official status of the receiver, like that of a sheriff or of an administrator, does not accompany him beyond the territorial jurisdiction of the court appointing him. Being the mere arm of a court whose process can have no extraterritorial potency, his home-conferred status and powers are necessarily confined to the territorial limits within which the process of the appointing court is effective.[32] This rule applies

---

[30] Receiverships of railways traversing several states, are familiar instances. High, Receivers, 44, 388a; Wilmer *v.* Railway Co., 2 Woods 409. See *Ancillary Receivers, infra,* § 510.

[31] See *infra*, n. 32.

[32] Booth *v.* Clark, 17 How. (U. S.) 322; Hale *v.* Allinson, 188 U. S. 56; Great Western Mining, etc., Co. *v.* Harris, 198 U. S. 561; monographic note 4 L. R. A. (N. S.) 824; 3 Va. Law Reg. 831; High, Receivers 239 *et seq.* The difficulty is frequently met by procuring an *assignment* (voluntarily, or under order of the court) to the receiver, so as to vest title in him as trustee. See *infra*, § 507; High, Receivers 443 *et seq.*

where the receiver of one Federal court without title [32a] sues in another Federal court outside of the circuit; [33] and whether the receiver sues in his own name or that of the main defendant [34] and in spite of the circumstance that the suit is expressly directed by the court appointing him. [35]

§ 506. Suits by foreign receivers, continued—relaxation of the rule by comity.—Notwithstanding the established rule denying to a receiver the privilege of maintaining a suit in a foreign jurisdiction *as a matter of right,* the courts are more and more evincing a disposition to accord recognition to foreign receivers from motives of *interstate comity;* and numerous instances of such comity are to be found in the reports.

This comity is usually extended on such terms as to preserve the rights of citizens of the state whose comity is thus invoked —and hence it will not be extended to the prejudice of citizens who have acquired rights against the *res* in the foreign jurisdiction, nor when it would contravene the laws or public policy of the state. [36]

10. *Assignees and Statutory Receivers.*

§ 507. Foreign receivers, continued—rule inapplicable to assignee or statutory receivers.—Of course a wholly different situation is presented where the receiver has *title* to the *res* which he is seeking to recover in the foreign jurisdiction. It is the lack of title that defeats his claim is recognition as of right. [37]

§ 508. Receiver as assignee. — Hence if the receiver holds an *assignment* from the real owner (normally the main

---

[32a] See *supra,* § 501, *infra,* § 507.

[33] Brigham *v.* Luddington, 12 Blatchf. 237; High, Receivers 239. See Federal Judicial Code, 56.

[34] Great Western Mining, etc., Co. *v.* Harris, 198 U. S. 561; High, Receivers 239.

[35] Sterrett *v.* Second Nat. Bank, (C. C. A.), 246 Fed. 753, 3 A. L. R. 256 (annotated), affirmed 248 U. S. 73.

[36] High, Receivers 239-241; Folger *v.* Columbia Ins. Co., 99 Mass. 267, 96 Am. Dec. 747; note 6 Am. St. Rep. 185; Holbrook *v.* Ford, 153 Ill. 633, 46 Am. St. Rep. 917; Straughan *v.* Hallwood, 30 W. Va. 274. 8 Am. St. Rep. 49, and extensive note; Grogan *v.* Egbert (W. Va.), 28 S. E. 714; note 26 C. C. A. 49-58.

[37] See *Title of Receiver, supra,* § 484.

defendant in the original suit)—or is exercising powers under a valid *statute* of the state of his appointment, which in terms, or by implication, vests him with title and control of the *res,* wheresoever situated—then the question of his recognition by the courts of a foreign state is no longer one of *comity,* but he is entitled to demand recognition as a matter of *right.* In such a situation, the receiver is not the representative of a foreign court, but, *pro hac vice,* is the *legal holder (as trustee) of the right or title* that he is asserting, under the term of an express trust.[88]

§ 509. Statutory receivers.—So, where the statutes of the state under whose laws a corporation is organized provide that a particular official, whether called receiver, statutory assignee, commissioner, or by other designation, shall take charge of its affairs upon insolvency, and the authority so bestowed by statute is in such terms as to make the receiver a *quasi* assignee and representative of the corporation, such a provision is in effect a *part of its corporate charter.* A corporation may under the law of its creation, or under the domestic law to which it is subject, have one set of officers for the management of its affairs while engaged in *active operations,* and another to take charge of and wind up its affairs upon its *insolvency.* In a proper case, therefore, the property and effects of such a corporation vest in such statutory official, as *quasi* assignee, by force of the statute, and he has the same powers and title in a foreign state as in the state of his appointment.[89]

---

[88] Hawkins *v.* Glenn, 131 U. S. 319; Bernheimer *v.* Converse, 206 U. S. 516; Howarth *v.* Lombard, 175 Mass. 570, 56 N. E. 888, 891; High, Receivers 241a, 244; authorities n. 39 *infra.* In such case, the description of himself as "receiver" would be immaterial, as merely *descriptio personae.* High, Receivers 244; *supra,* §§ 481, 501.

[89] Bockover *v.* Life Association, 77 Va. 85, 6 Am. and Eng. Corp., Cas. 603; Relfe *v.* Rundle, 103 U. S. 222; Bernheimer *v.* Converse, 206 U. S. 516. And refusal by the court of another state to recognize such a statutory receiver is a violation of the full faith and credit clause of the Constitution of the United States. Converse *v.* Hamilton, 224 U. S. 243—a case of a statutory receiver suing in a foreign state, in a court of law, and in his own name as statutory receiver. See Sterrett *v.* Second Nat. Bank (C. C. A.), 246 Fed. 753, 3 A. L. R. 256 (monographic note), affirmed 248 U. S. 73—where the terms of the statute were held not sufficient to invest the receiver with the character and title of assignee.

The same result follows, as before noted [40] where the receiver sues to recover property *taken from his possession,* since he has special or possessory title.

11. *Ancillary Receivers.*

§ 510. Ancillary receivers.—In order to avoid the difficulties that hamper the receiver when he attempts to assert dominion over assets in a foreign jurisdiction, it is common practice for the original plaintiffs, or some of them, to institute an equity suit in the foreign state, and to secure the appointment there of an *ancillary receiver,* with authority to take possession of all the assets of the insolvent within that jurisdiction.

Whether the domiciliary receiver may himself institute such suit for an ancillary receivership will depend on the question, already discussed,[41] whether he is an *assignee,* or otherwise has title to the assets which he is seeking to recover, or whether he is an *ordinary chancery receiver,* and therefore dependent on the comity of the foreign court.[42]

The foreign court, in the ancillary proceeding, will give such a direction to the assets within its jurisdiction as the nature of the situation may demand, looking eventually to their transmission to the domiciliary receiver in the home state—but usually taking care that the claims of local creditors who have secured liens on the estate prior to the ancillary receivership are first satisfied.[43]

12. *Receivers' Certificates.*

§ 511. Receivers' certificates. — In the foreclosure of mortgages of railways, and doubtless of other public service companies which, from their nature and from public necessity, must notwithstanding the receivership be operated as going concerns, courts of equity possess the power when the physical con-

---

[40] *Supra,* § 501.

[41] *Supra,* § 507-509.

[42] High. Receivers 306a-306b, 375a; Mahon *v.* Ongley Electric Co., 159 N. Y. 196, 50 N. E. 805. The erection of ancillary receiverships is quite common in Federal court proceedings for the foreclosure of mortgages on railroads whose lines run through several states. By comity, the same receiver is appointed in each court, and the court first appointing the receiver is permitted to assume the general administration of the assets. Central Trust Co. *v.* East Tenn.. etc., R. Co.. 30 Fed. 895; Platt *v.* Philadelphia, etc., R. Co.. 54 Fed. 569; Clyde *v.* Richmond & D. R. Co., 56 Fed. 539; High, Receivers 375a.

[43] High, Receivers 47, 306-306b.

dition of the property demands it, and for purposes of necessary repairs and equipment, to authorize the receiver *to borrow money on the credit of the entire corporate assets* under the control of the court, and to issue debentures or certificates of indebtedness therefor. Such certificates are known as *"receivers' certificates."* When issued *by consent* of the parties in interest, or, under proper circumstances, *without such consent, and after due notice to the bondholders, or other lienors, whose priorities are thus displaced,* such certificates may be, and usually are, by order of the court, constituted *liens superior to all antecedent liens on the property.*

§ **512. The same.**—The theory upon which such action is justified is that the court having undertaken, through the receivership, the administration of the assets as a trust fund for the benefit of the bondholders and at their request, may rightfully preserve the assets at the expense of the fund; and since the maintenance and operation of the railway are essential to protect the interests of the public, as well as to preserve the custom, good-will and corporate rights and franchises of the corporation, the necessary expenses of such maintenance and operation should properly be borne by the trust subject.[44] The rule does not apply to receiverships of *purely private corporations, except where all lien-holders consent.*[45]

A few cases have extended the principle to receiverships of purely private corporations, but the propriety of these decisions is doubtful.[46] Where, however, the *preservation* (as contrasted with the profitable *operation*) of the property makes it necessary, the propriety of issuing such certificates, *not as a lien superior to existing liens,* or as a superior lien *by consent of all prior lienors,* is undoubted, even in the case of private corporations or (in principle) of individuals.[47]

---

[44] Wallace *v.* Loomis, 97 U. S. 146; High, Receivers 398c. *et seq.*

[45] High, Receivers 312b-312d; Fidelity Insurance, etc., Co. *v.* Roanoke Iron Co., 68 Fed. 623; monographic note, 26 C. C. A. 350-372.

[46] See Karn & Hickson *v.* Rorer Iron Co., 86 Va. 754; Prof. Burks, 4 Va. Law Reg. 373. In Osborne *v.* Big Stone Gap, etc., Co., 96 Va. 58, the Virginia court seems to approve of the application of the principle to *private corporations,* provided *due notice* is given to the creditors interested. But as no such notice was given, the approval was *obiter.*

[47] See Jerome *v.* McCarter, 94 U. S. 734; Kent *v.* Lake Superior Canal Co., 144 U. S. 75.

CHAPTER XXXIV.

Appeals.[1]

§ 512½. Preliminary.—It is not the purpose of this chapter to attempt more than an outline of the subject of appeals in equity. The procedure is largely statutory, and reference must be made to the statute for details.

The topic of *Appeal and Error* is one of the most comprehensive in the law—not because of inherent difficulties, but because practically in every case appealed, counsel for the appellee is disposed to raise every possible question of procedure in the higher court. These questions the court must decide, and thus decided they find their way into the reports, and serve to swell the volume of case law under this title.

§ 513. Use of terms—appeal—writ of error—supersedeas.—Where the appellate court assumes the review of a chancery case the proceeding is designated as an *appeal;* and the parties are known, respectively, as *appellant* and *appellee.*

Where the higher court thus assumes the review of proceedings in an *action at law,* the jurisdiction is exercised though a *writ of error* issued to the lower court. Here the parties are known as *plaintiff in error* and *defendant in error,* respectively.

Where the higher court thus grants an appeal or writ of error, and it is desired to *stay the hand of the appellee* or defendant in error until the case can be reviewed and disposed of above, a writ of *supersedeas* is granted for the purpose, as supplementary to the appeal or writ of error.[2]

§ 514. Prerequisites of an appeal—(a) subject-matter.—As a prerequisite to an appeal in any case in Virginia, there must be involved matter of sufficient importance to warrant a rehearing of the case by the Court of Appeals, and the cause must have reached a certain stage in its progress towards

---

[1] See Va. Code 1919, ch. 267, and the revisor's voluminous annotations.
[2] *Id.* § 6349.

finality. These prerequisites of subject-matter involved, the
statute[3] prescribes as follows:

(a) Subject-matter.
- (1) Title or bounds of *lands;* or
- (2) A *freehold or franchise;* or
- (3) Some matter not merely pecuniary (*e. g.* custody of a child, divorce, etc.) ; or
- (4) An amount or value equal to $300, exclusive of costs.[4]

§ 515. The same—(b) stage of the cause.—If one of
the foregoing prerequisites obtains, an appeal lies, *provided the
case has progressed far enough,* and the action of the court is of
sufficient moment, to warrant an appeal *at that stage of the
cause.* This stage is fixed by the statute[5] as follows: That is
to say, an appeal lies (assuming the existence of a prerequisite
subject-matter as above shown) from

Stage of the cause.
- (a) Any *final* decree;
- (b) Any *interlocutory* decree, which
  - (1) Dissolves an *injunction;*[6] or
  - (2) Requires *money to be paid;* or
  - (3) Requires *title* or *possession* of property to be changed; or
  - (4) Adjudicates the *principles of a cause.*

§ 516. The same—time limit.—Appeals are limited to
one year after final decree.[7]   Hence, until a final decree has
been entered, there is *no time limit* to an appeal from an *interlocutory* decree.

But if the appeal be from a final decree *refusing a bill of review* to a decree ren⸱ered more than six months prior thereto,

---

[3] Va. Code 1919, § 6337. For certain exceptions, see §§ 6336–6337.
See also Va. Const. § 88.
[4] For the effect of a consolidation of several causes, on the amount
involved in the appeal, see *ante* §§ 349 *et seq.*
[5] Id. § 6336.
[6] Where an injunction is refused, application may be made direct
to the appellate court, on the original papers. Id. § 6320. See
Injunctions, ante, ch. xxvii.
[7] Va. Code 1919, § 6337.

the appeal may not be had except within six months from the decree so refusing a bill of review.[8]

§ 517. Method of appeal.—The procedure in appellate proceedings is largely a matter of local statute law. In many states an appeal may be had as a *matter of right*, with no discretion in the lower or the higher court to grant or disallow.

But in Virginia no appeal may be taken except it be allowed by the appellate court, or one of the judges thereof, on a written petition clearly and distinctly assigning the errors complained of, and accompanied by a certified transcript of the record in the cause.[9] Reference must be had to the statute for particulars.

In case the proposed appellant desires to stay further proceedings in the lower court, in the interval between the entry of the decree and the granting of the appeal, he may secure a suspension from the lower court, for a reasonable time, on motion, and the giving of a bond of indemnity.[10]

§ 518. Transcript of the record.—This is furnished by the clerk, but may not be delivered to the party proposing to appeal until notice of an intention to apply for such transcript has been given to the other party, or his counsel.[11]

On allowance of the appeal, the clerk of the appellate court is required to have the record printed for the use of the court and counsel,[12] and to issue proper process against the parties interested other than the appellant.[13]

§ 519. Appeal bond.—Except where the appeal is proper to protect the estate of a decedent, infant, convict or insane person, or the interest of a county, city or town in Virginia, the appeal is ineffective until bond be given,[14] in a penalty to be fixed by the appellate court, or judge granting the appeal. If the decree is for *payment of money*, enforcement of which has

---

[8] Id.

[9] Id. §§ 6336-6348. See Acts 1920, p. 416, giving counsel the right of oral argument in presenting the petition.

[10] Id. § 6338.

[11] Id. § 6339.

[12] Id. § 6357.

[13] Id. § 6350.

[14] Id. § 6351.

been suspended by a *supersedeas,* the bond in no case may be less than the amount so decreed, or payment of which has been so stayed, with interest and costs—the condition of the bond being for the performance and satisfaction of the decree, or that portion so stayed, in case the decree be affirmed, or the appeal or *supersedeas* be dismissed; together with all damages, costs and fees that may be awarded by the appellate court, etc.

§ 520. The record in a chancery suit—bills of exception.—The difference in the practice at law and in chancery, is strikingly exemplified in the matter of the *record.* At law the record is a bare skeleton, containing merely the pleadings, empaneling of the jury, the verdict and the judgment—none of the numerous motions, exceptions to evidence, instructions given or refused, nor the evidence itself, being a part of the record, unless made so by a *bill of exceptions.*

On the other hand, in chancery every step taken in the cause, and every document filed therein, from the *subpœna* to the final decree, constitutes, or should constitute, a part of the record, without special order to that effect. Hence there is no such thing in chancery as a *"bill of exceptions."* [15]

---

[15] See Livingston *v.* Story, 12 Pet. 339; Barrett *v.* McAllister (W. Va.), 12 S. E. 1106. The case of Winston *v.* Gordon, 115 Va. 899, illustrates bills of exception taken on trial of an *issue out of chancery.* While the "bill of exceptions" is thus unknown in the equity practice, there are still *"exceptions"* in equity—as to answer (though abolished in Virginia); to a master's or receiver's report; to testimony offered, etc. But these, when properly filed, become parts of the record as of course. It has been heretofore pointed out that these exceptions should be specifically brought to the attention of the court, and the *court's action thereon shown in the decree,* otherwise on appeal they will, as a general rule, be taken to have been waived.

APPENDIX I.

FORMS.

In the following pages are presented the forms in a chancery suit, from the *subpœna* to the final decree, in a suit for the specific performance of a contract for the sale of real property. Among a few other additional forms, are the bill, answers, and decree of sale, in a suit for the sale of infants' lands.

I.

The Proceedings in a Suit for Specific Performance—By Vendor against Vendee.*

1. THE MEMORANDUM OR PRÆCIPE.

To the clerk of the Circuit Court of Albemarle County:

John A. Kendrick

v.

Peter Quinby.

Issue *subpœna in chancery* against the defendant, to the sheriff of Albemarle County. To first March rules.

Feb. 1, 1920.   LEMON & HERBERT,
for complainant.

2. THE SUBPOENA.

The Commonwealth of Virginia,

To the Sheriff of Albemarle County, Greeting:

We command you that you summon *Peter Quinby* to appear before the judge of our Circuit Court for the County of Albemarle, at the clerk's office of our said court, at rules to be holden therefor, on the *first Monday in March next,* to answer *a bill in chancery* exhibited against him in our said court by *John A. Kendrick.* And have then there this writ.

---

*Errors have been intentionally made, in order to illustrate to the student the proper methods of taking advantage of them.

Witness William L. Maupin, the Clerk of our said court, at the courthouse thereof, this the 1st day of February, in the year of our Lord 1920, and of our foundation the one hundred and forty-fourth.

(Signed)   WILLIAM L. MAUPIN,
Clerk.

3. THE BILL.   [*By vendor, for specific performance*].

To the Honorable John W. Fishburne, Judge of the Circuit Court of Albemarle County:

The bill of your complainant, John A. Kendrick, of Albemarle county, Virginia, respectfully shows unto your honor:

1. That by a written contract bearing date on the first day of June, 1910, between your complainant and a certain Peter Quinby, of the same county, hereinafterwards named as defendant, your complainant agreed to sell to the said defendant, and the said defendant agreed to purchase from your complainant, a certain house and lot situated in the village of Keswick in said county, on the corner of Main Street and Maple Avenue, as the streets are designated on the plan of said village, which said lot is more fully described in the said written contract, a duplicate-original of which contract, signed by both parties, is herewith filed, marked "Exhibit 101," and asked to be read as a part of this bill.

2. By the terms of said contract, the defendant was required to pay, as the purchase price of said property, the sum of six thousand dollars, as follows, to-wit: Fifteen hundred dollars ($1,500.) in cash, and the remainder, to-wit, four thousand and five hundred dollars ($4,500.), in three (3) equal annual installments of fifteen hundred dollars ($1.500.) each, represented by the three promissory notes of the defendant, bearing even date with said contract, and payable to your complainant in one, two and three years after date, respectively, with legal interest from date, until paid—all of which will more fully and at large appear by reference to said written contract hereinbefore referred to as Exhibit 101, and filed with this bill.

3. Your complainant further shows that in pursuance of the terms of said contract, the said defendant paid to your com-

plainant the cash payment of fifteen hundred dollars ($1,500.),
and executed and delivered to complainant the three promissory
notes as aforesaid. The said defendant also took possession of
the premises, as he was entitled to do under the said contract,
and has been ever since, and is now, in complete possession and
enjoyment thereof.

4. Your complainant further shows that since the cash payment aforesaid, the said defendant has paid nothing whatsoever
of the balance due under the terms of said contract, and by virtue of the promissory notes aforesaid, and in spite of complainant's numerous and urgent requests to do so. All of said notes
are long since past due, with the interest accrued thereon. They
are herewith filed, marked "Exhibits 102a," "102b" and "102c,"
respectively, and prayed to be read as parts of this bill.

5. Your complainant is advised that by virtue of the foregoing facts, he is entitled to come into a court of equity praying
for a decree for the specific performance of the said contract by
the said defendant; and, in case the said defendant shall fail or
refuse to perform his promises when so required by the court's
decree, that the court will treat the said contract as creating, by
implication of equity, a lien on said premises, in favor of complainant, for the security of the unpaid purchase money aforesaid; and that the court in this proceeding will enforce the said
lien by subjecting the said property to payment of the balance
due as aforesaid.

Your complainant is further advised that in case of a sale of
the said property, for the enforcement of his lien aforesaid, a
sufficient sum shall not be realized to satisfy the balance due,
the court will render a personal decree against the defendant
for the residue.

6. Your complainant hereby avers his willingness and ability
to make proper conveyance of the said premises to said defendant, with perfect legal title, as soon as the said purchase money
has been paid to him. And complainant hereby offers to file
such conveyance, duly executed, among the papers in this cause,
whenever the court may so order.[1]

---

[1] In some jurisdictions it is held that complainant vendor in a suit
for specific performance must *file a deed of conveyance along with his*

7. In consideration of the premises, and forasmuch as compainant is without remedy save in a court of equity where matters of this kind are only and properly cognizable, your complainant prays:

(1) That the said Peter Quinby be made a party defendant to this bill, and may answer the same, but not under oath.

(2) That a decree be entered against the said defendant requiring him, within such reasonable time as the court may order, to pay to your complainant the unpaid purchase money, with the interest thereon, as aforesaid; and, in default of such payment, that the said premises may be sold under the orders and direction of the court, and that the proceeds, or so much thereof as may be necessary, be paid over to your complainant to satisfy the balance due him as aforesaid, together with the costs of this suit, including a fee of one hundred and fifty dollars ($150.) to complainant's attorney herein.[2]

(3) That in case of the defendant's default in payment of the balance due to complainant, and a deficiency for that purpose shall result from a sale of the said property, a personal decree may be entered against the defendant for such deficiency.

(4) That all such other things be ordered and done as may be necessary for the complete disposition of this cause; and for such other relief, both general and special, as to equity may seem meet and the nature of the case may require.

And your complainant will ever pray, etc.

Lemon & Herbert,

Charlottesville, Va.,

Solicitors for Complainant.

---

bill—though the better rule is *contra*. This clause, as here worded, would probably comply with the rule of practice even in those states holding the minority view. The latter view was maintained in Wood *v.* Walker, 92 Va. 24, but, as shown by Judge Burks in a criticism of this ruling, in 1 Va. Law Reg. 442, it was probably erroneous. There is a distinct ruling to the contrary by Staples, J., in Whitten *v.* Saunders, 75 |Va. 563, 570, nor does the minority view seem based on any sound reason.

[2] See *post,* for defendant's demurrer to this prayer for an attorney's fee.

4. DEMURRER TO BILL.

Kendrick   The demurrer of Peter Quinby to a bill of com-
   v.   plainant exhibited against him in the Circuit Court
Quinby.   of Albemarle county by John A. Kendrick.

This defendant says that the said bill is insufficient in law, and especially in this: (1) That the said complainant has not tendered along with his bill a proper deed of conveyance of the said premises to this defendant; and for further cause of demurrer, (2) that the said bill seeks an allowance to complainant's counsel for an attorney's fee of one hundred and fifty dollars, without any special allegations rendering such an allowance, or any allowance, proper; for which second cause this defendant demurs to so much of said bill as prays for such inequitable allowance. And for further cause of demurrer, (3) that the bill shows on its face that the plaintiff's alleged cause of action did not arise within five years before the institution of this suit.

APPLEBY & PEARMON,

   Solicitors for Defendant.

5. ORDER OF THE COURT: *Over-ruling demurrer to bill in part.*

Kendrick   This cause came on this day to be heard on the
   v.   bill of the plaintiff and the exhibits filed therewith,
Quinby.   and on the demurrer of the defendant to said bill,
               and was argued by counsel.

On consideration whereof, the court deeming as not well taken the first cause in said demurrer alleged, namely, that the plaintiff has not tendered a conveyance with his bill, doth overrule the said demurrer as to said first cause alleged.

And the court being of opinion that the question of the statute of limitations may not be raised by demurrer, doth likewise overrule the said demurrer as to said third cause alleged.

And as to the second cause of said demurrer, namely, the insufficiency of said bill in failing to allege proper or any grounds for the allowance of the attorney's fee therein prayed, the court doth sustain the same. But leave is given to the plaintiff to amend his bill in that respect if he shall be so advised.

6. DEFENDANT'S PLEA: *Statute of limitations.*

Kendrick
v.
Quinby.

The plea of Peter Quinby to a bill of complaint filed against him in the Circuit Court of Albemarle county, by John A. Kendrick.

For plea to the said bill, and to the whole and every part thereof, and to all and every the relief therein prayed, this defendant says that neither the complainant's alleged grounds of relief, nor any claim in said bill asserted, arose within five (5) years before the bringing of this suit.

Wherefore defendant prays judgment whether he shall be compelled to make answer to said bill, and prays to be hence dismissed with his reasonable costs and charges in this behalf expended.

APPLEBY & PEARMON,

Solicitors for Defendant.

7. ENTRY BY CLERK: *Plea set down for argument.*

[Title of the cause].

On motion of the plaintiff, by counsel, defendant's plea is set down for argument.

8. ORDER OF THE COURT: *Plea disallowed*

[Title of the cause].

This cause came on this day to be again heard on the papers formerly read, and on the plea the defendant, set down for argument on the plaintiff's motion, and was argued by counsel.

On consideration whereof, the court being of opinion that the statute of limitations set up in said plea is not a valid defense to the whole of the relief prayed in the bill; and the said plea being to the whole of such relief, and not to a part thereof, the court doth for that cause disallow the said plea, but without prejudice to the respondent's right, by answer, to assert the same defense to that portion of the bill which prays for a personal decree. And the defendant is ordered to answer the bill within fifteen days from the date of this order.

9. DEFENDANT'S ANSWER.

The answer of Peter Quinby to a bill of complaint filed against him in the Circuit Court of Albemarle county, by John A. Kendrick.

This respondent [reserving to himself the benefit of all just exceptions which may be had or taken to said bill by reason of its many errors and imperfections, both of form and substance] [3] for answer to said bill, or to so much thereof as he is advised it is material that he should answer, answering says:

1. That the allegations of the first and second clauses of the said bill, with respect to the contract of sale and purchase between respondent and complainant, of the premises therein referred to, are substantially true, and that the paper Exhibit "101" filed with the bill is a duplicate original of said contract; and that Exhibits 102a, 102b and 102c are the original promissory notes executed by respondent according to the terms of the said contract. It is also true that respondent has been in possession of the said premises since the execution of said contract and of said notes.

2. But it is not true that respondent has made no payment on the said deferred installments of purchase money. On the contrary respondent avers that he has, from time to time, made numerous payments on said notes, amounting in the aggregate to two thousand and seven hundred dollars ($2,700), in addition to the cash payment of one thousand and five hundred dollars ($1,500). Respondent files herewith, as a part of this answer, a more accurate and more detailed statement of such payments, with their respective amounts and dates—such statement being marked Exhibit "P. Q." Respondent also files as a part of this answer, receipts for each payment claimed, signed by Adam L. Henderson, attorney for complainant, which said attorney had due authority to receive such payments on behalf of the complainant and to give receipts therefor. These receipts are marked Exhibits ".P. Q. 1", "P. Q. 2" and "P. Q. 3", respectively.

3. Respondent, further answering, says that having full confidence in the integrity of the complainant, respondent accepted without question the assurance of complainant that the complainant had complete and perfect title to said property, with right to convey the same by his sole deed when said purchase money was paid. But respondent has since ascertained from reputable

---

[3] Old form—may be omitted.

sources, and hence avers and charges, that at the time the said contract was made, the complainant was not an unmarried person as he fraudulently induced respondent to believe, but that he was then the husband of a living wife, to-wit, Sarah O. Kendrick (who was Sarah Owen), who is still living, and who was then, and is now, a person *non compos mentis*, and who is now, and has been for many years, confined in the State Hospital for the Insane at Staunton. And respondent is advised that the said wife of the complainant has a contingent right of dower in the premises in controversy in this suit, and hence that should respondent be compelled to pay the balance of said purchase money, the complainant would be wholly unable to convey to respondent a complete title to said property. Respondent is therefore advised that not only will the court not compel him to accept an imperfect title to the said premises, but will, in a proper proceeding, rescind the said contract *ab initio,* and will require the complainant to repay to respondent the various sums heretofore paid by respondent to complainant as payment for said premises as aforesaid, with interest from the respective dates of such payments.

Respondent is further advised that while such failure of title is a perfect defense to the bill of the complainant, it will be necessary in order to obtain the affirmative relief of rescission to which respondent is entitled, that he file a cross-bill in this suit, unless the court should see fit to treat respondent's answer as a cross-bill, which respondent now prays that the court will. do.

3. And for a further defence in this behalf, respondent alleges—and the same appears from the face of the bill—that the indebtedness asserted in the bill did not arise within five years from the institution of this suit. Wherefore respondent is advised, and therefore avers, that no personal decree may be rendered against him in this suit, because any such personal recourse is barred by the statute of limitations.

And having fully answered, respondent prays to be hence dismissed with his reasonable costs in this behalf expended.

APPLEBY & PEARMON,
    Solicitors for Respondent.

10. PLAINTIFF'S MOTION TO STRIKE OUT.[4]

[On motion to strike out the defense of the statute of limitations set up in the answer foregoing, it is assumed that the court denies the motion—thus in effect (since the facts appear from the bill itself) ruling that the prayer of the bill for a personal decree against the defendant is denied, because defendant's personal liability is barred by the statute of limitations.]

11. GENERAL REPLICATION TO ANSWER.[5]

Kendrick
v.
Quinby.

For replication to said answer, the plaintiff, by counsel, says that the matters and things in said answer alleged as defenses to the plaintiff's bill are not true.

LEMON & HERBERT,
   for complainant.

12. CROSS-BILL BY DEFENDANT: *Praying rescission of contract and return of payments made.*

To the Honorable the Judge of the Circuit Court of Albemarle county:

The cross-bill of your complainant, Peter Quinby, respectfully shows unto your honor:

1. That there is pending in your Honor's court a certain suit in chancery, under the short style of Kendrick *v.* Quinby, in which suit a certain John A. Kendrick is complainant, and your complainant herein is defendant.

2. That the purpose of the said suit is to compel the specific performance of a certain contract for the sale and purchase of certain real property, in which contract the said Kendrick was vendor and your complainant was vendee—all of which will more fully and at large appear, reference being had to the pleadings and exhibits in said original suit, which said pleadings and exhibits are prayed to be taken as parts of this cross-bill, as fully and effectually as if herein specifically recited.

---

[4] See Text, *ante*, § 248.
[5] Rarely written out at length, and usually appearing in the record only by clerk's entry on his docket *"Gen'l. Repl'n,"* or recited in the first decree as having been filed. Now required to be entered, as of course, by the clerk. Va. Code 1919, § 6138.

3. Making specific reference to said contract, your complainant charges that the said Kendrick, plaintiff in said original bill, agreed, upon the payment of six thousand dollars ($6,000.) of purchase money, payable as shown in said contract, to convey to your complainant a perfect title to the premises in the said bill and proceedings mentioned.

4. Your complainant further shows that believing that the defendant herein was an unmarried person (as he falsely pretended to be) and had complete title in himself to said premises, and could convey to your complainant a perfect title thereto by his sole deed, your complainant entered into said contract in good faith, and, in like faith, undertook to pay the purchase money according to the terms of the said contract.

5. Your complainant further shows that he made the cash payment called for by the terms of said contract, to-wit, one thousand and five hundred dollars ($1,500.), on the day the said contract bears date, to-wit, June 1, 1910; and that subsequently he paid various large sums of money to the said Kendrick, through the latter's duly authorized attorney, a certain Adam L. Henderson, as credits on complainant's notes held by said Kendrick, and representing the deferred installments of purchase money due under said contract.

Your complainant has already filed with his answer in the said original suit, a detailed statement of all the payments so made by him under said contract—which statement is designated as Exhibit "P. Q.", and now prayed to be read, along with the vouchers accompanying the same, as a part of this cross-bill as if copied herein at large. The aggregate principal amount of such payments, including the said cash payment of fifteen hundred dollars ($1,500.), is forty-two hundred dollars ($4,200), as shown in the exhibit last mentioned.

6. Your complainant further shows to the court that in spite of the said Kendrick's reiterated assertions to the contrary, fraudulently made to induce your complainant to enter into the said contract, the said Kendrick was not, at the time the said contract was made, an unmarried person; but on the contrary complainant avers and charges that he was at that time, and is now, the husband of one Sarah O. Kendrick (formerly Sarah

Owen), who is still alive, and a lunatic, and is now, and for many years previously has been, confined in the State Hospital for the Insane at Staunton.

Your complainant is advised that the said wife has a contingent right of dower in the property so contracted to be sold to your complainant, by reason whereof it will be impossible for the defendant herein to make to your complainant a complete title to said premises after the payment of said purchase money —and hence that not only will the court for that reason refuse the relief of specific performance prayed for in said original bill, but that, on this cross-bill filed for the purpose, the court, if satisfied of the truth of the allegations hereinbefore made, will rescind the said contract *ab initio,* and will require the said defendant herein to repay to your complainant all moneys paid to said defendant under said contract, with interest from the date of such payments, respectively.

Your complainant is further advised that on a decree for a rescission of the said contract, and for a return of the purchase money so paid, he will be entitled, in equity, to assert a lien on the premises in question to secure performance by the defendant of such personal decree as may be rendered against him under the prayers of this cross-bill.

Being without other remedy, your complainant prays that he may be permitted to file this his cross-bill in said suit; that the said John A. Kendrick, complainant in the original bill, be made a party defendant hereto, and may answer the same, but not under oath; that the contract in the bill and proceedings mentioned may, for the reasons hereinbefore assigned, be declared null and void and of no effect; that the defendant herein be decreed to repay to your complainant the said sum of forty-two hundred dollars (4,200.), with interest from the respective dates of such payments; that complainant's equitable lien aforesaid be recognized, and, if necessary, enforced; and for such other relief, both general and special, as to equity may seem meet and the nature of the case require. And your complainant will ever pray, etc.

Appleby & Pearmon,

Solicitors for Complainant in Cross-Bill.

13. PLAINTIFF'S DEMURRER TO CROSS-BILL.[6]

Kendrick The demurrer of John A. Kendrick to a cross-
v. bill filed against him in the Circuit Court of Albe-
Quinby. marle county, in a suit in chancery therein pending
under the short style of Kendrick *v.* Quinby:

This defendant in said cross-bill says that the said cross-bill is not sufficient in law, and especially in this, to-wit: (1) Because, assuming the existence of this defendant's alleged wife and her alleged insanity, there is no allegation that she is incurably insane, and hence, so far as concerns the allegations of said cross-bill, the said wife, if she in fact exists, may recover her sanity in time to unite with this defendant in making title to the complainant in the cross-bill; (2) Because, in spite of the alleged insanity of the said wife, the court has full power in this suit to require this defendant to give proper indemnity to the complainant against any loss or damage to accrue by reason of such alleged contingent right of dower in said alleged wife of defendant, which indemnity is already under the control of the court in the form of the unpaid purchase money due by said complainant to this respondent in the cross-bill.

Wherefore defendant demurs to said cross-bill, and to every part thereof, and to all and every the relief therein prayed for, and says that the same is not sufficient in law. He therefore prays judgment whether he shall be required to answer the same.

LEMON & HERBERT,
For Defendant in Cross-Bill.

14. ORDER OF THE COURT: *Demurrer to cross-bill overruled.*

Kendrick This cause came on this day to be again heard
v. on the papers formerly read, on the cross-bill of
Quinby. the defendant, filed by leave of court, and on the
plaintiff's demurrer to said cross-bill and was argued by counsel.

On consideration whereof, the court being of opinion that the allegation of present insanity of the wife of the defendant in the cross-bill is sufficient for the purposes of the said cross-bill—

---

[6] Both grounds of demurrer overruled—see *infra.*

and the court being further of opinion that it would be contrary
to the rules of equity to compel or allow a vendor-husband to
accept indemnity against the contingent dower right of his wife,
the court doth overrule the said demurrer for both causes alleged.

15. plaintiff's answer to cross-bill.

The answer of John A. Kendrick to a cross-bill of complaint
filed against him by a certain Peter Quinby, in a certain suit in
chancery depending in the circuit court of Albemarle county, in
which suit this respondent is plaintiff, and the complainant in
said cross-bill is defendant.

For answer to said cross-bill, this respondent says:

1. That the allegations of said cross-bill with reference to
the marriage of this respondent to a certain Sarah Owen, are
wholly false and without any foundation whatsoever. On the
contrary, respondent distinctly and unequivocally denies that he
was ever married to the said Sarah Owen, or to any other person whomsoever; but he avers that at the time the contract
which is the foundation of this controversy was made, he was
an unmarried person, and has so continued to the present moment. Respondent is at a loss to understand why the complainant in the cross-bill should have set up a defense which he must
have known was utterly unfounded, unless it should have been
for the purpose of prolonging this litigation, and thus securing
to himself a continued use of the said property of which he has
so long enjoyed possession without complying with the terms
of the contract under which he secured such possession.

2. Further answering, this respondent, with equal emphasis
and directness, denies that the said complainant has at any time
paid to him, in person or through his duly authorized agent or
attorney, or through any other person, any such sums of money
as complainant in his said cross-bill has so recklessly alleged, or
any other sums at any time, or in any manner, save the cash
payment made at the time the said contract was entered into, as
shown in the original bill. If any such payments were made to
the said Adam L. Henderson, as attorney for respondent, as
alleged in the cross-bill (which payments respondent does not

admit were in fact made), such payments were made wholly at the risk of the said complainant, since respondent here and now, in the most emphatic manner, denies that said Adam L. Henderson ever had authority, express or implied, from repondent to act as his agent or attorney in connection with this contract, or in any other matter. And respondent further denies that he ever received any of said alleged payments, or any portion thereof, from or through the said Adam L. Henderson, or any other person.

And having fully answered, respondent prays to be dismissed from the proceedings on said cross-bill, with his reasonable costs about his defense in this behalf expended.

Lemon & Herbert,

For respondent in Cross-Bill.

[To this answer complainant in the cross bill files a *general replication.*]

16. THE TESTIMONY.

[The whole case, on bill and cross-bill, and the several defensive pleadings, is now ready for the taking of testimony. A careful study of the pleadings will indicate what the issues are, namely, (1) *Has the plaintiff a living wife,* who is entitled to dower in the property in controversy? (2) *What payments has the defendant made to the plaintiff,* under the contract, and what is the balance due?

The questions of (1) *attorney's fees;* (2) *necessity of filing a conveyance with the bill;* (3) *compelling defendant to accept indemnity against the contingent right of dower* in the alleged wife of plaintiff; (4) *the right of defendant to a rescission,* if the alleged wife of plaintiff is alive; and (5) *the statute of limitations*—have all been settled by the decision of the court on the several objections to pleadings in the form of (a) demurrer to the bill, (b) plea set down for argument, and (c) demurrer to cross-bill.

The evidence to be taken, therefore, will be confined to the two issues of fact recited above.]

17. DEPOSITIONS.

Kendrick
 v.   On Original Bill.
Quinby
 and
Quinby
 v.   On Cross-Bill.
Kendrick

The depositions of A, B, C and others taken, in pursuance of the notice hereto attached, [or taken by consent of parties] before me, Howard Winston, a Notary Public in and for the county of Albemarle, in the state of Virginia, on the 14th day of November, 1921, at my office in the Colonnade Club Building, West Lawn, University of Virginia, between the hours of 9 A. M. and 6 P. M., to be read as evidence in behalf of the plaintiff in the original bill, [or for the defendant, as the case may be] in a certain suit in chancery depending in the Circuit Court of Albemarle county, under the style of *Kendrick* v. *Quinby,* on original bill, and *Quinby* v. *Kendrick,* on cross-bill.

Present:

John R. Lemon, for complainant.

R. C. Appleby, for respondent.

The witnesses whose several depositions follow, being duly sworn to speak the truth, the whole truth and nothing but the truth, depose and say:

First witness: *James Aday.*

1st question by plaintiff's counsel: Please state your age, residence and occupation.

Answer: James Aday—Preston Heights, University, Va.—Law student.

2nd question: Please state whether you know the plaintiff in this suit, how long you have known him, and what your relations with him have been and are.

Answer: I do. I have known him intimately for four years, and our relations have been quite close and friendly, etc., etc.

Cross-examination by defendant's counsel.

1st Cross-question: Please say whether, etc., etc., etc.

Re-examination by counsel for plaintiff.

1st question: In your answer to Mr. Appleby's 14th cross-question you say, etc., etc. Please explain precisely what you mean by that answer. Etc., etc., etc.

And further the deponent saith not.

(Signed) JAMES ADAY.

Second witness: Benj. Brown.

[Examined in chief—cross-examined and re-examined, and deposition signed, as in the case of the first witness.

If there are other witnesses to be examined at the same sitting, their depositions follow. When the depositions at that sitting are closed, the notary attaches a certificate substantially in the following form:]

I, Howard Winston, a notary public in and for the county of Albemarle in the state of Virginia, do certify that the foregoing depositions of James Aday, Benjamin Brown, etc., etc., were duly taken, sworn to and subscribed before me at the time and place and for the purpose in the caption mentioned.

Given under my hand [and seal[7]] this the 14th day of November, 1921.

(Signed) HOWARD WINSTON,
Notary Public.

My commission expires March 3, 1923.

18. DECREE: *Dismissing cross-bill, and order of reference to a master.*

Note for decree, December Term 1921.

John A. Kendrick ⎫
    v.   ⎬ On Original Bill.
Peter Quinby ⎭

and

Peter Quinby ⎫
    v.   ⎬ On Cross-Bill.
John A. Kendrick ⎭

This cause came on this day to be again heard on the papers

---

[7] The use of the notary's seal is almost universal, but it is not required in Virginia where the attested document is taken and is to be used within the state.

formerly read, on the answer of the defendant Peter Quinby, to the original bill, with geneneral replication thereto, on the cross-bill of the said defendant Peter Quinby, filed by leave of court, and on the exhibits therewith filed, on the answer of the plaintiff to said cross-bill, with general replication thereto, and on the depositions of witnesses for both plaintiff and defendant, and was argued by counsel.

On consideration whereof, the court being satisfied from the testimony that the plaintiff is not the husband of a living wife, and that, in consequence, the title to the property in the bill and proceedings mentioned is not now, and was not at the commencement of this suit, encumbered by the contingent right of dower as alleged in the answer and cross-bill of the defendant, but that, on the contrary, the plaintiff is able and willing to perform his contract by conveying a perfect title to the defendant, it is adjudged, ordered and decreed that the cross-bill of the defendant be and the same is hereby dismissed at the costs of the said defendant.

And the court being unable at this time to ascertain from the testimony what amounts the defendant has paid to the plaintiff on said contract of sale and purchase, and what balance actually remains unpaid, the court doth adjudge, order and decree that this cause be referred to one of the masters of this court, with directions to take, state and settle an account showing what the said balance due under said contract is, with the date or dates from which the same, or the several parts thereof, bear interest. And said master will report to the next term of this court how he has executed this decree, for such further order in the premises as the court may be advised.

Kendrick
    v.   19. MASTER'S REPORT.
Quinby.

Commissioner's Office,
Jan. 13, 1922.

To the Honorable John W. Fishburne, Judge of the Circuit Court of Albemarle County.

The undersigned master begs leave respectfully to report that in accordance with the directions of a decree of your honor's court, entered at the December term, 1921, in the above entitled cause, and after giving due notice to the parties thereto, the undersigned proceeded on the third day of January, 1922, to take said account. Both parties appeared in person and by counsel, and much testimony, both in the form of depositions of witnesses and of documents, was introduced on such hearing. All of the testimony introduced before the master is herewith returned for the inspection of the court. The proceedings were adjourned from time to time to suit the convenience of the parties; and the report is made up as of the 12th day of January, 1922.

The conclusion of the undersigned is herewith submitted in the form of a statement marked "Master's Exhibit number 1." From this statement it appears that the defendant made sundry payments from time to time under the contract in question, some of which payments were made to the plaintiff personally, but most of them were made to one Adam L. Henderson, as attorney for the plaintiff. The plaintiff, in his pleadings and by his evidence before the master, denied the authority of the said attorney to represent him in the matter, but the master is of opinion that the defendant has established the contrary by a preponderance of testimony, and the account has been made up on the basis of the validity of all payments so made to said Henderson in that behalf.

The statement referred to shows a balance of principal due the plaintiff of $2,375, with interest thereon from July 17, 1915, until paid, and the master recommends a decree for that amount in the plaintiff's favor.

Respectfully submitted,

W. R. Sewell,
Master.

Master's fee: [8]

     47 hours at $1.—$47.

       Paid by plaintiff.

W. R. S.

---

[8] The master is required to make affidavit that he was diligently employed for the number of hours stated in his report. Va. Code 1919. § 3482.

20. plaintiff's exceptions to report:

[Title of the   The plaintiff by counsel excepts to the report
cause.]   of W. R. Sewell, master, filed in this cause on
                  January 13, 1922, and for ground of exception
asserts that the finding of the master that the said Adam L.
Henderson was in fact plaintiff's attorney, and authorized to receive payments from the defendant on the plaintiff's behalf, is
based on no valid testimony in the cause, but rests chiefly on
hearsay testimony, to which the plaintiff duly excepted when it
was offered, as will appear by reference to the depositions fi!␣d
with the said report. The plaintiff makes special reference to
the depositions of P, Q, R and S, filed with the master's report,
as being the only testimony offered by defendant to establish
said Henderson's authority, none of which depositions, nor all
combined, would even tend to prove such authority, if the hearsay and incompetent testimony therein were excluded.

Respectfully submitted.

Lemon & Herbert,
for Complainant.

21. decree: *Sustaining exceptions to master's report, and ordering payment by defendant.*

Note for decree February term, 1922.

Kendrick   This cause came on this day to be again heard on
   v.   the papers formerly read, and on the report of W.
Quinby.   R. Sewell, master filed on the 13th day of January,
              1922, and on the plaintiff's exceptions to said report,
and was argued by counsel.

On consideration whereof, the court being satisfied from an
examination of the said report and of the testimony excepted to,
that the plaintiff's exceptions to said testimony, and to said report, are well taken, doth sustain the said exceptions, and doth
reject the findings of the master in the particulars following, to-
wit: That is to say, the court finds, and so adjudges, that the
defendant is not entitled to credit for any of the payments
shown by the master's statement to have been made to Adam L.
Henderson, alleged attorney for plaintiff, but is entitled to credit
only for such payments as are shown by said statement to have

been made to the plaintiff personally. And it appearing that
the rejected credits may be ascertained by a mere inspection of
the said report and statement, and that the balance then due the
plaintiff may be ascertained by a statement made up at the bar
of the court by counsel, under direction of the court, the court
deems it unnecessary to refer the said report back to the master for further proceedings. In other particulars the said report
is confirmed.

Adopting, therefore, the statement so made up at the bar of
the court, as exhibiting the true state of the account between the
parties, and which is ordered to be filed with the papers in this
cause, and it appearing from such statement that the balance so
due is represented by what follows, the court doth adjudge, order and decree that the defendant do, within 60 days from the
entry of this decree, pay to the plaintiff the sum of $3,650, with
legal interest thereon from the 13th day of August, 1917, until
paid, together with the costs of this suit.

The court doth further adjudge, order and decree that before
demanding payment of the sum hereinbefore decreed, the plaintiff shall file with the clerk of this court, as a part of the record
in this cause, a proper deed of conveyance, properly executed,
acknowledged and certified, conveying the property in the bill
and proceedings mentioned to the defendant, or to such person
as he may, in writing, filed with the papers in this cause, direct—
such conveyance to contain the usual covenants of warranty,
and to be delivered by the clerk to the defendant, upon written
acknowledgment of the plaintiff, or his counsel, that the defendant has fully satisfied this decree.

And the court doth retain the cause for such further proceedings as may be necessary, in case the defendant shall neglect or
refuse to obey the mandate of this decree.

Notes on the foregoing decree.

1. If the defendant performs the decree, he receives his conveyance, and the plaintiff his purchase money, so that there is
no need of further continuing the cause on the docket. In which
case, on motion of the plaintiff, an order is entered that "the
objects of this suit having been accomplished it is ordered to be
stricken from the docket."

2. If the decree be not performed, the plaintiff will ask for a decree subjecting the property to his vendor's (legal) lien, as set out in the bill—in which case there may be the following further proceedings—the precise proceedings depending somewhat on circumstances:

1. Decree appointing a special commissioner to make sale of the property, on terms prescribed in the decree.

2. Sale by the commissioner.

3. Report of sale, by the commissioner to the court.

4. Confirmation of the sale by the court—or rejection and order for a re-sale.

5. Order to commissioner, to collect the purchase money, as the installments fall due.

6. Reports of the commissioner, from time to time, showing the amount of his collections.

7. Orders, from time to time, directing the commissioner to pay over to plaintiff such balance as he has in his hands, as a credit on plaintiff's debt.

8. After the purchase money is paid in full by the purchaser at the judicial sale, an order is made appointing a special master (or commissioner) to convey the title to the purchaser.

9. After plaintiff's balance is all paid, and the costs provided for, an order is entered directing the net balance to be paid over to the defendant.

10. Filing of commissioner's final report—its confirmation by the court, and an order dismissing the cause from the docket.

II.

Suit for sale of Infants' Lands.
Under Virginia Code 1919, Chapter 217.
(See the Text, *ante*, chapter xxx.)

1. THE BILL.

To the Honorable Archibald D. Dabney, Judge of the Corporation Court of the City of Charlottesville.

The Bill of Allan W. Perkins, guardian of the infant defendants hereinafterwards named, respectfully represents unto your Honor:

1. That by an order of your honor's court entered at the December term thereof, 1921, your complainant was duly appointed guardian of John Winston Aday, Thomas Quincey Aday, and Lucy Blanton Aday, aged respectively fifteen (15), thirteen (13) and nine (9) years, the children of Henry Aday, and his wife, Lucy B. Aday (née Blanton), of the City of Charlottesville, and both now deceased.

Your complainant duly qualified as such guardian, by giving the required bond and taking the prescribed oath, as will appear from a certified copy of the said order of appointment and qualification filed herewith, marked "Exhibit 1", and asked to be read as a part of this bill.

2. The mother of the said infants, the said Lucy B. Aday, died several years ago, intestate, and without leaving any estate of value.

3. The father of the said infants, the said Henry P. Aday, died on the 17th day of July, 1921, in the City of Charlottesville, where he had long resided. During his lifetime he had accumulated a considerable estate, all of which, by his will, admitted to probate in in your honor's court, at the November term thereof, 1921, he devised and bequeathed, in absolute estate, to his said three surviving children, equally to be divided amongst them. A verified copy of such will is herewith filed as a part of this bill, marked "Exhibit 2."

4. The estate so devised and bequeathed to said infants, and now in the possession and control of your complainant as their guardian, consists of both real and personal estate, and is probably worth at present market prices from $50,000 to $60,000.

5. The personal estate so passing to said infants, and now in possession and control of your complainant as their guardian, is as follows:

(a) Household and kitchen furniture, books, silverware, pictures and like articles contained in the testator's late residence, worth probably $1000.

(b) Fifty (50) shares of the stock of the Charlottesville Woolen Mills, of the estimated market value of $6000.

(c) Cash in bank (the Peoples National Bank of Charlottesville), to complainant's credit as guardian, $2752.63.

(d) Sundry unsettled open accounts due the testator's estate, and now in course of collection by the executor, of unknown and doubtful value, and which on a liberal estimate will not realize more than $250.

So far as complainant is informed and believes, the property mentioned above is all of the personal estate belonging to said infants.

6. The real estate belonging to said infants, and all derived under the testator's will before mentioned, consists of the following parcels:

(A) The late dwelling house of the testator, known as 1396 University Place, in the City of Charlottesville—still occupied as a home by said infants, who are under the care of their aunt, Anna R. Simpson, widowed sister of the said testator.

(B) Three store houses, adjoining each other, in the same city, known as Nos. 1132, 1134 and 1136 W. Main Street. The assessed value of the three is $47,000, but the market value is probably $50,000 or more. They are all occupied by good tenants, and produce a net annual rental of about $3,000.

(C) Four vacant lots in University Place, adjoining the home place above mentioned. These lots were purchased by the said testator shortly before his death, with a view of building thereon, and selling the lots and buildings at a profit, but the prosecution of the enterprise was halted by his death. These lots are described as lots Nos. 187, 188, 189, and 190, as designated on a plat of University Place, recorded in the clerk's office of your honor's court, in deed-book 46, pages 641-642. A certified copy of the deed of conveyance from the testator's grantor, the University Place Company, is herewith filed as a part of this bill, marked "Exhibit 3" and prayed to be taken as a part of this bill.

All of the foregoing parcels of realty are held and owned by said infants as tenants in common, and in fee simple estate.

So far as your complainant is informed and believes the foregoing is a complete list of all the real estate owned by the infant defendants—and as already stated, the whole thereof was derived through the will of their father, Henry P. Aday, deceased.

7. Your complainant further represents that the four vacant lots last above described, are not only not income-producing, but they require a considerable annual outlay in the form of state and city taxes. They are assessed for taxation at $3000 each, and the annual tax-bill on these lots alone amounts to something over $150 a year.

The said lots are well located, and are in a very desirable locality, and are likely to increase somewhat in value in the future. But after giving the matter careful consideration, and after conference with several real estate experts in whose judgment and integrity he has confidence, your complainant is confirmed in his own judgment that the interests of his said wards would be promoted by a sale of these lots, and a re-investment of the proceeds in some safe income-producing security. It is the purpose of this bill to secure a decree from your honor's court, authorizing and directing such a sale for reinvestment as indicated.

8. Your complainant further shows that inasmuch as the infant defendants acquired title to the said lots through the will of their father, the said Henry P. Aday, the same would descend to the kindred on their father's side, should all of said infants die before attaining their majority. The said Henry P. Aday left surviving him two sisters, namely, Anna R. Simpson, widow, and Susan R. Ramsay, now the wife of Robert A. Ramsay—both residents of the City of Charlottesville—and three nephews, children of a pre-deceased brother Thomas L. Aday, namely, John M. Aday, Samuel M. Aday, and Rufus B. Aday, all adults, all non-residents of this commonwealth, and all three residing at Tulsa, Oklahoma.

In case the said infants should all die before attaining their majority the following persons, therefore, would be their heirs, towit: Anna R. Simpson, Susan R. Ramsay, John M. Aday, Samuel M. Aday and Rufus B. Aday.

9. In addition to the kindred on the father's side, the next of kin on the mother's side, in case the said infants should all die during their minority, would be two widowed sisters of the mother, namely, Anne Hathaway Allen, of Charlottesville, and Martha Blanton Willoughby, of Richmond, Va., who would be co-distributees with the father's next of kin above mentioned.

It follows that in case the said infant defendants all died before attaining their majority, the following would be their *distributees* towit: Anna R. Simpson, Susan R. Ramsay, John M. Aday, Samuel M. A'day, Rufus B. Aday, Anne Hathaway Allen and Martha Blanton.Willoughby.   All of these are, therefore, hereinafterwards prayed to be made parties defendant to this bill, as required by the statute in such cases made and provid~d.

10. The premises considered, your complainant prays that the said infant wards, John Winston Aday, Thomas Quincey Aday, and Lucy Blanton Aday, as well as the said Anna R. Simpson, Susan R. Ramsay, John M. Aday, Samuel M. Aday, Rufus B. Aday, Anne Hathaway Allen and Martha Blanton Willoughby be made parties defendant to this bill, and may answer the same; but answers under oath are waived as to all of the defendants save as to such as by law are required to answer under oath; that a competent and discreet attorney at law be appointed guardian *ad litem* to represent the interests of said infants in this proceeding, who, as well as the said John Winston Aday, the infant defendant who is over fourteen years of age, may be required to answer this bill on oath in proper·person; that the four vacant lots above mentioned may be sold under orders of the court, and the proceeds properly invested in other income-producing securities; that a proper counsel's fee be allowed to complainant's counsel in this cause; that all other necessary and proper proceedings may be had and taken for accomplishing the prayers of this bill; and for such other relief, both general and special, as to equity may seem meet and the nature of the case may require.

And your complainant will ever pray, etc.

(signed)   Allan W. Perkins,
Guardian.

Duke & Duke,
  For Complainant.

Virginia, City of Charlottesville, Towit:

I, Louise F. Wheeler, a Notary Public in and for the state and city aforesaid, do certify that Allan W. Perkins, whose name as guardian is signed to the foregoing bill of complaint, this day personally appeared before me in my said city, and made oath that the matters and things stated in said bill as of his own knowledge are true, and that those stated as on the information of others he believes to be true.

Given under my hand this the 21st day of January, 1922.

(Signed)   LOUISE F. WHEELER,
Notary Public.

My commission expires March 16th, 1923.

2. ANSWER OF INFANTS BY GUARDIAN AD LITEM.

The joint answers of John W. Aday, Thomas Q. Aday and Lucy B. Aday, infants under the age of twenty-one years, by Albert S. Bolling, their guardian *ad litem*, appointed by the court, as a competent and discreet attorney at law, to defend their interests in this cause, to a bill of complaint filed against these respondents and others, in the Corporation Court of the City of Charlottesville, by Allan W. Perkins, guardian of these respondents.

These respondents, by their said guardian *ad litem*, for answer to said bill, say that they are infants of tender years, and therefore incapable of knowing or defending their rights in the premises. They therefore submit their interests to the protection of the court, and pray that no decree may be rendered to their prejudice.

And having fully answered they pray to be hence dismissed.

                          Thomas Q. Aday,
                          John W. Aday,
                          Lucy B. Aday.

(Signed)   ALBERT S. BOLLING,
Guardian ad Litem.

Virginia, City of Charlottesville, Towit:

I, Louise F. Wheeler, a notary public in and for the state and city aforesaid, do certify that Albert S. Bolling, whose name as guardian *ad litem,* is signed to the foregoing answer, this day personally appeared before me, in my said city, and made oath that to the best of his knowledge and belief, the matters and things stated in the said answer are true.

Given under my hand, this the 25th day of January, 1922.[9]

(Signed) Louise F. Wheeler,
Notary Public.

My commission expires March 16th, 1923.

3. answer of infant over 14 years of age.

The separate answer of John W. Aday, in proper person, to a bill of complaint filed against him and others, in the Corporation Court of Charlottesville, by Allan W. Perkins, guardian of this respondent.

For answer to said bill, this respondent adopts the answer already filed in his behalf and that of his infant co-defendants by Albert S. Bolling, his guardian *ad litem,* in which answer this respondent, along with his infant co-defendants, has placed his interests herein under the protection of the court, and prayed that no decree be entered herein to his prejudice.

This respondent, who is now in his sixteenth year, as stated in the bill, has heard the said bill read, and believes that he understands the allegations therein and the purpose thereof. He believes the allegations of the bill to be true, and its purpose to be to the interest of himself and his infant co-defendants. So far as he lawfully may, therefore, he concurs in the prayers of the bill.

And having fully answered he prays to be hence dismissed.

(Signed) John W. Aday.

Albert S. Bolling,
For Respondent.

[Append personal affidavit of the infant respondent.]

4. answer of guardian ad litem in proper person.[10]

The answer, in proper person, of Albert S. Bolling guardian *ad litem* of the infant defendants John W. Aday, Thomas Q. Aday and Lucy B. Aday, duly appointed to defend their inter-

---

[9] Oath probably not necessary here.

[10] The practice prevailing in some of the circuits of Virginia, of filing a merely perfunctory answer on the part of the guardian *ad litem* in proper person, is clearly not within the spirit and intent of the

ests in this suit, to a bill of complaint filed against such infant defendants and others, in the Corporation Court of the City of Charlottesville, by Allan W. Perkins, guardian of said infants.

This respondent, for answer to said bill, says that he has carefully read the same, and is fully informed as to the purposes thereof; that, as a resident of the City of Charlottesville for many years, respondent is familiar with all of the real property mentioned in the bill, and also with the general circumstances of the infant defendants, which he believes to be truly stated in the bill. He concurs in the opinion of the guardian, expressed in the bill, that the vacant lots therein described should be sold, and the proceeds reinvested in some safe, income-producing securities; and that such sale and reinvestment would clearly promote the interests of the infant owners, and, so far as he knows, will not violate the rights of any other persons.

And having fully answered he prays to be hence dismissed, with his reasonable costs and charges.

(Signed) ALBERT S. BOLLING,

Guardian ad Litem.

[Append personal affidavit of guardian ad litem.]

5. DECREE OF SALE.[11]

Allan W. Perkins, Guardian of
    John W. Aday, Thomas Q. Aday and
    and Lucy B. Aday, infants....................Plaintiff.
        v.
    John W. Aday, Thomas Q. Aday and
    Lucy B. Aday, infants; Anna R. Simpson
    Susan R. Ramsay, John M. Aday,
    Samuel M. Aday, Rufus B. Aday,
    Anne Hathaway Allen and Martha
    Blanton Willoughby ....Defendants.

---

statute. The purpose of requiring the personal answer of the guardian ad litem is, that the court may have the benefit of his personal knowledge of the situation, and his personal opinion as to the propriety of the sale, or other disposition of the infant's property. If he have not proper information, it is his duty to acquire it by investigation.

[11] Since the court here is exercising a limited statutory jurisdiction, it is important that the decree expressly recite all essential jurisdictional steps, so as to foreclose any collateral questioning of the procedure in the future. As to the conclusiveness of such recitals, see the Text, ante, § 40.

This cause came on this day to be heard on the bill of the plaintiff, duly verified as required by law, and the exhibits filed therewith; on the joint answers of John W. Aday, Samuel M. Aday, and Lucy B. Aday, infant defendants, by Albert S. Bolling, their guardian *ad litem,* a competent and discreet attorney-at-law, duly appointed to defend their interests herein, and under the oath of said guardian *ad litem;* on the separate answer, in proper person, of the infant defendant John W. Aday, who is over fourteen years of age, and under the oath of the said infant defendant, in proper person; on the separate answer, in proper person, of Albert S. Bolling guardian *ad litem* of said infant defendants, under the oath of said guardian *ad litem,* —to none of which answers does the plaintiff deem it necessary to reply; on the bill taken for confessed as to the defendants Anna R. Simpson, Susan R. Ramsay, Anne Hathaway Allen and Martha Blanton Willoughby, upon whom process appears to have been duly served, and they failing to appear and answer or otherwise respond to said process; on the bill set for hearing as to the non-resident defendants John M. Aday, Samuel M. Aday and Rufus B. Aday, against whom the plaintiff appears to have proceeded by order of publication as required by law, and they still failing to enter their appearance herein; and on the testimony of witnesses taken in the presence of the said guardian *ad litem,* and was argued by counsel.

On consideration whereof, being satisfied from the testimony of witnesses taken and certified as required by law, and independently of any admissions in the several answers filed herein, that a sale of the vacant lots of ground in the bill and proceedings mentioned will promote the interests of the infant defendants, owners thereof, and that the rights of no other person will be violated thereby, the court doth adjudge, order and decree that Allan W. Perkins and Albert S. Bolling, who are hereby appointed special commissioners for the purpose, do, after advertising the time, terms and place of sale for at least three times a week for two successive weeks in the Charlottesville Progress, and in such other manner as they may deem best calculated to give due publicity to the said sale, expose the said four lots of ground, in the bill and proceedings mentioned,—described as lots Nos. 187, 188, 189 and 190, as designated on the plat of University Place—for sale by way of public auction on the premises, on the following terms towit: One fourth of the purchase money to be paid in cash, and the residue in equal installments, maturing six, twelve and eighteen months after date, respectively, with interest from date, the deferred installments represented by negotiable notes of the purchaser, or purchasers, payable to the order of the court in this cause, and containing waiver of homestead exemption. But the said commissioners shall not proceed to the execution of this decree until they (or that one who shall serve hereunder) shall have executed bond before the clerk of this court, in the penalty of $10,000, with good security to be approved by the said clerk, conditioned for the faithful performance of their duties hereunder.

And said commissioners will report to the next term of this court how they have executed this decree.

[The further proceedings differ in nowise from proceedings in other chancery suits.]

III.

Order of Reference in a Creditors' Suit.

[Title of cause.]

.... On consideration whereof the court doth adjudge, order and decree that this cause be, and the same is hereby, referred to one of the masters (or commissioners) of this court, with directions to take, state and settle an account showing:

1. What estate, real or personal, is owned by the defendant, the Charlottesville Canning Company, (Inc.), and subject to the claims of its creditors.

2. All delinquent taxes on the real estate belonging to the defendant, the Charlottesville Canning Company, (Inc.), with the interest thereon, as required by law.

3. What claims asserted, or to be asserted, in this cause, constitute liens on the assets of the said company, with their several amounts and their respective priorities.

4. All other valid claims against said company, not reduced
to judgment, or otherwise charged as liens on such assets.

5. Any other matters deemed pertinent by said master, or required to be stated by any party in interest.

And the said master shall give notice of the time and place for
the taking of such account, by a publication thereof once a week
for four successive weeks in the Charlottesville Progress, which
publication shall be equivalent to personal notice to all parties in
interest.

And said master will report to a future term of this court
how he has executed this decree.

IV.

The Master's Deed.

THIS DEED, made this the 21st day of January, 1922, between Charles W. Allen, special commissioner as hereinafter-
ward shown, of the one part, and Patrick C. Callaway, of the
other part.

WHEREAS, in a certain suit in chancery depending in the
Circuit Court of the County of Albemarle, under the short style
of Amiss *et al. v.* The Charlottesville Canning Co., (Inc.) *et al.*,
by a decretal order of the said court, entered at its April term,
1921, the party of the first part was authorized and directed to
convey, with special warranty of title, to the party of the second
part, the real property hereinafterwards described—all of which
will more fully and at large appear by reference to the proceedings in the court and cause aforesaid; and

WHEREAS, in pursuance of the statute in such cases made
and provided,[12] the names of the parties on whose behalf this
conveyance is made, are here set out, to-wit,

(A, B, C, D, E, etc.)

NOW, THEREFORE, in consideration of the premises, and
in execution of the authority and directions of the decretal order aforesaid, the party of the first part, special commissioner
as aforesaid, doth hereby grant and convey, with special warranty of title, unto the party of the second part, the following

---

[12] For this awkward and apparently useless clause, see Va. Acts
1918, p. 444, and comments thereon, *ante*, § 310.

described real property, situated in Albemarle County, in the State of Virginia, to-wit:

[Here insert description.]

This is the same property [or a portion of the same property] which was conveyed to William R. Blackshear by Henry T. Lyne and wife, by their joint deed, bearing date on the 17th day of May, 1906, and recorded in the clerk's office of the Circuit Court of said county, in deed book 178, on pages 56-58, and to which deed reference is here made for a more accurate description of the property intended to be conveyed hereby.

Witness the following signature and seal, on the day and year first aforesaid.

(Signed)   CHARLES W. ALLEN, [SEAL].
Special Commissioner.

[To be acknowledged and certified as in case of other deeds of conveyance.]

V.

Other Forms in Equity.

Subjoined are a few other familiar forms used in the equity practice, with which the young practitioner should cultivate a close and intimate acquaintance.

1. AFFIDAVITS.

(1) *Virginia Form.*[13]

Virginia,

     County of Albemarle, to-wit:

1, Howard Winston, a Notary Public (or a justice of the peace, or a commissioner in chancery) for the State and county aforesaid do certify that Peter Quinby whose name is signed to the foregoing answer, this day made oath before me, in my said county, that the matters and things therein stated as of his own knowledge are true, and those stated as on the information of others he believes to be true.

---

[13] This form of affidavit, practically universal in Virginia, differs from that prevailing generally in other states in the following particulars: (1) It is wholly the language of the notary; (2) It is not signed by the affiant; and (3) the notarial seal is not affixed.

Affidavits taken by a Virginia notary, for use in other states should, of course, conform to the general and not to the local practice.

Given under my hand this the 17th day of January, 1922.

(Signed)   Howard Winston,
Notary Public.

My commission expires March 3, 1923.

(2) *The more usual form of Affidavit in other States.*

State of Kentucky,

County of Jefferson, to-wit:

Peter Quinby being duly sworn [on the Holy Evangely of Almighty God] deposes and says that the matters and things in the foregoing answer, stated as of his own knowledge, are true, and those stated as on information and belief he believes to be true.

(Signed) Peter Quinby.

Sworn to and subscribed before me, by the affiant, Peter Quinby, who is well known to me, this the 17th day of January, Anno Domini, 1922.

(Signed)   Adam Beasley,

(official seal)   *Notary Public.*

My commission expires March 3, 1925.

2. preliminary injunction order.

On the motion of the plaintiff, an injunction is awarded against the defendant, the Chesapeake and Ohio Railway Company, restraining and prohibiting the said defendant, its agents and servants, from entering, or in anywise trespassing upon or injuring, the lot of ground in the bill mentioned, until the further order of this court.

But the plaintiff shall not have the benefit of this order until he, or some one for him, shall have entered into bond, before the clerk of this court, with good security to be approved by said clerk, in the penalty of five hundred dollars ($500), conditioned to answer all costs and damages which may be awarded against him in case this injunction shall be dissolved.

(Signed)   John W. Fishburne, *Judge.*

To the Clerk of the Circuit Court of Albemarle county.

3. rule to show cause.

(1) *On petition filed.*

On the motion of Hiram Q. Abernathy, he hath leave to file

his petition in this cause, which is accordingly done. And on like motion a rule is awarded against Aaron Applegarth and Amelia Applegarth, his wife, defendants named in the said petition, to appear here on the first day of the April term of this court next, to show cause if any they have or can show why the prayer of the said petition shall not be granted.

(2) *On Contempt Charge.*

It being represented to the court by affidavits filed by the plaintiff in this cause that the defendant, the Chesapeake & Ohio Railway Company, and its chief engineer Robert C. Calloway, are in contempt of this court in having violated the injunction heretofore awarded the plaintiff in this cause, enjoining and restraining the said defendant and its agents and servants from entering or otherwise trespassing upon or injuring the property of the plaintiff in the bill and proceedings mentioned, on the motion of the plaintiff a rule is awarded against the said defendant, the Chesapeake and Ohio Railway Company, and the said Robert C. Calloway to appear here tomorrow morning at ten o'clock to show cause if any they have or can show why they shall not be attached or otherwise proceeded against according to law, for their said contempt.

APPENDIX II

The Federal Equity Rules of 1912

RULE 1.

DISTRICT COURT ALWAYS OPEN FOR CERTAIN PURPOSES—ORDERS AT CHAMBERS.

The district courts, as courts of equity, shall be deemed always open for the purpose of filing any pleading, of issuing and returning mesne and final process, and of making and directing all interlocutory motions, orders, rules and other proceedings preparatory to the hearing, upon their merits, of all causes pending therein.

Any district judge may, upon reasonable notice to the parties, make, direct, and award, at chambers or in the clerk's office, and in vacation as well as in term, all such process, commissions, orders, rules and other proceedings, whenever the same are not grantable of course, according to the rules and practice of the court.

2.

CLERK'S OFFICE ALWAYS OPEN, EXCEPT, ETC.

The clerk's office shall be open during business hours on all days, except Sundays and legal holidays, and the clerk shall be in attendance for the purpose of receiving and disposing of all motions, rules, orders and other proceedings which are grantable of course.

3.

BOOKS KEPT BY CLERK AND ENTRIES THEREIN.

The clerk shall keep a book known as "Equity Docket," in which he shall enter each suit, with a file number corresponding to the folio in the book. All papers and orders filed with the clerk in the suit, all process issued and returns made thereon, and all appearances shall be noted briefly and chronologically in this book on the folio assigned to the suit and shall be marked with its file number.

The clerk shall also keep a book entitled "Order Book," in which shall be entered at length, in the order of their making, all orders made or passed by him as of course and also all orders made or passed by the judge in chambers.

He shall also keep an "Equity Journal," in which shall be entered all orders, decrees and proceedings of the court in equity causes in term time.

Separate and suitable indices of the Equity Docket, Order Book and Equity Journal shall be kept by the clerk under the direction of the court.

4.

NOTICE OF ORDERS.

Neither the noting of an order in the Equity Docket nor its entry in the Order Book shall of itself be deemed notice to the parties or their solicitors; and when an order is made without prior notice to, and in the absence of, a party, the clerk, unless otherwise directed by the court or judge, shall forthwith send a copy thereof, by mail, to such party or his solicitor and a note of such mailing shall be made in the Equity Docket, which shall be taken as sufficient proof of due notice of the order.

5.

MOTIONS GRANTABLE OF COURSE BY CLERK.

All motions and applications in the clerk's office for the issuing of mesne process or final process to enforce and execute decrees; for taking bills *pro confesso;* and for other proceedings in the clerk's office which do not require any allowance or order of the court or of a judge, shall be deemed motions and applications grantable of course by the clerk; but the same may be suspended, or altered, or rescinded by the judge upon special cause shown.

6.

MOTION DAY.

Each district court shall establish regular times and places, not less than once each month, when motions requiring notice and hearing may be made and disposed of; but the judge may at any time and place, and on such notice, if any, as he may consider reasonable, make and direct all interlocutory orders, rulings and proceedings for the advancement, conduct and hearing of causes. If the public interest permits, the senior circuit judge of the circuit may dispense with the motion day during not to exceed two months in the year in any district.

7.

PROCESS, MESNE AND FINAL.

The process of subpœna shall constitute the proper mesne process in all suits in equity, in the first instance, to require the defendant to appear and answer the bill; and, unless otherwise provided in these rules or specially ordered by the court, a writ of attachment, and, if the defendant cannot be found, a writ of sequestration, or a writ of assistance to enforce a delivery of possession, as the case may require, shall be the proper process to issue for the purpose of compelling obedience to any interlocutory or final order or decree of the court.

8.

ENFORCEMENT OF FINAL DECREES.

Final process to execute any decree may, if the decree be solely for the payment of money, be by a writ of execution, in the form used in the district court in suits at common law in actions of *assumpsit*. If the decree be for the performance of any specific act, as, for example, for the execution of a conveyance of land or the delivering up of deeds or other documents, the decree shall, in all cases, prescribe the time within which the act shall be done, of which the defendant shall be bound, without further service, to take notice; and upon affidavit of the plaintiff, filed in the clerk's office, that the same has not been complied with within the prescribed time, the clerk shall issue a writ of attachment against the delinquent party, from which, if attached thereon, he shall not be discharged, unless upon a full compliance with the decree and the payment of all costs, or upon a special order of the court, or a judge thereof, upon motion and affidavit, enlarging the time for the performance thereof. If the delinquent party cannot be found a writ of sequestration shall issue against his estate, upon the return of *non est inventus*, to compel obedience to the decree. If a mandatory order, injunction or decree for the specific performance of any act or contract be not complied with, the court or a judge, besides, or instead of, proceedings against the disobedient party for a contempt or by sequestration, may by order direct that the act required to be done, so far as practicable, by some other person appointed by the court or judge, at the cost of the disobedient party, and the act, when so done, shall have like effect as if done by him.

9.

WRIT OF ASSISTANCE.

When any decree or order is for the delivery of possession, upon proof made by affidavit of a demand and refusal to obey the decree or order, the party prosecuting the same shall be entitled to a writ of assistance from the clerk of the court.

10.

DECREE FOR DEFICIENCY IN FORECLOSURES, ETC.

In suits for the foreclosure of mortgages, or the enforcement of other liens, a decree may be rendered for any balance that may be found due to the plaintiff over and above the proceeds of the sale or sales, and execution may issue for the collection of the same, as is provided in rule 8 when the decree is solely for the payment of money.

11.

PROCESS IN BEHALF OF AND AGAINST PERSONS NOT PARTIES.

Every person, not being a party in any cause, who has obtained an order, or in whose favor an order shall have been made, may enforce obedience to such order by the same process as if he were a party; and every person, not being a party, against whom obedience to any order of the court may be enforced, shall be liable to the same process for enforcing obedience to such orders as if he were a party.

12.

ISSUE OF SUBPŒNA—TIME FOR ANSWER.

Whenever a bill is filed, and not before, the clerk shall issue the process of subpœna thereon, as of course, upon the application of the plaintiff, which shall contain the names of the parties and be returnable into the clerk's office twenty days from the issuing thereof. At the bottom of the subpœna shall be placed a memorandum, that the defendant is required to file his answer or other defense in the clerk's office on or before the twentieth day after service, excluding the day thereof; otherwise the bill may be taken *pro 'confesso.* Where there are more than one defendant, a writ of subpœna may, at the election of the plaintiff, be sued out separately for each defendant, or a joint subpœna against all the defendants.

13.

MANNER OF SERVING SUBPŒNA.

The service of all subpœnas shall be by delivering a copy thereof to the defendant personally, or by leaving a copy thereof at the dwelling-house or usual place of abode of each defendant, with some adult person who is a member of or resident in the family.

14.

ALIAS SUBPŒNA.

Whenever any subpœna shall be returned not executed as to any defendant, the plaintiff shall be entitled to other subpœnas against such defendant, until due service is made.

15.

PROCESS, BY WHOM SERVED.

The service of all process, mesne and final, shall be by the marshal of the district, or his deputy, or by some other person specially appointed by the court or judge for that purpose, and not otherwise. In the latter case, the person serving the process shall make affidavit thereof.

16.

DEFENDANT TO ANSWER—DEFAULT—DECREE PRO CONFESSO.

It shall be the duty of the defendant, unless the time shall be enlarged, for cause shown, by a judge of the court, to file his answer or other defense to the bill in the clerk's office within the time named in the subpœna as required by rule 12. In default thereof the plaintiff may, at his election, take an order as of course that the bill be taken *pro confesso;* and thereupon the cause. shall be proceeded in *ex parte.*

17.

DECREE PRO CONFESSO TO BE FOLLOWED BY FINAL DECREE—SETTING ASIDE DEFAULT.

When the bill is taken *pro confesso* the court may proceed to a final decree at any time after the expiration of thirty days after the entry of the order *pro confesso,* and such decree shall be deemed absolute, unless the court shall, at the same term, set aside the same, or enlarge the time for filing the answer, upon cause shown upon motion and affidavit. No such motion shall be granted, unless upon the payment of the costs of the plaintiff up to that time, or such part thereof as the court shall deem reasonable, and unless the defendant shall undertake to file his answer within such time as the court shall direct, and submit to such other terms as the court shall direct, for the purpose of speeding the cause.

18.

PLEADING—TECHNICAL FORMS ABROGATED.

Unless otherwise prescribed by statute or these rules, the technical forms of pleadings in equity are abolished.

19.

AMENDMENTS GENERALLY.

The court may at any time, in furtherance of justice, upon such terms as may be just, permit any process, proceeding, pleading or record to be amended, or material supplemental matter to be set forth in an amended or supplemental pleading. The court, at every stage of the proceeding, must disregard any error or defect in the proceeding which does not affect the substantial rights of the parties.

20.

FURTHER AND PARTICULAR STATEMENT IN PLEADINGS MAY BE REQUIRED.

A further and better statement of the nature of the claim or defense, or further and better particulars of any matter stated in any pleading, may in any case be ordered, upon such terms, as to costs and otherwise, as may be just.

21.

SCANDAL AND IMPERTINENCE.

The right to except to bills, answers, and other proceedings for scandal or impertinence shall not obtain, but the court may, upon motion or its own initiative, order any redundant, impertinent or scandalous matter stricken out, upon such terms as the court shall think fit.

22.

ACTION AT LAW ERRONEOUSLY BEGUN AS SUIT IN EQUITY—TRANSFER.

If at any time it appear that a suit commenced in equity should have been brought as an action on the law side of the court, it shall be forthwith transferred to the law side and be there proceeded with, with only such alteration in the pleadings as shall be essential.

23.

MATTERS ORDINARILY DETERMINABLE AT LAW, WHEN ARISING IN SUIT IN EQUITY TO BE DISPOSED OF THEREIN.

If in a suit in equity a matter ordinarily determinable at law arises, such matter shall be determined in that suit according to the principles applicable, without sending the case or question to the law side of the court.

24.

SIGNATURE OF COUNSEL.

Every bill or other pleading shall be signed individually by one or more solicitors of record, and such signatures shall be considered as a certificate by each solicitor that he has read the pleading so signed by him; that upon the instructions laid before him regarding the case there is good ground for the same; that no scandalous matter is inserted in the pleading; and that it is not interposed for delay.

25.

BILL OF COMPLAINT—CONTENTS.

Hereafter it shall be sufficient that a bill in equity shall contain, in addition to the usual caption:

First, the full name, when known, of each plaintiff and defendant, and the citizenship and residence of each party. If any party be under any disability that fact shall be stated.

Second, a short and plain statement of the grounds upon which the court's jurisdiction depends.

Third, a short and simple statement of the ultimate facts upon which the plaintiff asks relief, omitting any mere statement of evidence.

Fourth, if there are persons other than those named as defendants who appear to be proper parties, the bill should state why they are not made parties—as that they are not within the jurisdiction of the court, or cannot be made parties without ousting the jurisdiction.

Fifth, a statement of and prayer for any special relief pending the suit or on final hearing, which may be stated and sought in alternative forms. If special relief pending the suit be desired the bill should be verified by the oath of the plaintiff, or someone having knowledge of the facts upon which such relief is asked.

26.

JOINDER OF CAUSES OF ACTION.

The plaintiff may join in one bill as many causes of action, cognizable in equity, as he may have against the defendant. But when there are more than one plaintiff, the causes of action joined must be joint, and if there be more than one defendant the liability must be one asserted against all of the material defendants, or sufficient grounds must appear for uniting the causes of action in order to promote the convenient administration of justice. If it appear that any such causes of action cannot be conveniently disposed of together, the court may order separate trials.

27.

STOCKHOLDER'S BILL.

Every bill brought by one or more stockholders in a corporation against the corporation and other parties, founded on rights which may properly be asserted by the corporation, must be verified by oath, and must contain an allegation that the plaintiff was a shareholder at the time of the transaction of which he complains, or that his share had devolved on him since by operation of law, and that the suit is not a collusive one to confer on a court of the United States jurisdiction of a case of which it would not otherwise have cognizance. It must also set forth with particularity the efforts of the plaintiff to secure such action as he desires on the part of the managing directors or trustees, and, if necessary, of the shareholders, and the causes of his failure to obtain such action, or the reasons for not making such effort.

28.

AMENDMENT OF BILL AS OF COURSE.

The plaintiff may, as of course, amend his bill before the defendant has responded thereto, but if such amendment be filed after any copy has issued from the clerk's office, the plaintiff at his own cost shall furnish to the solicitor of record of each opposing party a copy of the bill as amended, unless otherwise ordered by the court or judge.

After pleading filed by any defendant, plaintiff may amend only by consent of the defendant or leave of the court or judge.

29.

DEFENSES—HOW PRESENTED.

Demurrers and pleas are abolished. Every defense in point of law arising upon the face of the bill, whether for misjoinder, nonjoinder, or insufficiency of fact to constitute a valid cause of action in equity, which might heretofore have been made by demurrer or plea, shall be made by motion to dismiss or in the answer; and every such point of law going to the whole or a material part of the cause or causes of action stated in the bill may be called up and disposed of before final hearing at the discretion of the court. Every defense heretofore presentable by plea in bar or abatement shall be made in the answer and may be separately heard and disposed of before the trial of the principal case in the discretion of the court. If the defendant move to dismiss the bill or any part thereof, the motion may be set down for hearing by either party upon five days' notice, and, if it be denied, answer shall be filed within five days thereafter or a decree *pro confesso* entered.

30.

ANSWER—CONTENTS—COUNTER-CLAIM.

The defendant in his answer shall in short and simple terms set out his defense to each claim asserted by the bill, omitting any mere statement of evidence and avoiding any general denial of the averments of the bill, but specifically admitting or denying or explaining the facts upon which the plaintiff relies, unless the defendant is without knowledge, in which case he shall so state, such statement operating as a denial. Averments other than of value or amount of damage, if not denied, shall be deemed confessed, except as against an infant, lunatic or other person *non compos* and not under guardianship, but the answer may be amended, by leave of the court or judge, upon reasonable notice, so as to put any averment in issue, when justice requires it. The answer may state as many defenses, in the alternative, regardless of consistency, as the defendant deems essential to his defense.

The answer must state in short and simple form any counter-claim arising out of the transaction which is the subject-matter of the suit, and may, without cross-bill, set out any set-off or counter-claim against the plaintiff which might be the subject of an independent suit in equity against him, and such set-off or counter-claim, so set up, shall have the same effect as a cross-suit, so as to enable the court to pronounce a final judgment in the same suit both on the original and cross-claims.

<h3 style="text-align:center">31.</h3>

REPLY—WHEN REQUIRED—WHEN CAUSE AT ISSUE.

Unless the answer assert a set-off or counter-claim, no reply shall be required without special order of the court or judge, but the cause shall be deemed at issue upon the filing of the answer, and any new or affirmative matter therein shall be deemed to be denied by the plaintiff. If the answer include a set-off or counter-claim, the party against whom it is asserted shall reply within ten days after the filing of the answer, unless a longer time be allowed by the court or judge. If the counter-claim is one which affects the rights of other defendants they or their solicitors shall be served with a copy of the same within ten days from the filing thereof, and ten days shall be accorded to such defendants for filing a reply. In default of a reply, a decree *pro confesso* on the counter-claim may be entered as in default of an answer to the bill.

<h3 style="text-align:center">32.</h3>

ANSWER TO AMENDED BILL.

In every case where an amendment to the bill shall be made after answer filed, the defendant shall put in a new or supplemental answer within ten days after that on which the amendment or amended bill is filed, unless the time is enlarged or it is otherwise ordered by

a judge of the court; and upon a default, the like proceedings may
be had as upon an omission to put in an answer.

33.

TESTING SUFFICIENCY OF DEFENSE.

Exceptions for insufficiency of an answer are abolished. But if
an answer set up an affirmative defense, set-off or counter-claim,
the plaintiff may, upon five days' notice, or such further time as
the court may allow test the sufficiency of the same by motion to
strike out. If found insufficient but amendable, the court may allow
an amendment upon terms, or strike out the matter.

34.

SUPPLEMENTAL PLEADING.

Upon application of either party the court or judge may, upon
reasonable notice and such terms as are just, permit him to file and
serve a supplemental pleading, alleging material facts occurring after
his former pleading, or of which he was ignorant when it was made,
including the judgment or decree of a competent court rendered
after the commencement of the suit, determining the matters in controversy or a part thereof.

35.

BILLS OF REVIVOR AND SUPPLEMENTAL BILLS—FORM.

It shall not be necessary in any bill of revivor or supplemental
bill to set forth any of the statements in the original suit, unless
the special circumstances of the case may require it.

36.

OFFICERS BEFORE WHOM PLEADINGS VERIFIED.

Every pleading which is required to be sworn to by statute, or
these rules, may be verified before any justice or judge of any court
of the United States, or of any State or Territory, or of the District
of Columbia, or any clerk of any court of the United States, or of
any Territory, or of the District of Columbia, or any notary public.

37.

PARTIES GENERALLY—INTERVENTION.

Every action shall be prosecuted in the name of the real party
in interest, but an executor, administrator, guardian, trustee of an
express trust, a party with whom or in whose name a contract has
been made for the benefit of another, or a party expressly author-

ized by statute, may sue in his own name without joining with him the party for whose benefit the action is brought. All persons having an interest in the subject of the action and in obtaining the relief demanded may join as plaintiffs, and any person may be made a defendant who has or claims an interest adverse to the plaintiff. Any person may at any time be made a party if his presence is necessary or proper to a complete determination of the cause. Persons having a united interest must be joined on the same side as plaintiffs or defendants, but when anyone refuses to join, he may for such reason be made a defendant.

Anyone claiming an interest in the litigation, may at any time be permitted to assert his right by intervention, but the intervention shall be in subordination to, and in recognition of, the propriety of the main proceeding.

38.

REPRESENTATIVES OF CLASS.

When the question is one of common or general interest to many persons constituting a class so numerous as to make it impracticable to bring them all before the court, one or more may sue or defend for the whole.

39.

ABSENCE OF PERSONS WHO WOULD BE PROPER PARTIES.

In all cases where it shall appear to the court that persons, who might otherwise be deemed proper parties to the suit, cannot be made parties by reason of their being out of the jurisdiction of the court, or incapable otherwise of being made parties, or because their joinder would oust the jurisdiction of the court as to the parties before the court, the court may, in its discretion, proceed in the cause without making such persons parties; and in such cases the decree shall be without prejudice to the rights of the absent parties.

40.

NOMINAL PARTIES.

Where no account, payment, conveyance, or other direct relief is sought against a party to a suit, not being an infant, the party, upon service of the subpœna upon him, need not appear and answer the bill, unless the plaintiff specially requires him to do so by the prayer; but he may appear and answer at his option; and if he does not appear and answer he shall be bound by all the proceedings in the cause. If the plaintiff shall require him to appear and answer he shall be entitled to the costs of all the proceedings against him, unless the court shall otherwise direct.

41.

SUIT TO EXECUTE TRUSTS OF WILL—HEIR AS PARTY.

In suits to execute the trusts of a will, it shall not be necessary to make the heir at law a party; but the plaintiff shall be at liberty to make the heir at law a party where he desires to have the will established against him.

42.

JOINT AND SEVERAL DEMANDS.

In all cases in which the plaintiff has a joint and several demand against several persons, either as principals or sureties, it shall not be necessary to bring before the court as parties to a suit concerning such demand all the persons liable thereto; but the plaintiff may proceed against one or more of the persons severally liable.

43.

DEFECT OF PARTIES—RESISTING OBJECTION.

Where the defendant shall by his answer suggest that the bill of complaint is defective for want of parties, the plaintiff may, within fourteen days after answer filed, set down the cause for argument as a motion upon that objection only; and where the plaintiff shall not so set down his cause, but shall proceed therewith to a hearing, notwithstanding an objection for want of parties taken by the answer, he shall not at the hearing of the cause, if the defendant's objection shall then be allowed, be entitled as of course to an order to amend his bill by adding parties; but the court shall be at liberty to dismiss the bill, or to allow an amendment on such terms as justice may require.

44.

DEFECT OF PARTIES—TARDY OBJECTION.

If a defendant shall, at the hearing of a cause, object that a suit is defective for want of parties, not having by motion or answer taken the objection and therein specified by name or description the parties to whom the objection applies, the court shall be at liberty to make a decree saving the rights of the absent parties.

45.

DEATH OF PARTY—REVIVOR.

In the event of the death of either party the court may, in a proper case, upon motion, order the suit to be revived by the substitution of the proper parties. If the successors or representatives of the deceased party fail to make such application within a reasonable time, then any other party may, on motion, apply for such relief, and the court, upon any such motion, may make the necessary orders for notice to the parties to be substituted and for the filing of such pleadings or amendments as may be necessary.

46.

TRIAL—TESTIMONY USUALLY TAKEN IN OPEN COURT— RULINGS ON OBJECTIONS TO EVIDENCE.

In all trials in equity the testimony of witnesses shall be taken orally in open court, except as otherwise provided by statute or these rules. The court shall pass upon the admissibility of all evidence offered as in actions at law. When evidence is offered and excluded, and the party against whom the ruling is made excepts thereto at the time, the court shall take and report so much thereof, or make such a statement respecting it, as will clearly show the character of the evidence, the form in which it was offered, the objection made, the ruling, and the exception. If the appellate court shall be of opinion that the evidence should have been admitted, it shall not reverse the decree unless it be clearly of opinion that material prejudice will result from an affirmance, in which event it shall direct such further steps as justice may require.

47.

DEPOSITIONS—TO BE TAKEN IN EXCEPTIONAL INSTANCES.

The court, upon application of either party, when allowed by statute, or for good and exceptional cause for departing from the general rule, to be shown by affidavit, may permit the deposition of named witnesses, to be used before the court or upon a reference to a master, to be taken before an examiner or other named officer, upon the notice and terms specified in the order. All depositions taken under a statute, or under any such order of the court, shall be taken and filed as follows, unless otherwise ordered by the court or judge for good cause shown: Those of the plaintiff within sixty days from the time the cause is at issue; those of the defendant within thirty days from the expiration of the time for the filing of plaintiff's depositions; and rebutting depositions by either party within twenty days after the time for taking original depositions expires.

48.

TESTIMONY OF EXPERT WITNESSES IN PATENT AND TRADE-MARK CASES.

In a case involving the validity or scope of a patent or trademark, the District Court may, upon petition, order that the testimony in chief of expert witnesses, whose testimony is directed to matters of opinion, be set forth in affidavits and filed as follows: Those of the plaintiff within forty days after the cause is at issue; those of the defendant within twenty days after plaintiff's time has expired; and rebutting affidavits within fifteen days after the expiration of the time for filing original affidavits. Should the opposite party desire the production of any affiant for cross-examination, the court or judge shall, on motion, direct that said cross-examination and any re-examination take place before the court upon the trial, and unless the affiant is produced and submits to cross-examination in compliance with such direction, his affidavit shall not be used as evidence in the cause.

49.

EVIDENCE TAKEN BEFORE EXAMINERS, ETC.

All evidence offered before an examiner or like officer, together with any objections, shall be saved and returned into the court. Depositions, whether upon oral examination before an examiner or like officer or otherwise, shall be taken upon questions and answers reduced to writing, or in the form of narrative, and the witness shall be subject to cross and re-examination.

50.

STENOGRAPHER—APPOINTMENT—FEES.

When deemed necessary by the court or officer taking testimony, a stenographer may be appointed who shall take down testimony in shorthand, and, if required, transcribe the same. His fee shall be fixed by the court and taxed ultimately as costs. The expense of taking a deposition, or the cost of a transcript, shall be advanced by the party calling the witness or ordering the transcript.

51.

EVIDENCE TAKEN BEFORE EXAMINERS, ETC.

Objections to the evidence, before an examiner or like officer, shall be in short form, stating the grounds of objection relied upon, but no transcript filed by such officer shall include argument or debate. The testimony of each witness, after being reduced to writing, shall be read over to or by him, and shall be signed by him in the presence of the officer; provided, that if the witness shall refuse to sign his deposition so taken, the officer shall sign the same, stating upon the record the reasons, if any, assigned by the witness for such refusal. Objection to any question or questions shall be noted by the officer upon the deposition, but he shall not have power to decide on the competency or materiality or relevancy of the questions. The court shall have power, and it shall be its duty, to deal with the costs of incompetent and immaterial or irrelevant depositions, or parts of them, as may be just.

52.

ATTENDANCE OF WITNESSES BEFORE COMMISSIONER, MASTER OR EXAMINER.

Witnesses who live within the district, and whose testimony may be taken out of court by these rules, may be summoned to appear before a commissioner appointed to take testimony, or before a master or examiner appointed in any cause, by subpœna in the usual form, which may be issued by the clerk in blank and filled up by the party praying the same, or by the commissioner, master, or examiner, requiring the attendance of the witnesses at the time and place specified, who shall be allowed for attendance the same compensation as for attendance in court; and if any witness shall refuse to appear or give evidence it shall be deemed a contempt of the court, which being certified to the clerk's office by the commissioner, master, or examiner, an attachment may issue thereupon by order of the court or of any judge thereof, in the same manner as if the contempt were for not attending, or for refusing to give testimony in the court.

In case of refusal of witnesses to attend or be sworn or to answer any question put by the commissioner, master or examiner or by counsel or solicitor, the same practice shall be adopted as is now practiced with respect to witnesses to be produced on examination before an examiner of said court on written interrogatories.

53.

NOTICE OF TAKING TESTIMONY BEFORE EXAMINER, ETC.

Notice shall be given by the respective counsel or parties to the opposite counsel or parties of the time and place of examination before an examiner or like officer for such reasonable time as the court or officer may fix by order in each case.

54.

DEPOSITIONS UNDER REV. STAT. §§ 863, 866, 867—CROSS-EXAMINATION.

After a cause is at issue, depositions may be taken as provided by

Sections 863, 865, 866 and 867, Revised Statutes. But if in any case no notice has been given the opposite party of the time and place of taking the deposition, he shall, upon application and notice, be entitled to have the witness examined orally before the court, or to a cross-examination before an examiner or like officer, or a new deposition taken with notice, as the court or judge under all the circumstances shall order.

55.

DEPOSITIONS DEEMED PUBLISHED WHEN FILED.

Upon the filing of any deposition or affidavit taken under these rules or any statute, it shall be deemed published, unless otherwise ordered by the court.

56.

ON EXPIRATION OF TIME FOR DEPOSITIONS, CASE GOES ON TRIAL CALENDAR.

After the time has elapsed for taking and filing depositions under these rules, the case shall be placed on the trial calendar. Thereafter no further testimony by deposition shall be taken except for some strong reason shown by affidavit. In every such application the reason why the testimony of the witness cannot be had orally on the trial, and why his deposition has not been before taken, shall be set forth, together with the testimony which it is expected the witness will give.

57.

CONTINUANCES.

After a cause shall be placed on the trial calendar it may be passed over to another day of the same term, by consent of counsel or order of the court, but shall not be continued beyond the term save in exceptional cases by order of the court upon good cause shown by affidavit and upon such terms as the court shall in its discretion impose. Continuances beyond the term by consent of the parties shall be allowed, on condition only that a stipulation be signed by counsel for all the parties and that all costs incurred theretofore be paid. Thereupon an order shall be entered dropping the case from the trial calendar, subject to reinstatement within one year upon application to the court by either party, in which event it shall be heard at the earliest convenient day. If not so reinstated within the year, the suit shall be dismissed without prejudice to a new one.

58.

DISCOVERY—INTERROGATORIES—INSPECTION AND PRODUCTION OF DOCUMENTS—ADMISSION OF EXECUTION OR GENUINENESS.

The plaintiff at any time after filing the bill and not later than twenty-one days after the joinder of issue, and the defendant at any time after filing his answer and not later than twenty-one days after the joinder of issue, and either party at any time thereafter by leave of the court or judge, may file interrogatories in writing for the discovery by the opposite party or parties of facts and documents material to the support or defense of the cause, with a note at the foot thereof stating which of the interrogatories each of the parties is required to answer. But no party shall file more than one set of interrogatories to the same party without leave of the court or judge.

If any party to the cause is a public or private corporation, any opposite party may apply to the court or judge for an order allowing him to file interrogatories to be answered by any officer of the corporation, and an order may be made accordingly for the examination of such officer as may appear to be proper upon such interrogatories as the court or judge shall think fit.

Copies shall be filed for the use of the interrogated party, and shall be sent by the clerk to the respective solicitors of record, or to the last known address of the opposite party, if there be no record solicitor.

Interrogatories shall be answered, and the answers filed in the clerk's office, within fifteen days after they have been served, unless the time be enlarged by the court or judge. Each interrogatory shall be answered separately and fully and the answers shall be in writing, under oath, and signed by the party or corporate officer interrogated. Within ten days after the service of interrogatories, objections to them, or any of them, may be presented to the court or judge, with proof of notice of the purpose so to do, and answers shall be deferred until the objections are determined, which shall be at as early a time as is practicable. In so far as the objections are sustained, answers shall not be required.

The court or judge, upon motion and reasonable notice, may make all such orders as may be appropriate to enforce answers to interrogatories or to effect the inspection or production of documents in the possession of either party and containing evidence material to the cause of action or defense of his adversary. Any party failing or refusing to comply with such an order shall be liable to attachment, and shall also be liable, if a plaintiff, to have his bill dismissed, and if a defendant, to have his answer stricken out and be placed in the same situation as if he had failed to answer.

By a demand served ten days before the trial, either party may call
on the other to admit in writing the execution or genuineness of
any document, letter or writing, saving all just exceptions; and if
such admission be not made within five days after such service, the
costs of proving the document, letter or writing shall be paid by
the party refusing or neglecting to make such admission, unless at
the trial the court shall find that the refusal or neglect was reasonable.

59.

REFERENCE TO MASTER—EXCEPTIONAL, NOT USUAL.

Save in matters of account, a reference to a master shall be the
exception, not the rule, and shall be made only upon a showing
that some exceptional condition requires it. When such a reference is made, the party at whose instance or for whose benefit it is
made shall cause the order of reference to be presented to the master for a hearing within twenty days succeeding the time when the
reference was made, unless a longer time be specially granted by
the court or judge; if he shall omit to do so, the adverse party shall
be at liberty forthwith to cause proceedings to be had before the
master, at the costs of the party procuring the reference.

60.

PROCEEDINGS BEFORE MASTER.

Upon every such reference, it shall be the duty of the master, as
soon as he reasonably can after the same is brought before him, to
assign a time and place for proceedings in the same, and to give
due notice thereof to each of the parties, or their solicitors; and
if either party shall fail to appear at the time and place appointed,
the master shall be at liberty to proceed *ex parte*, or, in his discretion, to adjourn the examination and proceedings to a future day,
giving notice to the absent party or his solicitor of such adjournment; and it shall be the duty of the master to proceed with all
reasonable diligence in every such reference, and with the least
practicable delay, and either party shall be at liberty to apply to the
court, or a judge thereof, for an order to the master to speed the
proceedings and to make his report, and to certify to the court or
judge the reason for any delay.

61.

MASTER'S REPORT—DOCUMENTS IDENTIFIED BUT NOT
SET FORTH.

In the reports made by the master to the court, no part of any
state of facts, account, charge, affidavit, deposition, examination, or

answer brought in or used before him shall be stated or recited. But such state of fact, account, charge, affidavit, deposition, examination, or answer shall be identified, and referred to, so as to inform the court what state of facts, account, charge, affidavit, deposition, examination, or answer were so brought in or used.

62.

POWERS OF MASTER,

The master shall regulate all the proceedings in every hearing before him, upon every reference; and he shall have full authority to examine the parties in the cause, upon oath, touching all matters contained in the reference; and also to require the production of all books papers writings, vouchers, and other documents applicable thereto; and also to examine on oath, *viva voce*, all witnesses produced by the parties before him, or by deposition, according to the acts of Congress or otherwise, as here provided; and also to direct the mode in which the matters requiring evidence shall·be proved before him; and generally to do all other acts, and direct all other inquiries and proceedings in the matters before him, which he may deem necessary and proper to the 'justice and merits thereof and the rights of the parties.

63.

FORM OF ACCOUNTS BEFORE MASTER.

All parties accounting before a master shall bring in their respective accounts in the form of debtor 'and creditor; and any of the other parties who shall not be satisfied with the account so brought in shall be at liberty to examine the accounting party *viva voce*, or upon interrogatories, as the master shall direct.

64.

FORMER DEPOSITIONS, ETC., MAY BE USED BEFORE MASTER.

All affidavits, depositions and documents which have been previously made, read, or used in the court upon any proceeding in any cause or matter may be used before the master.

65.

CLAIMANTS BEFORE MASTER EXAMINABLE BY HIM.

The master shall be at liberty to examine any creditor or other person coming in to claim before him, either upon written interrogatories or *viva voce*, or in both 'modes, as the nature of the case may appeal to him to require. The 'evidence upon such examinations shall be taken down by the master, or by some other person by his order and in his presence, if either party requires it, in order that the same may be used by the court if necessary.

66.

RETURN OF MASTER'S REPORT—EXCEPTIONS—HEARING.

The master, as soon as his report is ready, shall return the same into the clerk's office and the day of the return shall be entered by the clerk in the Equity Docket. The parties shall have twenty days from the time of the filing of the report to file exceptions thereto, and if no exceptions are within that period filed by either party, the report shall stand confirmed. If exceptions are filed, they shall stand for hearing before the court, if then in session, or, if not, at the next sitting held thereafter, by adjournment or otherwise.

67.

COSTS ON EXCEPTIONS TO MASTER'S REPORT.

In order to prevent exceptions to reports from being filed for frivolous causes, or for mere delay, the party whose exceptions are overruled, shall, for every exception overruled, pay five dollars costs to the other party, and for every exception allowed shall be entitled to the same costs.

68.

APPOINTMENT AND COMPENSATION OF MASTER.

The District Courts may appoint standing masters in chancery in their respective districts (a majority of all the judges thereof concurring in the appointment), and they may also appoint a master *pro hac vice* in any particular case. The compensation to be allowed to every master shall be fixed by the district court; in its discretion, having regard to all the circumstances thereof, and the compensation shall be charged upon and borne by such of the parties in the cause as the court shall direct. The master shall not retain his report as security for his compensation; but when the compensation is allowed by the court, he shall be entitled to an attachment for the amount against the party who is ordered to pay the same, if, upon notice thereof, he does not pay it within the time prescribed by the court.

69.

PETITION FOR REHEARING.

Every petition for a rehearing shall contain the special matter or cause on which such rehearing is applied for, shall be signed by counsel, and the facts therein stated, if not apparent on the record, shall be verified by the oath of the party or by some other person. No rehearing shall be granted after the term at which the final decree of the court shall have been entered and recorded, if an appeal lies to the Circuit Court of Appeals or the Supreme Court. But if no appeal lies, the petition may be admitted at any time before the end of the next term of the court, in the discretion of the court.

70.

SUITS BY OR AGAINST INCOMPETENTS.

Guardians *ad litem* to defend a suit may be appointed by the court, or by any judge thereof, for infants or other persons who are under guardianship, or otherwise incapable of suing for themselves. All infants and other persons so incapable may sue by their guardians, if any, or by their *prochein ami;* subject, however, to such orders as the court or judge may direct for the protection of infants, and other persons.

71.

FORM OF DECREE.

In drawing up decrees and orders, neither the bill, nor answer, nor other pleadings, nor any part thereof, nor the report of any master, nor any other prior proceeding, shall be recited or stated in the decree or order; but the decree and order shall begin, in substance, as follows: "This cause came on to be heard (or to be further heard, as the case may be) at this term, and was argued by counsel; and thereupon, upon consideration thereof, it was ordered, adjudged and decreed as follows, viz:" (Here insert the decree or order.)

72.

CORRECTION OF CLERICAL MISTAKES IN ORDERS AND DECREES.

Clerical mistakes in decrees or decretal orders, or errors arising from any accidental slip or omission, may, at any time before the close of the term at which final decree is rendered, be corrected by order of the court or a judge thereof, upon petition, without the form or expense of a rehearing.

73.

PRELIMINARY INJUNCTIONS AND TEMPORARY RESTRAINING ORDERS.

No preliminary injunction shall be granted without notice to the opposite party. Nor shall any temporary restraining order be granted without notice to the opposite party, unless it shall clearly appear from specific facts, shown by affidavit or by the verified bill, that immediate and irreparable loss or damage will result to the applicant before the matter can be heard on notice. In case a temporary restraining order shall be granted without notice, in the contingency specified, the matter shall be made returnable at the earliest possible time, and in no event later than ten days from the date of the order, and shall take precedence of all matters, except older matters of the same character. When the matter comes up for hearing the party who obtained the temporary restraining order shall proceed with his application for a preliminary injunction, and if he does not do so the court shall dissolve his temporary restraining order. Upon two days' notice to the party obtaining such temporary restraining order, the opposite party may appear and move the dissolution or modification of the order, and in that event the court or judge shall proceed to hear and determine the motion as expeditiously as the ends of justice may require. Every temporary restraining order shall be forthwith filed in the clerk's office.

74.

INJUNCTION PENDING APPEAL.

When an appeal from a final decree, in an equity suit, granting or dissolving an injunction, is allowed by a justice or a judge who took part in the decision of the cause, he may, in his discretion, at the time of such allowance, make an order suspending, modifying or restoring the injunction during the pendency of the appeal, upon such terms, as to bond or otherwise, as he may consider proper for the security of the rights of the opposite party.

75.

RECORD ON APPEAL—REDUCTION AND PREPARATION.

In case of appeal:

(a) It shall be the duty of the appellant or his solicitor to file with the clerk of the court from which the appeal is prosecuted, together with proof or acknowledgment of service of a copy on the appellee or his solicitor, a *præcipe* which shall indicate the portions of the record to be incorporated into the transcript on such appeal. Should the appellee or his solicitor desire additional portions of the record incorporated into the transcript, he shall file with the clerk of the court his *præcipe* also within ten days thereafter, unless the time shall be enlarged by the court or a judge thereof, indicating such additional portions of the record desired by him.

(b) The evidence to be included in the record shall not be set forth in full, but shall be stated in simple and condensed form, all parts not essential to the decision of the questions presented by the appeal being omitted and the testimony of witnesses being stated only in narrative form, save that if either party desires it, and the court or judge so directs, any part of the testimony shall be reproduced in the exact words of the witness. The duty of so condensing and stating the evidence shall rest primarily on the appellant, who shall prepare his statement thereof and lodge the same in the clerk's office for the examination of the other parties at or before the time of filing his *præcipe* under paragraph (a) of this rule. He shall also notify the other parties or their solicitors of such lodgment and shall name a time and place when he will ask the court or judge to approve the statement, the time so named to be at least ten days after such notice. At the expiration of the time named or such further time as the court or judge may allow, the statement, together with any objections made or amendments proposed by any party; shall be presented to the court or the judge, and if the statement be true, complete and properly prepared, it shall be approved by the court or judge, and if it be not true, complete or properly prepared, it shall be made so under the direction of the court or judge and shall then be approved. When approved, it shall be filed in the clerk's office and become a part of the record for the purposes of the appeal.

(c) If any difference arise between the parties concerning directions as to the general contents of the record to be prepared on the appeal, such difference shall be submitted to the court or judge in conformity with the provisions of paragraph (b) of this rule, and shall be covered by the directions which the court or judge may give on the subject.

76.

RECORD ON APPEAL—REDUCTION AND PREPARATION—COSTS—CORRECTION OF OMISSIONS.

In preparing the transcript on an appeal, especial care shall be taken to avoid the inclusion of more than one copy of the same paper and to exclude the formal and immaterial parts of all exhibits, documents and other papers included therein; and for any infraction of this or any kindred rule the appellate court may withhold or impose costs as the circumstances of the case and the discouragement of like infractions in the future may require. Costs for such an infraction may be imposed upon offending solicitors as well as parties.

If, in the transcript, anything material to either party be omitted by accident or error, the appellate court, on a proper suggestion or its own motion, may direct that the omission be corrected by a supplemental transcript.

77.

RECORD ON APPEAL—AGREED STATEMENT.

When the questions presented by an appeal can be determined by the appellate court without an examination of all the pleadings and evidence, the parties, with the approval of the District Court or the judge thereof, may prepare and sign a statement of the case showing how the questions arose and were decided in the District Court, and setting forth so much only of the facts alleged and proved, or sought to be proved, as is essential to a decision of such questions by the Appellate Court. Such statement, when filed in the office of the clerk of the District Court, shall be treated as superseding, for the purposes of the appeal, all parts of the record other than the decree from which the appeal is taken, and, together with such decree, shall be copied and certified to the Appellate Court as the record on appeal.

78.

AFFIRMATION IN LIEU OF OATH.

Whenever under these rules an oath is or may be required to be taken, the party may, if conscientiously scrupulous of taking an oath, in lieu thereof make solemn affirmation to the truth of the facts stated by him.

79.

ADDITIONAL RULES BY DISTRICT COURT.

With the concurrence of a majority of the circuit judges for the circuit, the District Courts may make any other and further rules and regulations for the practice, proceedings and process, *mesne* and final, in their respective districts, not inconsistent with the rules hereby prescribed, and from time to time alter and amend the same.

80.

COMPUTATION OF TIME—SUNDAYS AND HOLIDAYS.

When the time prescribed by these rules for doing any act expires on a Sunday or legal holiday, such time shall extend to and include the next succeeding day that is not a Sunday or legal holiday.

81.

THESE RULES EFFECTIVE FEBRUARY 1, 1913
—OLD RULES ABROGATED.

These rules shall be in force on and after February 1, 1913, and shall govern all proceedings in cases then pending or thereafter brought, save that where in any then pending cause an order has been made or act done which cannot be changed without doing substantial injustice, the court may give effect to such order or act to the extent necessary to avoid any such injustice.

All rules theretofore prescribed by the Supreme Court, regulating the practice in suits in equity, shall be abrogated when these rules take effect.

TABLE OF CASES

INDEX

FORMS.   [REFERENCES ARE TO PAGES.]   PAGES